CHINA AND INTERNATIONAL DISPUTE RESOLUTION IN THE CONTEXT OF THE 'BELT AND ROAD INITIATIVE'

T0382161

Written by eminent international judges, scholars and practitioners, this book offers a timely study of China's role in international dispute resolution in the context of the construction of the 'Belt and Road Initiative' (BRI). It is the first comprehensive assessment of China's policy and practice in international dispute resolution, providing in-depth analysis of the law and practice in the fields of international trade, commerce, investment and international law of the sea, as they relate to BRI dispute resolution. This book will be an indispensable reading for scholars and practitioners with an interest in China and international dispute resolution. It also constitutes an invaluable reference for anyone interested in the changing international law and order, in which China is playing an increasingly significant role, particularly through the BRI construction.

WENHUA SHAN (PhD, Trinity College, Cambridge) is Ministry of Education Yangtze River Chair Professor of International Economic Law and the founding Dean of the School of Law at Xi'an Jiaotong University, PR China. He is also the founding Director of the Silk Road Institute for Interactional and Comparative Law (SRIICL). He has taught as Professor of International Law at Oxford Brookes University and UNSW Sydney, and has been a Senior Fellow of the Lauterpacht Centre for International Law at the University of Cambridge, Assistant President, Xi'an Jiaotong University, and Deputy Director-General of the Judicial Case Academy at the Supreme People's Court, PR China. He has published over a dozen books in international and comparative law with leading English and Chinese publishers, including CUP and OUP, and numerous articles in journals such as the *European Journal of International Law* and *American Journal of Comparative Law*. He is the founding Editor-in-Chief of *The Chinese Journal of Comparative Law* and founding General Editor of the "China and International Economic Law Series" and "Silk Road Studies in International Economic Law". As Conciliator of the International Centre for the Settlement of Investment Disputes (ICSID), Expert Member of the International Commercial Expert Committee of the Supreme People's Court of China, Executive President of the China International Investment Arbitration Forum (CIIAF) and Arbitrator of the China International

Economic and Trade Arbitration Commission (CIETAC) among others, Shan has practised international and Chinese laws since 1992.

SHENG ZHANG is Associate Professor at Xi'an Jiaotong University School of Law. He is Deputy Secretary-General of the China International Investment Arbitration Forum and an editor of *The Chinese Journal of Comparative Law*. He mainly focuses on international investment law and comparative law. He was a visiting scholar at the Lauterpacht Centre for International Law and the Max-Planck Institute for Comparative and International Private Law. He has published articles in the *European Journal of International Law, Journal of International Dispute Settlement, The Chinese Journal of Comparative Law* and *Columbia FDI Perspectives.*

JINYUAN SU is Professor of International Law at Xi'an Jiaotong University School of Law. He was an Erin J. C. Arsenault Fellow (2014–2015) at the McGill Institute of Air and Space Law and a visiting research fellow (2009–2010) at the Lauterpacht Centre for International Law, University of Cambridge. Dr Su's research interests lie in outer space law, the law of the sea and international aviation law. His articles are published in international peer-reviewed journals such as *Chinese Journal of International Law, International & Comparative Law Quarterly, Asian Journal of International Law, Ocean Development & International Law* and *The International Journal of Marine and Coastal Law.*

CHINA AND INTERNATIONAL DISPUTE RESOLUTION IN THE CONTEXT OF THE 'BELT AND ROAD INITIATIVE'

Edited by

WENHUA SHAN
Xi'an Jiaotong University

SHENG ZHANG
Xi'an Jiaotong University

JINYUAN SU
Xi'an Jiaotong University

CAMBRIDGE
UNIVERSITY PRESS

CAMBRIDGE
UNIVERSITY PRESS

University Printing House, Cambridge CB2 8BS, United Kingdom

One Liberty Plaza, 20th Floor, New York, NY 10006, USA

477 Williamstown Road, Port Melbourne, VIC 3207, Australia

314-321, 3rd Floor, Plot 3, Splendor Forum, Jasola District Centre, New Delhi - 110025, India

103 Penang Road, #05-06/07, Visioncrest Commercial, Singapore 238467

Cambridge University Press is part of the University of Cambridge.

It furthers the University's mission by disseminating knowledge in the pursuit of education, learning and research at the highest international levels of excellence.

www.cambridge.org
Information on this title: www.cambridge.org/9781009306058
DOI: 10.1017/9781108561976

© Cambridge University Press 2020

First published 2020
First paperback edition 2022

A catalogue record for this publication is available from the British Library

ISBN 978-1-108-47339-2 Hardback
ISBN 978-1-009-30605-8 Paperback

CONTENTS

FIGURES

TABLES

CONTRIBUTORS

JUDGE JAMES RICHARD CRAWFORD is currently a member of the International Court of Justice. Prior to his election to the Court, he acted as counsel in numerous cases before the International Court of Justice and other international tribunals, and as an arbitrator in twenty-six international arbitrations. He was Whewell Professor of International Law at the University of Cambridge and has published widely in the fields of statehood, collective rights, investment law and international responsibility. Recent works include *The International Law of Responsibility* (co-edited, OUP, 2010), *The Cambridge Companion to International Law* (co-edited, CUP, 2012) and *Brownlie's Principles of Public International Law* (9th edition, OUP, 2019). He was the first Australian member of the United Nations International Law Commission and in that capacity was responsible for the ILC's work on the International Criminal Court (1994) and for the second reading of the ILC Articles on State Responsibility (2001). He has been Yangtze River Chair Professor of International Law (by Ministry of Education) and the Honorary Director of the Silk Road Institute for International and Comparative Law of XJTU.

MICHAEL HWANG currently practises as a barrister, primarily servicing lawyers as independent counsel and arbitrator. He has received specialist training in both domestic and international arbitration (as well as mediation), and has lectured and written extensively on international arbitration and mediation. He is active in domestic and international disputes (under ICC, CIETAC, UNCITRAL, LCIA, ICSID, AAA, BANI and SIAC Rules) as counsel and arbitrator as well as mediator. His arbitrations and mediations have involved disputes in a host of countries all over the world. He is an accredited arbitrator to sixteen national arbitration centres as well as the Permanent Court of Arbitration and ICSID. Dr Hwang received his legal education at Oxford University (both at undergraduate and post-graduate levels) where he was a College Scholar and prizewinner. He then took up a teaching appointment at the Faculty of Law at the University of

Sydney before returning to Singapore to commence private practice in 1968. In 1991, Dr Hwang was appointed a Judicial Commissioner of the Supreme Court (a full time post equivalent to the office of an acting High Court Judge) for a fixed term which expired at the end of 1992. He returned to private practice at the beginning of 1993, and was Head of the Litigation Department of the law firm of Allen & Gledhill, Singapore (currently Singapore's largest law firm). He retired from the firm at the end of 2002 to establish an independent practice as a barrister and chartered arbitrator. In 1997, Dr Hwang was appointed one of the first twelve Senior Counsel of the Supreme Court of Singapore (an appointment equivalent to that of Queen's Counsel in England). He has (at different times) acted as Visiting Professor as well as Adjunct Professor at the National University of Singapore, and has been conferred with an Honorary LLD Degree by the University of Sydney.

LIM SI CHENG is an Associate in the International Arbitration practice of Mayer Brown's Singapore office. He is a former Associate at Michael Hwang Chambers, and an LLB (Hons) graduate from Durham University.

DAVID HOLLOWAY is a barrister practicing from Outer Temple Chambers, London, Dubai and Abu Dhabi. He has acted as counsel in cases before the English courts at all levels and before international tribunals. He is additionally admitted as an advocate at the DIFC Courts in Dubai and as a registered foreign lawyer (Hong Kong). In addition to professional practice, he is an academic, teaching and researching in the areas of international commercial law. He is currently Senior Lecturer at the Law School of the University Of Birmingham and Director of the LLM in International Commercial Law offered at the University's Dubai Campus. He has previously held faculty appointments at the University of Edinburgh, City University of Hong Kong and Xi'an Jiaotong University. He has published widely in the areas of international trade and international arbitration. He is General Editor of International Arbitration Law Review and co-author of Schmitthoff, the law and practice of International Trade. He sits as an arbitrator and is a panel arbitrator with many leading arbitral institutions and is also a part time Tribunal Member of the Hong Kong Board of Review (Tax Appeals Tribunal).

E.U. PETERSMANN is a professor of the European University Institute. He has combined legal practice (e.g., as legal advisor in German, EU, GATT, WTO and UN institutions) with academic teaching at universities in Germany, Switzerland, Italy, the United States, China and India for more than thirty-five years. He has been a secretary, member or chairman of GATT/WTO dispute settlement panels and chaired the International Trade Law Committee of the International Law Association from 1999 to 2014. He has published 30 books and more than 300 contributions to books and journals on international law. He is Emeritus Professor of international and European law and former head of the Law Department at the European University Institute, Florence (Italy).

GUOHUA YANG is a professor at Tsinghua University Law School. He worked in the Chinese Ministry of Commerce from 1996 to 2014; he was the first Director and later Deputy Director General for WTO Legal Affairs within the Ministry responsible for WTO cases related to China. He also has a rich background on trade policy making and international cooperation. For example, he was the head of Chinese delegations for intellectual property rights dialogues with the United States, the EU, Japan, Russia, Switzerland and Brazil, and for international conferences at Asia–Pacific Economic Cooperation (APEC) and United Nations Commission on International Trade Law (UNCITRAL), etc. He is Executive Vice Chairman, WTO Law Research Society of China Law Society (China WTO Law Society); Arbitrator, International Economic and Trade Arbitration Commission (CIETAC, China) and South China International Economic and Trade Arbitration Commission/Shenzhen Court of International Arbitration (SCIA, China); Member, Expert Group for Commercial and Maritime Trials, Supreme Court, China; Member, Indicative List for dispute settlement panels, WTO Secretariat; Associate Editor, *Journal of World Trade*; Distinguished Legal Scholar Award, Beijing Law Society (1999). He was also IP attaché at the Chinese Embassy in the United States, Washington, DC (January 2006– September 2008). He graduated from Peking University Law School in 1996 (PhD) and Wuhan University Law School in 1994 (LLM).

MEG KINNEAR is currently the Secretary-General of the International Centre for Settlement of Investment Disputes (ICSID) at the World Bank. She was formerly the Senior General Counsel and Director General of the Trade Law Bureau of Canada, where she was responsible for the conduct of all international investment and trade litigations involving Canada, and participated in the negotiations of bilateral investment agreements. In November 2002, Ms Kinnear was also named Chair of the Negotiating Group on Dispute Settlement for the Free Trade of the Americas Agreement. From October 1996 to April 1999, Ms Kinnear was Executive Assistant to the Deputy

Minister of Justice of Canada. Prior to this, Ms Kinnear was Counsel at the Civil Litigation Section of the Canadian Department of Justice (from June 1984 to October 1996) where she appeared before federal and provincial courts as well as domestic arbitration panels. Ms Kinnear was called to the Bar of Ontario in 1984 and the Bar of the District of Columbia in 1982. She received a Bachelor of Arts (BA) from Queen's University in 1978, a Bachelor of Laws (LLB) from McGill University in 1981, and a Master of Laws (LLM) from the University of Virginia in 1982. Ms Kinnear has published numerous articles on international investment law and procedure and is a frequent speaker on these topics. She is a co-author of *Investment Disputes under NAFTA* (published in 2006 and updated in 2008 and 2009). She also co-authored texts on Canadian legal procedure including *Federal Court Practice* (1988–90, 1991–92, and 1993–2009 annually) and 1995 Crown Liability and Proceedings Act Annotated (1994).

WEI SHEN is KoGuan Distinguished Professor of Law, Shanghai Jiao Tong University Law School; PhD (London School of Economics and Political Science), LLM (University of Cambridge), LLM (University of Michigan), LLM and LLB (East China University of Political Science and Law); attorney-at-law, New York. Professor Shen is the former Dean of Shandong University Law School, China. Professor Shen is also Global Professor of Law, New York University School of Law, BFLC Adjunct Professor of Law, National University of Singapore, and has been included in Marquis *Who's Who* (2011 onwards). Professor Shen is an arbitrator with Shanghai Arbitration Commission, Hong Kong International Arbitration Centre, Shanghai International Arbitration Centre and Shenzhen International Court of Arbitration. He is an associate member of the International Academy of Comparative Law (*Académie international de droitcomparé*). He is a member of Moody's China Academic Advisory Panel and Honorary Fellow of Asian Institute of International Financial Law, University of Hong Kong.

PENG WANG is an associate professor at the School of Law of Xi'an Jiaotong University, China, and was a visiting scholar at the University of Cambridge Lauterpacht Centre for International Law. Dr Wang teaches courses on international economic law, international investment law and arbitration, international law and international relations, and has contributed to academic journals such as *ICSID Review*, *The Journal of World Investment & Trade*, *Polish Yearbook of*

International Law, *Chinese Journal of Comparative Law* and *Transnational Dispute Management*, among others.

ANATOLE BOUTE is a professor at the Chinese University of Hong Kong, specializing in the fields of energy, environmental and investment law. His research focuses on the legal aspects of the transition of energy systems towards sustainability, with a special interest for energy market reforms in emerging economies. He graduated in political sciences (2003) and law (2004) from the University of Leuven and holds an advanced master (LLM) in energy and environmental law (2005) from the same university. In 2005, he was called to the Brussels Bar where he practiced until 2009 with the energy law team of Janson Baugniet. He advised on and was involved in litigation concerning the promotion of renewable energy sources, energy efficiency, greenhouse gas emissions trading, the liberalization of energy markets and nuclear energy. He is the author of *Russian Electricity and Energy Investment Law* (Brill Nijhoff, 2015) and of articles in several internationally peer reviewed journals, including the *Fordham International Law Journal*, *ICSID Review*, *Common Market Law Review*, *Transnational Environmental Law*, *Journal of Environmental Law*, *European Law Review*, *Europe–Asia Studies*, and *Energy Policy*. In 2009, he received the Willoughby Prize for his articles published in the *Journal of Energy & Natural Resources Law*.

NATALIE KLEIN is a professor at UNSW Sydney's Faculty of Law, Australia. She was previously at Macquarie University where she served as Dean of Macquarie Law School (2011–17), as well as Acting Head of the Department for Policing, Intelligence and Counter-Terrorism at Macquarie (2013–14). Professor Klein has been a visiting fellow at the Lauterpacht Centre for International Law at the University of Cambridge and MacCormick Fellow at the University of Edinburgh. She is currently a non-resident fellow at the Lakshman Kadirgamar Institute in Sri Lanka. Prior to joining Macquarie, Professor Klein worked in the international litigation and arbitration practice of Debevoise & Plimpton LLP, served as counsel to the government of Eritrea (1998–2002) and was a consultant in the Office of Legal Affairs at the United Nations. Her masters and doctorate in law were earned at Yale Law School, and she is a fellow of the Australian Academy of Law.

KEYUAN ZOU is Harris Professor of International Law at the Lancashire Law School of the University of Central Lancashire (UCLan), UK. He specializes in international law, in particular law of the sea and international environmental law. Before joining UCLan, he worked at Dalhousie University (Canada), Peking University (China), University of Hannover (Germany) and National University of Singapore. He has published over sixty refereed English papers in over thirty international journals including *Asian Yearbook of International Law, Asia-Pacific Journal of Environmental Law, Chinese Journal of International Law, Columbia Journal of International Affairs, Criminal Law Forum, German Yearbook of International Law, International Journal of Marine and Coastal Law, International Lawyer, Journal of Environmental Law, Journal of International Maritime Law, Journal of International Wildlife Law and Policy, Journal of Maritime Law and Commerce, Lloyd's Maritime and Commercial Law Quarterly, Marine Policy, Maritime Policy and Management, Netherlands International Law Review, Ocean Development and International Law, Ocean Yearbook, Singapore Journal of International and Comparative Law, Ocean and Coastal Management* and *Yearbook of Law and Legal Practice in East Asia.*

BINGBING JIA is Professor of International Law at the Tsinghua University Law School, Beijing, China. He studied law at Peking University and obtained his PhD in 1995 at the University of Oxford. Previously he was a legal officer at the UN ICTY. He is a member of the Curatorium of The Hague Academy of International Law. He is a member of the board of editors of the *Chinese Journal of International Law, Journal of International Criminal Justice, American Journal of International Law* and the *Chinese Yearbook of International Law.* His research interests include the law of peace, international humanitarian and criminal law.

JIANGYU WANG (SJD & LLM, University of Pennsylvania; MJur, Oxford; MPhil in Laws, Peking University; LLB, China University of Political Science and Law) is Professor of Law and Director of the Centre for Chinese and Comparative Law at the School of Law of City University of Hong Kong. He is also a joint Editor-in-Chief of *The Chinese Journal of Comparative Law* (Oxford University Press) and subject editor of the *Asian Journal of Comparative Law* (Cambridge University Press). Before coming to Hong Kong, he held a tenured appointment at the National University of Singapore Faculty of Law while he served as the Director of the Asian Law Institute (ASLI). His teaching and research interests include international economic law, international law and international relations, Chinese and comparative corporate and securities law, law and development, and the Chinese legal system.

ABBREVIATIONS

APEC	Asia–Pacific Economic Cooperation
ASEAN	Association of Southeast Asian Nations
BIT	Bilateral investment treaty
BRI	Belt and Road Initiative
CAFTA	China–ASEAN Free Trade Agreement
CETA	Comprehensive Economic and Trade Agreement
CICC	China's International Commercial Court
CIETAC	China International Economic and Trade Arbitration Commission
CJEU	Court of Justice of the European Union
CPC	Communist Party of China
DIFC	Dubai International Financial Centre
ECT	Energy Charter Treaty
ECtHR	European Court of Human Rights
EEZ	Exclusive economic zone
EU	European Union
FCNs	Treaties of friendship, commerce and navigation
FDI	Foreign direct investment
FTAs	Free trade agreements
GATT	General Agreement on Tariffs and Trade
GDP	Gross domestic product
GVCs	Global value chains
G20	Group of 20
HKIAC	Hong Kong International Arbitration Centre
ICJ	International Court of Justice
ICSID	International Centre for the Settlement of Investment Disputes
ICTR	International Criminal Tribunal for Rwanda
IDSM	Investment dispute settlement mechanisms
IMO	International Maritime Organization
ISDS	Investor–State dispute settlement
ITA	Information technology agreement
ITLOS	International Tribunal for the Law of the Sea
ITO	International Trade Organization
LICs	Low-income countries

MAI	Multilateral agreement on investment
MIDR	Multilateral investment dispute resolution
MOU	Memorandum of understanding
NAFTA	North American Free Trade Agreement
NYC	New York Convention
OECD	Organization for Economic Co-operation and Development
PCA	Permanent Court of Arbitration
RCEP	Regional Comprehensive Economic Partnership Agreement
RTAs	Regional trade agreements
SIAC	Singapore International Arbitration Centre
SMEs	Small and medium-sized enterprises
SOEs	State-owned enterprises
TIWG	Trade and Investment Working Group
TPP	Trans-Pacific Partnership Agreement
TTIP	Transatlantic Trade and Investment Partnership Agreement
UDHR	Universal Declaration of Human Rights
UN	United Nations
UNCITRAL	United Nations Commission on International Trade Law
UNCLOS	United Nations Convention on the Law of the Sea
UNCTAD	United Nations Conference on Trade and Development
VCLT	Vienna Convention on the Law of Treaties
WHO	World Health Organization
WTO	World Trade Organization
WITO	World Investment and Trade Organization
WIPO	World Intellectual Property Organization

Introduction

WENHUA SHAN, JINYUAN SU AND SHENG ZHANG

For most of its recorded 5,000-year history, China has been a prosperous and influential nation in the Far East. The international order that it shaped in this region is unique in post-Westphalian terms. Despite the fact that it claimed to be the 'Middle Kingdom' and maintained suzerain–vassal relations with neighbouring countries, it was seldom aggressive in its interactions with the outside world, and the peace and order sustained under its predominance was beneficial to the countries in the region. This changed fundamentally due to the late Qing Government's isolation policy of the eighteenth century, which, by way of reaction, brought it under the sway of European powers.

After several decades of war, China became genuinely independent, but remained troubled by civil wars and domestic turbulence. Since 1978, it has experienced rapid economic and social development. In 2011, it became the world's second largest economy, a title Japan had held for over four decades. It is projected to overtake the United States as the global economic leader between 2020 and 2030. Whereas the accuracy of this prediction remains to be tested by time, it is believed by many that the world's economy and politics is undergoing a shift of gravity from the west to the east.

The impact of this shift cannot be underestimated, certainly not in a rise of China's magnitude and a noted change of its approach towards international engagements. In September 2013, as the concept of Silk Road Economic Belt was introduced by Chinese President Xi Jinping during a visit to Kazakhstan, the Chinese government embarked on the 'Belt and Road Initiative' (BRI). In March 2015, the Chinese National Development and Reform Commission, Ministry of Foreign Affairs and Ministry of Commerce jointly released an action plan on the principles, framework, and cooperation priorities and mechanisms under the BRI. For the first time, China tabled a grand strategic conception in a bid to enhance international cooperation and global governance, and led its implementation. Since 2013, the BRI has developed from a concept to a key platform for building a community of a shared future for mankind, and a public good for the world. The concept of the BRI has also been referred to in resolutions adopted by the United Nations (UN) General Assembly and Security Council. In Resolution 2,274 (2016) on the mandate of the UN Assistance Mission in Afghanistan adopted in March 2017, the Security Council called for strengthening regional trade and transit through regional development initiatives, including the BRI.[1] In November 2017, at its 71st session, the General Assembly adopted Document A/71/9, encouraging member states to boost economic development in Afghanistan and the region through the BRI and other initiatives.[2]

But the BRI is not only an economic project; it also has inextricable links to law and order. Cooperation among countries in the context of the BRI cannot succeed without rules and the rule of law. As pointed out by China's State Councillor and Foreign Minister Wang Yi at the Forum on Belt and Road Legal Cooperation in July 2018, 'regulations and the rule of law provide the green light for the BRI to go global, as well as the safety valve to cope with different types of risks and challenges'.[3] Given that the implementation of the BRI involves extensive government-to-government, government-to-enterprise and enterprise-to-enterprise transactions, a sound legal system including an effective and efficient dispute settlement mechanism is an imperative to coordinate the interests of the diverse parties and solve their disputes that arise in such transactions.

Indeed, the role of China in international law particularly in international dispute settlement has become one of the most intriguing topics.

Traditionally, China was very conservative in submitting to the jurisdiction of international tribunals due to its miserable and humiliating experience of foreign oppression and invasion since the Opium War in the 1840s. China has stood firmly in seeking to solve international disputes by way of negotiations on the basis of equality and the Five Principles of Peaceful Coexistence. Such a position has been scrutinized

---

[1] United Nations Security Council, Resolution 2274(2016), S/RES/2274(2016), www .securitycouncilreport.org/atf/cf/%7B65BFCF9B-6D27-4E9C-8CD3-CF6E4FF96FF9% 7D/s_res_2274.pdf
[2] United Nations General Assembly, Resolution adopted by the General Assembly on 17 November 2016 on the Situation in Afghanistan, A/RES/71/9, https://undocs.org/A/ RES/71/9
[3] China Daily, Legal Support to Boost Belt and Road Initiative, 3 July 2018, www .chinadaily.com.cn/m/chinalic/2018–07/03/content_36503057.htm

under a harsh spotlight during the South China Sea arbitration brought by the Philippines.

In sharp contrast with China's conservative approach to dispute settlements under public international law, China has become one of the most active users of the WTO dispute settlement mechanism. Meanwhile, China has adopted a more liberal approach to international investment dispute settlement by embracing a full-scale investor–state arbitration mechanism. As a result, Chinese investors have started to make good use such mechanism provided by the over 130 investment treaties that China has entered into. China and its investors' participation in trade and investment dispute settlement have helped in boosting its confidence in the international dispute settlement system as a whole. Though it remains to be seen how far will China go in engaging international dispute settlement, particularly in public international law fields.

Against these backdrops, the appropriate time has come to consider the unique characteristics of China's engagement in the international dispute settlement. While there have been some examinations of China's participation in the individual fields of international law and dispute settlement, this book distincts itself from existing scholarship by considering international dispute settlement as a whole in the context of the BRI, identifying broad themes including international investment, commercial, WTO and maritime dispute settlements.

This book presents contributions from eminent judges, legal scholars and practitioners from Europe, the United Kingdom, the United States of America, Australia and China in a variety of areas of international law with close relevance to China.

H. E. Judge James Crawford (Chapter 1) considers that an effective dispute resolution system is important to the success of the BRI. It could help to offset the fears that may otherwise turn trade and investment away. With predictable legal protections underwriting their participation in the scheme, trade and investment might more readily be encouraged to flow the full length of the BRI. The BRI will operate through, rather than aiming to replace, existing legal frameworks of cooperation and economic integration. Given that the types of disputes that might arise in the context of the BRI are notably diverse, no single mechanism of dispute settlement is possible.

Michael Hwang SC, David Holloway and Lim Si Cheng (Chapter 2) examine the dispute solution options the contracting parties have when their cross-border transaction turn sour. The traditional answer is that international arbitration is the best option to govern cross border disputes. Yet recent trends have improved the enforceability of foreign judgments. They argue that the foreign judgment is catching up with the foreign arbitral award in terms of enforceability. After introducing the consistent enforceability of foreign judgments in common law countries, they highlight a number of contemporary trends that are gradually improving the enforceability of foreign judgments in civil law countries. In the end, they discuss the fledgling potential of the 2005 Hague Convention on Choice of Court Agreements to standardize the law and practice of enforcement of judgments made by designated courts in exclusive choice of court agreements.

Ernst-Ulrich Petersmann (Chapter 3) discusses legal methodology problems of multilevel trade and investment regulation and explores related problems of adjudication involving investment projects in the context of BRI involving more than 65 countries. The very limited number of investor–state arbitration proceedings initiated so far by foreign companies against China – or by Chinese companies against foreign host states – suggests that alternative dispute resolution may become one of the important 'legal innovations' of BRI. Yet, the involvement of third parties as 'mediators' or 'conciliators' in dispute settlement proceedings also raises questions of 'justice' and of legal methodology that are easier to resolve by embedding BRI regulations into multilateral trade, investment and UN law.

Guohua Yang (Chapter 4) analyses the trade outcomes of the G20 Hangzhou Summit by revealing its position on strengthening the multilateral trading system, advancing negotiations on Doha issues, ratifying the Trade Facilitation Agreement, opposing protectionism on trade and its support for plurilateral trade agreements like the Environmental Goods Agreement. He points out that the G20 Hangzhou Summit will be beneficial to the development of both the WTO and G20. He also discusses specifically the importance of including issues in regional trade arrangements, the possibility of establishing a World Investment and Trade Organization (WITO) and the role of China in this aspect.

Meg Kinnear (Chapter 5) examines the role of the International Centre for the Settlement of Investment Disputes (ICSID) in investor–state dispute settlement. After briefly introducing the creation of the ICSID, she argues that ICSID dispute settlement is one of the mechanisms available should disputes arise under the BRI, and that the ICSID's special attributes will make it a particularly effective vehicle in this context. Further, she introduces the ICSID's efforts to modernize its rules.

Wei Shen (Chapter 6) explores the BRI and China's bilateral investment treaty (BIT) regime in the context of expropriation. He focuses on the notion of expropriation and the related compensation standard by examining expropriation clauses in China's existing BITs. China's BITs have been experiencing a generational evolution. Since 2006, when China signed a BIT with India, China has included the concept of indirect expropriation in its BITs. Yet most of the BITs between China and BRI counterparties were signed before 2006, which suggests that the expropriation and compensation standards in these existing BITs were not up to higher standards for protecting China's outbound investment into BRI counterparties. A sensible approach to fill in the gap is to have a BIT network covering China and BRI countries and applying the doctrines of indirect expropriation and the 'Hull Formula' to compensate expropriated investment.

Peng Wang (Chapter 7) looks at the reform of investor–state dispute settlement from the perspective of fast resolution, party autonomy and cost management. He proposes a Chinese perspective on a Multilateral Investment Dispute Resolution (MIDR) system of balance between public legitimacy management and private efficiency refinement. The institutional structure of the MIDR should be of internal balance, moderating three tensions between state and arbitrator, between investor and host state, and between state and arbitral tribunal during ex ante and ex post process of dispute resolution. The process of establishment of the MIDR should be one of external balance, moderating tensions between the procedure and substance of the MIDR, between the MIDR and existing institutions, and between the legal rights of MIDR stakeholders and the political will of leading states.

Anatole Boute (Chapter 8) discusses the added value that the Energy Charter Treaty (ECT) can potentially offer to Chinese external energy security by protecting Chinese outbound investments in countries along the Belt and Road. The geographical scope of the ECT to a large extent covers China's main energy partners along the 'Silk Road Economic Belt'. In addition, participating in the modernization of the ECT could help China shape the treaty to reflect the special characteristics of its foreign energy investments and adjust this mechanism to the benefit of China's increasing energy activities in the large number of BRI counterparties.

Natalie Klein (Chapter 9) investigates dispute settlement relating to the maritime dimensions of the BRI, and explores the potential use of the dispute settlement mechanism of the United Nations Convention on the Law of the Sea (UNCLOS) in relation to possible disputes relating to three subjects that may arise pursuant to the BRI: ports, navigation and military activities. She observes that there is undoubtedly an important role for judges or arbitrators to play in ensuring that the implementation of the BRI remains consistent with the rights and obligations agreed under UNCLOS. How successfully this role will be played will ultimately depend on the precise details of any dispute and the final decisions of a particular court or tribunal, including the enforcement of those decisions. Courts or tribunals will likely see themselves as having a critical position in ensuring that the balance of interests agreed in the UNCLOS is not jeopardized by the national strategies or priorities of any one state party.

Keyuan Zou (Chapter 10) analyses the legal issues arising from state practice in the implementation of the UNCLOS, particularly relating to the practice in east Asia concerning maritime dispute settlement. He discusses the general legal framework including the UNCLOS, and how states in East Asia solve their disputes in a peaceful manner. Unlike Europe or America, the Asian cultures are quite divergent. Such divergence has different impacts on the attitudes and policies of Asian countries towards the settlement of disputes. It may also be an obstacle to the regional integration of effective control of disputes as well as to the general acceptance of the international judicial bodies whose foundation was based essentially on western legal systems. The questions about 'the efficacy of future global initiatives that are perceived to be Western in origin and orientation, and how they can be amenably incorporated into the legal systems and cultures of non-Western countries'[4] should be timely and properly answered.

Bingbing Jia (Chapter 11) examines an issue of treaty interpretation arising from a moment's reflection on the dispute settlement mechanisms established in the UNCLOS. Those mechanisms, with primarily the International Tribunal for the Law of the Sea and Arbitral Tribunals established under Annex VII of the Convention making waves in recent times, are designed solely to deal with disputes concerning the interpretation or application of the Convention. Any dispute that may eventually seize those mechanisms for solution will be primarily related to treaty interpretation. Besides, while hugely important, the UNCLOS does not provide for all matters in the oceans. Professor Jia tries to investigate

---

[4] See Douglas M. Johnston, 'Environmental Law as "Sacred Text": Western Values and Southeast Asian Prospects', in Douglas M. Johnston and Gerry Ferguson (eds.), *Asia-Pacific Legal Development* (Vancouver: UBC Press, 1998), at 416.

what should be done in interpreting the UNCLOS, if it is silent on matters indispensable for proper interpretation of some of its rules.

Jiangyu Wang (Chapter 12) takes up the South China Sea arbitration case between China and the Philippines concerning maritime entitlements in the South China Sea. The relevant arbitral tribunal ruled in favor of the Philippines, first on jurisdiction and admissibility issues in October 2015, and finally on the merits in July 2016. China has not only refused to accept the tribunal's jurisdiction but also vigorously attacked the validity and legality of the final award. China's handling of this case has several implications for its approach to international dispute settlement. The South China Sea Arbitration may have given China two takeaways: the appreciation of the importance of using international law and the understanding that foreign countries – led by the United States – again are using international law as a disguise to violate China's sovereignty. A combination of these two factors will strengthen the prevailing attitude of treating international law as a tool to protect China's national interest, rather than a serious belief in international rule of law.

This edited volume is an outcome of an international conference held in October 2016 to commemorate the 10th anniversary of the Silk Road Institute for International and Comparative Law (SRIICL) at the School of Law of Xi'an Jiaotong University. As can be seen from the preceding chapters, it might well be the case that no 'one size fits all' dispute settlement mechanism may be found for all transactions under the BRI, as rightly pointed out by Crawford. However, this does not prevent states along the BRI countries to consider creating new or adapting old mechanisms to better fit their needs of dispute settlement. As this book goes to press, China has already set up two new courts (in Xi'an and Shenzhen respectively) devoted to commercial disputes arising out of international transactions particularly along the BRI countries. The courts, which intend to provide an 'integrated dispute resolution (IDR) mechanism by closely cooperating with arbitration and conciliation institutions,[5] have already settled a number of cases.[6] Clearly law is playing an increasingly important role in the BRI implementation, and it is natural to start with procedural rules and mechanisms. This book is certainly not the end but the beginning of the discussions on BRI dispute settlement.

[5] Wenhua Shan, IDR – The Chinese Solution for International Commercial Dispute Settlement (in Chinese), Legal Daily, 13 November 2018.
[6] Qiao Wenxin, The First International Commercial Court of the Supreme People's Court effectively concluded the first five cases, People's Court Daily, 30 December 2019.

As with every book, this book cannot be ready without the help and cooperation offered by many friends and colleagues. We would like to take this opportunity to thank the contributors for their dedication and hard work, without which the book would have not come into shape. We would also like to thank Joe Ng, Gemma Smith and James Baker from Cambridge University Press for their patience and constant encouragement throughout the process of preparing the book. Last but not least, we shall thank all the participants of the 'SRIICL at 10th' conference, including the supporting staff and the volunteers, for their contribution to such a fruitful and most memorable event!

PART I

China, BRI and International Dispute Resolution

China and the Development of an International Dispute Resolution Mechanism for the Belt and Road Construction

JAMES CRAWFORD AC[*]

Sometime in the 1970s, archaeologists unearthed a tomb in Turfan (China), an important trading centre along the ancient Silk Road. The tomb was some 1,300 years old, dating to a time when trade along the ancient Silk Road was in full swing. In the tomb lay the remains of an Iranian merchant, entombed in accordance with Zoroastrian beliefs, and in a garment made from pieces of paper.[1]

The papers, pieced together, revealed the record of a case that the deceased's brother had brought before a Chinese court. He had testified that his brother had died in the desert while on a business trip with his 'two camels, four cattle and ... [one] donkey'. Prior to his death, the deceased had loaned '275 bolts of silk' to his Chinese business partner. Following his death, his brother petitioned the court for relief in the form of the return of the silk to him. The court ruled in his favour, ordering that 'as his brother's survivor, the Iranian was entitled to the silk'.[2]

From this simple tale we can draw lessons about the dangers of the desert along the Silk Road; the modest size of the merchant convoys that travelled along it (evidently not all of these were large caravans); and the partnership that it fostered between the Chinese and migrants from distant places and different cultures. We are reminded of the technological advancements that exchanges along the Silk Road brought. At the

---

[*] Judge, International Court of Justice. Thanks to my associate, Rosalind Elphick for assistance with the original version of this paper, which was delivered as a keynote address at a conference in Xi'an in November 2016. Rose Cameron and Iulia Joffé assisted with updating the text, which, however, expresses the author's personal views only.
[1] Hansen, *The Silk Road: A New History* (2012) 3.
[2] Ibid.

time of this entombment, paper was an extremely valuable commodity and the secret of its manufacture was known only to the Chinese.[3] The secret would, however, soon be carried along the Silk Road to change, and record, the history of the world.[4] Moreover, the Zoroastrian style of the Iranian's entombment suggests the religious tolerance that was apparently typical of the cities along the Road.[5]

But the story also offers a glimpse into justice at the time. As early as the seventh century CE, disputes could be settled through organised, third-party dispute resolution mechanisms. Moreover, Chinese courts were open to hearing complaints raised by foreign merchants. And the law appears to have been applied without parochialism in a dispute between a foreign and a local merchant. An investment and a trader were protected by operation of the law.

The ancient Silk Road is being reinvented today as the Belt and Road Initiative (BRI). It is a substantial strategic scheme, potentially involving more than sixty countries. Most of these are either developing or least-developed economies. The Initiative spans the promotion of trade links, capital flows, infrastructure investment and policy coordination among participant states. It is unparalleled in terms of China's financial commitment.[6]

An initiative of this size and potential reach presents a legal protection and enforcement challenge much different to that which exists on the domestic plane, even in a country as large and dynamic as China. Nevertheless, as we contemplate the design of an effective dispute resolution mechanism, even in the much changed setting of modern-day China and the vastly different embodiment of the Road idea, the story revealed by the Iranian tomb in Turfan may help to identify what we are looking for: a dispute resolution mechanism that is accessible to all

---

[3] The Silk Road Foundation, 'The History of Paper', www.silk-road.com/artl/papermaking .shtml (accessed 30 August 2019).

[4] Hansen, 6.

[5] Grenet, *Comparative Studies of South Asia, Africa and the Middle East* (2007) 27, 463–78; Foltz, *Religions of the Silk Road: Premodern Patterns of Globalization* (2016) 4, 20, 63, 126, 157.

[6] European Parliament, 'One Belt, One Road (OBOR): China's Regional Integration Initiative' (July 2016) 1, 5–6, www.europarl.europa.eu/RegData/etudes/BRIE/2016/586608/EPRS_BRI (2016)586608_EN.pdf (accessed 30 August 2019). China is reported to have budgeted $1 trillion for infrastructure projects: The Economist, 'The New Silk Road' (12 September 2015), www.economist.com/news/special-report/21663326-chinas-latest-wave-globali sers-will-enrich-their-countryand-world-new-silk-road (accessed 30 August 2019); Public Broadcasting Service, 'China Is Spending Nearly $1 Trillion to Rebuild the Silk Road' (2 March 2016), www.pbs.org/newshour/making-sense/china-is-spending-nearly-1-trillion- to-rebuild-the-silk-road/ (accessed 30 August 2019).

participants all the way down to the individual merchant; a mechanism that is impartial, and one that ensures effective legal protection.

Of course, the BRI is primarily an economic and political project. Its legal aspect is underdeveloped. But good ideas are not necessarily achieved by means of the law, and a lawyer, not least an international lawyer, might have no specific role to play. Or that role might be a straightforward one of legal maintenance, from appropriation to audit, one might say, leaving the real work to the entrepreneurs. The legal articulation so far officially offered is all modern boilerplate, thoroughly conventional. A classic example from Chinese authorities: 'The Belt and Road Initiative is a way for win-win cooperation that promotes common development and prosperity and a road towards peace and friendship by enhancing mutual understanding and trust, and strengthening all-round exchanges ... It promotes practical cooperation in all fields, and works to build a community of shared interests, destiny and responsibility featuring mutual political trust, economic integration and cultural inclusiveness.'[7] This is all praiseworthy, no doubt – but there is very little legal substance here, even in terms of modalities.

1.1 How Can International Law Be Harnessed to Promote This Initiative?

But I am asked to speak as a lawyer. As such, I am predisposed to think of law as functional, a way of doing, not just of speaking. One thing is likely: with increased economic integration comes a potential increase in trade and investment disputes. Moreover, within the cadre of the BRI, these disputes are set to occur in and between developing and least-developed states. The relative instability of these states extends to their domestic legal systems, which can be incomplete and changeable. Additionally, by including states such as Syria and Afghanistan in its ambit, the Project has assumed an element of risk, even high risk.[8] An effective dispute resolution mechanism could help to offset the fears that may otherwise

---

[7] National Development and Reform Commission, Ministry of Foreign Affairs, and Ministry of Commerce of the People's Republic of China, with State Council authorization, 'Vision and Actions on Jointly Building Silk Road Economic Belt and 21st-Century Maritime Silk Road' (28 March 2015) section III (emphasis added), http://en.ndrc.gov.cn /newsrelease/201503/t20150330_669367.html (accessed 30 August 2019).

[8] See also Shengli Jiang, 'Establishment of an International Trade Dispute Settlement Mechanism under the Belt and Road Initiative' in Yun Zhao (ed.), *International Governance and the Rule of Law in China under the Belt and Road Initiative* (Cambridge University Press 2018) 305.

turn trade and investment away from such volatile places. With predictable legal protections underwriting their participation in the scheme, trade and investment might more readily be encouraged to flow the full length of the Belt and Road.

Another concern is that several of the routes China has identified for the Belt and Road will pass directly through zones that are the subject of serious territorial and sovereignty disputes. One proposed route is set to pass through Kashmir. A second crosses through China's disputed border with Bhutan, a state with which China has had no formal diplomatic relations for over two decades.[9] And it is difficult to escape the fact that the maritime belt starts in the South China Sea. It is inevitable that China will face issues in these regions.

1.2   How Does Chinese Strategy Envision Dispute Resolution within the BRI?

This question is made interesting due to the Initiative's unprecedented project design. In March 2015, the National Development and Reform Commission, the Ministry of Foreign Affairs and the Ministry of Commerce jointly released the Initiative's blueprint.[10] This is a broadly phrased document. It makes it clear that the project has no specific implementation or governance structure. Moreover, no-one seems to see the need to create one. A key passage in the document reads as follows:

> The development of the Belt and Road should mainly be conducted through policy communication and objectives coordination. It is a pluralistic and open process of cooperation which can be highly flexible, and *does not seek conformity*. China will join other countries along the Belt and Road to substantiate and improve the content and mode of the Belt

---

[9] Andrea Matles Savada, 'China', in Bhutan: A Country Study. Washington: GPO for the Library of Congress (1991), http://countrystudies.us/bhutan/51.htm (accessed 30 August 2019); Hong Kong Trade Development Council, 'Bhutan: Market Profile', http://china-trade-research.hktdc.com/business-news/article/One-Belt-One-Road/Bhutan-Market-Profile/obor/en/1/1X3CGF6L/1X0A3OW4.htm (accessed 30 August 2019).

[10] National Development and Reform Commission, Ministry of Foreign Affairs, and Ministry of Commerce of the People's Republic of China, with State Council authorization (March 2015), http://en.ndrc.gov.cn/newsrelease/201503/t20150330_669367.html (accessed 30 August 2019). This document will be referred to as the 'Action Plan'.

and Road cooperation ... and align national development programs and
regional cooperation plans.[11]

This approach departs sharply from the model of existing, treaty-based
integration projects, such as the EU or NAFTA.[12] We are accustomed to
seeing a clear legal framework in place – setting out the overarching
strategy and applicable norms, as well as identifying the participating
states and the geographical scope of the project – and to seeing it before
the implementation phase begins. The BRI does not offer these old
comforts. There is no 'Belt and Road' convention for the parties to adhere
to in order to join in the Initiative, nor is the number of countries or the
nature of their participation in it fixed by any specific agreement.

But making this kind of comparison is not useful, because the BRI is
not law, nor is it multilateral. It is simply the external policy of a single
state. As such, there is no reason why it should not be malleable and even
abstruse. The Memoranda of Understanding that China has signed with
some Belt and Road states[13] do not significantly alter this picture, given
that they are couched in explicitly aspirational language.[14]

Does this mean that international law is irrelevant to the project? Not
necessarily. As China outlines in its *Action Plan*, it aims to 'take full
advantage of the existing bilateral and multilateral cooperation mechanisms' in the implementation of its scheme.[15] In short, the Belt and Road
will operate through, rather than aiming to replace, existing international
law frameworks of cooperation and economic integration.

There are a number of these in place. For example, China has concluded bilateral investment treaties (BITs) with 86 of the 137 states that it
has identified as potential partners in the BRI.[16] A number of regional

---

[11] *Action Plan*, section VIII (emphasis added).
[12] See Jaemin Lee, 'The Belt and Road Initiative under Existing Trade Agreements', in
Yun Zhao (ed.), *International Governance and the Rule of Law in China under the Belt
and Road Initiative* (Cambridge: Cambridge University Press 2018) 62–63.
[13] For example, Poland, Serbia, Czech, Bulgaria and Slovakia. See Xinhuanet 'China, CEE
Countries Sign Memo to Promote Belt and Road Initiative' (27 November 2015), www
.chinadaily.com.cn/2015-11/27/content_22522636.htm (accessed 30 August 2019).
[14] For example, the Memorandum of Understanding on Cooperation Concerning the
Eurasia Initiative and the Silk Road Economic Belt and the 21st Century Maritime Silk
Road Between Ministry of Strategy and Finance of Korea and National Development and
Reform Commission of China (24 October 2016).
[15] *Action Plan*, section V.
[16] This number is based on a study of the BITs listed at http://investmentpolicyhub
.unctad.org/IIA/CountryBits/42, cross-referenced with the states listed as forming part
of the 'Belt and Road Initiative' at http://beltandroad.hktdc.com/en/country-profiles
/country-profiles.aspx. See also Wei Shen, 'The Belt and Road Initiative, Expropriation

and preferential trade agreements are in place: the China–ASEAN Free Trade Agreement (CAFTA), Asia–Pacific Economic Cooperation, the Free Trade Agreement of the Asia Pacific, the EU–China Trade and Cooperation Agreement and the China–Pakistan FTA. China is also a member of the WTO, along with 111 of the Belt and Road states.[17] Remarkably, the only participants that are not members are Palestine, Iran and Bhutan,[18] and Bhutan and Iran have both formally triggered the accession process.[19] China is a party to both ICSID and the New York Convention, along with 105 and 106 of its envisioned partner states respectively. China also joins forty-seven of the Belt and Road states in membership of the Permanent Court of Arbitration.

Moreover, the *Action Plan* outlines China's aim to sign new 'cooperation MOUs or plans', to develop 'bilateral cooperation pilot projects' and to establish 'bilateral joint working mechanisms'.[20] To this end, China has actively promoted the upgrading of CAFTA[21] and is in negotiation to conclude the China and the Gulf Cooperation Council,[22] a BIT with the EU[23] and a Regional Comprehensive Economic Partnership (which proposes to establish free trade between Brunei, Myanmar, Cambodia, Indonesia, Laos, Malaysia, the Philippines, Singapore, Thailand, Vietnam, Australia, China, India, Japan, South Korea and New Zealand).[24]

---

and Investor Protection under BITs', in Yun Zhao (ed.), *International Governance and the Rule of Law in China under the Belt and Road Initiative* (Cambridge University Press 2018) 135–36.

[17] WTO, 'Members and Observers' (2016), www.wto.org/english/thewto_e/whatis_e/tif_e/org6_e.htm (accessed 30 August 2019).

[18] Ibid.

[19] On Bhutan: WTO, 'Accessions: Bhutan' (2016), www.wto.org/english/thewto_e/acc_e/a1_bhoutan_e.htm (accessed 30 August 2019). On Iran: WTO, 'Accessions: Iran' (2016), www.wto.org/english/thewto_e/acc_e/a1_iran_e.htm (accessed 30 August 2019).

[20] *Action Plan*, section V.

[21] The State Council Information Office of the People's Republic of China, 'China, ASEAN seals deal to upgrade bilateral FTA' (23 November 2015), www.scio.gov.cn/32618/Document/1456293/1456293.htm (accessed 30 August 2019).

[22] China FTA Network, 'China-GCC FTA' (12 May 2016), http://fta.mofcom.gov.cn/topic/engcc.shtml (accessed 30 August 2019).

[23] European Parliament 'EU and China Comprehensive Agreement on Investment (EU–China CAI)', www.europarl.europa.eu/legislative-train/api/stages/report/current/theme/a-balanced-and-progressive-trade-policy-to-harness-globalisation/file/eu-china-investment-agreement (accessed 30 August 2019).

[24] China FTA Network, 'China-RCEP' (22 August 2016), http://fta.mofcom.gov.cn/list/rcepen/enrcepnews/1/encateinfo.html (accessed 30 August 2019).

The web of legal ties means that there will be few Belt and Road states in which transnational trade and investment would enjoy no legal protection. Only a handful of states have not concluded BITs with China: these being Afghanistan, Bhutan, the Maldives, Montenegro, Nepal and Timor-Leste (note also that BITs signed between China and Jordan in 2001,[25] and China and Brunei in 2000,[26] have yet to come into force).[27] Palestine has BITs in place with only four other Belt and Road states, not including China,[28] and two of these – that with Jordan and Turkey – are not yet in force.[29] But Palestine has acceded to the Hague Convention for the Pacific Settlement of International Disputes, and has established FTAs with the European Union and the Arab League.[30] Bhutan has not concluded BITs with any states[31] and is not yet a member of the WTO. It is, however, a member of SAFTA and the Bay of Bengal Initiative for Multi-Sectoral Technical and Economic Cooperation.[32]

Thus, a number of dispute resolution mechanisms are already in place. Each BIT has a built-in investor–state dispute settlement mechanism, for example, and Chinese claimants (including SOEs) have commenced a number of investor–state arbitrations – though as yet only three have

[25] Investment Policy Hub, 'Jordan', https://investmentpolicy.unctad.org/country-navigator/109/jordan (accessed 30 August 2019).

[26] Investment Policy Hub, 'Brunei Darussalam', https://investmentpolicy.unctad.org/country-navigator/32/brunei-darussalam (accessed 30 August 2019).

[27] Ministry of Commerce, Chinese People's Republic, 'Bilateral Investment Treaty' (31 March 2016), http://english.mofcom.gov.cn/article/bilateralchanges/201603/20160301287079.shtml (accessed 30 August 2019).

[28] Investment Policy Hub, 'Egypt – State of Palestine BIT (1998)' https://investmentpolicy.unctad.org/international-investment-agreements/treaties/bilateral-investment-treaties/1384/egypt–state-of-palestine-bit-1998 (accessed 30 August 2019). Investment Policy Hub, 'State of Palestine – Russian Federation BIT (2016)' https://investmentpolicy.unctad.org/international-investment-agreements/treaties/bilateral-investment-treaties/3786/state-of-palestine–russian-federation-bit-2016 (accessed 30 August 2019).

[29] Investment Policy Hub, 'Jordan – State of Palestine BIT (2012)' https://investmentpolicy.unctad.org/international-investment-agreements/treaties/bilateral-investment-treaties/2174/jordan–state-of-palestine-bit-2012 (accessed 30 August 2019). Investment Policy Hub, 'Turkey – State of Palestine BIT (2018)' https://investmentpolicy.unctad.org/international-investment-agreements/treaties/bilateral-investment-treaties/3832/turkey–state-of-palestine-bit-2018 (accessed 30 August 2019).

[30] Permanent Court of Arbitration, 'New PCA Member State: Palestine' (15 March 2016), https://pca-cpa.org/en/news/new-pca-member-state-palestine/ (accessed 30 August 2019); Investment Policy Hub, 'State of Palestine', https://investmentpolicy.unctad.org/country-navigator/161/state-of-palestine (accessed 30 August 2019).

[31] Investment Policy Hub, 'Bhutan: BITs', https://investmentpolicy.unctad.org/country-navigator/25/bhutan (accessed 30 August 2019).

[32] Investment Policy Hub, 'Bhutan: TIPs', https://investmentpolicy.unctad.org/country-navigator/25/bhutan (accessed 30 August 2019).

been commenced against it.[33] China is already an active participant in WTO dispute settlement processes: it has brought 20 cases, acted as respondent in 43 and participated as a third party in 173.[34] But the *Action Plan* does not identify any vision for dispute resolution beyond these existing mechanisms.

1.3   What Are the Possibilities for a 'Belt and Road' Dispute Resolution Mechanism?

A combination of mediation and arbitration appears to be the popular choice here.[35] The Supreme People's Court of the People's Republic of China has ventured an opinion (in July 2015) indicating as much. It instructed the courts below it to 'give support to the resolution of disputes by the Chinese and foreign parties through mediation, arbitration, and other non-litigation forms' and 'promote the improvement of the joint working mechanism for commercial mediation, arbitration mediation, people's mediation, administrative mediation, industrial mediation, and judicial mediation'.[36]

I understand that the International Academy of the Belt and Road in its *Blue Book on the Dispute Resolution Mechanism for the Belt and Road* advocated the creation of a uniform dispute resolution mechanism adopting the approach of mediation followed by arbitration.[37]

---

[33] *Hela Schwarz GmbH* v. *People's Republic of China*, ICSID Case No ARB/17/19; *Ekran Berhad* v. *People's Republic of China* (ICSID Case No ARB/11/15); *Ansung Housing Co, Ltd.* v. *People's Republic of China* (ICSID Case No ARB/14/25). For cases brought by Chinese investors, see, for example: *Tza Yap Shum* v. *Republic of Peru* (ICSID Case No ARB/07/6); *Ping An Life Insurance Company of China* v. *Kingdom of Belgium* (ICSID Case No ARB/12/29); *Sanum Investments Limited (Investor/Claimant)* v. *Laos* (PCA Case No 2013-13); *Beijing Urban Construction Group Co. Ltd.* v. *Republic of Yemen* (ICSID Case No ARB/14/30).

[34] World Trade Organisation, 'Disputes by Country/Territory' (2016), www.wto.org/eng lish/tratop_e/dispu_e/dispu_by_country_e.htm (accessed 30 August 2019).

[35] See also Sienho Yee, 'Dispute Settlement on the Belt Road: Ideas on System, Spirit and Style' (2018) 17 CJIL 907.

[36] Chinese Supreme People's Court, 'Several Opinions on Providing Judicial Services and Guarantee for the Building of One Belt One Road by People's Courts (No. 9 [2015] of the Supreme People's Court)' (16 June 2016) para 11 (unofficial translation).

[37] Xinhua Finance Agency, 'Blue Book the Dispute Resolution Mechanism for B&R Was Issued' (12 October 2016), http://en.xfafinance.com/html/13th_Five-year_Plan /Development_Policy/2016/267617.shtml (accessed 30 August 2019); Yuen, Script of Presentation at the 5th Asia Pacific ADR Conference (12 October 2016) para 15, www .doj.gov.hk/eng/public/pdf/2016/sj20161012e2.pdf (accessed 30 August 2019).

Arbitration is also the model of dispute resolution which the Asian Infrastructure Investment Bank's Articles of Agreement have been drafted to include.[38]

The China International Economic and Trade Arbitration Commission (CIETAC) launched its Investment Arbitration Rules in December 2017, which are the first set of investment arbitration rules promulgated by the Chinese arbitral institution.[39] This step will likely pave the way for the CIETAC and its rules to be adopted more widely in future investment agreements or instruments involving Chinese parties.[40]

On 23 January 2018, China's Central Leading Group for Comprehensively Deepening Reforms released plans for the establishment of a Belt and Road dispute settlement mechanism.[41] On 1 July 2018, China's Supreme People's Court followed up this announcement with issuing the 'Provisions on Several Issues Regarding the Establishment of the International Commercial Court'.[42]

The Provisions include nineteen articles that provide a skeleton for the Belt and Road dispute settlement mechanism.[43] According to the Provisions, the Belt and Road dispute settlement mechanism will comprise two international commercial courts (collectively known as the China International Commercial Court (CICC)): one in Xi'an addressing commercial disputes from projects on the Silk Road Economic Belt, and one in Shenzhen addressing disputes from the 21st Century Maritime Silk Road.[44]

---

[38] Asian Infrastructure Investment Bank, Articles of Agreement, Article 55, www.aiib.org /en/about-aiib/basic-documents/_download/articles-of-agreement/basic_document_ french_bank_articles_of_agreement.pdf (accessed 30 August 2019).

[39] Jue Jun Lu, 'Dispute Resolution Along the Belt and Road: What Does the Future Hold?' (2 August 2018), http://arbitrationblog.practicallaw.com/dispute-resolution-along-the-belt-and-road-what-does-the-future-hold/ (accessed 30 August 2019).

[40] Ibid.

[41] Guo Liqin, *China Will Set Up a New International Commercial Court in Beijing, Xi'an and Shenzhen*, Yicai (24 January 2018), https://perma.cc/7C2U-43UG (accessed 30 August 2019).

[42] Provisions of the Supreme People's Court on Several Issues Regarding the Establishment of the International Commercial Court, http://cicc.court.gov.cn/html/1/219/199/201/817 .html (accessed 30 August 2019).

[43] Zachary Mollengarden, '"One-Stop" Dispute Resolution on the Belt and Road: Toward an International Commercial Court with Chinese Characteristics' (2019) 36(1) *Pacific Basin Law Journal* 65, 101.

[44] Mollengarden (n 38) 74.

The CICC will be a 'permanent adjudication organ' of the Chinese Supreme Peoples' Court.[45] According to Article 11 of the Provisions, the CICC will be a 'one-stop' mechanism, acting as a 'dispute resolution platform' through which 'mediation, arbitration, and litigation are efficiently linked'. How this one-stop dispute resolution mechanism will work in practice remains to be seen.

The CICC will be comprised exclusively of Chinese nationals,[46] and parties may only be represented by Chinese qualified attorneys.[47] The judges of the CICC, however, will be supported by an International Commercial Expert Committee, the members of which will serve as mediators in international commercial disputes[48] and assist with the interpretation of foreign law.[49]

As a member of the International Court of Justice, I would be remiss if I did not note that arbitration is not the only possibility. The Chinese Supreme People's Court in its July 2015 opinion acknowledged 'the advantages of various dispute resolution methods in resolving disputes and conflicts involved in the construction of the "Belt and Road"' and 'diversified demands of the Chinese and foreign parties for the resolution of disputes'.[50] A unified system does not have to identify a single mechanism for all types of disputes – as Part XV of UNCLOS shows. For example, it would be possible for 'mixed' (state–private actor) disputes to be referred to one mechanism, while interstate disputes were referred to another. The International Court is an option that I would encourage policymakers to consider as a possible forum for the latter.

The International Court offers various advantages. It is outside the Belt and Road states and thus offers geographic neutrality; the diversity and size of the bench is aimed at political and ideological neutrality. Although the Court has general jurisdiction, it has a proven track record in the

---

[45] Provisions of the Supreme People's Court on Several Issues Regarding the Establishment of the International Commercial Court, http://cicc.court.gov.cn/html/1/219/199/201/817 .html (accessed 30 August 2019), Article 1.

[46] Jue Jun Lu, 'Dispute Resolution Along the Belt and Road: What Does the Future Hold?' (2 August 2018), http://arbitrationblog.practicallaw.com/dispute-resolution-along-the-belt-and-road-what-does-the-future-hold/ (accessed 30 August 2019).

[47] Mollengarden (n 38) 101.

[48] Provisions of the Supreme People's Court on Several Issues Regarding the Establishment of the International Commercial Court, Article 12.

[49] Ibid, Article 8.4.

[50] Chinese Supreme People's Court, 'Several Opinions on Providing Judicial Services and Guarantee for the Building of One Belt One Road by People's Courts (No. 9 [2015] of the Supreme People's Court)' (16 June 2016) para 11 (unofficial translation).

settlement of certain types of disputes that are of particular relevance to the BRI, such as territorial disputes (including as they relate to maritime delimitation). The Court's position at the informal apex of the international judicial system gives it unique authority, borne out by scholarly studies revealing rather high levels of compliance with its decisions.[51] In cases of non-compliance, aggrieved states may refer their cases to the Security Council, 'which may, if it deems necessary, make recommendations or decide upon measures to be taken to give effect to the judgment',[52] giving their cause a heightened profile irrespective of the Council's ability or inclination to respond effectively.

The working methods of the Court also provide certain advantages to litigant states. Chief among these is the amount of time and energy that is given to each case. Each dispute is heard by a full bench. That is, at least fifteen (plus ad hoc judges, if any) judicial minds are brought to bear on every case. Moreover, the judges must vote separately on each aspect of the Court's decision. The process is both inclusive and painstaking.

Over the years, the Court has shown itself responsive to criticism by adjusting a number of its working methods. Answering concerns of slowness, for example, it has shortened the time-limits for written proceedings; undertaken several cases at once; and shortened the length of time allowed for deliberations. The timescale for processing new cases is now comparable to those of an arbitral tribunal.

It is worth recalling also that China is already a party to the Statute of the Court, along with every one of its potential Belt and Road partners, aside from Palestine.[53] Furthermore, there is always a Chinese judge on the Court.

1.4   Is A 'Belt and Road' Dispute Resolution Mechanism Desirable?

In assessing our response to this question, we would need to think carefully about the advantages and disadvantages – specific to the BRI – attendant on adding a new layer of jurisdiction to an already complicated web of international arrangements. Proliferation of dispute

---

[51] Paulson (2004) 98 *AJIL* 434; Schulte, *Compliance with Decisions of the International Court of Justice* (2005); Llamzon (2007) 5 *EJIL* 815.
[52] UN Charter, Article 94(2)(g).
[53] United Nations, 'Member States', www.un.org/en/member-states/ (accessed 30 August 2019).

resolution mechanisms has sparked some anxiety and created difficult problems of delineation, not least under Part XV of UNCLOS.

To be sure, globalisation has deeply affected the content and modes of enforcement of international law. It is creating strong pressures for regulation and enforcement mechanisms in some fields, encouraging the emergence of branch-specific mechanisms. Apart from UNCLOS, we have witnessed the emergence of international criminal tribunals, human rights courts, GATT panels and various modes of arbitration.

The proliferation of institutions designed to administer specific substantive fields of international law has brought some benefits. A problem arising within a specific area of law can be dealt with by a tribunal that is dedicated to problem-solving of that specific kind. Regional mechanisms are able to offer a level of geopolitical sensitivity that can be lacking from less focussed tribunals. This can have a real impact on the tribunal's interpretation of the respective rights of the parties, particularly in cases that call for an assessment of the equities.

But the type of dispute settlement mechanism that is appropriate will depend on the particular facts, the parties involved and their preferences. In my experience, states like to be able to draw on the fullest range of possibilities when choosing a dispute resolution mechanism for a particular dispute.

Complicating the picture in the Belt and Road context is the fact that its envisioned partners belong to an array of regional organizations – the European Union, the Arab League, the African Union and the Association of Southeast Asian Nations, for example. States' ability to commit to a Belt and Road dispute resolution mechanism might be affected by these other affiliations.

1.5 Conclusion

There is to my mind no clear winner in this assessment. The types of disputes that might arise in the context of the BRI are notably diverse, and this quite apart from the amorphous subject matter covered by its objectives. Perhaps the answer is that no *single* mechanism is possible.

A Chinese proverb on the virtues of third party dispute resolution comes to mind: 'Settling a dispute through the law is like losing a cow for the sake of a cat.' There is a perception that judicial dispute settlement can be time-consuming, costly and unpredictable. This no doubt cuts across the Chinese interest in encouraging the settlement of differences through negotiation or mediation before turning to tribunals.

One Belt, One Road, One Clause for Dispute Resolution?

MICHAEL HWANG, DAVID HOLLOWAY AND LIM SI CHENG

2.1 Introduction

The One Belt One Road initiative is an international project with an extraordinary ambition. It aims to invest in the history of civilisations by revitalising the overland and maritime routes of the ancient Silk Road. The initiative is anticipated to impact the lives of over 62 per cent of the world's population and around 31 per cent of the world's GDP.[1] More than sixty countries have indicated their commitment to participate in the One Belt One Road initiative (the 'OBOR initiative').[2]

The global academic community views the OBOR initiative in a generally positive light. Economists welcome it as a steady step towards growth in world trade.[3] Political scientists view it as a sturdy anchor against antiglobalisation sentiments.[4] Historians celebrate it because it refreshes global interest in a fascinating but understudied area of world

---

[1] HKTDC, 'Belt and Road Basics', http://bit.ly/2sm0vqo (accessed 25 September 2017).

[2] HKTDC, 'Country Profile', http://bit.ly/2tXlzFR (accessed 25 September 2017).

[3] An example of an economic analysis of the OBOR initiative can be found in H. Chen, 'China's "One Belt, One Road" Initiative and Its Implications for Sino-African Investment Relations', *Transnational Corporations Review*, 8(3) (2016), 178.

[4] See for example N. Casarini, 'When All Roads Lead to Beijing. Assessing China's New Silk Road and Its Implications for Europe', *The International Spectator*, 51(4) (2016), 95; W. Liu and M. Dunford, 'Inclusive Globalization: Unpacking China's Belt and Road Initiative', *Area Development Policy*, 1(3) (2016), 323; A. Grimmel and S. My Giang, 'Why China's "One Belt, One Road" Initiative Should Be Taken More Seriously by the EU and How It Can Be an Interregional Success' (*LSE EUROPP blog*, 11 April 2017), http://bit.ly/2tALKEl (accessed 25 September 2017); and B. Zheng, 'China's "One Belt, One Road" Plan Marks the Next Phase of Globalization' (*The Huffington Post*, 18 May 2017), http://bit.ly/2uB811V (accessed 25 September 2017). Of course, this is not to deny that some political scientists are less enamoured by the OBOR initiative: see A. Cooley, 'The Emerging Political Economy of OBOR: The Challenges of Promoting Connectivity in

history.[5] But the members of the legal profession are in a more pensive mood, because they are thinking about the capacity of the law at all levels – national, transnational and international – to facilitate the resolution of commercial disputes[6] between enterprises that may arise in the course of the implementation of the OBOR initiative.[7] What dispute resolution options do contracting parties have when their cross-border transactions turn sour? And which of these options best guarantees that winning parties get their money back?

The traditional answer to these questions is that international arbitration is the best option to govern cross-border disputes. The purported basis for this is that 164 States (the 'NYC States') have ratified the 1958 New York Convention on the Recognition and Enforcement of Foreign Arbitral Awards (the '1958 New York Convention'),[8] making the arbitral award the most widely enforceable type of legal order in the world. So, an arbitral award obtained in one NYC State will readily be enforced in another NYC State, subject to certain limited grounds for the setting aside and non-recognition of arbitral awards under the 1958 New York Convention. On the other hand, foreign judgments are perceived to be less widely enforceable, due to the unfavourable treatment of foreign judgments by national laws and the lack of a multilateral treaty regulating foreign judgments. International litigation is perceived to be the poor cousin of international arbitration.

The purpose of this chapter is to investigate these assumptions in the light of some recent trends that have improved the enforceability of foreign judgments. It argues that the foreign judgment is catching up with the foreign arbitral award in terms of enforceability. International litigation is slowly emerging as a credible alternative to international arbitration. Global trends are challenging the claim that the arbitration clause is (and will always be) the only viable dispute resolution clause. To

Central Asia and Beyond' (Centre for Strategic & International Studies, October 2016), http://bit.ly/2shZSyH (accessed 25 September 2017).
[5] In fact, one historian's book recently topped the bestseller lists in China! See University of Oxford, 'Historian's Book Tops Bestseller Charts in China', http://bit.ly/2qtqwUV (accessed 25 September 2017).
[6] Inter-State disputes and investor–State disputes may also arise from the OBOR initiative, but they are beyond the scope of analysis of this chapter. We will only focus on the dispute resolution mechanisms that are available to private parties in commercial disputes.
[7] See G. Wang, 'The Belt and Road Initiative in Quest for a Dispute Resolution Mechanism', *Asia Pacific Law Review*, 7 June 2017, http://bit.ly/2thxXjY (accessed 25 September 2017).
[8] UNCITRAL, 'Status: Convention on the Recognition and Enforcement of Foreign Arbitral Awards (New York, 1958)', http://bit.ly/2tX1Jul (accessed 25 September 2017).

make this argument, this chapter will proceed in the following manner. First, it will demonstrate the consistent enforceability of foreign judgments in common law countries (Section 2.2). Second, it will highlight a number of contemporary trends that are gradually improving the enforceability of foreign judgments in civil law countries (Section 2.3). Finally, it will discuss the fledgling potential of the 2005 Hague Convention on Choice of Court Agreements to standardise the law and practice of enforcement of judgments made by designated courts in exclusive choice of court agreements (Section 2.4).

2.2   Common Law Countries

A number of participating countries in the OBOR initiative apply the common law of recognition and enforcement of foreign judgments, including Malaysia, Singapore, Brunei, New Zealand and South Africa.[9] Several territories in civil law countries also apply the common law, including Hong Kong (in China) and the Dubai International Financial Centre (the DIFC) (in UAE).[10]

The common law generally adopts a pro-enforcement attitude to foreign judgments. This is because the common law adheres to a doctrine of obligation, according to which 'the judgment of a court of competent jurisdiction over the defendant imposes a duty or obligation on the defendant to pay the sum for which judgment is given, which the courts in [a common law] country are bound to enforce'.[11] The result of this is that the common law courts 'have never thought it necessary to investigate what reciprocal rights of enforcement are conceded by the foreign country, or to limit their exercise of jurisdiction to that which they would recognise in others'.[12] In other words, reciprocity is not a requirement for the enforcement of a foreign judgment in the eyes of a common law court.

Beyond the general attitude of the common law, there is another reason why foreign judgments are generally as enforceable as foreign arbitral awards in common law countries. The reason is that the common law approach to the enforcement of foreign judgments shares three

---

[9]   HKTDC (n 2).
[10] Ibid.
[11] *Schibsby* v. *Westenholz* (1870) L.R. 6 Q.B. 155, 159 (per Blackburn J), following *Russell* v. *Smyth* (1842) 9 M. & W. 810, 819 and *Williams* v. *Jones* (1845) 13 M. & W. 628, 633.
[12] *Adams* v. *Cape Industries Plc* [1990] Ch. 433, 552.

important similarities with the approach of international arbitration to the enforcement of foreign arbitral awards.

First, the common law and the regime of international arbitration both provide that the enforcing court is not permitted to review the foreign judgment or arbitral award (as the case may be) on the merits. Under common law, it is established that 'a foreign judgment could not be re-examined on the merits provided the foreign court had jurisdiction according to the English rules of the conflict of laws'.[13] Under the 1958 New York Convention, recognition or enforcement of a foreign arbitral award may be refused on one of the grounds set out in Article V, none of which enables the defendant to argue that the arbitral tribunal has made an error of fact or law. The UNCITRAL Model Law on International Commercial Arbitration (the 'Model Law') also does not provide for such a ground.[14]

Second, the common law and the 1958 New York Convention prescribe the same ground for the staying of enforcement proceedings. Under common law, although a foreign judgment may be considered final and conclusive notwithstanding the existence of a pending appeal in the foreign country,[15] a stay of execution 'in a proper case ... would no doubt be ordered pending a possible appeal'.[16] Under the 1958 New York Convention, the enforcing court may stay the proceedings if an application for the setting aside or suspension of the arbitral award has been made to the competent authority of the country in which, or under the law of which, the arbitral award was made.[17]

---

[13] Lord Collins of Mapesbury (ed), *Dicey, Morris & Collins on the Conflict of Laws* (15th ed., Sweet & Maxwell 2012) 721. See *Henderson* v. *Henderson* (1844) 6 Q.B. 288; *Bank of Australasia* v. *Harding* (1850) 9 C.B. 661; *De Cosse Brissac* v. *Rathbone* (1861) 6 H. & n. 301; *Godard* v. *Gray* (1870) L.R. 6 Q.B. 139.

[14] N. Blackaby and C. Partasides, *Redfern and Hunter and International Arbitration* (6th ed., Oxford University Press 2015) 595: 'in [the Model Law] there is no possibility for challenging an award on the basis of mistake of law, however narrow'. See also UNCITRAL 2012 Digest of Case Law on the Model law on International Commercial Arbitration (United Nations Publication 2012) 140: 'A great number of cases underline that the Model Law does not permit review of the merits of an arbitral award. This has been found to apply in principle to issues of law as well as to issues of fact.' In *PT Perusahaan Gas Negara (Persero) TBK* v. *CRW Joint Operation* [2010] SGHC 202 [10], the Singapore High Court remarked: 'It is trite law that the court will not interfere with an arbitral award even if the award was made on a misapplication of the law or contains errors of fact.'

[15] Collins (n 13) 677–78.

[16] Ibid. 678.

[17] Article V(1)(e) 1958 New York Convention. See also Article 36(1)(a)(v) UNCITRAL Model Law.

Third, the common law and the 1958 New York Convention provide similar defences to the enforcement of foreign judgments and awards. These pertain to (a) jurisdiction, (b) public policy, (c) fraud and (d) breach of natural justice, and we will discuss each aspect in turn.

(a) *Jurisdiction*. Under common law, a foreign judgment will not be enforced if the foreign court lacked 'international jurisdiction' to give that judgment.[18] A foreign court has international jurisdiction if the judgment debtor (i) was present in the foreign country at the time the foreign proceedings were instituted;[19] (ii) was a claimant or counter-claimant in the foreign proceedings; (iii) had submitted to the foreign proceedings by way of appearance; or (iv) had earlier agreed to submit to the jurisdiction of the foreign court.[20] Under the 1958 New York Convention, a foreign arbitral award may be refused enforcement if the arbitral tribunal lacked the jurisdiction to arbitrate the dispute, that is, if the arbitral agreement was invalid[21] or the arbitral award dealt with a dispute that fell outside the terms of the submission to arbitration.[22] The upshot is that, although the concept of jurisdiction differs between the two regimes, both regimes allow the defendant to challenge the foreign judgment or arbitral award on the basis of lack of jurisdiction in its respective conceptions in the two regimes.

(b) *Public policy*. Under common law, a foreign judgment will not be enforced if to do so would be contrary to national public policy. As Scarman J (as he then was) held, 'an English court will refuse to apply a law which outrages its sense of justice and decency'.[23] Likewise, under the 1958 New York Convention, a foreign arbitral award will not be enforced if the arbitral award conflicts with national public policy.[24] The authors of *Redfern and Hunter on International*

---

[18] Collins (n 13) 725.

[19] The common law requirement of presence has since been amended by section 32 UK Civil Jurisdiction and Judgments Act 1982. Presence is no longer sufficient as a matter of UK law. The bringing of the foreign proceedings must also not conflict with any agreement under which the dispute was to be settled otherwise than by proceedings in the foreign court.

[20] Collins (n 13) 692.

[21] Article V(1)(a) 1958 New York Convention. See also Articles 34(2)(a)(i) and 36(1)(a)(i) Model Law.

[22] Article V(1)(c) 1958 New York Convention. See also Articles 34(2)(a)(iii) and 36(1)(a)(iii) Model Law.

[23] *Re Fuld's Estate (No 3)* [1968] P 675, 698.

[24] Article V(2)(b) 1958 New York Convention. See also Articles 34(2)(b)(ii) and 36(1)(b)(ii) Model Law.

Arbitration observe that '[m]ost developed arbitral jurisdictions have similar conceptions of public policy'.[25] For example, 'German courts have held that an award will violate public policy if it conflicts with fundamental notions of justice, *bonos mores*, or conflicts with principles that are fundamental national or economic values'.[26] Likewise, the Singapore Court of Appeal has stated that public policy is violated if upholding the arbitral award would '"shock the conscience" . . . or is "clearly injurious to the public good or . . . wholly offensive to the ordinary reasonable and fully informed member of the public" . . . or where it violates the forum's most basic notion of morality and justice'.[27]

(c) *Fraud*. Under common law, a foreign judgment will not be enforced if it is tainted by fraud on the part of the judgment creditor or the foreign court.[28] Under the 1958 New York Convention, while fraud is not expressly stipulated to be a ground for refusal of enforcement or for setting aside, most authorities permit the inclusion of fraud under the heading of public policy.[29] Several national laws also include fraud as a separate ground for setting aside or for refusal of enforcement.[30]

(d) *Breach of natural justice*. Under common law, a foreign judgment will not be enforced if the proceedings in which the foreign judgment was obtained were opposed to 'natural justice'.[31] These principles of natural justice involve 'first of all that the court . . . has given notice to the litigant that they are about to proceed to determine the rights between him and the other litigant; the other is that having given him that notice, it does afford him an opportunity of substantially presenting his case before the court'.[32] Under the 1958 New York Convention, the failure to give the defendant proper notice of the appointment of the arbitrator or of the proceedings, or the opportunity to present his case, will entitle the defendant to the refusal of enforcement of the arbitral award.[33] While there is no express

---

[25] Blackaby and Partasides (n 14) 598.
[26] Ibid.
[27] *PT Asuransi Jasa Indonesia (Persero)* v. *Dexia Bank SA* [2006] SGCA 41 [59].
[28] Collins (n 13) 727.
[29] G. Born, *International Commercial Arbitration*, vol. II (2nd ed., Kluwer Law International 2014) 3704.
[30] See section 24(a) International Arbitration Act (Cap 143A) of Singapore.
[31] Collins (n 13) 740.
[32] *Jacobson* v. *Frachon* (1927) 138 L.T. 386, 392.
[33] Article V(1)(b) 1958 New York Convention. See also Articles 34(2)(a)(ii) and 36(1)(a)(ii) Model Law.

provision to deal with the lack of impartiality and independence on the part of the arbitral tribunal (which is widely regarded as a form of breach of natural justice), 'it is nonetheless clear that an arbitrator's lack of independence and/or impartiality can be a basis for denying recognition of an award',[34] whether one regards it as a violation of public policy,[35] a deprivation of the opportunity to present one's case[36] or a failure to constitute the arbitral tribunal in accordance with the agreement of the parties.[37] Certain national laws also expressly stipulate 'breach of natural justice' as a ground to set aside or refuse to enforce an award.[38]

The discussion above makes it clear that the principles of the common law and the Model Law have developed along the same lines of thinking. Both regimes do not permit the enforcing court to review the foreign judgment or award on the merits. Both regimes allow the aggrieved defendant to stay the proceedings on the basis of the existence of an appeal or setting-aside proceedings (as the case may be) in the forum court. Both regimes allow the defendant to challenge the propriety of the foreign court or arbitral proceedings by reference to jurisdiction, fraud, breach of natural justice or public policy. So, if parties anticipate that enforcement proceedings would be instituted in a particular common law country in the event of a dispute because their assets are located in that country, there should be very few surprises if the parties decide to submit to foreign court proceedings instead of arbitral proceedings. The foreign judgment should be just as enforceable as a foreign arbitral award in that common law country.

To be sure, the two regimes do not completely mirror each other, and there may be defences that only one of the regimes recognises. For example, the common law requires the foreign judgment to be final and conclusive, with the result that provisional orders that fail to deal with the merits of the case are unenforceable.[39] On the other hand, the

---

[34] Born (n 29) 3587.

[35] Articles 34(2)(b)(ii) and 36(1)(b)(ii) Model Law.

[36] Articles 34(2)(a)(ii) and 36(1)(a)(ii) Model Law.

[37] Articles 34(2)(a)(iv) and 36(1)(a)(iv) Model Law.

[38] See section 24(b) Singapore International Arbitration Act (Cap 143A) and section 36(3)(b) New Zealand Arbitration Act 1996.

[39] A. Briggs, *The Conflict of Laws* (3rd ed., Oxford University Press 2013) 168: '"final" means that the decision cannot be reopened in the court which made the ruling, even though it may be subject to appeal to a higher court; and "conclusive" that it represents the court's settled answer on the substance of the point adjudicated. For this reason, a foreign freezing order will not be recognized, as it is neither predicated upon a final

2006 version of the Model Law allows for the enforcement of interim measures, which are defined as temporary measures to:

(a) maintain or restore the status quo pending determination of the dispute;
(b) take action that would prevent, or refrain from taking action that is likely to cause, current or imminent harm or prejudice to the arbitral process itself;
(c) provide a means of preserving assets out of which a subsequent award may be satisfied; or
(d) preserve evidence that may be relevant and material to the resolution of the dispute.[40]

But all in all, there are more similarities than dissimilarities between the two regimes. Insofar as common law countries are concerned, the enforceability of foreign arbitral awards and judgments are more or less on par.

The pro-enforcement attitude of the common law countries is further seen in the statutes enacted by these countries to govern the enforcement of judgments from the courts of certain specified countries.[41] The purpose of enacting these statutes is to streamline the process of enforcing judgments from these countries. Under English common law, a foreign judgment is not directly enforceable, and the judgment creditor must go through the trouble of bringing an action on the foreign judgment to obtain an English judgment.[42] In contrast, under the UK Administration of Justice Act 1920 and the Foreign Judgments (Reciprocal Enforcement) Act 1933, a judgment creditor simply registers the foreign judgment with the High Court in England, which, upon registration, will have the same effect as an

---

determination of the validity of the claim nor usually incapable of review and revision by the court which ordered it.'

[40] Article 17(2) Model Law.

[41] For example, the UK has enacted the Administration of Justice Act 1920 to govern the recognition and enforcement of judgments obtained in Commonwealth countries, and the Foreign Judgments (Reciprocal Enforcement) Act 1933 for judgments obtained in countries to which the Queen has directed to extend the Act. See also the Singapore Reciprocal Enforcement of Foreign Judgments Act (Cap 265) and the Reciprocal Enforcement of Commonwealth Judgments Act (Cap 264); the Australian Foreign Judgments Act 1991; and the New Zealand Reciprocal Enforcement of Judgments Act 1934.

[42] See Briggs (n 39) 139: 'It is sometimes said that at common law one enforces a foreign judgment by bringing an action on the judgment. It may be true that this is the effect of the common law, but as it is written the proposition is liable to mislead: one obtains an English judgment, and enforces that.'

English judgment for the purposes of execution.[43] So, if these statutes are to be remembered for anything, it is that they serve to expedite, not hinder, the enforceability of foreign judgments. They simplify the process to make foreign judgments more enforceable. This is all achieved without departing greatly from the substantive requirements of common law. As Briggs notes, 'the substantive terms of the statutes which determine the entitlement to register the judgment are very close to the common law as this was understood at the date of enactment, with the consequence that in substance, although not in form, recognition will depend on the rules of the common law'.[44]

2.3 Civil Law Countries

There are also growing signs to indicate that the enforceability of foreign judgments in civil law countries in the OBOR initiative are slowly improving. Civil law countries are becoming increasingly receptive to enforcing foreign judgments. To appreciate these trends, it is necessary to first examine the traditionally conservative attitudes of these civil law countries. This will enable us to better appreciate the significance of these positive trends.

2.3.1 The Traditional Positions

Traditionally, the laws of civil law countries on the enforcement of foreign judgments were thought to be lamentably diverse. There was very little uniformity between the laws of civil law countries. Different civil law countries imposed different hurdles to the enforcement of foreign judgments. For example, some civil law countries only require the absence of an earlier local judgment on the same dispute.[45] Other civil law countries additionally require the absence of earlier local proceedings.[46] Even when civil law countries impose the same hurdle,

---

[43] Section 2(2) UK Foreign Judgments (Reciprocal Enforcement) Act 1933 and section 9(3) UK Administration of Justice Act 1920.

[44] Briggs (n 39) 164.

[45] For example, Article 380 of the Qatari Civil and Commercial Procedure Law No. 13 of 1990 provides: 'Execution may not be ordered unless the following is verified: [...] The judgment or order is not inconsistent with the judgment or order that was issued before by a court in Qatar', http://bit.ly/2uisKaN (accessed 25 September 2017).

[46] For instance, Article 412(1)(4) of the Russian Civil Procedure Code No. 138-FZ of 14 November 2002 (as amended on 6 February 2012) provides: 'A rejection of a forcible execution of the decision of a foreign court may be admissible [if] ... in the

they may have different conceptions of what that hurdle entails. For instance, in relation to jurisdiction, some countries require that the dispute does not fall within the 'exclusive jurisdiction' of the local courts.[47] Other countries simply require that the local courts do not have 'jurisdiction' over the dispute.[48] Still other countries require that the foreign court has jurisdiction under the law of the country in which the foreign court is situated.[49] These are all very different conceptions of the same requirement of jurisdiction, effected through different phraseologies of the same hurdle. Finally, even when civil law countries adopt the same phraseology in relation to the same hurdle, their local courts may have different interpretations of what that hurdle entails. Public policy is a clear example. Both Polish and Turkish laws provide for a 'public policy' hurdle,[50] but what is contrary to Polish public policy

proceedings of a court in the Russian Federation there is a case instituted on the dispute between the same parties, for the same object and on the same grounds before the case was instituted in the foreign court', http://bit.ly/2sR2eYe (accessed 25 September 2017).

[47] For example, Article 169(6) of the Iranian Civil Judgments Enforcement Act 1977 provides: 'Civil Judgments issued by foreign courts are enforceable in Iran if they satisfy the following conditions, unless a different procedure is mentioned by the law: [. . .] The subject matter of the judgment should not be exclusively within the jurisdiction of the Iranian Courts', http://bit.ly/2tkmouU (accessed 25 September 2017). See also Article 412(1)(3) of the Russian Civil Procedure Code (n 46): 'A rejection of a forcible execution of the decision of a foreign court may be admissible [if] . . . the consideration of the case is referred to the exclusive cognisance of the courts in the Russian Federation.'

[48] Article 11 of the Saudi Arabian Enforcement Law (Royal Decree No. M/53 of 2013) 'states that (subject to relevant treaties and conventions) an Enforcement Judge may only enforce on the basis of reciprocity and after being satisfied that (i) Saudi courts do not have jurisdiction to adjudicate the dispute': S. Al-Ammari and T. Martin, 'Arbitration in the Kingdom of Saudi Arabia', *Arbitration International*, 30(2) (2014), 387, 403–04. See also Article 439(4) of the Vietnamese Code of Civil Procedure 2015 (No. 92/2015/QH13), which provides that a civil judgment or decision of a foreign court shall not be recognised or enforced in Vietnam if 'the foreign Courts that have issued the judgments/decisions do not have jurisdiction to settle civil cases as prescribed in Article 440 of this Code', http://bit.ly/2tp7sfn (accessed 25 September 2017).

[49] For example, Article 235(2)(a)–(b) of the UAE Federal Law No. 11 of 1992 concerning Civil Procedures provides: 'it shall not be possible to order the execution before the verification of the following: (a) That the state's courts are not authorised to examine the litigation in which the decision or the order has been delivered and that the foreign courts which have delivered it are authorised therewith according to the international rules of the judicial jurisdiction decided in their law. (b) That the decision or the order has been delivered from an authorised court according to the law of the country in which it has been issued', http://bit.ly/2t1dSOD (accessed 25 September 2017).

[50] See Article 1146(1)(7) of the Polish Code of Civil Procedure of 17 November 1964 (available in English at http://bit.ly/2s8ORzE, accessed 25 September 2017) and Article 54(1)(c) of the Turkey Act on Private International and Procedural Law (Act No. 5718) (available in English at http://bit.ly/2tsXZTf, accessed 25 September 2017).

may be consistent with Turkish public policy (this diversity exists among common law countries too).

We can see the diversity of the approaches of the civil law countries in the OBOR initiative when we compare the civil procedure codes of these countries. While it may not be possible to analyse the attitude of every civil law country participant in the OBOR initiative, it is possible to sift out the countries with larger populations, higher gross domestic product (GDP) or GDP per capita, and look at their civil procedure codes to examine the hurdles they impose on the enforcement of foreign judgments. We have done exactly that, and the results of our analysis are set out in Table 2.1. Let us turn our attention to the table's results.

As can be seen, there are nine 'hurdles to enforcement' at the top of the table and fourteen civil law countries at the left side of the table. The ticks indicate the hurdles that the corresponding civil law country imposes in its civil procedure code. Based on the table's results, we can observe that the approaches of the civil law countries are unhappily diverse, in that different countries impose different hurdles. A judgment creditor cannot expect to encounter the same hurdles when seeking to enforce his judgment in different civil law countries. We have not even considered the limitation periods for the bringing of a claim on a foreign judgment, which are likely to differ from country to country. These procedural differences will only add to the difficulty of enforcing foreign judgments in civil law countries.

Another gloomy observation to be made from the table is that most civil law countries impose a criterion of reciprocity. Some of these countries require reciprocity in the narrow sense, in that they require the existence of a binding treaty between the civil law country and the foreign country for the mutual recognition and enforcement of foreign judgments (which we shall call 'treaty reciprocity').[51] Other countries require reciprocity in the broad sense, in that they do not require the existence of a treaty relationship but only require the existence of some reciprocal relationship between the foreign court and the local courts

---

[51] For example, Article 391 of the Uzbek Code of Civil Procedure provides that the procedure for the enforcement of foreign judgments is determined by the provisions of the relevant international treaty. This 'effectively means that if there is no treaty between Uzbekistan and country of origin of the judgment, then such award cannot be enforced and thus will have to be re-tried by Uzbek state courts': N. Yuldashev and M. Ruziev, 'Uzbekistan' in M. Madden (ed.), *Litigation and Dispute Resolution* (4th ed., Global Legal Group 2015) 324.

Table 2.1 *Hurdles of enforcement in selective civil law countries in the BRI*

Civil law country		Hurdles to Enforcement							
	Reciprocity	Due process	No fraud	Public policy	No earlier judgment	No earlier proceedings	Jurisdiction	Legal effect	No mistake of law or fact
China (excluding Hong Kong)	✓	✓		✓	✓		✓ (non-statutory)	✓	✓
Philippines	✓ (non-statutory)	✓	✓	✓	✓ (non-statutory)		✓	✓	✓
Indonesia	**Judgment creditors must relitigate[52]**								
Thailand	**Judgment creditors must relitigate[53]**								
Vietnam		✓		✓	✓	✓	✓	✓	
Kazakhstan	✓				**'to be determined by law'**				
Uzbekistan	✓								
Egypt	✓	✓		✓	✓		✓	✓	
Qatar	✓	✓		✓	✓		✓	✓	
Turkey	✓	✓		✓			✓	✓	

52 By the phrase 'judgment creditors must relitigate', we mean that the only available option to the judgment creditor is to argue on the merits of the case again before the courts of the civil law country concerned. This is because there is no provision in the law of the civil law country which allows the creditor to request the enforcement of foreign judgments without having to argue on the merits of the case.

53 Some Thai judgments have used common law-type reasoning as to the requirements for enforcing foreign judgments but the legal basis for this is uncertain. See Section 3 of the Act on Conflict of Laws, B.E. 2481 and the 1918 Supreme Court decision in case no. 585/2461.

('broad reciprocity').[54] Whatever the precise requirements of the civil law countries may be, the bottom line is that all civil law countries in the table above (with the exception of Poland, discussed below) require *some* form of reciprocity. This can be problematic in terms of enforceability.

For civil law countries which require treaty reciprocity, enforcement will not be possible if the civil law country does not have treaty relations with the foreign country. For civil law countries which require broad reciprocity, uncertainty arises as to what exactly is required before a reciprocal relationship is deemed to exist. Must there be *possible* reciprocity, in the sense that, based on the requirements of the law of the foreign country, the foreign court is likely to enforce a judgment of the local court on terms similar to the local court's law? Or must there be *proven* reciprocity, in the sense that there must have been an earlier case in which the foreign court had enforced the local court's judgment? Furthermore, what happens when a person obtains a judgment from country X which happens to require broad reciprocity, and seeks to enforce that judgment in country Y which also requires broad reciprocity? Will country Y's courts enforce country X's judgment, absent a treaty relationship between country X and Y? In our view, this is the critical weakness of broad reciprocity, because it creates a tiresome 'waiting game'[55] as the courts of each country sit idly for the other court to make the first move. No one benefits from the gridlock, so there is a real concern over whom we are sacrificing the judgment creditor for.[56]

---

[54] For example, Article 282 of the Chinese Civil Procedure Law 2013 requires the People's Court to enforce a foreign judgment 'after examining it in accordance with the international treaties concluded or acceded to by the People's Republic of China or with the principle of reciprocity'. This translation is provided by W. Zhang, 'Recognition and Enforcement of Foreign Judgments in China: A Call for Special Attention to Both the "Due Service Requirement" and the "Principle of Reciprocity"', *Chinese Journal of International Law*, 12(1) (2013), 143, 150. This would also appear to be the position in Vietnam, see Article 423(1)(b) of the 2015 CPC and the case of *Choongnam Spinning Ltd HCM City* first instance court decision No.2083/2007/QĐST-KDTM, the Appeal Court of the Supreme Court in Ho Chi Minh City, decision No. 62/2008/QDKDTM-PT.

[55] Such a waiting game has occurred between the courts of China and Japan. As Zhang (n 54) 172 notes, 'because Chinese courts refused to recognize Japanese judgments in the past, Japanese courts subsequently referred to such cases and refused to recognize Chinese judgments. A vicious circle is thus formed and continuously reinforced between China and Japan.'

[56] Reciprocity has aptly been described as 'a misplaced retaliation against private parties for acts of foreign states unrelated to the dispute': P. de Miguel Asensio, 'Recognition and Enforcement of Judgments in Intellectual Property Litigation: The CLIP Principles' in J. Basedow, T. Kono & A. Metzger (eds.) *Intellectual Property in the Global Arena* (Mohr Siebeck 2010). Indeed, Professor Adrian Briggs rejects reciprocity as a basis for the

2.3.2 The Silver Lining in the Cloud

We have seen in the above discussion that the laws of civil law countries suffer from two weaknesses, namely diversity and reciprocity. You may even be convinced at this junction that the enforcement of foreign judgments in civil law countries is a lost cause. But there are positive trends to indicate that things are looking up for the enforcement of foreign judgments in civil law countries, which are enabling foreign judgments to slowly attain similar levels of enforceability in civil law countries as arbitral awards. Let me address the two issues of diversity and reciprocity in turn.

With regard to diversity, our response is that diversity is not a unique problem to international litigation. Diversity also exists in international arbitration. The 1958 New York Convention permits States parties to refuse the recognition and enforcement of arbitral awards on a variety of grounds stipulated in Article V, including grounds of non-arbitrability and public policy. These grounds are prone to diverse interpretations in national courts the world over. There is in fact a growing body of academia that deals with the question of whether national courts have interpreted the 1958 New York Convention grounds in a consistent manner.[57] So we should neither be alarmed by diversity nor expect complete uniformity. At any rate, the laws of civil law countries are not so diverse that they include hurdles beyond the scope of imagination of international arbitration. Civil law countries impose requirements of jurisdiction, due process and public policy, which are familiar concepts in international arbitration. The only hurdle which international arbitration is foreign to is the hurdle of 'no mistake of law or fact', but this hurdle is only imposed by the Philippines. In any case, the Philippine Supreme Court declared in the 2005 case of *Bank of the*

---

enforcement of foreign judgments: see A. Briggs, 'The Principle of Comity in Private International Law' in *Collected Courses of the Hague Academy of International Law*, vol 354 (Brill | Nijhoff 2012).

[57] See for instance G. Bermann, 'Interpretation and Application of the New York Convention by National Courts' in M. Schauer and B. Verschraegen (eds.), *Ius Comparatum – Global Studies in Comparative Law*, vol 24 (Springer 2017); H. Kronke et al. (eds.), *Recognition and Enforcement of Foreign Arbitral Awards: A Global Commentary on the New York Convention* (Kluwer Law International 2010); A. van den Berg (ed.), *ICCA Congress series no. 9 – Improving the Efficiency of Arbitration Agreements and Awards: 40 Years of Application of the New York Convention* (Kluwer Law International 1999); and M. Hwang & S. Lee, 'Survey of South East Asian Nations on the Application of the New York Convention', *Journal of International Arbitration*, 25(6) (2008), 873.

Philippine Islands Securities Corporation v. *Edgardo v Guevara*[58] that the Philippine courts are not allowed to delve into the merits of a foreign judgment.

As regards the issue of reciprocity, we have two points to make. First, there are early signs to indicate that the winds are changing. Civil law countries are gradually repealing the requirement of reciprocity. Poland is a recent example. In 1932, the Polish Code of Civil Procedure required the existence of a treaty relationship. In 1996, Poland substituted the treaty requirement with a reciprocity requirement. In 2008, Poland abolished the reciprocity requirement altogether. In so doing, Poland joined the growing list of civil law countries that have abolished reciprocity, including Venezuela, Lithuania, Bulgaria, Macedonia, Spain, Montenegro and France. Even where countries retain the reciprocity requirement, there is a burgeoning trend of countries interpreting the requirement in a more liberal manner. We have two cases in mind which vividly illustrate this trend.

The first case is a Russian case called *Rentpool B.V.* v. *Podjemnye Tekhnologii*,[59] decided by the Abitrazh (Commercial) Court of Moscow in 2009. In Russia, the Civil Procedure Code imposes the requirement of a treaty between the foreign country and Russia. Article 409(1) provides that 'the decisions of foreign courts, including decisions on the approval of an amicable settlement, shall be acknowledged and executed in the Russian Federation if this is stipulated in the international treaty of the Russian Federation'.[60] Traditionally, Russian courts have 'applied this requirement literally, refusing to recognise or enforce foreign judgments in the absence of a treaty obligation to do so'.[61] However, in *Rentpool B.V.* v. *Podjemnye Tekhnologii*, the Abitrazh (Commercial) Court of Moscow formally acknowledged that it was not necessary to establish the existence of a treaty relationship. Broad reciprocity was sufficient.[62]

---

[58] *Bank of the Philippine Islands Securities Corporation* v. *Edgardo v Guevara* GR No. 167052, available in English at http://bit.ly/2s8Twlk (accessed 25 September 2017).
[59] *Rentpool B.V.* v. *Podjemnye Tekhnologii*, Decision of the Commercial Court of Moscow Region No. A41-9613/09 of 5 June 2009, available in English at http://bit.ly/2snZ5k4 (accessed 25 September 2017).
[60] (n 46).
[61] B. Elbalti, 'Reciprocity and the Recognition and Enforcement of Foreign Judgments: A Lot of Bark But Not Much Bite', *Journal of Private International Law*, 13(1) (2017), 184, 197.
[62] The decision was later reaffirmed by the Cassation Court of Moscow Circuit on 29 June 2009 and the Federal Supreme Court of the Republic of Russia on

The next case is an even more recent case decided by a Chinese court in late 2016. The Chinese Code of Civil Procedure imposes the requirement of broad reciprocity. Article 282 requires the people's court to examine the application for enforcement 'according to the international treaties concluded or accede to by the PRC or based on the principle of reciprocity'.[63] Conventionally, the practice of the Chinese courts has been to deny, in the absence of an applicable treaty, the enforcement of foreign judgments on the basis of lack of reciprocity.[64] However, in the 2016 case of *Kolmar Group AGC v. Jiangsu Textile Industry (Group) Import & Export* ('Kolmar Group'),[65] a Chinese court enforced a foreign judgment on the basis of broad reciprocity for the first time in reported Chinese legal history. The Nanjing Intermediate People's Court enforced a judgment issued by the High Court of Singapore, holding that the requirement of (broad) reciprocity was satisfied given that the Singapore courts had previously enforced a judgment issued by the Jiangsu Suzhou Intermediate People's Court in *Giant Light Metal Technology (Kunshan) Co Ltd* v. *Aksa Far East Pte Ltd*.[66] There is now a very recent second case in 2020 where a Chinese court has recognized and enforced a Singapore judgment. This is a decision of the Wenzhou Intermediate People's Court *Oceanside Development Group Ltd v (1) Chen Tong Kao (2) Chen Xiu Dan (Case No [2017]Zhe.03.X.W.R.7)* where the Court granted its order of enforcement despite the Singapore judgment having been obtained in default of an order of court requiring the submission of a cash bond as a condition of being granted leave to defend.[67] The upshot of the above is that, insofar as we perceive the imposition of reciprocity to be a problem, we can take comfort in the fact that the tides are gradually turning and civil law countries are slowly knocking down the walls of reciprocity. This has occurred along two lines

---

7 December 2009 (ruling No BAC-12688/09). Subsequent cases have followed suit: see Elbalti (n 61) 199.

[63] Zhang (n 54).

[64] Ibid.

[65] *Kolmar Group A.G. v. Jiangsu Textile Industry (Group) Import & Export Co Ltd* (2016) Su01 Assisting Foreign Recognition No 3. The gradual loosening of the reciprocity requirement in China is reflected by the joint declaration in the 2nd China–ASEAN Justice Forum on 8 June 2017, which China participated in. The seventh consensus of the declaration was to promote the mutual recognition of civil and commercial judgments.

[66] *Giant Light Metal Technology (Kunshan) Co Ltd* v. *Aksa Far East Pte Ltd* [2014] SGHC 16.

[67] See Meng Yu, 'Again! Chinese Court Recognizes a Singapore Judgment', China Justice Observer, 8 March 2020, available in English at www.chinajusticeobserver.com/a/again-chinese-court-recognizes-a-singapore-judgment (accessed 27 June 2020).

of development: (a) the trend of civil law countries repealing the reciprocity requirement completely; and (b) the trend of civil law countries interpreting the reciprocity requirement in a more liberal fashion.

Before we move on to our second response, we should also mention a third case that overcame the hurdle of enforceability of foreign judgments in Dubai outside the DIFC. The case is called *DNB Bank ASA v. Gulf Eyadah Corporation & Gulf Navigation Holding PJSC*,[68] and it was decided by the DIFC Court of Appeal in early 2016. As readers may know, the DIFC is an autonomous region within Dubai which has adopted the common law system. The rest of Dubai employs the civil law system, as do the other Emirates of the UAE. The consequence of this is that the hurdle of reciprocity applies to the enforcement of foreign judgments in Dubai outside the DIFC, but does not apply to the enforcement of foreign judgments within the DIFC. The open question, however, was whether judgment creditors who have assets in Dubai outside the DIFC could use the DIFC courts as a conduit, that is, enforce their foreign judgment in the DIFC courts and take the DIFC court's judgment to the Dubai courts for enforcement. This was the question that the DIFC Court of Appeal had to decide in *DNB Bank ASA* v. *Gulf Eyadah Corporation & Gulf Navigation Holding PJSC*. And this was the question that the DIFC court answered in the affirmative, based on its interpretation of the provisions of Dubai Law No. 12 of 2004, as amended by Dubai Law No. 16 of 2011 (among other legislation), which is the relevant statute governing the relationship between the Dubai courts and the DIFC courts. The decision enables judgment creditors to enforce their foreign judgments in Dubai via the conduit of the DIFC courts if the creditors' assets are located in Dubai. This is yet another example of a civil law country gradually expanding the enforceability of foreign judgments within its jurisdiction.

Our second response to the issue of reciprocity is that it is important that we do not overstate the problems that arise from reciprocity. The fortunate reality is that many countries have entered into a range of bilateral and multilateral treaties for the mutual recognition and enforcement of judgments to overcome the hurdle of reciprocity. Even countries which do not have many treaty relations with other countries are at least parties to regional treaties for the mutual enforcement of judgments. In

---

[68] *DNB Bank ASA v Gulf Eyadah Corporation and Gulf Navigation Holdings PJSC* [2015] DIFC CA 007. The judgment was delivered by the principal author in his capacity as Chief Justice of the DIFC courts.

Central Asia, there is a treaty between Armenia, Belarus, Kazakhstan, Kyrgyzstan, Moldova, Russia, Turkmenistan, Tajikistan, Ukraine and Uzbekistan called the 1993 Minsk Convention on Legal Assistance and Legal Relations in Civil, Family and Criminal Matters to govern the mutual recognition and enforcement of judgments. In the Middle East, there are several regional treaties for the mutual recognition and enforcement of judgments to which many Arab and north African countries are parties, including the 1983 Riyadh Arab Agreement for Judicial Cooperation and the 1996 GCC Convention for the Execution of Judgments, Delegations and Judicial Notifications. These regional treaties will assume a critical role in the OBOR initiative, as many parties to these treaties are also participants in the initiative. Judgments obtained in one party's courts may therefore be enforced in another party's courts in accordance with the terms of the applicable treaty.

Even where there is no applicable treaty, there is still some light at the end of the tunnel for the judgment creditor. Not all civil law countries require treaty reciprocity. Some civil law countries only require broad reciprocity. This preserves the possibility of enforcing the judgments of common law countries in these civil law countries and safeguards the enforceability of common law judgments. Indeed, as we have seen above, the Nanjing Intermediate People's Court enforced a Singapore judgment in *Kolmar Group* on the basis that the High Court of Singapore had previously enforced a Chinese judgment, notwithstanding the absence of a treaty between China and Singapore for the mutual recognition and enforcement of judgments.

Furthermore, in many civil law countries which require broad reciprocity, the position is unsettled as to whether broad reciprocity means *possible* or *proven* reciprocity. The courts have had little opportunity to contemplate this matter. So there remains a possibility for these courts to adopt the conception of possible reciprocity (which is the easier standard of the two to satisfy) when the appropriate case arises. This is important because it paves the way for a potential solution to the waiting game impasse we discussed above. The solution is for the courts (or the governments, depending on which the competent body is) of civil law countries which require broad reciprocity to enter into bilateral memorandums of understanding ('MOUs') that, short of imposing binding obligations on the parties, affirm their shared understanding that, for the sole purpose of overcoming the waiting game impasse, the requirement of broad reciprocity is mutually satisfied. Such an MOU will not be easy to formulate, and its inchoate legal nature will require skilful drafting. But if it is pulled off successfully, it can serve to crystallise the reciprocity relationship between the two countries and encourage the courts of one country to take the first move and enforce the other court's foreign judgment when the opportune moment arises.

A similar (but not identical) development has already occurred between the DIFC courts and other foreign courts. The DIFC courts have taken the initiative to enter into memorandums of guidance ('MOGs') with an increasing number of foreign courts to 'set out the parties' understanding of the procedures for the enforcement of each party's money judgments in the other party's courts'.[69] Typically, an MOG would state that 'the parties desire and believe that the cooperation demonstrated by this memorandum will promote a mutual understanding of their laws and judicial processes and will improve public perception and understanding'.[70] While the MOGs do not go so far as to affirm reciprocity between the courts, the MOG model can usefully be transposed to the context of civil law countries which encounter the waiting game conundrum. Our point here is that there is no need for countries to take the more drastic measure of repealing the requirement of broad reciprocity if they are willing to enter into MOUs for the mutual affirmation of reciprocity. Insofar as we cannot expect the universal removal of the broad reciprocity requirement anytime soon, the MOU remains the most practical solution to the barrier of reciprocity that judgment creditors face today.

2.4   2005 Hague Convention on Choice of Court Agreements

We now turn to the final section of our chapter, which is the Convention of 30 June 2005 on Choice of Court Agreements (the '2005 Hague Convention'). The 2005 Hague Convention is the latest global effort to regulate the treatment of exclusive choice of court agreements and the enforcement of judgments of designated courts. It has the potential to equalise the enforceability of foreign judgments and arbitral awards. It affirms the principle that the merits of a judgment are non-reviewable,[71]

---

[69] See for example paragraph 1 of the Memorandum of Guidance – Enforcement between DIFC Courts and the Supreme Court of Singapore (19 January 2015) http://bit.ly/2u68JFg (accessed 25 September 2017).

[70] See for example paragraph 3 of the Memorandum of Guidance between the Dubai International Financial Centre Courts and The High Court of Kenya, Commercial & Admiralty Division (27 November 2014), http://bit.ly/2twZvVx (accessed 25 September 2017).

[71] Article 8(2) 2005 Hague Convention.

which is a position shared by international arbitration. It permits the enforcing court to postpone enforcement if the judgment is appealable or is being appealed against in the country of origin,[72] which is a position shared by common law countries in respect of foreign judgments as well as international arbitration in respect of foreign arbitral awards. Most importantly, it imposes grounds for the refusal of enforcement of foreign judgments which resemble the grounds in the 1958 New York Convention. Article 9 of the 2005 Hague Convention provides that a Contracting State may refuse enforcement if, inter alia: (a) the agreement was null and void;[73] (b) a party lacked the capacity to conclude the agreement;[74] (c) the defendant was not duly notified of the document which instituted the foreign proceedings;[75] (d) the judgment was obtained by fraud;[76] and (e) enforcement would be manifestly incompatible with the public policy of the Contracting State (including fundamental principles of procedural fairness).[77] These are all familiar grounds in the world of international arbitration.

Furthermore, Article 2(2) of the 2005 Hague Convention specifically provides that the Convention will not apply to the following matters:

(a) the status and legal capacity of natural persons
(b) maintenance obligations
(c) other family law matters, including matrimonial property regimes and other rights or obligations arising out of marriage or similar relationships
(d) wills and succession
(e) insolvency, composition and analogous matters
(f) the carriage of passengers and goods
(g) marine pollution, limitation of liability for maritime claims, general average, and emergency towage and salvage
(h) anti-trust (competition) matters
(i) liability for nuclear damage
(j) claims for personal injury brought by or on behalf of natural persons
(k) tort or delict claims for damage to tangible property that do not arise from a contractual relationship

---

[72] Article 8(4) 2005 Hague Convention.
[73] Article 9(a) 2005 Hague Convention.
[74] Ibid.
[75] Article 9(c) 2005 Hague Convention.
[76] Article 9(d) 2005 Hague Convention.
[77] Article 9(e) 2005 Hague Convention.

(l) rights in rem in immovable property, and tenancies of immovable property
(m) the validity, nullity, or dissolution of legal persons, and the validity of decisions of their organs
(n) the validity of intellectual property rights other than copyright and related rights
(o) infringement of intellectual property rights other than copyright and related rights, except where infringement proceedings are brought for breach of a contract between the parties relating to such rights, or could have been brought for breach of that contract
(p) the validity of entries in public registers

Many of these areas are considered to be non-arbitrable under Article V (2)(a) of the 1958 New York Convention. Gary Born writes that

> typical examples of nonarbitrable subjects include specific categories of disputes involving criminal matters; domestic relations and succession; bankruptcy; trade sanctions; certain competition claim; consumer claims; labor or employment grievances; and certain intellectual property matters. In general, the type of disputes which are nonarbitrable arise from a common set of considerations, typically involving public rights, or interests of third parties, which are the subjects of uniquely governmental authority.

So, if there is one treaty that promises to advance the transnational enforceability of foreign judgments today, it is the 2005 Hague Convention, which was painstakingly negotiated since 1996.[78] Membership in the Convention is steadily growing. As at the time of writing (May 2020) the EU has signed as a bloc, and Denmark, the UK, Mexico, Montenegro, North Macedonia, Singapore, China and the USA have also signed independently (although China, North Macedonia, Ukraine and the USA have not yet ratified the Convention. Thirteen of the signatories are participants in the OBOR initiative (Bulgaria, Croatia, Czech Republic, Estonia, Hungary, Latvia, Lithuania, Poland, Romania, Slovakia, Slovenia, Singapore and Ukraine). In certain regions, countries are also calling upon neighbouring countries to join the 2005 Hague Convention.[79] If this momentum continues, we may one day be able to

---

[78] For a historical overview of the 2005 Hague Convention, see P. Nygh and F. Pocar, *Report on the Preliminary Draft Convention on Jurisdiction and Foreign Judgments in Civil and Commercial Matters* (August 2000), http://bit.ly/2snq6UF (accessed 25 September 2017).
[79] Singapore in one example in the ASEAN region. See S. Menon, 'ASEAN Integration through Law' (August 2013), http://bit.ly/2traAXJ (accessed 25 September 2017) and

confidently describe the 2005 Hague Convention as the 'litigation counterpart'[80] of the 1958 New York Convention.

Of course, the 1958 New York Convention and the 2005 Hague Convention are not completely identical, and there are some differences between the two regimes which affect enforceability. Some grounds for refusal of enforcement under the 2005 Hague Convention do not exist under the 1958 New York Convention. These include where: (a) the judgment is inconsistent with an earlier judgment in the enforcing court's State or a third State in a dispute between the same parties;[81] (b) the judgment awards damages that do not compensate a party for actual loss suffered;[82] and (c) the judgment has no effect or is unenforceable in the State of origin.[83] None of these grounds appear in the 1958 New York Convention. Furthermore, while the Model Law provides for the enforcement of interim measures, the 2005 Hague Convention specifically provides that interim measures are not governed by the Convention.[84] So there are undeniable differences between the two regimes to be aware of, but they are not so serious as to completely set back the enforceability of foreign judgments in comparison to the enforceability of foreign arbitral awards.

A. Reyes, 'ASEAN and the Hague Conventions', *Asia Pacific Law Review*, 22(1) (2014), 25, 40.

[80] R. Brand and P. Herrup, *The 2005 Hague Convention on Choice of Court Agreements: Commentary and Documents* (Cambridge University Press 2008) 3.

[81] Article 9(f)–(g) 2005 Hague Convention. However, note that in principle, 'national court judgments and arbitral awards should have the same preclusive effects in arbitral proceedings as in national court litigation ... Rules of preclusion are elements of the applicable law, which the arbitral tribunal is bound to apply ... An arbitral tribunal's failure to give preclusive effect to a prior and valid judicial judgment would be subject to serious enforceability challenges in many jurisdictions' on the ground of public policy: Born (n 29) 3774. So, even though the ground of 'earlier inconsistent judgment' is not expressly stated in the 1958 New York Convention, it may arguably be subsumed under the rubric of public policy.

[82] Article 11(1) 2005 Hague Convention.

[83] Article 8(3) 2005 Hague Convention. A commentary on Article 8(3) may be found in Brand and Herrup (n 79) 274–75: 'Having effect means that it is legally valid and operative. If it does not have effect, it will not constitute a valid determination of the parties' rights and obligations ... Likewise, if the judgment is not enforceable in the State of origin, it should not be enforced elsewhere under the Convention. It is of course possible that the judgment will be effective in the State of origin without being enforceable there. Enforceability may be suspended pending an appeal (either automatically or because the court so ordered).'

[84] Articles 4 and 7 2005 Hague Convention.

2.5 Conclusion

Our conclusions are as follows.

(a) In common law countries, the enforcement of foreign judgments shares a number of essential similarities with the enforcement of foreign arbitral awards under the 1958 New York Convention, with the result that the foreign judgment is no less enforceable than foreign arbitral awards in common law countries.

(b) In civil law countries, although there are issues of diversity which undermine the predictability of success of enforcing foreign judgments in these countries, the problem of diversity is not as crippling as we think when we realise that civil law countries impose ordinary hurdles to enforcement such as jurisdiction, public policy and due process, which are all familiar concepts to the world of international arbitration.

(c) The only unusual hurdle to the enforcement of foreign judgments is reciprocity, of which different civil law countries have different conceptions (some being treaty reciprocity and others being broad reciprocity). But let us not disregard the fact that an increasing number of civil law countries are repealing the requirement of reciprocity, or are interpreting the requirement more liberally.

(d) Even where civil law countries have not repealed the requirement of broad reciprocity, there is a way to overcome the waiting game impasse other than through repeal. The solution lies in entering into bilateral MOUs with other civil law countries which impose the requirement of broad reciprocity that, short of imposing treaty-like obligations on the parties, affirm the mutual satisfaction of the broad reciprocity requirement.

(e) The entry into force of the 2005 Hague Convention will only consolidate the steady improvement of the transnational enforceability of foreign judgments. Not only are the merits of foreign judgements non-reviewable under the Convention, the grounds for the refusal of enforcement under the Convention replicate (for the most part) the grounds for the refusal of enforcement under the 1958 New York Convention.

(f) The consequence of the above is that the enforceability of foreign judgments is firmly catching up with the enforceability of foreign arbitral awards. The conventional belief that the arbitration clause is the only viable dispute resolution clause is increasingly being challenged. Countries such as Singapore have anticipated this global trend and have seized the opportunity, establishing international commercial courts in addition to existing arbitration institutions in the faith that the enforceability of the judgments of these courts will improve with time.

(g) The authors regret that, owing to time constraints, it has not been possible to update this article with a discussion of the Hague Convention on the Recognition and Enforcement of Foreign Judgments in Civil or Commercial Matters which was launched on 2 July 2019. This will complement the Hague Convention on Choice of Court Agreements 2005.

PART II

China, BRI and International Trade Dispute Resolution

3

Trade and Investment Adjudication Involving 'Silk Road Projects'

Legal Methodology Challenges

ERNST-ULRICH PETERSMANN[*]

I Introduction

The 2013 One Belt, One Road (OBOR) initiative by the Chinese President Xi Jinping envisages investing more than $1 trillion for the construction and infrastructure of a 'Silk Road Economic Belt' (following the ancient silk road from China through central Asia and the Middle East to Europe) and for a '21st Century Maritime Silk Road' (linking China to Southeast Asia and East Africa) so as to promote international policy coordination, infrastructure facilities connectivity, unimpeded trade, financial integration as well as human 'people-to-people bonds' among more than sixty-five countries bordering these 'Silk Roads'.[1] The realization of this ambitious financial, investment, trade and policy cooperation will depend, inter alia, on multilevel private and public, national and international legal regulation. Even though the design of OBOR cooperation seems to evolve pragmatically,[2] its legal coherence and legitimacy

---

The author wishes to thank Professor W. Zhou from UNSW Law School at Sydney (Australia) for constructive criticism of an earlier draft. The contribution is based on my lecture at the 10th Anniversary International Symposium on 'China and the Development of International Dispute Resolution System in the Context of the "Belt and Road Initiative."'

[1] Details of the Chinese OBOR Initiative can be found at http://en.ndrc.gov.cn/newsrelease/201503/t20150330_669367.html. Trade over the silk roads by land and by sea is documented from about 200 BC up to the fall of Constantinople in 1453 BC; it connected the economic centers from the east to the west ends of Asia, Arabia (e.g. Baghdad, Damascus, Cairo), Venice and Rome.

[2] An illustration are the annual '16+1' meetings of China with sixteen central and eastern European countries (including eleven EU Member States) which, in spite of the permanent secretariat for 'Cooperation between China and Central and Eastern European Countries',

will require mutually consistent rule of law and dispute settlement mechanisms, as illustrated by the establishment of the Chinese-European Arbitration Centre at Hamburg (Germany) and of China–Africa Joint Arbitration Centres at Johannesburg (South Africa) and Shanghai (China). The limited number of investor–state arbitration proceedings initiated so far by foreign companies against China – or by Chinese companies against foreign host states[3] – seems to confirm the Chinese preference for alternative dispute settlement methods that avoid recourse to international or domestic courts (e.g. also in view of the often inadequate independence and judicial expertise of local courts in some African and Asian countries). Promotion of such alternative dispute resolution may become one of the important 'legal innovations' of China's OBOR cooperation. Yet, also involvement of third parties (as mediators or conciliators) in dispute settlement proceedings raises questions of 'justice' and of legal methodology.

II   How to Promote Legitimacy of OBOR Regulations? Lessons from the Past

Since ancient times, legal rules and institutions (like markets) have proven to be indispensable instruments for international trade (*lex mercatoria*) and for the peaceful governance of peoples. Chinese civilization is older – and was for many centuries more developed (e.g. in terms of inventions like printing, paper making, the compass, gunpowder, locks for canals) – than European civilization. Yet, the 'political invention' of constitutionalism – as a legal limitation on feudal powers (like the decision of the Ming emperor in China in 1480 to forbid overseas trade and exploration) and as the legal foundation of liberty and welfare of citizens – emerged in Europe about 500 BC in response to the rivalry among city republics around the Mediterranean, that is, millennia before China adopted its first Constitution of 1911. Democratic and republican constitutionalism holds that, in order to limit abuses of power, enhance

---

seem to focus more on bilateral discussions than on the few high profile infrastructure projects (like the Belgrade–Budapest high-speed railway that Chinese companies plan to build).

[3] Even though China has signed more than 130 bilateral investment treaties (BITs), there seem to have been only two complaints initiated against China under the ICSID rules so far, and only five arbitration complaints initiated by Chinese foreign investors against foreign host states; cf. Y. Hua, *China's Legal Obligations in the Field of Foreign Investment: How Trade Agreements Influence the Formation of Investment Agreements*, doctoral thesis defended on 15 June 2017 in the EUI at Florence.

the input and output legitimacy of law and governance, be socially accepted as legitimate and voluntarily complied with, and progressively institutionalize 'public reason', all three basic functions of law need to be justified both *among citizens* as ultimate sources of legal legitimacy and 'constituent powers', as well as *vis-à-vis citizens* as 'democratic principals' of governments, to which citizens delegate only limited 'constituted powers':

- the *instrumental function* of law for the normative ordering of social cooperation (e.g. the need for protecting equal individual rights for welfare-increasing cooperation among free and reasonable citizens);
- the *systemic function* of law for justifying the reasonable coherence of legal 'primary rules of conduct' and 'secondary rules' of recognition, change and adjudication (e.g. the need for promoting the consistency of utilitarian trade and investment rules with the human rights, rule of law and democracy principles that have become recognized by all UN member states as integral parts of UN law); and
- the *cultural function* of law for transforming the 'law in the books' into social facts ('living law') through 'legal socialization' and 'institutionalization of public reason' inducing legal subjects to voluntarily comply with legal rules and principles (e.g. the obligation of each WTO member under Article XVI(4) WTO Agreement to 'ensure the conformity of its laws, regulations and administrative procedures with its obligations as provided in the annexed Agreements').

1   Diversity of Chinese and Western Legal Traditions and Constitutionalism

The bestselling book by Peter Frankopan, *The Silk Roads. A New History of the World*, begins with the childhood recollection of the author that the 'accepted and lazy history of civilization . . . is one where Ancient Greece begat Rome, Rome begat Christian Europe, Christian Europe begat the Renaissance, the Renaissance the Enlightenment, the Enlightenment political democracy and the industrial revolution. Industry crossed with democracy in turn yielded the United States, embodying the rights to life, liberty and the pursuit of happiness'.[4] His book documents how this biased, western vision of history based on a 'mantra of the political,

---

[4] P. Frankopan, *The Silk Roads. A New History of the World*, London: Bloomsbury 2015, at xiii.

cultural and moral triumph of the West' ignores many older civilizations (notably in Asia) and the dark sides of European civilization (like imperial 'opium wars' in Asia, genocide in Europe). Yet, the postwar elaboration of international monetary, trade and investment law continues to be mainly shaped by European and North American countries and by their bilateral and multilateral trade and investment agreements. Will the comparatively fewer Asian initiatives for new regional and multilateral trade and investment rules and organizations – like the Association of Southeast Asian Nations (ASEAN), the Regional Comprehensive Economic Partnership (RCEP), the Trans-Pacific Partnership Agreement (TPP), the China-led OBOR project and the Asian Infrastructure Investment Bank – lead to substantive changes in international economic law (IEL)?

Until World War II, Asian traditions of justifying law and governance vis-à-vis citizens fundamentally differed from those in European and North American constitutional democracies. For instance, while democratic, republican and cosmopolitan constitutionalism were discussed in Europe and legally evolved since the ancient Athenian democracy and Roman republic 2,500 year ago, republican constitutionalism emerged in China only since 1911. Since Plato's *The Republic* (ca. 375 BC), the metaphor of the 'state ship' is used in western republicanism for describing the legal structure that protects society from the dangerous waters surrounding it. The Chinese proverb attributed to the Confucian philosopher Xunzi (298–220 BC) used the same metaphor of the 'state ship' in a significantly different way: 'The heavens create the people and appoint the ruler. The ruler is like a boat, the people are like the water. The water may support the boat, and it may also capsize it.' In the western metaphor, society and its rulers are on the boat together; the captain acts as an *agent* of the people who are the democratic principal and constituent power. The Chinese metaphor described the people as keeping the state afloat without being on board the ship and without being capable of reforming or steering it. Such 'preconceptions' of law, the state and of citizens are bound to influence legal interpretations. For instance, the 1982 Constitution of the People's Republic of China is based on the democratic principle that 'all power belongs to the people' (Article 2). Democratic constitutions derive from this principle the need for protecting human rights and delegation of limited powers to democratically elected legislative, executive and judicial government branches so as to protect constitutional, participatory, representative and deliberative self-government of, by and for citizens and peoples. China's constitution, however, emphasizes the need for 'dictatorship by the proletariat' (Preamble) and the 'people's democratic dictatorship led by the working class' (Article 1), as postulated by Karl Marx based on his claims to know 'historic truth' about the domination of the human condition by materialism. Authoritarian claims to know 'truth' seem to be related also to the neglect for individual rights in the two philosophical schools of Confucianism and Legalism in China, which

> shared a vision of society in which individual lives were led within hierarchies and social distinctions and proper behavior derived from an individual's status in those hierarchies ... Western thought makes the individual the bearer of rights and bases rights on the fundamental dignity and equality of every human being. There were no such concepts in Chinese thought; in the Confucian view, 'identity constantly changes, varying with the context; duties and, correspondingly, rights/rites are also constantly being redefined as other actors change'.[5]

The Confucian view of subordinating individual rights and corresponding duties to collective interests continues to inform many Chinese and Marxist conceptions of individual rights in modern China.[6] It reflects patriarchal and communitarian, socialist traditions that are fundamentally different from the more antagonistic, western conceptions of human and constitutional rights as constitutional constraints aimed at protecting diverse individuals and peoples – as constituent powers and democratic principals vis-à-vis all governance agents – by corresponding legal duties of governments with only limited, delegated and separated, regulatory powers. Article 51 of China's Constitution of 1982[7] illustrates how

[5] S. B. Lubman, *Bird in a Cage: Legal Reform in China after Mao*, Stanford University Press 1999, 15–16, 19.

[6] Cf. J. Chan, *Confucian Perfectionism. A Political Philosophy for Modern Times*, Princeton University Press 2014 (arguing that China should adopt liberal democratic institutions that are shaped by the Confucian conception of the good rather than the liberal conception of equal rights).

[7] Article 51 of the 1982 Constitution sets clear limits upon the free exercise of rights by emphasizing the subordination of the individual to the community: 'in exercising freedoms and rights, citizens of the People's Republic of China may not infringe upon the interest of the state, of society or of the collective or upon the lawful freedom and rights of other citizens'. In the Chinese constitutional order, human rights must conform to state-sponsored policies as determined by the communist party (as the ultimate elite and authority) in order to maintain the 'social harmony between individual and state interests' (similar to the Confucian emphasis on maintaining harmony inside the family as the existential unity of human relationships). Conflict (as opposed to social harmony) is considered an ethical and ontological evil that needs to be limited through proletarian 'class struggles' and redistribution of benefits rather than through rights-based constitutionalism and adjudication.

Chinese conceptions of individual 'freedoms and rights' differ from 'Kantian interpretations' of respect for 'human dignity' in terms of equal freedoms as 'first principle of justice' asserting moral and constitutional priority over governmental limitations of the diverse civil, political, economic, social and cultural human and constitutional rights and corresponding governmental 'duties to protect'. Yet, both Chinese and Western lawyers acknowledge that the multilevel nature of modern human rights law and constitutional law require respect for legitimate 'constitutional pluralism' depending on the diverse 'constitutional contracts', democratic preferences and ratification of human rights treaties in different jurisdictions. As modern China and other Asian countries adopt ever more legislation and international agreements protecting trading rights, investment rights, intellectual property rights and other economic, social, constitutional and human rights, generalizations contrasting 'rights in the east' and in 'the west' may no longer be justifiable. For instance,

- in 2011, China's patent office received more patent applications than any other patent office in the world;
- China also seems to comply with most WTO rules and WTO dispute settlement rulings as well as with international investment law and adjudication.

Yet, China has chosen a power-oriented approach disregarding its legal and judicial obligations under the UN Convention on the Law of the Sea (UNCLOS).[8] China's political use of history for justifying its territorial and maritime claims over large swaths of the South China Sea reflects long-standing imperial strategies reflecting the ancient Chinese board game *wei qui* (also known in the west by its Japanese name *go*), such as building artificial islands and extending military positions surrounding oil, gas and other natural resources aimed at occupying territories and excluding other countries without regard to international law (e.g. the UNCLOS provisions on exclusive economic zones and archipels). Also, inside China the Constitution of 1982 is not effectively enforced in domestic courts; even though most other UN member states have recognized constitutionalism as a reasonable self-restraint on the bounded

---

[8] See China's rejection of the arbitration award of 12 July 2016 under UNCLOS Annex VII concerning the Chinese claims to control more than 80 per cent of the South China Sea without regard to UNCLOS obligations: Permanent Court of Arbitration Case No 2013–19 in the matter of the South China Sea Arbitration (*The Republic of the Philippines* v. *The Peoples Republic of China*). The award is published on the PCA website at www.pcacases.com/web/view/7.

rationality and 'animal instincts' of human beings and as the most important 'political invention' for decentralized, citizen-driven protection of public goods (PGs), China's communist party avoids applying 'national constitutionalism' for protecting citizens against abuses of power. Yet, China increasingly uses legal self-commitments to UN, WTO, investment and regional law for justifying China's market liberalization and regulations of non-market concerns.[9] Can utilitarian OBOR regulations effectively protect transnational PGs (e.g. as defined by UN and WTO law) without regard to democratic and republican constitutionalism?

The effectiveness of the Chinese regulatory system (e.g. for obtaining compliance with patent targets set by the central government) has been explained in terms of an authoritarian 'pressure driving mechanism'.[10] Yet, China's communist governance cannot be unilaterally imposed on other OBOR countries. UN human rights law and democratic constitutionalism proceed from the 'Kantian premise' that – because the limits of cognitive human reason (e.g. in terms of time, space, causality, subjective human senses) exclude knowledge of 'absolute truth' – constitutional protection of individual autonomy rights (e.g. to choose one's individual conceptions of a 'good life' and of 'social justice', including individual and democratic freedoms to 'falsify' claims of truth) offer more efficient and more legitimate information, coordination and sanctioning mechanisms for providing private and public goods demanded by citizens. Republican constitutionalism focuses on participatory rights as incentives for citizens to use their 'republican virtues' and assume responsibility for protecting the collective supply of PGs (*res publica*). As illustrated by the *Kadi*-case law of the European Court of Justice (CJEU) limiting the domestic implementation of UN Security Council 'smart sanctions' against alleged terrorists if such sanctions violate fundamental rights protected in European Union law,[11] multilevel judicial protection of rule of law in constitutional democracies is committed to

---

[9] Cf. P. D. Farah & E. Cima (eds), *China's Influence on Non-Trade Concerns in International Economic Law*, Routledge: New York 2016. Also, Chinese human rights scholarship transcends Confucian Chinese traditions and Marxist ideologies in response to China's ratification of UN human rights conventions and human rights discourse outside China (e.g. justifying human rights as protecting human freedoms, basic interests and capabilities).

[10] Cf. X. Yang, Pressure Driving Mechanism: A Concise History of the Concept, in: *Social Science* 2012, 11; W. Cheng & P. Drahos, *How China Built the World's Biggest Patent Office: The Pressure Driving Mechanism* (unpublished manuscript 2017).

[11] On the '*Kadi* jurisprudence' annulling – on grounds of human rights violations – the EU implementation of 'smart sanctions' ordered by the UN Security Council against alleged terrorists, see: M. Avbelj et al. (eds.), *Kadi on Trial: A Multifaceted Analysis of the Kadi Trial*, London: Routledge 2014.

interpreting also international treaty obligations in conformity with the fundamental rights of citizens as constitutional restraints on abuses of political power. Just as China has accepted multilevel trade adjudication as an integral part of WTO law and multilevel investment adjudication as provided for in international investment agreements, OBOR regulations should remain consistent with multilevel judicial remedies in additional areas of international cooperation (like government procurement, labour rights, environmental protection) in order to protect transnational OBOR cooperation in accordance with UN legal guarantees accepted by OBOR countries. Multilevel judicial governance must remain embedded in republican constitutionalism in order to remain legitimate and voluntarily complied with by governmental and non-governmental actors and litigants. As constitutionalism is about limiting abuses of power and justifying third-party adjudication in terms of protecting equal rights and due process of law, the legitimacy of transnational OBOR cooperation is bound to depend on multilevel respect for the existing international legal and constitutional obligations of OBOR countries. Even if communist rulers avoid 'constitutional governance' inside China, many OBOR cooperation partners will make their transnational economic cooperation with China conditional on respect for the 'constitutional principles' underlying their respective national constitutions and UN human rights law.[12]

2   From 'Western' leadership towards Chinese Leadership through the OBOR Project?

The OBOR project – even though primarily motivated by domestic policy goals (e.g. to improve the connectivity of western China with western trading partners) – pursues more ambitious goals to refashion the global economic order compared with the postwar reconstruction promoted by the US Marshall Plan. Yet, the postwar US leadership was embedded into US initiatives for the multilateral Bretton Woods Agreement (1944) and the UN Charter (1945), as promoted by US Secretary of State Cordell Hull (whose leadership was rewarded with the Nobel Peace Prize in 1945).[13] In

---

[12] On 'economic constitutionalism' and 'justice as respect for human rights' in IEL see: E. U. Petersmann, *International Economic Law in the 21st Century. Constitutional Pluralism and Multilevel Governance of Interdependent Public Goods*, Oxford: Hart 2012.

[13] On Cordell Hull's strategic leadership see: K. Dam, C. Hull, The Reciprocal Trade Agreements Act and the WTO, in: E. U. Petersmann (ed.), *Reforming the World Trading System. Legitimacy, Efficiency, and Democratic Governance*, Oxford University Press 2005, 83–98.

the Preamble of the UN Charter, 'We the Peoples of the United Nations determined', inter alia, 'to establish conditions under which justice and respect for the obligations arising from treaties and other sources of international law can be maintained'. This rules-based, universalist US strategy (in contrast to the nationalist 'America First' strategies of US President Trump) was further specified in the 1948 Universal Declaration of Human Rights (UDHR) and its 'recognition of the inherent dignity and of the equal and inalienable rights of all members of the human family (as) the foundation of freedom, justice and peace in the world' (Preamble). Yet, the 2017 British 'Brexit' decision and US President Trump's power-oriented rejection of multilateral agreements[14] may signal the end of Anglo-Saxon leadership for protecting international PGs. Will China's G-20 initiatives – at the G-20 summit in Shanghai in 2016 – for non-binding 'Guiding Principles for Global Investment Policymaking', and more recent proposals for China's membership in the Transatlantic Partnership Agreement (TPP), lead to transformation of the WTO into a new World Investment and Trade Organization, as recently suggested by Chinese academics[15] so as to promote more legal and institutional coherence between regional and worldwide trade and investment rules and institutions?

The term 'constitutionalism' refers to three complementary 'political inventions' that respond to the 'bounded rationality' of human beings and underlie also mega-regional free trade agreements (FTAs) like the TPP:[16]

1. A *legal self-commitment* to constitution, limitation, regulation and justification of multilevel governance of PGs based on agreed 'principles of justice' of a higher legal rank with due respect for 'constitutional pluralism' (cf. the TPP provisions on environmental protection, good governance, protection of human, labor, investor and intellectual property rights and transnational rule of law);

2. A *political self-commitment* to 'constitutionalizing' law and governance through (a) legislative, (b) administrative, (c) judicial and (d)

---

[14] Examples include Trump's dismissal of the United Nations (UN) as a 'social club'; his criticism of NATO as 'obsolete'; his support for disintegration of the EU; his withdrawal from the TPP and from the 2015 Paris Agreement on Climate Change Prevention; and his re-negotiating of the North American Free Trade Agreement (NAFTA) and of other multilateral agreements.

[15] *World Investment and Trade Organization: Is It Possible for Global Governance? G20, TPP and WTO*, Chinese Initiative of International Law, WTO Public Forum September 2017.

[16] For details see: E. U. Petersmann, *Multilevel Constitutionalism for Multilevel Governance of Public Goods – Methodology Problems in International Law*, Oxford: Hart 2016.

international rules and institutions so as to institutionalize public reason and specify the agreed 'principles of justice', which – in spite of the ancient origins of constitutionalism – remain imperfectly realized in national and multilevel governance of PGs (cf. the TPP provisions on dispute settlement and domestic implementation of TPP law); and

3. A *methodological self-commitment* (as explicitly reflected also in the Preamble and Article 31(3) of the Vienna Convention on the Law of Treaties, VCLT) to interpreting and restraining the 'rules of recognition, change and adjudication' of 'legal systems' in conformity with human rights and other 'principles of justice' aimed at limiting abuses of power in the real constitution.

US President Trump's disregard for multilateral UN and trade agreements raises some serious questions: Will Chinese leadership in the OBOR project help to counter the present risks of unravelling the global trading and economic order? Or will resistance by Chinese rulers against constitutional restraints limiting their 'communist party state' – notably their rejection of the 'democratic ideals of 1789' underlying UN and European human rights law – encourage power politics also beyond state borders (e.g. unilateral occupation of large parts of the South China Sea)?

As globalization transforms ever more *national* into *transnational* PGs[17] which no single state can protect unilaterally without international law and multilevel governance institutions: Can the multilevel OBOR governance be constituted, limited, regulated and justified without 'multilevel constitutionalism' through 'bilateral deals' (following the power-oriented policy paradigm of US President Trump)? Who protects the universally recognized civil, political, economic, social and cultural rights of citizens if 'the sovereign sleeps'[18] and transnational PGs (like

---

[17] Economists tend to define pure PGs (like sunshine, clean air, inalienable human rights) by their non-rival and non-excludable use that prevents their production in private markets. Most PGs are 'impure' in the sense of being either non-rival (e.g. 'club goods') or non-excludable (like common pool resources). Political and legal 'republican theories' tend to focus on whether republican 'common goods' for everyone (in contrast to the diverse private interests of citizens) are defined and implemented through participatory procedures and democratic conceptions of public interests (e.g. in protecting the republican values of 'freedom as non-domination', political equality, self-government and 'civic virtues' of citizens). On the different kinds and 'collective action problems' of PGs see Petersmann (note 16).

[18] The distinction between 'sovereignty' and 'government' appointed by the sovereign people was increasingly discussed since the 16th century in view of the impossibility of

mutually beneficial monetary, trading, investment, environmental, security and rule of law systems) are governed through ever more complex networks (like global markets and supply chains for international production of goods) driven by interest group politics? Can the 'disconnect' of the intergovernmental UN/WTO governance from citizens and peoples as constituent powers and democratic principals of all governance agents be limited so as to better protect human rights, rule of law and democratic governance in UN/WTO practices? Are authoritarian rulers right that economic poverty may justify prioritizing 'justice as economic efficiency'[19] over protecting 'justice as human rights'? Is the 'invisible hand development paradigm' (e.g. the assumption that private market competition and private law coordination can produce PGs) consistent with the universal recognition of human rights and with the need for reducing unnecessary poverty and environmental destruction?[20]

3 Why the Legitimacy of OBOR Law and Governance Depends on Constitutionalism?

Can the OBOR project be successfully designed and implemented on purely utilitarian principles of governance? Bilateral 'OBOR deals'

---

applying the Athenian model of permanent self-governance through democratic assemblies in city-republics to nation states with vast territories and people. Hobbes's suggestion in *De Cive* (1642) that the sovereign – after appointing a government – may be considered as 'sleeping', contributed to the invention in the 18th century of 'constitutional democracy' constituting, limiting, regulating and justifying limited government powers through democratically agreed, constitutional rules of a higher legal rank and constitutional rights of citizens aimed at 'constitutionalizing' the overall structures of society; cf. R. Tuck, *The Sleeping Sovereign: The Invention of Modern Democracy*, Cambridge University Press 2016.

[19] By treating citizens as mere objects of governmental 'utility maximization' and neglecting human rights, utilitarian focus on efficient production and distribution offers no guarantee for taking into account the non-economic dimensions of human welfare, for instance whenever restrictive business practices or emergency situations increase prices depriving poor people of effective access to water, essential food and medical services. The utilitarian assumption that morality consists in weighing and aggregating costs and benefits so as to 'maximize happiness' (e.g. by governmental redistribution of the 'gains from trade' at the whim of the rulers) risks being inconsistent with the moral principles underlying modern human rights (like respect for human dignity and 'inalienable' human rights).

[20] For a famous criticism of the privatization and 'commodification' of natural resources, human resources and financial resources see the 1944 book by K. Polanyi, *The Great Transformation: The Political and Economic Origins of our Time* (new edition, with an introduction by J. Stiglitz, Boston: Beacon Press 2004). For a criticism of the regulatory neglect of 'market failures' and 'governance failures' in UN/WTO law see Petersmann (note 12).

between China and recipient countries risk conflicting with existing multilateral agreements, as recently recalled by the EU investigations into China's construction of a railway link between Belgrade and Budapest and its alleged violation of EU regulations stipulating public tenders for large transport projects.

The insight that human rights and constitutionalism promote 'reasonableness' and limit rational egoism of individuals underlies UN human rights conventions that are ratified also by China (e.g. the International Covenant on Economic, Social and Cultural Rights). The conferral of the 2017 Nobel Prize for economics on R. Taler 'for his contribution to behavioural economics' reflects similar economic insights that 'bounded rationality' – for instance by the selfish *homo economicus* maximizing individual preferences through cost–benefit calculations in economic markets as well as in 'political markets' – remains part of the 'human condition' shaping also economic behavior, such as human responses to the 'three principles' of

- 'thinking automatically' (e.g. 'fast' and 'spontaneous' rather than 'deliberative' and 'reasonable slow thinking');
- 'thinking socially' (e.g. adjusting to social contexts of corruption); and
- 'thinking with mental models' that depend on the situation and the culture (e.g. in under-regulated financial industries profiting from tax avoidance and circumvention of the law).[21]

Constitutionalism is a rational response to this human condition (like risks of rational egoism and of limited human reasonableness) by committing all human beings and citizens to respect for equal human rights, rule of law, democratic input legitimacy, republican output legitimacy, inclusive democratic rule justifications, and democratic and judicial accountability. Also beyond state borders, republican and cosmopolitan constitutionalism includes and protects persons and citizens affected by public and private power through equal rights and remedies in multilevel 'bottom-up governance' of transnational PGs (like the international division of labour based on global supply chains).[22] The EU law principles of multilevel legal and judicial protection of

---

[21] Cf. *World Development Report 2015: Mind, Society and Behavior*, Washington: World Bank 2015 (discussing rational choice theory, behavioral economics, public choice and deliberative democracy theories on how individuals, institutions, and societies make legally relevant decisions, enact laws, or adapt to them).

[22] Kantian arguments for constitutional, cosmopolitan and international rights to equal freedoms are based not only on moral 'categorical imperatives' and a priori reasons for

- fundamental rights (e.g. as protected in the EU Charter of Fundamental Rights as an integral part of the 2009 Lisbon Treaty and European constitutional law);
- constitutional, representative, participatory and deliberative democracy (cf. Articles 2, 9–12 TEU); and
- related constitutional principles (e.g. of conferral of limited powers, subsidiarity, proportionality, rule of law)

may offer the most developed 'multilevel constitutional law for multilevel governance of PGs'.[23] Yet, just as the UK and United States remain reluctant to limit their national sovereignty by multilevel governance and judicial institutions, so are many Asian governments rejecting European constitutional law as a model for cooperation among Asian countries with different legal and cultural traditions. Such insistence on diversity and constitutional pluralism must be respected. Yet, Chinese citizens should not forget their own historical experiences that the widespread poverty inside China during the decades prior to its economic liberalization policies since 1978 was unnecessary and caused by government failures. Just as China's self-commitment to GATT/WTO law helped lift hundreds of millions of poor people out of poverty by embedding the 'open door policies' initiated by President Deng Xiaoping into the legal framework of GATT/WTO, so could embedding of China's OBOR project into multilateral trade, investment and regional agreements contribute to legitimizing OBOR governance and related adjudication through multilevel legal restraints on 'market failures' and 'government failures' inducing private and public, national and transnational actors to limit their rational pursuit of self-interests.[24]

reconciling 'the choice of one … with the choice of another in accordance with a universal law of freedom' (I. Kant, *The Metaphysics of Morals*, Cambridge University Press 1996, at 230). Kant also argued that a peaceful international order can be developed only through cosmopolitan law (*Weltbürgerrecht*) that transforms the classical law among nations (*Völkerrecht*) through multilevel constitutional guarantees of equal cosmopolitan rights of citizens; cf. J. Bohman and M. Lutz-Bachmann (eds.), *Perpetual Peace. Essays on Kant's Cosmopolitan Ideal*, Cambridge University Press 1997. Regional economic integration law among the twenty-seven EU Member States and their promotion of 'cosmopolitan rights' and 'democratic peace' for over sixty years are often seen as empirical evidence confirming Kantian legal philosophy.

23 Cf. Petersmann (note 16).
24 On the increasing references to human rights in investor–state arbitration, see V. Kube & E. U. Petersmann, 'Human Rights Law in International Investment Arbitration', *Asian Journal for WTO & Health Law and Policy* 11 (2016), 67–116.

4 Constitutional Pluralism Calls for Respecting the Diversity of 'Principles of Justice'

Constitutionalism is about 'imagined orders' based on inter-subjectively shared beliefs (e.g. 'social contracts') rather than about objective 'truth'. It must respect culturally diverse traditions of 'constitutional pluralism' and of legitimate contestation, for instance

- by foreign 'market citizens' contesting discrimination of foreigners; or
- by 'cosmopolitan citizens' challenging harmful 'externalities' (like transboundary pollution and climate change) and related 'discourse failures' in foreign jurisdictions (e.g. in US politics disregarding global PGs like climate change).

By empowering citizens and foreigners to locally engage with, invoke and enforce international rules and human rights in domestic jurisdictions, 'cosmopolitan constitutionalism' can promote the legal coherence and effectiveness of multilevel regulation and judicial protection of transnational PGs.[25] Theories and 'principles of justice' differ according to the diverse 'contexts of justice'. For example,

- dispute settlement procedures may be justified by diverse principles of 'procedural justice';
- constitutional assemblies and courts of justice may be designed very differently depending on the agreed principles of 'constitutional justice';
- the allocation of equal civil, political, economic, social and cultural rights of citizens may be justified by different principles of 'distributive justice';
- principles of 'corrective justice' may justify very different remedies (e.g. retrospective reparation of injury in investment courts, only prospective remedies in WTO dispute settlement procedures);
- principles of 'commutative justice' may justify particular interpretations of contractually agreed rights, duties and reciprocity principles (as illustrated by the 'violation', 'non-violation' and 'situation complaints' provided for in Article XXIII GATT); and
- 'equity principles' may justify particular legal and judicial responses to unforeseen challenges.[26]

---

[25] Cf. E. U. Petersmann, Cosmopolitan Constitutionalism: Linking Local Engagement with International Economic Law and Human Rights, in: L. Biukovic & P. Pitman (eds.), *Local Engagement with International Economic Law and Human Rights*, Cheltenham: Elgar Publishing 2017, 26–54.
[26] Cf. R. Forst, *Contexts of Justice: Political Philosophy beyond Liberalism and Communitarianism*, Berkeley: University of California Press 2002.

Impartial third-party adjudication is a much older paradigm of 'constitutional justice' than democratic 'constitutional contracts'. Impartial 'courts of justice' fit republican, cosmopolitan and economic definitions of PGs (e.g. in terms of non-exclusive and non-exhaustive access for all) and are essential for legitimizing legal regulation also of OBOR projects involving countries with diverse legal traditions. 'Constitutional justice' principles, including UN legal principles, aim at limiting power-oriented conceptions of PGs (e.g. unilateral occupation of large parts of the South China Sea in violation of UNCLOS obligations) and of majoritarian politics. Constitutionalism requires international and domestic courts and their participation in multilevel governance of PGs treaties so that treaty interpretations remain justifiable 'in conformity with the principles of justice', including also 'human rights and fundamental freedoms for all', as recalled in the Preamble and Article 31 of the 1969 VCLT. National and regional courts throughout Europe – like the CJEU, the European Free Trade Area (EFTA) Court, the European Court of Human Rights (ECtHR), and national courts cooperating with these European courts – are all committed to 'constitutional methodologies' aimed at protecting fundamental rights of citizens and transnational rule of law based on coherent 'principles of justice' respecting the legitimacy of 'constitutional pluralism' and of legal diversity. Yet, the legal and judicial traditions in many African and Asian countries are obviously different and may legitimately prioritize alternative dispute resolution methodologies.

EU law illustrates how democratic, cosmopolitan and judicial conceptions of 'constitutional justice' can complement each other in justifying citizen-oriented, multilevel governance of transnational PGs and of 'common pool resources'. The universal recognition of 'inalienable' human rights and fundamental freedoms calls for interpreting the rights of citizens and peoples and the corresponding duties of states, governments and international organizations as reciprocal principal–agent relationships.[27] Chinese law and the Chinese OBOR initiative could be strengthened and legitimized through 'republican constitutionalism' recognizing and empowering citizens as owners of PGs. By embedding principles of procedural, distributive, corrective, commutative justice

---

[27] On this need for reconciling the three competing conceptions of 'international law among states', 'international law among peoples', and 'cosmopolitan international law based on universal human rights' see, E. U. Petersmann, 'Human Rights, International Economic Law and "Constitutional Justice"', *European Journal of International Law* 19 (2008), 769–98.

and equity into 'constitutional justice principles', modern international law and multilevel governance of PGs can be designed more legitimately and more effectively, for instance by limiting 'constitutional nationalism' through multilevel protection of citizens across national frontiers. Complementing 'republican' by 'economic conceptions' of PGs can help clarify the collective action problems impeding 'constitutional justice' (e.g. in common market and competition law). Citizens must hold rulers more accountable for justifying their widespread disregard for the customary rules of treaty interpretation so that 'PGs treaties' are construed as protecting rights not only of governments, but also of citizens as the main economic actors, 'democratic principals' and 'constituent powers' of multilevel governance agents. As illustrated by widespread corruption problems and civil society contestation of law and governance in many OBOR countries, the voluntary compliance by private and public actors with multilevel OBOR regulations will depend no less on bottom-up support by civil society of 'just rules' than on legal and judicial attempts at their 'top-down enforcement' by governance institutions.

III   Legal Methodology Problems of Trade and Investment Adjudication Involving Silk Road Projects

The term 'legal methodology' refers to the 'best way' for identifying law, the methods of legal interpretation, the 'primary rules of conduct' and 'secondary rules of recognition, change and adjudication', the relationship between 'legal positivism', 'natural law' and 'social theories of law', and the 'dual nature' of modern legal systems. The etymological origins of the word methodology – the Greek word *meta-hodos*, referring to 'following the road' – suggest that globalization and multilevel governance of transnational PGs (like human rights, rule of law, democratic peace, mutually beneficial monetary, trading, development, environmental, communication and legal systems promoting 'sustainable development') require reviewing legal methodologies in order to find 'better ways' enabling citizens and peoples to increase their social welfare through rules-based global cooperation.

Section II explained why constitutionalism as (1) a normative conception for the input legitimacy of public law, (2) a sociological conception for the output legitimacy of public law, and (3) a legal methodology for interpreting and developing PGs systems – has proven to be the most important 'political invention' for protecting PGs both inside and beyond states. Constitutionalism suggests that law – including IEL and regulations of OBOR projects – must be understood and developed with due regard to the dynamic interactions between the 'law in the books', the 'law in action', and the underlying 'principles of justice' justifying law and governance vis-à-vis citizens. Transforming national into multilevel constitutionalism is required, inter alia, by

- the universal recognition of human rights;[28]
- the transformation of national into transnational PGs due to globalization;
- the need for limiting 'collective action problems' in multilevel governance of transnational 'aggregate PGs'; and
- the greater effectiveness of citizen-driven 'bottom-up network governance' compared with intergovernmental 'top-down chessboard governance'[29] or authoritarian 'pressure driving mechanisms'.[30]

This comparatively greater effectiveness of 'cosmopolitan international law' empowering citizens at home and abroad is illustrated by numerous empirical examples like:

- national and international contract, commercial and investment law (e.g. protecting 'global supply chains') enforced through multilevel cooperation among national and international tribunals (e.g. based

---

[28] Similar to the recognition of the 'trinity' of human rights, rule of law and democratic governance inside constitutional democracies and in an increasing number of regional institutions (like the EU and the Council of Europe), also UN institutions recognize 'that human rights, the rule of law and democracy are interlinked and mutually reinforcing and that they belong to the universal and indivisible core values and principles of the United Nations' (UN GA Res. 64/116 of 15 January 2010). From the point of view of legal methodology, it remains contested whether democratic governance and rule of law can be deduced – as principles of positive international law – from the government obligations to respect, protect and fulfil human rights; or whether – in order to become positive international law – they must be inductively proven to have also been specifically endorsed by states, for instance in the numerous UN and regional human rights conventions and related resolutions of UN and regional institutions recognizing legal duties to the democratic exercise of governance powers. Arguably, both the inductive as well as the deductive methodology justify the same conclusion that – since the UDHR of 1948 – all UN member states have consented to UN and regional treaties and resolutions recognizing legal duties to protect democratic governance and related human rights (like freedom of opinion, freedom of assembly, freedoms to participate in representative governments and in regular elections of democratic institutions).

[29] Cf. A. M. Slaugther, *The Chess-Board and the Web. Strategies of Connection in a Networked World*, New Haven: Yale University Press 2017 (elaborating strategies for designing, improving and managing social networks for resolving collective action problems at local, national and transnational levels of governance).

[30] See above note 10.

on the 1958 New York Convention and the 1966 Convention establishing the International Centre for the Settlement of Investment
Disputes, ICSID)
- rights-based common market, competition, labour laws and environmental regulations as enforced by the CJEU and the EFTA Court in
  cooperation with national courts
- regional human rights regimes enforced by national and regional
  human rights courts (e.g. in Africa, Europe and Latin America)
- international criminal law as enforced through multilevel cooperation
  among national and international criminal courts
- multilevel tobacco control regulations in the context of the World
  Health Organization (WHO) and its Framework Convention on
  Tobacco Control (FCTC)[31]
- internet regulation and its decentralized enforcement through multilevel arbitration procedures (e.g. administered by the World
  Intellectual Property Organization, WIPO)
- consular and refugee regulations protecting individual rights and
  judicial remedies.[32]

1   From Democratic, Republican and Cosmopolitan Constitutionalism to 'Constitutional Pluralism'

Since the Athenian democracy and the Roman republic some 2,500 years
ago, constitutionalism continues to dynamically evolve in response to
diverse legal cultures, regulatory contexts and 'collective action problems'. For instance:

- Emancipatory 'constitutionalism 1.0' constituted, limited, regulated
  and justified legislative, executive and judicial powers for republican
  (self)government (e.g. from the Athenian democracy and Roman
  republic to the Constitutions of the USA 1787, India 1949 and China
  1982).

---

[31] On their multilevel judicial enforcement see L. Gruszczynski, 'The WTO and FCTC
Dispute Settlement Systems: Friends or Foes?', *Asian Journal of WTO & Health Law and
Policy* 12 (March 2017) 105–34.
[32] For empirical evidence confirming the greater effectiveness of citizen-driven 'cosmopolitan international law' empowering citizens through individual rights, remedies and
'network governance' see R. Pierik & W. Werner (eds.), *Cosmopolitanism in Context.
Perspectives from International Law and Political Theory*, Cambridge University Press
2010; Petersmann (note 12), at 59 ff, 321 ff.

- The post-World War II 'human rights constitutionalism 2.0' further limited governance powers by multilevel human rights and judicial remedies (notably in European law); yet it failed to effectively 'constitutionalize' foreign policy powers (e.g. in UN/GATT politics) that often continue to tax, restrict and regulate citizens in their transnational cooperation without effective protection of human rights, rule of law and democratic self-governance.
- Multilevel 'EU constitutionalism 3.0' (e.g. based on Articles 2, 3, 6, 21 Lisbon Treaty and the EU Charter of Fundamental Rights) succeeded in 'constitutionalizing' the common market integration and some foreign policy areas (as illustrated by the *Kadi* jurisprudence and the European Economic Area Agreement between the EU and EFTA member states).[33]

Section I argued that globalization and its transformation of national into transnational PGs (like human rights, open monetary, trading, investment, legal security and environmental protection systems) require 'cosmopolitan UN/WTO constitutionalism 4.0'. UN/WTO governance of global PGs remains, however, legally 'disconnected' from effective democratic control, 'cosmopolitan rights' and judicial remedies of citizens. Due to inadequate restraints on foreign policy powers, intergovernmental power politics continues to prevail over citizen-oriented 'cosmopolitan' and 'constitutional conceptions' of UN/WTO law and governance. The 'America First' policies of US President Trump illustrate how governments and diplomats often pursue rational self-interests (e.g. in satisfying domestic interest groups in exchange for their political support, limiting the legal and judicial accountability of foreign policies vis-à-vis adversely affected citizens); 'global democracy', 'global justice', diplomatic and inter-governmental 'top-down UN/WTO constitutionalism' remain utopias. Yet, the historical evolution from 'constitutionalism 1.0' to democratic 'European constitutionalism 3.0' suggests that functionally limited 'multilevel constitutionalism 4.0' may be a politically realistic methodology for making multilevel governance of transnational PGs more legitimate and effective, for instance by setting incentives for civil society support of transnational PGs regimes limiting toxic tobacco consumption (e.g. in the context of the 2003 FCTC) and climate change (e.g. in the context of the 2015 Paris Agreement). Arguably, also European constitutional law offers lessons for extending 'republican'

[33] For different distinctions between 'constitutionalism 1.0, 2.0 and 3.0' see A. Somek, *The Cosmopolitan Constitution*, Oxford University Press 2014.

and 'cosmopolitan constitutionalism' beyond national borders; even in different legal contexts of transnational economic cooperation among national republics without effective 'democratic constitutionalism' (e.g. among China and Pakistan in the context of their OBOR cooperation), citizen-driven 'republican constitutionalism' and inclusive decision-making processes can limit 'collective action problems' in multilevel governance of transnational PGs (like the OBOR project of building transnational infrastructures connecting China with Afghanistan and Pakistan across areas dominated by militant local tribes). For instance:

- constitutional and 'cosmopolitan interpretations' of multilevel trade and investment regulations (e.g. by national and international courts of justice) can protect legal rights and judicial remedies of non-governmental actors and transnational rule of law, thereby limiting abuses of public and private powers;
- as illustrated by European economic integration law, legal empowerment of 'citizen struggles for justice' can promote other PGs like undistorted market competition and 'democratic peace';
- the customary law requirements of treaty interpretation 'in conformity with the principles of justice', including also 'human rights and fundamental freedoms for all' (as codified in the Preamble and Article 31 VCLT), can promote multilevel 'judicial dialogues' and strengthen the 'instrumental' and 'systemic functions' of law as well as the input and output legitimacy of intergovernmental lawmaking and multilevel governance.

2   How to Design OBOR Dispute Settlement Procedures?

The effectiveness of international courts of justice and of their multilevel cooperation with national courts is evaluated best by a 'goal-based approach'[34] that examines not only compliance with court judgments (which may depend more on the nature of remedies issued by a court than on the perceived quality of the court's procedures and reasoning), the usage rates of courts (which may be low due to dispute avoidance through out-of-court settlements) and the impact of courts on state conduct (e.g. compliance with minimalist judicial remedies that may

---

[34] Cf. Y. Shany, 'Assessing the Effectiveness of International Courts: A Goal-Based Approach', *American Journal of International Law* 106 (2012), 225–70.

fail to protect agreed treaty objectives effectively). Most international courts are mandated to also pursue broader goals such as:

- applying, interpreting and, if necessary, clarifying and enforcing the applicable international law rules and principles so as to strengthen the rule of law in the competent jurisdictions
- resolving international disputes and related legal problems
- supporting the operation of related international legal regimes
- legitimizing related rules and institutions.

International judicial effectiveness in realizing the legal and judicial dispute settlement objectives may depend on numerous other factors like the interests of state parties, interest groups and affected individuals; the tribunal's composition, formal authority (e.g. to compel compliance with the law), independence, human and financial resources; the reputation, functional capacity (e.g. depending on assistant staff and case load) and fact-finding capability of tribunals; their persuasive judicial reasoning, 'judicial dialogues' (e.g. with the disputing parties, third parties and other courts with 'overlapping jurisdictions'), the nature of the rules and rule violations concerned, and on judicial cooperation with domestic institutions concerned.[35]

So far, the OBOR project does not envisage the establishment of new national or international dispute settlement venues with specific dispute settlement goals, structures, processes, outcomes, stakeholders and constituencies (e.g. bearing the costs of permanent tribunals). As the WTO Dispute Settlement Understanding pursues 'providing security and predictability to the multilateral trading system' (Article 3 DSU) and most countries participating in the OBOR project are WTO member states, the WTO trade, investment, government procurement and dispute settlement rules and procedures might offer the most appropriate jurisdiction for settling related disputes also among countries cooperating in OBOR projects.[36] Similarly, as bilateral and regional investment rules and

---

[35] Cf. L. Helfer & A. M. Slaughter, 'Toward a Theory of Effective International Adjudication', *Yale Law Journal* 107 (1997), at 273 ff.

[36] If the WTO dispute settlement system is evaluated from the perspective of its much more frequent use by WTO Members since 1995 (e.g. 524 regular requests for consultations, 56 additional 'compliance disputes' pursuant to Article 21.5 DSU, over 350 WTO dispute settlement decisions issued by May 2017) compared with other worldwide dispute settlement systems (e.g. only twenty-three cases and six verdicts issued by the International Criminal Court since 2002; only twenty-five cases dealt with by the International Tribunal for the Law of the Sea since 1995), statistical analyses confirm the comparatively 'prompt settlement' of disputes 'essential to the effective functioning of the WTO' (Article 3(3) DSU). Yet, the WTO

arbitration procedures aim at protecting and reconciling both the public interests of the home and host states involved as well as the private interests of foreign investors (e.g. in full security of their property and investor rights), investment disputes arising from the implementation of OBOR projects might be submitted to existing investment jurisdictions (e.g. based on the more than 130 investment treaties concluded by China with other countries).[37] The private contract and commercial law disputes arising from joint ventures and other cooperation among Chinese and foreign companies and investors may be submitted and resolved most effectively by submission to one of the numerous private commercial law centres and established arbitration procedures in China and other countries attracting OBOR investment projects.[38] To the extent OBOR projects are financed by international and national development banks (like China Development Bank, a state lender which has already granted loans worth more than $160 billion to countries involved in OBOR projects), such financing is usually based on contracts incorporating the public procurement regulations of the banks concerned and requiring borrowers and contractors to use such procedures for funded procurements.[39] Comparative studies of recent arbitration reforms and of alternative dispute resolution methods in Asian countries identify new

dispute settlement system remains subject to power politics (e.g. political refusal to provide adequate legal and translation staff enabling compliance with the very tight DSU deadlines for WTO panel and Appellate Body proceedings) and to delaying tactics (e.g. more than 90 per cent of the thirty-three 'compliance panels' pursuant to Article 21(5) DSU found that the WTO member concerned had not complied fully with the DSB ruling, triggering subsequent requests in twenty-one of these disputes for DSB authorization of 'suspension of concessions' as countermeasures, notably against the United States and the EU). Moreover, in 27 out of 122 reports issued by the WTO Appellate Body, the latter was unable 'to complete the analysis' and, after having (partially) reversed the panel's findings, to resolve the dispute by remanding it back to the original WTO panel. However, evaluation of the WTO dispute settlement system from a different benchmark than its frequent use and comparatively speedy dispute settlement (e.g. since 2013 duration of about thirty-four months of WTO dispute settlement proceedings) – for example, in the light of Article 3(2) DSU ('providing security and predictability to the multilateral trading system'; 'clarify the existing provisions of those agreements in accordance with customary rules of interpretation of public international law') – could justify more criticism (e.g. in terms of neglecting the customary law requirement of interpreting treaties in conformity with 'human rights and fundamental freedoms for all', as recalled in the Preamble and Article 31(3) of the VCLT).

[37] Cf. J. Chaisse (ed.), *China's Three-Prong Investment Strategy: Bilateral, Regional and Global Tracks*, Oxford University Press 2017.

[38] Cf. J. Paulsson (ed.), *International Handbook on Commercial Arbitration*, The Hague: Kluwer 2015 (describing commercial arbitration in China in vol. 1).

[39] Cf. S. Williams-Elegbe, *Public Procurement and Multilateral Development Banks: Law, Practice and Problems*, Oxford: Hart 2017.

Asian approaches to modernization of arbitration and mediation procedures.[40]

3   Legitimacy Challenges of International Trade and Investment Adjudication

The legitimacy of courts (e.g. understood as socially accepted authority) depends not only on the internal rules constituting the legal regimes in which the courts operate. It is also influenced by the 'principles of justice' underlying and embedding legal and judicial systems. Judicial jurisprudence may generate additional legitimacy promoting social acceptance by the constituencies concerned.[41] Due to the lack of judicial independence inside China's 'communist party state', many foreign actors perceive the 'source legitimacy', 'procedural legitimacy' and 'result-based legitimacy' of Chinese courts as inadequate, even if national courts inside China offer 'low-cost judgments' compared with more expensive arbitration or international dispute settlement procedures. Comparative studies of international trade and investment courts point to both 'converging developments' (e.g. in judicial interpretations of national treatment and most-favoured-nation treatment obligations in trade and investment agreements, proportionality balancing) and 'diverging structures' (e.g. regarding prospective remedies in WTO dispute settlement procedures, retroactive reparation of injury in investment arbitration, cooperation between national courts and investment arbitral tribunals, lack of cooperation among national and WTO trade tribunals).[42] Evaluating the legitimacy and comparative advantages of national, regional and worldwide trade and investment courts and of their increasing interactions raises also political, sociological and moral legitimacy questions going beyond 'positive law',[43] for instance whether the legitimacy of international courts is ultimately a matter of justifiability towards individuals (e.g. in terms of protecting citizens against arbitrary domination,

---

[40] Cf. A. Reyes & W. Gu (eds.), *The Developing World of Arbitration: A Comparative Study of Arbitration Reform in the Asia Pacific*, Oxford: Hart Publishing 2018.

[41] On ad hoc responses of investment arbitrators responding, for example, to WTO Appellate Body jurisprudence and 'judicial proportionality' reasoning in European courts see D. Schneiderman, 'Legitimacy and Reflexivity in International Investment Arbitration: A New Self-Restraint?', *Journal of International Dispute Resolution* 2 (2011), 471–95.

[42] Cf. J. Kurtz, *The WTO and International Investment Law: Converging Systems*, Cambridge University Press 2016; Y. Hua (note 3).

[43] Cf. G. Ulfstein, M. Zhang, R. Howse & H. Ruiz-Fabri (eds.), *The Legitimacy of International Trade Courts and Tribunals*, Cambridge University Press 2017.

protecting equal freedoms as individual rights) rather than only vis-à-vis government agents representing states (e.g. in terms of helping them solve collective action problems).[44] The behaviour of international judges is influenced not only by law, but also by political constraints and uncertainty depending on their independence, accountability and the multilevel allocation and separation of powers (e.g. regarding the reappointment of WTO Appellate Body judges and the adoption of Appellate Body reports by the political WTO Dispute Settlement Body). The recent 'blockage' of the re-appointment of WTO Appellate Body judges by the United States – based on US claims that they have 'exceeded their mandates' – reflects regrettable US power politics disregarding their DSU obligations (e.g. under Article 23(1)) and the legitimate use of the customary rules of treaty interpretation by the Appellate Body (as required by Article 3(2) DSU).

The election of authoritarian, political leaders and their 'populist policies' have recently led to increasing criticism of international courts, for instance by the administration of US President Trump (criticizing independent WTO adjudication), China (rejecting the arbitral jurisdiction and awards under the UNCLOS), Britain (rejecting the jurisdiction of the CJEU beyond the presumed entry into force of Brexit, and criticizing the jurisdiction of the ECtHR), as well as by European civil society (e.g. opposing the limitation of national court jurisdictions in favour of investor–state arbitration privileging foreign investors).[45] The horizontal and vertical allocation of judicial authority, its accountability, democratic control, moral justification and judicial interpretation of indeterminate 'legal principles' will inevitably remain contested also in the implementation of China's OBOR projects, for instance depending on whether international courts will be socially accepted also by non-governmental actors as judicial promoters of 'justice', rule of law and other PGs. Future legal and judicial practices in the implementation of OBOR projects will help to discover comparative advantages and 'best practices' of alternative judicial, mediation and conciliation procedures and multilevel institutions for dispute settlement.

---

[44] Cf. E. U. Petersmann, International Dispute Settlement and the Position of Individuals under EU and International Law, in M. Cremona & R. Wessels (eds.), *The European Union and International Dispute Settlement*, Oxford: Hart 2017, 213–34.

[45] Cf. E. U. Petersmann, Transatlantic Free Trade Agreements: Lack of EU Leadership for Reforming Trade and Investment Law?, in *Revue Internationale de Droit Economique* 2016, 455–80.

IV Some Policy Conclusions for the OBOR Project

The legitimacy of economic, financial and investment cooperation in the implementation of OBOR projects depends on rules-based legal frameworks, impartial dispute settlement procedures, predictability and compliance of governance with the rule of law as 'a principle of governance in which all persons, institutions and entities ... including the State itself, are accountable to laws that are publicly promulgated, equally enforced and independently adjudicated, and which are consistent with international human rights norms and standards' that have become part of universally recognized human rights principles.[46]

China's leadership in the OBOR project (e.g. as main provider of financial and technical resources, goods and services for OBOR projects) seems to entail predominantly bilateral legal structures without creation of new multilateral courts, multilateral political control mechanisms and new multilateral treaties protecting non-state actors. Hence, decentralized judicial institutions and coordination mechanisms (e.g. *litis pendens* principles for preventing simultaneous cases before competing courts, *res judicata* principles preventing subsequent cases before different courts, judicial comity principles promoting judicial dialogues and regard to precedents), judicial independence, bilateral or plurilateral procurement procedures, investment protection and dispute settlement agreements may be more appropriate in view of the enormous diversity of the more than sixty countries participating in OBOR projects. Even if governments remain the 'masters' of intergovernmental OBOR projects, implementation of the infrastructure, investment and economic projects depends on non-state actors and civil society interested in 'non-domination';[47] they are likely to evaluate the normative legitimacy and social acceptability of OBOR rules, institutions and projects from diverse local perspectives. Protecting legitimate rights and interests of non-governmental actors and local 'compliance communities' (e.g. interested in non-domination, protection of legitimate expectations, respect for human rights and rule of law) and promoting the 'inner morality of law' will be important for

---

[46] UN General Assembly Resolution A/RES/67/97 (2012) on 'The Rule of Law at National and International Levels'.
[47] On 'rule of men' as domination, and 'rule of law' as non-domination, see P. Pettit, *Republicanism. A Theory of Freedom and Government*, Oxford University Press 1997. According to Pettit, republicanism pursues non-domination in the sense of 'protection from the arbitrary use of political authority and coercive power'. For broader conceptions of republicanism focusing on multilevel governance of PGs see Petersmann (note 12).

successful implementation of OBOR projects and voluntary compliance with related contracts.[48]

As national courts in China and in some other OBOR partner countries are widely perceived as failing adequate legitimacy standards (like judicial independence from political interference, impartiality, due process of law, legal expertise in international law), the international agreements and economic contracts governing the relationships between OBOR donor and recipient countries, investors and their contractors should provide for the existing dispute settlement procedures in international trade, investment, commercial and contract law rather than for submission of disputes to national jurisdictions. The 'Chinese initiative' for joining the TPP Agreement and multilateralising mega-regional FTAs among WTO members deserves support by OBOR partner countries as the most efficient way of reforming WTO law.[49] The Chinese traditions favouring alternative dispute resolution methods (like mediation and conciliation procedures) should be institutionalized at national and regional levels of OBOR cooperation. Subsidiarity principles are important in designing dispute settlement procedures among and within constitutional democracies, provided their national courts are subject to effective constitutional restraints (e.g. in EU and EEA countries

---

[48] On the 'two moralities of duty and of aspiration', the 'inner morality of law' and related procedural and substantive 'rule of law criteria' (e.g. based on principles of general applicability, promulgation of rules, their non-retroactivity, clarity, consistency, respect for human capabilities, *stare decisis* and congruence) see: L. L. Fuller, *The Morality of Law*, Yale University Press (revised edn.) 1969. On the need for socially constructing law 'bottom up' by involving all citizens and actors concerned in the making, administration and adjudication of (inter)national rules see: J. Brunée & S. J. Toope, *Legitimacy and Legality in International Law: An Interactional Account*, Cambridge University Press 2010, at 86: 'Interactional law only emerges when shared understandings become fused with a "practice of legality", rooted in *Fuller's eight criteria of legality* and embraced by a community of practice that adheres to those criteria in day-to-day decision-making.' On Fuller's 'inner morality of law criteria' as constitutive elements of 'legality' and rule of law see Fuller at 197–200. On the interrelationships between Fuller's eight principles of *generality* (law must take the form of general rules), *publicity* (law must be published), *clarity* (law must be comprehensible and not overly vague), *consistency* (laws must not contradict one another), *feasibility* (it must be possible for people to comply with the law), *constancy* (law must not change too rapidly), *prospectivity* (law cannot be retroactive) and *congruence* (law must be administered and enforced as it is written) with human rights law see D. Luban, 'The Rule of Law and Human Dignity: Re-Examining Fuller's Canons', *Hague Journal of the Rule of Law* 2 (2010), at 29.

[49] See note 15 and E. U. Petersmann, CETA, TTIP and TISA: New Trends in International Economic Law, in S. Griller et al. (eds.), *Mega-Regional Agreements: TTIP, CETA, TISA. New Orientations for EU External Economic Relations*, Oxford University Press 2017, 17, 33 ff.

cooperating in OBOR projects). In countries without 'republican constitutionalism', however, constraining national governance institutions through international legal and judicial commitments (e.g. WTO law, international investment law) can improve domestic institutions, enhance legal security and reduce transaction costs, for instance by resorting to 'positive complementarity principles' based on cooperation between national and transnational courts and tribunals (like recognition and enforcement by national courts of transnational arbitral awards and international judgments). Multilevel judicial cooperation between international and national courts (e.g. based on 'preliminary rulings' by the CJEU, 'advisory opinions' by the EFTA Court and MERCOSUR courts) can legalize, 'judicialize' and legitimize international politics (e.g. among countries implementing OBOR projects) by compensating inadequate national judicial institutions by an 'integrated, multilevel judiciary' engaging in 'judicial dialogues', common judicial justifications, 'checks and balances', collective learning processes and 'public reason-giving'. Republican and cosmopolitan constitutionalism can substitute for the lack of democratic constitutionalism inside China and some other OBOR participants, for instance by limiting political and judicial powers and protecting 'countervailing rights' of citizens, companies and other nongovernmental actors, litigants and third parties affected by dispute settlement proceedings.

4

Why Don't We Have a WITO? G20, TPP and WTO

GUOHUA YANG

This chapter has been developed from a dozen lectures and seminars in the past year, including the SRIICL@10th International Symposium on China and the Development of International Dispute Resolution System in the Context of the "Belt and Road Initiative" (BRI), held in Xi'an, China on November 1, 2016.

The outbreak of the global financial crisis in 2008 led to the first G20[1] Leaders' Summit of November 14–15, 2008, in Washington, DC, which focused primarily on strengthening financial regulation, with agreement on a 47-point action plan to improve financial regulation over the medium term.[2] G20 leaders met on April 2, 2009, in London for the second time on coordinated fiscal and monetary stimulus measures, pledging the amount of $1.1 trillion to avert the threat of global depression. When sovereign debt became a serious problem in Europe, the third Summit on June 26–27, 2010, in Toronto committed to halve fiscal deficits by 2013 and stabilize or reduce sovereign debt ratios by 2016. Since then, G20 has emerged as a power of global economic governance, from its beginnings as meetings of finance ministers and central bank governors discussing international financial and monetary policies, reform of international financial institutions and world economic development initiated in 1999. Nowadays, the G20 Summit is not only a forum for leaders to express the positions of each country, but also an important place to make commitments and consolidate measures to maintain world

---

[1] Argentina, Australia, Brazil, Canada, China, France, Germany, India, Indonesia, Italy, Japan, Mexico, Republic of Korea, Russia, Saudi Arabia, South Africa, Turkey, the United Kingdom, the United States and the European Union (EU). See G20 official website, www .g20.org/gyg20/G20jj/201510/t20151027_871.html (visited on November 27, 2016).
[2] See G20 Leaders' Communique, November 15, 2008, at G20 official website, http://g20.org /English/Documents/PastPresidency/201512/P020151225609230748803.pdf (visited on November 14, 2016).

4

economic order and boost world economic development. With a membership of only twenty countries, it accounts for more than four-fifths of gross world product and three-quarters of global trade, and is home to almost two-thirds of the world's population. Against this backdrop, the G20 Hangzhou Summit attracted worldwide attention.[3]

From the perspective of trade and the WTO, the G20 Hangzhou Summit was also an event to focus attention on. As one of the most important international economic organizations, the WTO has established within twenty years its significant role in maintaining international trade rules and promoting economic development and world peace.[4] However, it has encountered unprecedented challenges in recent years, particularly the delay of concluding the Doha Round and limited outcomes from multilateral negotiations,[5] while regional trade negotiations are increasing rapidly and attracting attention previously focused on multilateral ones,[6] so that pessimistic comments like "Doha is dead" and "the WTO is in crisis" are often heard around the world.[7] Hence, the positions of the G20 leaders, all of whose countries are WTO members, achieved the same importance as during the financial and sovereign debt crises. Fortunately, people feel relaxed after reading the commitments from the Summit, whose details are discussed in Section 4.2. Nevertheless, these commitments, according to my understanding, would not automatically turn into positive outcomes in practice, which means that people from both governments and civil society need to work together to turn all those positions and principles into detailed measures beneficial to a multilateral framework; this is the focus of the present chapter. Finally, it should be pointed

---

[3] See G20 official website, www.g20.org/gyg20/G20jj/201510/t20151027_871.html; www .g20.org/gyg20/ljfhcg/201511/t20151106_1226.html (visited on November 14, 2016).

[4] "The WTO provides the multilateral framework of rules governing international trade relations, an essential mechanism for preventing and resolving trade disputes, and a forum for addressing trade related issues that impact all WTO members." See para. 11, G20 Trade Ministers Meeting Statement.

[5] The Doha Round negotiations were initiated in 2001 and only some progress on conclusion of a Trade Facilitation Agreement, elimination of export subsidies on agriculture products and enlargement of the Information Technology Agreement were made. See WTO official website, www.wto.org/english/tratop_e/dda_e/dda_e.htm (visited on November 17, 2016).

[6] There are about 300 effective regional trade agreements. See WTO official website, http:// rtais.wto.org/UI/PublicAllRTAList.aspx (visited on November 14, 2016).

[7] For example, before the WTO Ministerial Conference in 2015, the United States Trade Representative published an article saying "the Doha Round of talks ... simply has not delivered ... It is time for the world to free itself of the strictures of Doha." See www .ftchinese.com/story/001065260 (visited on November 17, 2017).

out that both the membership and objectives of the WTO and G20 are overlapping, so they are mutually beneficial to each other.

4.1 Significance of G20 Hangzhou Summit: Global and Trade Issues

G20 emerged from the global economic crisis, and the current global economic situation remains unoptimistic, as indicated by the G20 Hangzhou Summit Leaders' Communique (hereinafter Communique):

> [T]he global economic recovery is progressing, resilience is improved in some economies and new sources for growth are emerging. But growth is still weaker than desirable. Downside risks remain due to potential volatility in the financial markets, fluctuations of commodity prices, sluggish trade and investment, and slow productivity and employment growth in some countries. Challenges originating from geopolitical developments, increased refugee flows as well as terrorism and conflicts also complicate the global economic outlook. (para. 2)[8]

To address these challenges, the four principles (set out in Communique para. 6) of the Hangzhou Consensus reached by the leaders are comprehensive:

(a) **vision:** to "strengthen the G20 growth agenda to catalyze new drivers of growth, open up new horizons for development, lead the way in transforming our economies in a more innovative and sustainable manner"
(b) **integration:** to "pursue innovative growth concepts and policies by forging synergy among fiscal, monetary and structural policies, enhancing coherence between economic, labor, employment and social policies as well as combining demand management with supply side reforms, short-term with mid- to long-term policies, economic growth with social development and environmental protection"
(c) **openness:** to "build an open world economy, reject protectionism, promote global trade and investment, including through further strengthening the multilateral trading system, and ensure broad-based opportunities through and public support for expanded growth in a globalized economy"

---

[8] All the official documents mentioned in this article were downloaded from the G20 official website at www.g20.org (visited in November 2016).

(d) **inclusiveness:** to "ensure that our economic growth serves the needs of everyone and benefits all countries and all people including in particular women, youth and disadvantaged groups, generating more quality jobs, addressing inequalities and eradicating poverty so that no one is left behind."

As one of the principles, trade and investment-related "openness" is complementary to the other principles. For example, the objectives to "open up new horizons for development," forge "synergy among fiscal, monetary and structural policies" and ensure "economic growth serves the needs of everyone and benefits all countries and all people" will create a better environment for the growth of trade and investment, and this growth will in the end promote these objectives. So trade and investment is only part of the package within the G20 economic agenda, and this suggests to the WTO that trade is not independent of the other areas, although it is a trade organization whose goal is to establish and implement trade rules; and above all, the WTO should address more trade-related issues, including the issues raised in the regional trade negotiations. As a matter of fact, as discussed in Section 4.3.4, this may relate to the direction of the WTO's development in the future to meet the challenges mentioned at the beginning of this chapter.

Following the four principles, the Summit identified seven areas to take measures, that is, strengthening policy coordination, breaking a new path for growth, more effective and efficient global economic and financial governance, robust international trade and investment, inclusive and interconnected development, and further significant global challenges affecting the world economy (the UK's membership in the EU, sustainable development, climate change, refugee crisis, terrorism and antimicrobial resistance, etc.), among which the "robust international trade and investment" is most closely relevant to the WTO.

4.2   Outcomes of G20 Hangzhou Summit on Trade: Commitments, Principles and Actions

As mentioned in Section 1, one of the four principles of the Hangzhou Consensus is "openness" and the relevant area is "robust international trade and investment" in the seven areas (paras. 25–31, Communique) as further elaborated by the G20 Trade Ministers Meeting Statement (hereinafter Statement).[9]

---

[9] There are similar expressions on trade and investment in the G20 Action Plan on the 2030 Agenda for Sustainable Development, Annex II of the Communique.

4.2.1   Strengthening the Multilateral Trading System

This position is expressed in the Communique in the following way: "We reaffirm our determination to ensure a rules-based, transparent, non-discriminatory, open and inclusive multilateral trading system with the World Trade Organization playing the central role in today's global trade." (para. 26)

The Statement continues: "We reaffirm the central role of the WTO in today's global economy. The WTO provides the multilateral framework of rules governing international trade relations, an essential mechanism for preventing and resolving trade disputes, and a forum for addressing trade related issues that impact all WTO members. We remain committed to a rules-based, transparent, non-discriminatory, open and inclusive multilateral trading system and are determined to work together to further strengthen the WTO." (para. 11)

These principles, positions or statements mean something substantial and significant in the context of the challenges mentioned at the very beginning of this chapter. First, G20 members support the WTO. The WTO itself is also a model of a rules-based, transparent, non-discriminatory, open and inclusive system, establishing and implementing international trade rules in goods, service and intellectual properties, and it is a multilateral trading system due to its representativeness of the 164 members accounting for over 90 percent of global trade volume. In the past twenty years, the WTO has proved to be a very successful organization in maintaining world economic order and supporting economic development. It has further proved itself as a good example of global governance and international rule of law, such as through its effective dispute settlement system, so that people can hardly imagine a world without the WTO. Hence, the G20 support of the WTO means confirmation of its role in the global economy, and G20 members, also as WTO members, will contribute their efforts to meeting its challenges. Second, the WTO is complementary to the G20, which could be clearly seen from the objectives of the G20 as an economic forum and its emphasis on trade and investment.

G20 support is building confidence in the development of the WTO, which means that some of the most important members of the WTO are committed to "doing something" whenever the WTO is in crisis. It is worth pointing out that the G20 and WTO members are overlapping, and it is improper to separate G20 from the WTO, or to say that the G20 is helping the WTO. The correct understanding of G20 support would be that some members of the WTO, on an important occasion (G20 Hangzhou Summit), explicitly expressed their position supporting the multilateral trading system – understood as a rules-based, transparent, non-discriminatory, open and inclusive system – and this will further translate into implementation measures to address the challenges faced by the WTO. To be frank, the achievements of the WTO have come from the joint efforts of all members, including G20 members, and it is rational to clear all the barriers on the road of progress when it is absolutely unrealistic to replace the WTO with any other organizations.

4.2.2   Regional Trade Agreements and Protectionism

4.2.1.1   Regional Trade Agreements (RTAs)

Regional trade negotiations were identified at the beginning of this chapter as one of the challenges to the WTO. As a matter of fact, the relationship between the WTO multilateral system and RTAs has long been a topic discussed widely among governments and academia, so that two contradictory expressions, that is, "stepping stone" and "stumbling block," are invoked to explain the effects of the latter on the former.[10] Here, the Communique declares officially and authoritatively that "We note the important role that bilateral and regional trade agreements can play in liberalizing trade and in the development of trade rules, while recognizing the need to ensure they are consistent with WTO rules. We commit to working to ensure our bilateral and regional trade agreements complement the multilateral trading system, and are open, transparent, inclusive and WTO-consistent." (para. 27) And the Statement further elaborates that "We note the important role that bilateral and regional trade agreements (RTAs) can play in liberalizing trade and in the development of trade rules, while recognizing the need to ensure that they are consistent with the WTO rules and provisions and contribute to a stronger multilateral trading system. We encourage future RTAs by G20 members to be open to accession and include provisions for review and expansion." (para. 13)

With the role of RTAs recognized, "consistent," "complement" and "WTO-consistent" are emphasized in their relation with the WTO, which means that RTAs are subjected to the WTO. Recognition of and

---

[10] "Stepping stone" means that RTAs are a necessary step for a multilateral system, while "stumbling block" means that RTAs will be harmful to the development of a multilateral system.

consensus on this relationship mean a lot to G20 members who are both members of the WTO and parties to numerous RTAs, and the conflict between "stepping stone" and "stumbling block" is resolved. With this clarification, we understand the WTO remains the mainstream, while RTAs, no matter how prevalent they are becoming, are only supplementary to the multilateral system, so that whenever possible RTAs will return to the fold of the WTO.[11] Above all, this is not a baseless analogy since two paths of integrating the RTAs into the WTO have been identified, either explicitly or implicitly, in the outcomes of the Summit: "future RTAs by G20 members to be open to accession and include provisions for review and expansion" (para. 13, Statement) and "(issues addressed in RTAs) may be legitimate issues for discussions in the WTO" (para. 26, Communique; para. 15, Statement). The first of these shows a roadmap for accession and expansion of RTAs to the WTO, that is, a de facto multilateralization of RTAs, while the second will be explored in detail in Section 4.4.3 to justify a proposal for a new and enlarged organization, a World Investment and Trade Organization, or WITO.

Additionally, a monitoring system is mentioned specifically in the Statement: "We appreciate the factual overview of RTAs developments given by the WTO Director-General. We will work with other WTO members towards the transformation of the provisional Transparency Mechanism on RTAs into a permanent one and commit to lead by example in fully fulfilling related notification obligations." (para. 13) The provisional Transparency Mechanism on RTAs was established on December 14, 2006, according to the General Council Decision on the Transparency Mechanism for Regional Trade Agreements,[12] which includes "Early Announcement," "Notification," "Procedures to Enhance Transparency," "Subsequent Notification and Reporting," "Bodies Entrusted with the Implementation of the Mechanism" and "Technical Support for Developing Countries."[13] The provisional mechanism has been working,[14] and transforming it into a permanent one and

---

[11] As a matter of fact, Article 24 of GATT 1947 is about RTAs, which means the contracting parties/members of GATT/WTO can form free trade areas to increase "freedom of trade" between some parties while not raising barriers to the trade of other parties. That is to say, legally speaking, RTAs are already a legitimate part of the multilateral system.

[12] See WTO document WT/L/671 at www.wto.org.

[13] See WTO official website, www.wto.org/english/tratop_e/region_e/trans_mecha_e.htm (visited on November 14, 2016).

[14] Ibid.

committing to lead by example will definitely facilitate effective monitoring of RTAs.

4.2.1.2   Trade Protectionism

This is a biased term, so that many countries apply trade remedy measures like antidumping duties, countervailing duties and safeguard measures, while few would declare that these are "protectionism."[15] However, the Communique reiterates "opposition to protectionism on trade and investment in all its forms. We extend our commitments to standstill and rollback of protectionist measures till the end of 2018, reaffirm our determination to deliver on them and support the work of the WTO, UNCTAD and OECD in monitoring protectionism." (para. 28) The Statement elaborates:

> [T]he stock of restrictive measures affecting trade in goods and services has continued to rise, with about three quarters of the measures recorded since 2008 still in place, and the number of new trade-restrictive measures imposed by G20 economies affecting both goods and services has reached the highest monthly average registered since the WTO began its monitoring exercise in 2009. In response, we recommit to our existing pledge for both standstill and rollback of protectionist measures, and to extend it until the end of 2018. (para. 12)

So the trade-restrictive measures monitored by the WTO are identified as protectionist measures and subject to both standstill and rollback, whether they are antidumping duties, countervailing duties or safeguard measures. Above all, "the WTO, UNCTAD and OECD in monitoring protectionism" refers to "their regular reporting on restrictive measures affecting trade in goods and services, and investment." (para. 12, Statement)[16] With consolidated efforts by various organizations, trade protectionism by G20 members will become more transparent and be reduced, and with their example, global protectionism will come under control.

---

[15]   However, the Report on G20 Trade Measures prepared in response to the request in 2008 by G20 leaders to the WTO, together with the OECD and UNCTAD, to monitor and report publicly on G20 adherence to their undertakings on resisting trade and investment protectionism, includes these trade remedies. See the 16th report at www.wto.org/english/news_e/news16_e/g20_wto_report_november16_e.pdf (visited on November 16, 2016).

[16]   Ibid.

4.3   Actions

The commitments and principles on strengthening the WTO, disciplining RTAs and restricting protectionism are supported by a series of specific actions in order to make the outcomes of the G20 Hangzhou Summit on trade enforceable and effective rather than political and rhetorical only.

4.3.1   Post-Nairobi Work

The implementation of the outcomes from the Nairobi WTO Ministerial Conference in December 2015 is emphasized as a measure to support the WTO with priorities on "all three pillars of agriculture (i.e., market access, domestic support and export competition), non-agricultural market access, services, development, TRIPS and rules" (para. 26, Communique),[17] which signifies the importance of the WTO Doha Development Agenda and responds to doubts over the fate of multilateral trade negotiations, while the Communique expressly notes "work together with all WTO members with a sense of urgency and solidarity and with a view to achieving positive outcomes of the MC11 (the 11th Ministerial Conference) and beyond." (para. 26)

Multilateral trade negotiations will be promoted and the WTO will be strengthened if all WTO members follow the example of G20 members by participating with a view to achieving positive outcomes of the Ministerial Conferences.

4.3.2   Trade Facilitation Agreement

The Communique commits "to ratify the Trade Facilitation Agreement by the end of 2016 and call on other WTO members to do the same"(para. 27), which brought the first agreement reached since the launch of the WTO Doha Round in 2001 into effect on February 22, 2017. This is an agreement on the publication and availability of information, nondiscrimination and transparency, disciplines on fees and charges imposed on or in connection with importation and exportation, release and clearance of goods, freedom of transit, border agency cooperation, etc.,[18] which will "make

---

[17] The outcome contains a series of six Ministerial Decisions on agriculture, cotton and issues related to least-developed countries. See www.wto.org/english/thewto_e/minist_e/mc10_e/nairobipackage_e.htm (visited on November 15, 2016).

[18] See www.wto.org/english/thewto_e/minist_e/mc9_e/desci36_e.htm (visited on March 23, 2017).

a significant contribution to lowering trade costs and freeing up world trade." (para. 14, Statement)[19]

4.3.3   Environmental Goods Agreement (EGA) and Other Plurilateral Agreements

Unlike the multilateral Trade Facilitation Agreement joined by all the WTO members, the EGA, whose objectives include the lowering and elimination of tariffs and nontariff measures on certain products of pollution control, waste management and clean energy, will be a plurilateral agreement to be joined on a voluntary basis by some members. G20 EGA participants "welcome the landing zone achieved in the WTO EGA negotiations, and reaffirm their aim to redouble efforts to bridge remaining gaps and conclude an ambitious, future-oriented EGA that seeks to eliminate tariffs on a broad range of environmental goods by the end of 2016, after finding effective ways to address the core concerns of participants." (para. 27, Communique)[20]

The G20 position on plurilateral agreements is as follows: "WTO-consistent plurilateral trade agreements with broad participation can play an important role in complementing global liberalization initiatives" (para. 27, Communique). The Statement further notes the "Information Technology Agreement (ITA) and its Expansion Agreement, and negotiations on the Trade in Services Agreement and the Environmental Goods Agreement (EGA). WTO members who share the objectives of participants in such plurilateral agreements and negotiations should be encouraged to join. In particular . . . the confirmation by all G20 participants in the expanded Information Technology Agreement of their commitment to implement it without further delay." (para. 16)

From the history and development of GATT/WTO, plurilateral agreements have been just one step away from multilateral agreements, that is, the former made by some members would usually turn into the latter made by all members in the end.[21] Thus, naming the several ongoing

---

[19]   See www.wto.org/english/news_e/news17_e/fac_27feb17_e.htm (visited on March 4, 2017).

[20]   For environmental goods and services, see www.wto.org/english/tratop_e/envir_e/envir_neg_serv_e.htm (visited on November 15, 2016).

[21]   For example, the GATT Tokyo Round negotiations in the 1970s concluded some "codes" in subsidies and countervailing measures, technical barriers to trade, import licensing procedures, government procurement, customs valuation, antidumping, bovine meat arrangement, international dairy arrangement and trade in civil aircraft which were not accepted by all members, but later in the Uruguay Round negotiations in the 1980s–90s became multilateral, with a few exceptions on government procurement, bovine meat

agreements, setting a deadline for the EGA and committing to ITA are positive actions to conclude and enforce these agreements, and to turn them into multilateral ones.

4.3.4   Other Issues Related to Trade: Growth, Global Value Chains (GVCs) and Steel

The G20 leaders endorse the G20 Strategy for Global Trade Growth and commit to "lead[ing] by example to lower trade costs, harness trade and investment policy coherence, boost trade in services, enhance trade finance, promote e-commerce development, and address trade and development" (para. 29, Communique), because "these activities, by promoting trade opening and integration and supporting measures for economic diversification and industrial upgrading will contribute to global prosperity and sustainable development." (para. 7, Statement)

The Communique declares to "support policies that encourage firms of all sizes, in particular women and youth entrepreneurs, women-led firms and SMEs, to take full advantage of global value chains (GVCs), and that encourage greater participation, value addition and upward mobility in GVCs by developing countries, particularly low-income countries (LICs)" (para. 30), because "GVCs, encompassing regional value chains (RVCs), have become an important feature of the global economy, and are important drivers of world trade" (para. 21, Statement), and the concrete actions to these ends include to "continue their efforts to enhance capacity building to promote inclusive and coordinated global value chains, and will continue to seek to develop and implement initiatives to assist developing countries, particularly LICs, and SMEs in the areas that matter most to GVCs. Such initiatives could include appropriate infrastructure, technology support, access to credit, supply chain connectivity, agriculture, innovation and e-commerce, skills training and responsible business conduct." (para. 22, Statement)

The Summit also mentions the problem of excess capacity, especially in steel. It describes the situation thus: "the structural problems, including excess capacity in some industries, exacerbated by a weak global economic recovery and depressed market demand, have caused a negative impact on trade and workers ... excess capacity in steel and

arrangement, international dairy arrangement and trade in civil aircraft. See WTO official publication *Understanding the WTO* at www.wto.org/english/thewto_e/whatis_e/tif_e/understanding_e.pdf, 16–17 (visited on March 23, 2017).

other industries is a global issue which requires collective responses." Describing the, it says "subsidies and other types of support from government or government-sponsored institutions can cause market distortions and contribute to global excess capacity and therefore require attention." It gives these solutions: "to enhance communication and cooperation, and take effective steps to address the challenges so as to enhance market function and encourage adjustment. To this end, we call for increased information sharing and cooperation through the formation of a Global Forum on steel excess capacity, to be facilitated by the OECD with the active participation of G20 members and interested OECD members." (para. 31, Communique)

All the above are prominent issues in the world economy and related to the development of trade rules in the future, and actions taken on them will undoubtedly improve the global trade environment.

4.3.5   Institutional Arrangements

The Trade and Investment Working Group (TIWG) has been established to better coordinate efforts to reinforce trade and investment, the terms of reference of which include: to implement the commitments and instructions on trade and investment from previous Summits, Trade Ministers Meetings (TMMs) and Sherpa Meetings; to undertake related cooperation on trade and investment taking into account the priorities of the G20 Presidency; to discuss other trade and investment issues of common interest raised by G20 members. Its modalities are: it will be chaired by the Presidency and one co-chair from the members; it will be convened as required, but not more than three or four times throughout the year; finally, it will report on its work to the G20 Sherpa Meetings, TMMs and the G20 Leaders Summits. The TIWG is not only a mechanism to implement the commitments, but also signifies the institutionalization of the G20.

4.4   Development of the WTO

The above descriptions of the outcomes on trade and investment clearly show that the G20 supports the core role of the WTO as a multilateral system, promotes the Doha negotiations, and sets examples in ratifying Trade Facilitation Agreements and working against trade protectionism. It also declares its position on plurilateral agreements like the Environmental Goods Agreement. With the implementation of these commitments and actions, the WTO will have a better situation in which to develop.

However, these outcomes are not enough to keep the WTO at its core position in the global trade system, since they only confirm the current functions of the WTO and commit to continuing with the Doha negotiations; however, the Doha agenda was established back in 2001, and dramatic changes have taken place in the past sixteen years, including some new ways of doing trade on which RTAs are making rules. So the challenge before the WTO is not only to conclude the Doha negotiations, but also to react to developments in trade. In this respect, the G20 Hangzhou Summit indicates the direction for the WTO, that is, "a range of issues may be of common interest and importance to today's economy, and thus may be legitimate issues for discussions in the WTO, including those addressed in regional trade arrangements (RTAs)." (para. 26, Communique)

4.4.1   Issues in RTAs: TPP As an Example

In Section 4.2.1.1, brief mention was made of the path for RTAs returning to the WTO. As a matter of fact, this is also a significant path for the development of the WTO, that is, to integrate the issues covered and rules agreed in the RTAs into the WTO. All TRA participants are at the same time the WTO members, and they all need new rules to address the new issues, so why don't they work on including these rules into the WTO? Some of the difficult parts of negotiations are to agree on issues and write the rules, that is, the parties always debate on what issues should be included in the negotiations and what words should be used to reflect the outcomes, and the number of participants and decision-making mechanism will make some negotiations even more difficult, which is exactly the case with the WTO. Indeed, WTO negotiations have failed to solve these problems due to its large number of members (164) and decision-making mechanism (consensus). However, negotiations become easier when a sample text is presented to the participants. In the case of the WTO, many rules have been established among some members and the rational choice of the WTO is to turn its attention to consolidation of the tremendous body of RTAs rules for their multilateralization. In this respect, TPP is a perfect example and is becoming a good opportunity.

4.4.2   Trans-Pacific Partnership in General

The Trans-Pacific Partnership (TPP) is a regional economic agreement negotiated among twelve countries, Australia, Brunei Darussalam, Canada, Chile, Japan, Malaysia, Mexico, New Zealand, Peru, Singapore, the United States and Vietnam, and released on November 5, 2015.[22] It is

"a high-standard, ambitious, comprehensive, and balanced agreement that will promote economic growth; support the creation and retention of jobs; enhance innovation, productivity and competitiveness; raise living standards; reduce poverty in our countries; and promote transparency, good governance, and enhanced labor and environmental protections . . . ., with its new and high standards for trade and investment in the Asia Pacific, as an important step toward our ultimate goal of open trade and regional integration across the region." "Five defining features make the Trans-Pacific Partnership a landmark 21st-century agreement, setting a new standard for global trade while taking up next-generation issues. These features include: Comprehensive market access. The TPP eliminates or reduces tariff and non-tariff barriers across substantially all trade in goods and services and covers the full spectrum of trade, including goods and services trade and investment, so as to create new opportunities and benefits for our businesses, workers, and consumers. Regional approach to commitments.   The TPP facilitates the development of production and supply chains, and seamless trade, enhancing efficiency and supporting our goal of creating and supporting jobs, raising living standards, enhancing conservation efforts, and facilitating cross-border integration, as well as opening domestic markets. Addressing new trade challenges. The TPP promotes innovation, productivity, and competitiveness by addressing new issues, including the development of the digital economy, and the role of state-owned enterprises in the global economy. Inclusive trade. The TPP includes new elements that seek to ensure that economies at all levels of development and businesses of all sizes can benefit from trade. It includes commitments to help small- and medium-sized businesses understand the Agreement, take advantage of its opportunities, and bring their unique challenges to the attention of the TPP governments. It also includes specific commitments on development and trade capacity building, to ensure that all Parties are able to meet the commitments in the Agreement and take full advantage of its benefits. Platform for regional integration. The TPP is intended as a platform for regional economic integration and designed to include additional economies across the Asia-Pacific region."[23]*

---

[22] For the TPP text, see www.tpp.mfat.govt.nz/text (visited on March 23, 2017).

[23] The descriptions are from https://ustr.gov/about-us/policy-offices/press-office/press-releases/2015/october/summary-trans-pacific-partnership (visited on November 7, 2015).

The thirty chapters of the TPP begin with trade in goods and go on to include customs and trade facilitation, sanitary and phytosanitary (SPS) and technical barriers to trade (TBT) measures, trade remedies, investment, services, e-commerce, government procurement, intellectual property, labor rights, environment and other issues. It also covers dispute settlement, exceptions and institutional arrangements, which not only raises the standard of the classical issues on goods and services in RTAs, but also incorporates emerging and comprehensive issues, including those related to the Internet and the digital economy, state-owned enterprises (SOEs) in trade and investment, and small and medium-sized enterprises (SMEs). Above all, the TPP represents an agreement among a group of countries diverse in terms of region, language, history, scale and level of development.

The scope of the TPP goes far beyond that of the WTO, particularly in investment. In establishing investment rules, the TPP provides the basic investment protections found in other agreements related to investment, including (1) national treatment; (2) most-favored-nation treatment; (3) "minimum standard of treatment" for investments in accordance with customary international law principles; (4) prohibition of expropriation that is not for public purpose, without due process, or without compensation; (5) prohibition on "performance requirements" such as local content or technology localization requirements; (6) free transfer of funds related to an investment, subject to exceptions in the TPP to ensure that governments retain the flexibility to manage volatile capital flows, including through nondiscriminatory temporary safeguard measures (such as capital controls) restricting investment-related transfers in the context of a balance of payments crisis or the threat thereof, and certain other economic crises or to protect the integrity and stability of the financial system; and (7) freedom to appoint senior management positions of any nationality. TPP adopts a "negative list" basis, meaning that their markets are fully open to foreign investors, except where they have taken an exception (nonconforming measure) in one of two country-specific annexes: (1) current measures on which a Party accepts an obligation not to make its measures more restrictive in the future and to bind any future liberalization; and (2) measures and policies on which a Party retains full discretion in the future. The investment chapter also provides for neutral and transparent international arbitration of investment disputes, with strong safeguards to prevent abusive and frivolous claims and ensure the right of governments to regulate in the public interest, including on health, safety and environmental protection.[24]

4.4.3   The Idea of the WTIO

If the TPP text becomes "legitimate issues for discussions in the WTO," the trade rules would be automatically updated, and investment rules would be integrated into a multilateral system. The rationale behind this hypothesis is as follows: Trade rules established sixteen years ago by the WTO need to be updated and expanded to meet new developments in the world economy, but the Doha multilateral negotiations have failed to do that and are still struggling to finish the built-in agenda. As important engines of global economic growth and development, trade and investment are complements,[25] which means the lack of a multilateral framework of investment rules, itself a problem in the development of the world economy widely criticized,[26] is affecting the expansion of trade.

[24]   Ibid.
[25]   The Working Group on the Relationship between Trade and Investment was established by the WTO in 1996, and a report by this group was released in 1998, although no conclusions were made. See WTO document WT/WGTI/2 at www.wto.org.
  However, to assist the trade community in its evaluation of how the WTO should respond to the growing importance of investment, the WTO Secretariat published a report on "Trade and Foreign Investment" focusing on the economic, institutional and legal interlinkages between trade and investment in 1996, one of the conclusions of which was that trade and investment are two ways, sometimes alternatives, but increasingly complementary, of serving foreign markets. See www.wto.org/english/news_e/pres96_e/pr057_e.htm (visited on March 18, 2017).
  In a speech on 20 March 2017, the WTO Director-General mentioned "three major changes in the global economy invite us to take a fresh look at the relationship between trade and investment," the second of which is "the way trade and investment are increasingly interlinked in the real economy. Global value chains have spread design, manufacturing and assembly across borders to the most cost-efficient or skills-rich locations. With the rise of these 'world factories,' multinational companies view trade and investment as two sides of the same coin – they are interdependent elements of a single strategy. Some GVCs focus on consumer products, others on capital goods, others on services, agricultural, or natural resource production. But all rely on sophisticated trade and investment networks to deliver 'just-in-time' production. All of this is taking place against the backdrop of the sweeping digitization of our economies – further blurring the lines between trade and investment. So again, my point is simple: given that trade and investment flows are so intertwined, efforts to expand global trade are increasingly related to expanding global investment as well. Therefore developing a coherent policy approach to both is increasingly important. And again this is evolving." See www.wto.org/english/news_e/spra_e/spra162_e.htm (visited on March 24, 2017).
[26]   See Stephan W. Schill, *The Multilateralization of International Investment Law*, Cambridge University Press 2009. OECD chaired the negotiations of a draft

However, investment has long been part of the GATT/WTO[27] and better coordination of efforts has been called for recently.[28] The TPP provides a perfect text for a set of new rules, with trade rules updated and investment rules established and integrated. Above all, the TPP provides an example of a new organization, an organization of trade and investment, or WITO (World Investment and Trade Organization). The development of the world economy makes a WITO necessary, and the outcomes of G20 Hangzhou Summit make it feasible. The political will of the G20 leaders opens a window for RTA issues, like those in the TPP text, to come into the WTO, so the next step to implement, or an opportunity to create, could be proposals such as the WITO put forward and discussed among WTO members.

As one of the leaders of the G20, TPP and WTO, the United States has withdrawn from the TPP as an organization;[29] the TPP as a trans-pacific regional agreement may not reflect the development and diversity of WTO members across all continents; and in history it has never occurred that a whole set of agreements was accepted into an world organization.[30] However, we do not see any difficulties in discussing issues in the TPP text, which have been agreed and written into rules by some important members, in the WTO. Economically, these rules, with updated provisions on trade and a multilateral framework on investment, are necessary for traders, investors and governments. Politically, G20 leaders have

---

Multilateral Agreement on Investment in 1995–98. See www.oecd.org/investment/inter nationalinvestmentagreements/multilateralagreementoninvestment.htm (visited on November 16, 2016). The G20 Guiding Principles for Global Investment Policymaking is also an attempt at a multilateral framework of investment rules.

[27] For the history of GATT/WTO with investment, see Jurgen Kurtz, *The WTO and International Investment Law: Converging Systems*, Cambridge University Press 2016. The Havana Charter for an International Trade Organization in 1948, which did not come into force and left as its sole legacy the GATT, had specific provisions on investment (Article 12: International Investment for Economic Development and Reconstruction); and the successor WTO, although a trade organization, has the Agreement on Trade-Related Investment Measures and part of the General Agreement on Trade in Services related to investment, that is, rules on commercial presence. For these documents, see www.wto.org.

[28] For example, the Statement (para. 5) mentions that "G20 Leaders reaffirmed their strong commitment to better coordinate efforts to reinforce trade and investment."

[29] See https://ustr.gov/about-us/policy-offices/press-office/press-releases/2017/january/ US-Withdraws-From-TPP (visited on March 23, 2017).

[30] However, it should be pointed out that the TPP is built on the WTO rules, with frequent invocation of WTO agreements throughout the text, an example of which is the language in the Preamble: "Build on their respective rights and obligations under the Marrakesh Agreement Establishing the World Trade Organization."

endorsed RTA issues, including those in the TPP, as legitimate issues for discussions in the WTO, with reasonable expectation of positive reaction from the other leaders of WTO members. And finally, the text has been legally agreed. To simplify, the TPP is already a "mini-WITO," and the time has come to discuss the possibility of making it into a real WITO.

4.5   Conclusions and the Role of China

As a power of global governance, G20 is playing an increasing role in the development of trade and investment, in which the WTO is a significant part. In recent years the WTO has faced tremendous challenges, but the G20 Hangzhou Summit recognizes its central role in the global economy, commits to strengthening the multilateral system, and encourages the ongoing negotiations, showing absolute position and strong support for the WTO. Above all, it indicates directions for the development of the WTO, including discussion on issues in RTAs, which provides a perfect opportunity for updating trade rules and expanding investment.

As the host of this Summit, China distinguished itself as a leader in global governance. The emphasis on multilateral systems of trade and investment coincides with the progress of the Chinese economy in recent years, especially since its accession to the WTO in 2001. It is recognized that China has benefited from globalization and it came as no surprise to hear support from China for international cooperation at the recent World Economic Forum Annual Meeting.[31] So we would also not be surprised if China put forward the issue of TRAs, including those in the TPP, for discussions to update and expand the WTO as a means to implement the outcomes of the G20 Hangzhou Summit on trade and investment. However, the idea of a WITO may be too radical for a government to propose.[32]

---

[31] Chinese President Xi Jinping defended globalization at the World Economic Forum Annual Meeting 2017 by saying that "we should commit ourselves to growing an open global economy ... We must remain committed to developing global free trade and investment, promote trade and investment liberalization and facilitation through opening-up and say no to protectionism." See www.weforum.org/agenda/2017/01/full-text-of-xi-jinping-keynote-at-the-world-economic-forum/ (visited on March 24, 2017).

[32] After the G20 Hangzhou Summit, China proposed to the WTO a discussion of the issue of the eWTP, or the Electronic World Trade Platform, an outcome of the endorsement by the G20 of the B20 2016 Policy Recommendations submitted to G20 leaders in Hangzhou, China. See WTO official website, https://docs.wto.org/dol2fe/Pages/FE_Search/FE_S_S009-DP.aspx?language=E&CatalogueIdList=232908,232897,232898,232842,232840,232753,232654,232579,232511,232460&CurrentCatalogueIdIndex=9&FullTextHash= 371857150 (visited on November 27, 2016).

PART III

China, BRI and Investment Dispute Resolution

5

ICSID and the Evolution of ISDS

MEG KINNEAR[*]

For many commentators, the International Centre for Settlement of Investment Disputes (ICSID) is often seen as equivalent to Investor–State Dispute Settlement (ISDS). This view has much justification. The Convention on the Settlement of Investment Disputes between States and Nationals of Other States (the ICSID Convention),[1] established in 1966, is the only set of global rules created by States specifically for ISDS. Likewise, the ICSID Secretariat created by the Convention is the only global institution established by States to administer investment dispute settlement. ICSID has become the premier institution for international investment dispute settlement, having administered approximately 70 percent of all known ISDS cases in the world.[2] ICSID cases have contributed substantially to the development of international investment law jurisprudence, defining the application and scope of international investment treaties and contracts.[3] ICSID has also been a leader in modernizing ISDS over the years, including through the adoption of the first provisions in arbitral rules on transparency of the arbitral process, participation of amicus curiae, and expedited preliminary motions.

To better understand the importance of ICSID and ISDS, it is useful to recall the legal situation prior to the development of these mechanisms.

---

[*] This chapter is based on a speech presented by the author at the International Symposium on China and the Development of International Dispute Resolution System in the Context of the "Belt and Road" Construction, Xi'an, People's Republic of China, on November 1, 2016. For the purposes of its publication, the information contained has been updated as of December 31, 2018.

[1] Convention on the Settlement of Investment Disputes between States and Nationals of Other States (opened for signature March 18, 1965, entered into force October 14, 1966) (ICSID Convention).

[2] UNCTAD, "Investor-State Dispute Settlement: Review of Developments in 2016," IIA Issue Note, no. 1, 2017.

[3] Meg Kinnear et al. (eds.), *Building International Investment Law: The First 50 Years of ICSID* (Kluwer Law International 2015).

Historically, foreign investors and their investments were subject to the jurisdiction of the host State. Foreign investors alleging breach of international law by the host State had few effective options. If seeking a remedy in the host State, the primary recourse for a foreign investor was to initiate a claim in domestic courts, like every other national. However, such claims were not usually cognizable by domestic courts. Even if they were, sovereign immunity usually provided a complete defense to the claim. Moreover, foreign investors were not in the same position as nationals in many respects, potentially facing local bias against foreign interests, or an inadequate or nonindependent judiciary in the host State. If seeking a domestic remedy in its home State, the investor was likely to find its home State courts reluctant to take jurisdiction over a claim where the relevant facts took place abroad and the respondent was a foreign State.

Available remedies in international law were also limited. The main international recourses were "gunboat diplomacy," State-to-State dispute settlement, and diplomatic protection. The use of "gunboat diplomacy" meant the "threat or use of force to back up diplomatic protection claims."[4] This was a common practice of capital-exporting States until the late 1800s and early 1900s.

State-to-State dispute resolution was used in some cases where there was an agreement between two States to resolve a dispute. Ad hoc commissions and arbitral tribunals "were established to adjudicate specific claims or classes of claims involving a host state's treatment of foreign nationals and their property."[5] This type of mechanism required States to establish a special mechanism to resolve the dispute. Through diplomatic protection the investor's home State intervened by making a claim against the host State to obtain a remedy for the investor. Newcombe and Paradell have said that "the theory underlying the principle of diplomatic protection is that an injury to a state's national is an injury to the state itself, for which it may claim reparation from any responsible state."[6] States were often reluctant to espouse investor claims because of their broader concern about political relations with the host State.[7] Further, the decision to espouse a claim by the home State was

---

[4] Ibid., 9.
[5] Ibid., 7. This practice dates from the 1794 Treaty of Amity, Commerce, and Navigation between Great Britain and United States (Jay Treaty), which, among other things, established a commission to decide claims regarding the treatment of British and US nationals during and after the American Revolution.
[6] Ibid., 5.
[7] Ibid.

completely discretionary. Before the home State would espouse the claim, investors had to clear various procedural hurdles, including establishing that there was a strong claim, exhausting local remedies, convincing the home State to espouse the claim, and giving up control over the claim.

In addition to procedural hurdles, there were substantive gaps in customary international law. The substantive weaknesses included uncertainty over the standard of compensation for expropriation and a high and uncertain threshold to establish breach of the minimum standard of treatment. There was also an absence of protection in other areas, such as nondiscrimination, transfer of funds, and convertibility of currency obligations.

These gaps caused States to incorporate relevant substantive protections in treaties. The "treatification" of investment law began with the development of Treaties of Friendship, Commerce, and Navigation (FCNs). The FCNs were treaties that focused on developing trade and provided basic protection for the property of nationals of the other country. They are the precursors of modern BITs, and their coverage included the guarantee of "equitable treatment" and "most constant protection and security" to the property of foreign investors, "most-favored nation" treatment and "just compensation for expropriation." FCNs were no longer concluded after the 1960s when their main function was addressed through the GATT[8] for trade, and BITs started to regulate specific investment obligations.

The first bilateral investment treaty (BIT) was concluded in 1959 between the Republic of Pakistan and the Federal Republic of Germany[9]. This BIT offered State–State dispute settlement only. In 1966, the ICSID Convention was concluded, offering a facility and rules for investor–State arbitration and conciliation. In the late 1960s, BITs with ISDS began to be negotiated. The first BIT that allowed investors to commence arbitration was concluded in 1968 between the Netherlands and Indonesia.[10] Since the late 1980s, the number of investment treaties has increased from 265[11] to more than 3,324 by the end of

---

[8] General Agreement on Tariffs and Trade 1994, April 15, 1994, Marrakesh Agreement Establishing the World Trade Organization, Annex 1A, 1867 U.N.T.S. 187, 33 I.L.M. 1153 (1994) (GATT).

[9] The first bilateral investment treaty (BIT) was signed between the Republic of Pakistan and the Federal Republic of Germany on November 25, 1959, entered into force November 28, 1962.

[10] Agreement on economic cooperation between Netherlands and Indonesia, signed July 7, 1968, entered into force July 17, 1971.

[11] UNCTAD, WIR 2017, Figure III.

2016.[12] This growth has been accompanied by an increasing diversity in treaty partners, a noticeable trend towards negotiating agreements on a regional and multiregional basis, and rapid growth of foreign direct investment.[13] We are also seeing a phenomenon where some traditional capital-importing states have become capital-exporting states, and vice versa. More recently, we are seeing investment protections as a chapter of a free trade agreement rather than a stand-alone BIT.[14] Invariably, where investment obligations are available, the ICSID mechanism for dispute settlement is offered for dispute resolution.

5.1   The Creation of ICSID

With the increase in cross-border investment[15] in the last century, there also came a recognition that foreign investors could be in a particularly disadvantageous position, and that this ultimately acted as a barrier to further investment (or reinvestment), and hence a barrier to growth.

Historically, there have been numerous efforts to negotiate multilateral rules governing cross-border investment. However, consensus on substantive investment obligations has proved elusive. For example, the efforts to create an International Trade Organization in 1947–48 (ITO),[16] the Abs-Shawcross Draft in 1959,[17] the discussions on sovereignty over natural resources in the United Nations in the 1960s,[18] the unsuccessful Multilateral Agreement on Investment (MAI) from 1995 to

[12] In 2016, 37 new IIAs were concluded, bringing the total number of treaties to 3,324 by year's end, with 4 additional treaties concluded in 2017. UNCTAD, WIR 2017, *Trends in IIAs signed, 1980–2016*, 111 http://unctad.org/en/PublicationsLibrary/wir2017_en.pdf.

[13] UNCTAD's 2015 Investment Report shows that global FDI has quadrupled since 1995, with the growth in FDI being seen in developed and developing countries. Not surprisingly, dispute settlement is following the pattern of investments, showing a new diversity in the system.

[14] Examples: EU (Singapore–EU FTA [2014]), CETA (2016), Vietnam–EU FTA (2016), US–Trans-Pacific Partnership, Free Trade of the Americas (abandoned in 2000s), China–Korea–Japan (2012), RCEP (ongoing), African Continental Free Trade Agreement (ongoing).

[15] FDI has quadrupled in the past twenty years. UNCTAD Statistics, http://unctadstat .unctad.org/wds/ReportFolders/reportFolders.aspx.

[16] United Nations Conference on Trade and Employment, Havana, Cuba, March 24, 1948.

[17] 1959 Abs-Shawcross Draft Convention on Foreign Investment (April 1959) 9 JPL 116 (1960).

[18] The United Nations General Assembly, which, in 1952, passed the first of seven resolutions on Permanent Sovereignty Over Natural Resources, in Andrew Newcombe and Luis Paradell, *Law and Practice of Investment Treaties* (Kluwer Law International, 2009), 26.

1998,[19] and the failure to embrace investment in the Singapore Round of negotiations of the World Trade Organization (WTO) in 1996[20] demonstrate the difficulty of concluding a single set of substantive international investment rules.

Under the leadership of China, the G20 recently established a useful set of guiding principles for investment policy-making in July 2016.[21] These memorialize "first principles" upon which most governments agree today.[22] These first principles include: the recognition of the need to avoid protectionism, the importance of open, nondiscriminatory, transparent, and predictable conditions for investment, the importance of legal certainty and strong protection for investors and investments, including through dispute settlement and enforcement procedures; the importance of transparency, sustainable development, and inclusive growth, and the reaffirmation of the right to regulate in the public interest. These principles are a useful starting point for States and could anchor a more detailed multilateral consensus on substantive obligations in the future.

While consensus on substantive obligations has proved elusive, there has been very real consensus on process, in the form of ICSID. The 1966 ICSID Convention was negotiated by the Executive Directors of the World Bank States with significant support from the legal department of the World Bank.[23] The basic thesis behind the creation of ICSID was that States would benefit from having access to a facility where they could

[19] The Multilateral Agreement on Investment: Draft Consolidated Text, DAFFE/MAI(98)7/ REV1; The Multilateral Agreement on Investment: Commentary to the Consolidated Text, DAFFE/MAI(98)8/REV1.

[20] In the 2001 Doha Declaration, WTO members recognized "the case for a multilateral framework to secure transparent, stable and predictable conditions for long-term cross-border investment." Paragraph 20, Doha Declaration, November 14, 2001, 41 ILM 746.

[21] Following their meeting in Shanghai on July 9–10, 2016, the G20 Trade Ministers issued a statement reinforcing their determination to "promote inclusive, robust and sustainable trade and investment growth." At the same time, the Ministers agreed G20 Guiding Principles for Global Investment Policymaking.

[22] G20 Guiding Principles: www.oecd.org/daf/inv/investment-policy/G20-Guiding-Principles-for-Global-Investment-Policymaking.pdf.

[23] Report of the Executive Directors on the Convention on the Settlement of Investment Disputes between States and Nationals of Other States (March 18, 1965): "The Convention was formulated by the Executive Directors of the International Bank for Reconstruction and Development (the World Bank). On March 18, 1965, the Executive Directors submitted the Convention, with an accompanying Report, to member governments of the World Bank for their consideration of the Convention with a view to its signature and ratification. The Convention entered into force on October 14, 1966, when it had been ratified by 20 countries."

resolve disputes with investors. The World Bank was a logical place for this facility as it had expertise offering its "good offices" in several high-profile cross-border investment cases. For example, in 1951, the Bank offered to act as a trustee between Iran and the Anglo-Iranian Oil Company, after Iran had nationalized its oil industry and terminated its concessions.[24] In 1956, the Bank was involved in helping French and British shareholders settle their claims for compensation[25] after Egypt nationalized the Suez Canal Company. In 1958, the President of the Bank was asked to conciliate differences over the payment of the principle and interest on the City of Tokyo and French bonds.[26] These experiences led the President of the World Bank to endorse creation of a dispute settlement role on a permanent basis with a formal set of rules and a Secretariat to support the function. Hence, ICSID was born fifty years ago, to offer an impartial forum for dispute resolution.

The design of the ICSID Convention reflected the special role States conceived for it. Most importantly, it was created as an impartial and delocalized facility, meaning that proceedings would not take place in any local court system. This reinforced the international and depoliticized nature of the ICSID system and put disputing parties on a level playing field. One area where this is evident is in the nationality of the arbitrators appointed in ICSID cases. Each Member State can designate up to four persons to the Panel of Arbitrators and up to four persons to the Panel of Conciliators.[27] Arbitrators are named to these lists by all Member States, but cannot act in a case where either party to the dispute is a conational. On annulment, the Committee members cannot share the nationality of the disputing parties or of the nationalities of the tribunal members that rendered the award under review.

The ICSID Convention is an international treaty in and of itself, available to all member States of the World Bank. As such, there is no cost to join or maintain membership at ICSID. However, it is important to note that the mere fact of joining ICSID does not enable the use of the mechanism, and States must take the additional step of consenting to ICSID dispute settlement in writing in a contract, treaty, or investment law.

---

[24] Antonio Parra, *History of the ICSID Convention* (Oxford University Press 2012), 22–23.
[25] *Ibid*, 24.
[26] World Bank Press Release, City of Tokyo Bonds of 1912, April 4, 1960. The President delivered a plan to the parties in 1960 to aid in the conciliation of their differences. The conciliation was undertaken by the President of the Bank "in his personal capacity."
[27] ICSID Convention, art. 12–16.

ICSID is a nonprofit organization and provides a cost-effective and transparent fee structure for its services. It offers first-class hearing facilities and access to arbitration facilities around the world and is the only institution that can administer ISDS under the main set of rules: the ICSID Convention, ICSID Additional Facility, and UNCITRAL Arbitration Rules. The ICSID Secretariat provides parties and tribunals with expert support throughout the process and has unparalleled experience.

Perhaps the most significant advantage of ICSID is the simplified enforcement mechanism. Pursuant to Article 53(1) of the ICSID Convention, awards are binding on the parties and not subject to appeal or other remedy except as provided by the Convention. An award rendered under the ICSID Convention is automatically enforceable as a final judgment of the courts in every ICSID Member State, without the requirement of recognition and enforcement in the State where enforcement is sought.[28] This is an important advantage of ICSID that is not available in any other arbitration regime. By comparison, awards issued under the UNCITRAL Arbitration Rules are subject to the recognition and enforcement provisions under the New York Convention.[29] This means that they are liable to set aside in the place of arbitration, and enforcement can be refused in any State where it is sought.[30] Awards issued under the ICSID Convention are not subject to any of these risks since enforcement of the award is automatic under Article 54 of the ICSID Convention.

Today ICSID has 155 Member States[31] and 9 further signatory States. Joining ICSID signals a State's intent to encourage foreign investment and to respect the standards in its treaties and contracts.

ICSID registered its first case in 1972,[32] but few cases were registered until the mid-1990s and early 2000s. In 1969, ICSID published Model Clauses[33] which suggested ways in which States could incorporate an

---

[28] ICSID Convention, art. 54(1).

[29] Convention on the Recognition and Enforcement of Foreign Awards (opened for signature June 10, 1958, entered into force June 7, 1959) 330 UNTS 38 (New York Convention).

[30] Albert Jan van den Berg, *Should the Setting Aside of the Arbitral Award Be Abolished?*, 29 (2) ICSID Rev – FILJ 263, 283 (2014).

[31] ICSID, *List of Contracting States and Other Signatories of the Convention*, Doc ICSID/3, https://icsid.worldbank.org/en/Documents/icsiddocs/List%20of%20Contracting%20States%20and%20Other%20Signatories%20of%20the%20Convention%20-%20Latest.pdf.

[32] *Holiday Inns S.A. and others* v. *Morocco* (ICSID Case no. ARB/72/1).

[33] The ICSID Convention requires that the parties' consent to ICSID jurisdiction be in writing. The ICSID Model Clauses were written to suggest how model clauses could be recorded. ICSID Model Clauses, https://icsid.worldbank.org/en/Pages/resources/ICSID-Model-Clauses.aspx.

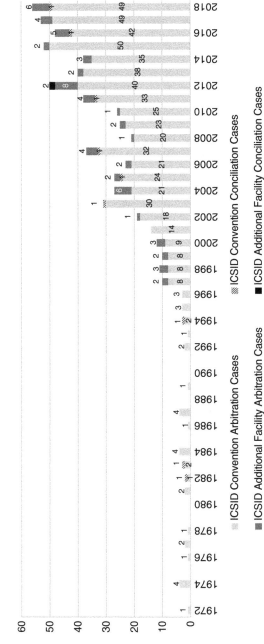

Figure 5.1 ICSID caseload – cases registered – 31 December 2018

ICSID clause into treaties or contracts. In 1978, the ICSID Additional Facility Rules were adopted.[34] These largely replicated the ICSID Rules, but extended their application to disputes between States and nationals of other States which fall outside the scope of the ICSID Convention.

In the last twenty years, the ICSID caseload has expanded significantly due to the combination of increased foreign investment and the conclusion of more investment treaties, contracts, and laws. On average, ICSID registers forty-five cases per year. In the past five decades, ICSID has registered a total of 721 cases, of which 258 are now pending before the Centre.

5.2   Other Work

As part of its mandate, ICSID promotes greater awareness of international law on foreign investment and the ICSID process. Throughout the years, ICSID has increased its capacity building with Member States. In 2018, ICSID gave over 120 presentations in twenty-seven different countries around the world. ICSID also publishes many specialized texts relating to international investment law and investment dispute settlement, including *the ICSID Review – Foreign Investment Law Journal*, published since 1986. The ICSID Review recently celebrated its thirtieth anniversary with three special themed issues of interest in international investment law.[35] ICSID also publishes two multivolume loose-leaf collections of Investment Treaties and Laws of the World. The Centre also issues consultation and background papers from time to time, including the 2016 Background Paper on Annulment, which provides data and updated charts concerning recent developments in annulment proceedings. The Centre prepared a set of Practice Notes for Respondents in ICSID Arbitration, which address questions frequently asked by ICSID Member States and provides practical organizational suggestions for responding to a Request for Arbitration and

---

[34] The Administrative Council adopted the Additional Facility Rules on September 27, 1978. They are (i) conciliation or arbitration proceedings for the settlement of investment disputes arising between parties one of which is not a Contracting State or a national of a Contracting State; (ii) conciliation or arbitration proceedings between parties at least one of which is a Contracting State or a national of a Contracting State for the settlement of disputes that do not directly arise out of an investment; and (iii) fact-finding proceedings.

[35] *30th Anniversary of the Review, Special Focus Issue on State-Owned Enterprises*, 31(1) ICSID Rev – FILJ (2016); *30th Anniversary of the Review, Special Focus Issue on the Intersection between Investment Arbitration and Public International Law*, 31(2) ICSID Rev – FILJ (2016), 255; *30th Anniversary of the Review, Special Focus Issue on Procedural Issues in Investment Treaty Arbitration*, 31(3) ICSID Rev – FILJ (2016), 505.

preparing for a case. In 2016, ICSID published a book that celebrates the first fifty years of ICSID, titled *Building International Investment Law: The First 50 Years of ICSID*. The book analyzes fifty landmark cases decided under its auspices. There is no doubt that ICSID has been a leader in innovation and has contributed enormously to the development and promotion of international investment law.

5.3   ICSID and OBOR

It is likely that a number of disputes will arise under the OBOR initiative given its cross-border character and extensive reach. Some of these will fall under ICSID jurisdiction based on the underlying contract, treaty, or law. The Centre is well suited to provide the necessary legal service, including a legal team and financial team that will provide administrative and financial support throughout the proceeding. ICSID offers first-class hearing facilities in Washington and Paris and is able to hold hearings in any of the World Bank offices around the world, with no rental fee. Moreover, ICSID has concluded cooperation agreements with other arbitration institutions to complement its ability to offer hearings anywhere in the world. In particular, ICSID has signed facilities cooperation agreements in Asia with the following institutions: China International Economic and Trade Arbitration Commission (CIETAC), Hong Kong International Arbitration Centre (HKIAC), Kuala Lumpur Regional Centre for Arbitration, (KLRCA), Seoul International Dispute Resolution Center (SIDRC), Shenzhen Court of International Arbitration (SCIA) and Maxwell Chambers and the Singapore International Arbitration Centre (SIAC).

5.4   Rule Amendments

In October 2016, ICSID began work on further updating and modernizing the ICSID Regulations and Rules. There have been four rounds of rule amendments following the adoption of the rules in 1967.[36]

The ICSID Rules were first amended by decision of the Administrative Council in 1984. These amendments were modest, simplifying certain provisions and updating others in the light of experience. The second set

---

[36] The Arbitration Rules were adopted on September 25, 1967, and were effective as of January 1, 1968. These were published with nonbinding explanatory notes: ICSID Arbitration Rules (1968).

of amendments was effective on January 1, 2003.[37] These amendments updated a few provisions of the ICSID Regulations and Rules and streamlined the Additional Facility Rules. Under the 2003 amendments, Arbitration Rule 1(3) made clear that in a typical three-member tribunal, the parties could appoint a conational as an arbitrator only with agreement of the other party. Rule 2 of the Institutional Rules codified the practice of the Secretariat to request that corporate claimants had to submit written evidence of the necessary internal steps to authorize the institution of a claim before the Centre. Arbitration Rules 4 and 9 modified the thirty-day time limit to "best efforts" regarding the appointment and/or disqualification of an arbitrator. The new amendments extended the short time limit imposed in Arbitration Rule 46 for the preparation of the award from 60 to 120 days.[38]

The current rules were approved in 2006 and came into effect on April 10, 2006. These amendments followed an extensive two-year period of public consultation. The consultation included a discussion paper released on October 22, 2004, on "Possible Improvements of the Framework for ICSID Arbitration"[39] and a working paper released on May 12, 2005, on "Suggested Changes to the ICSID Rules and Regulations."[40] This resulted in several proposals for amendments that have been groundbreaking for investment arbitration and ICSID practice.

The key amendments made in 2006 related to transparency, including public access to documents, public access to hearings, and amicus curiae participation. Arbitration Rule 48 was amended to require publication of awards with consent of the parties or excerpts of the legal reasoning adopted in an award where parties did not consent to publication.[41] In addition, the Centre can publish other material with the parties' consent (for example, decisions of the Tribunal, procedural orders, parties' submissions, transcripts and minutes of

---

[37] Approved on September 29, 2002.

[38] Antonio Parra, *The New Amendments to the ICSID Regulations and Rules and Additional Facility Rules*.

[39] ICSID, *Possible Improvements of the Framework for ICSID Arbitration, Discussion Paper* (October 22, 2004), https://icsid.worldbank.org/en/Documents/resources/Possible% 20Improvements%20of%20the%20Framework%20of%20ICSID%20Arbitration.pdf.

[40] ICSID, *Suggested Changes to the ICSID Rules and Regulations*, Working Paper of the ICSID Secretariat (May 12, 2005), https://icsid.worldbank.org/en/Documents/resources/ Suggested%20Changes%20to%20the%20ICSID%20Rules%20and%20Regulations.pdf.

[41] Aurelia Antonietti, *The 2006 Amendments to the ICSID Rules and Regulations and the Additional Facility Rules*, 21(2) ICSID Rev – FILJ 1, 442 (2006).

hearings, etc.)[42] Under amended Arbitration Rule 32(2), the Tribunal could allow other persons to attend or observe a hearing unless either party objected.[43] Arbitration Rule 37(2) made possible the participation of amicus curiae, called "a non-disputing party" in the ICSID system. Under this rule, the Tribunal has discretion to accept submissions by nondisputing parties after consulting with both parties.[44] This rule has subsequently been invoked more than forty-five times, and has resulted in amicus submissions from diverse parties such as environmental groups, trade associations, and the European Union.[45] Another key amendment was the adoption of Arbitration Rule 41(5). This rule introduces a procedure for the early dismissal by tribunals of claims that are manifestly without legal merit. The idea behind Rule 41(5) was that it would save time and cost for the parties if the Tribunal dismissed unmeritorious claims at an early stage.[46] Similar changes were included to the Additional Facility Rules in 2006.

The 2006 amendments incorporated important improvements to the system and have had far-reaching effects on the practice of investment arbitration. They have been widely emulated in the rules of other arbitral institutions, in newly negotiated investment treaties, and in parts of the Mauritius Convention and the UNCITRAL Rules on Transparency in Treaty-based Investor–State Arbitration.

In the public consultation leading to the 2006 Rule amendments, ICSID consulted with Member States on the creation of an

---

[42] ICSID Administrative and Financial Regulations (2006), Rule 22.

[43] In practice, hearings are broadcast to a separate room with a closed-circuit television feed or live through webcast. Broadcasts or webcasts can be interrupted whenever confidential information is referred to during the hearing.

[44] Under these amendments, the nondisputing role would be to assist the Tribunal in the determination of a factual or legal issue, providing a different perspective from that of the parties. In considering the request, the Tribunal should take certain factors in consider-ations, such as: whether the submission would address a matter within the scope of the dispute, whether the nondisputing party has a significant interest in the proceeding, and whether the nondisputing party submission would not disrupt the proceedings. ICSID, *Tables of Decisions in ICSID Cases, Decisions on Non-Disputing Party Participation*, https://icsid.worldbank.org/en/Pages/resources/Tables-of-ICSID-Decisions.aspx.

[45] Meg Kinnear, *The ICSID Rules Amendments* (April 2017), https://icsid.worldbank.org/en/Documents/about/ICSID%20Rules%20Amendment%20Process-ENG.pdf.

[46] Under this rule, there are two kinds of objections that can be raised by a respondent in this summary view: (1) a claim that has no substance on the merits; or (2) a claim that has no jurisdiction. The standard is comparatively high, "the basis of the expedited objection shall be that the claim is manifestly without legal merit." Antonietti (n 37), 440.

Appellate Body. The mechanism "would be intended to foster coherence and consistency in the caselaw emerging under investment treaties."[47] ICSID proposed a single ICSID Appeals Facility instead of having multiple mechanisms under individual IIAs. The proposal suggested that the facility would operate under a set of ICSID Appeals Facility Rules and would be available for cases under the ICSID Convention, ICSID Additional Facility, UNCITRAL, and other rules. It could also be incorporated by reference in investment laws, contracts, and treaties.[48] In 2006, there was general agreement by the Member States that the establishment of such procedures should be done through a single ICSID mechanism, but that an attempt to establish an ICSID mechanism would be premature.[49]

In recent years, there has been renewed interest in this concept by some States, for example, in the current proposals for CETA, the EU–Vietnam FTA, and other EU proposals.[50] Moreover, ICSID has been designated as the administering Secretariat for the First-Instance Tribunal in CETA[51] and has offered such services to all States.

5.4.1 Current Process

ICSID has commenced a further amendment process. The Secretariat launched this process in October 2016 by asking Member States for preliminary suggestions of topics or themes for possible amendment and to designate contact persons for the duration of the amendment process. The Secretariat has also invited suggestions from other stakeholders.[52] The goal of this round of amendments is mainly to keep the rules up to date and to continuously modernize based on experience. Given ICSID's administration of more than 700 cases, several lessons learned can be incorporated into the system. The amendments aim at making the process increasingly time and cost effective while maintaining due process and a balance between

---

[47] *Possible Improvements of the Framework for ICSID Arbitration*, October 22, 2004.
[48] ICSID, *Possible Features of an ICSID Appeals Facility*, para 2.
[49] Possible Improvements of the Framework for ICSID Arbitration, News from ICSID, vol. 21, no. 2, 2004.
[50] Article 8.28.2 CETA; Article 28.1 EUVFTA.
[51] *Ibid.*
[52] ICSID, *ICSID Rules and Regulations Amendment Process*, https://icsid.worldbank.org/en/amendments.

investors and States. The ICSID Secretariat has published four working papers containing proposals for amendments to the ICSID Rules,
the most recent in February 28, 2020. The fourth paper builds on the
proposals that were originally published in August 2018 (Working
Paper #1) and follows extensive consultations with ICSID Member
States and the public, and were further revised in Working Paper #2
and #3. The potential topics to be considered include appointment
of arbitrators, code of conduct for arbitrators, challenge of arbitrators, third-party funding, consolidation, modernizing means of communication, preliminary objections, first sessions, witnesses, expert
and other evidence, discontinuance, awards and dissents, security for
costs, allocation of costs, annulment, and publication of decisions
and orders.[53]

Given its role and importance in the system, ICSID will continue to
encourage the development of international investment law around the
world while focusing on how the system can best meet the needs of its
facility service users.

---

[53] ICSID, *List of Potential Rule Amendment Topics*, https://icsid.worldbank.org/en/
Documents/about/List%20of%20Topics%20for%20Potential%20ICSID%20Rule%
20Amendment-ENG.pdf; ICSID, *Working Paper #1 – Proposals for Amendments of the
ICSID Rules* (August 2018); ICSID, *Working Paper #2 – Proposals for Amendment of the
ICSID Rules* (March 2019).

6

Tackling Political Risks through Treatization along the Belt and Road: A Minilateral Solution

WEI SHEN

Born and inherited from the Chinese ideal of *tianxia* (literally meaning everything under the heavens), an enlightened realm,[1] China announced its One Belt and One Road Initiative (the OBOR initiative or more recently, B&R or BRI), that is, "the Silk Road Economic Belt and the 21st Century Maritime Silk Road" initiatives, in September 2014, right before the Asia-Pacific Economic Cooperation (APEC) summit held in Beijing.[2] Chinese government and officials advertised this initiative's exotic appeal to foreigners by using the unlovely acronym OBOR. The road refers to ancient maritime routes between China and Europe, while the belt describes the Silk Road's trails overland.

The sprawling OBOR initiative is to revivify, reinvigorate and resurrect the old Silk Road trading route that once carried treasures between China and the Mediterranean through Central Asia and the Middle East. In the seventh century, the Silk Road was a vast and ancient network of trade routes connecting Chinese merchants and those of Central Asia, the Middle East, Africa and Europe. That was a golden age when Chinese luxuries were coveted across the globe and the Silk Road was a conduit for diplomacy, political influence and, most importantly, economic expansion.

Unlike any existing kind of international pacts and treaties, the OBOR initiative is the Chinese government's primary foreign policy component,[3]

---

[1] Salvatore Babones, "American Tianxia: When Chinese Philosophy Meets American Power", June 22, 2017, Foreign Affairs. Available at www.foreignaffairs/com/articles/2017-06-22 (accessed April 3, 2020).

[2] President Xi Jinping first floated the idea of forming a "New Silk Road Economic Belt" in a speech at Nazarbayev University in Astana, Kazakhstan in September 2013. One month later, he made a pitch for a "21st Century Maritime Silk Road" when addressing Indonesia's parliament in Jakarta.

[3] Vassilis Ntousas, "Back to the Future: China's 'One Belt, One Road' Initiative," (2016) FEPS Policy Brief, p. 2.

global economic strategy and geopolitical project[4] to implement its Silk Road concept and to export its infrastructural investment-driven development model,[5] with a wide coverage of 55 percent of the world's GDP, 70 percent of global population, and 75 percent of the world's energy reserves. The OBOR initiative covers 3.8 billion people and economies totaling $21 trillion.[6] The OBOR is amorphous – it has no official list of member states, and is an open-ended regime technically embracing any country which wants to be part of it. China's rough count of OBOR members, at the initial stage, is sixty or so countries along the route.[7] The OBOR initiative encompasses countries that need to build more infrastructure projects but lack sufficient capital to finance needed projects. Effectively, the Silk Road will connect China's western region, including the predominantly Muslim Xinjiang province, with the Chinese-funded Pakistani port city of Gwadar, part of the China-Pakistan Economic Corridor with a variety of road, railway, port, old and gas projects in the amount of over US$46 billion.[8] Official figures say that there are 900 deals under way, worth $890 billion, and China may invest $4 trillion in OBOR countries.[9] The initiative effectively connects the supply and demand sides. Relatively poorer inland regions in China will also be key beneficiaries of this initiative.

The underlying rationale of the initiative is to apply a bonding approach instead of a more assertive, muscular diplomatic and military approach, by strengthening China's economic, political and even cultural connectivity with its neighboring nations. For instance, China is focused on securing a route to the Indian Ocean that would reduce dependence on the choke-point of the Strait of Malacca between the Malay Peninsula

---

[4] Jedrzej Gorski, Julien Chaisse, Manjiao Chi, Ahmad Manzoor, and Teresa Cheng, "One Belt One Road Initiative (OBOR): Editorial," (2017) 14(3) Transnational Dispute Management, available at www.transnational-dispute-management.com/article.asp?key=2469

[5] Julien Chaisse & Mitsuo Matsushita, "China's 'Belt and Road' Initiative: Mapping the World Trade Normative and Strategic Implication" (2018) 52(1) *Journal of World Trade* 163–186.

[6] "Belt and Road Initiative," The World Bank Brief, March 29, 2018, available at www.worldbank.org/en/topic/regional-integration/brief/belt-and-road-initiative (last accessed March 30, 2020).

[7] Zheping Huang, "Your Guide to Understanding OBOR, China's New Silk Road Plan," May 15, 2017, available at https://qz.com/983460/obor-an-extremely-simple-guide-to-understanding-chinas-one-belt-one-road-forum-for-its-new-silk-road/ (last accessed March 30, 2020).

[8] Farhan Bokhari, Lucy Hornby and Christian Shepherd, "China Urges Pakistan to Give Army Lead Role in Silk Road Project," *Financial Times*, July 21, 2016,

[9] "Our Bulldozers, Our Rules," *The Economist*, July 2, 2016, 29.

and the Indonesian island of Sumatra.[10] The Chinese government is trying to take advantage of a mostly benign security environment to achieve its aim of strengthening its global power without causing conflict. OBOR is viewed as a soft way to package this strategy. The OBOR initiative also fits the "China dream" of recreating a great past and its new image. China has made OBOR such a central part of its foreign policy. Economically, China also needs to implement this initiative to shift some vast manufacturing capacity overseas due to the rising compliance costs of environmental protection measures and anticorruption campaigns.[11] In a tactical response to the Western countries' concern, China plans to embed anti-graft officers in OBOR ventures abroad.[12] Through the OBOR initiative, China can extend its commercial influence, probably political influence as well, while reducing economic dependence on investment in infrastructure at home. However, the EU has expressed concerns regarding China's exporting of excess industrial capacity in key industries and has put in place some arrangements to address those concerns.[13] Given its effect, the Belt and Road initiative is labelled as a surplus recycling mechanism.[14]

In implementing the OBOR initiative, China wants to make use of this platform to deepen its economic ties with its neighboring countries. For instance, China made Pakistan an early stop on the One Road in 2015 with the China–Pakistan Economic Corridor (CPEC), a $46 billion bundle of road, railway, electricity, oil and gas projects that marked the largest foreign investment in Pakistan. On the other hand, these countries are wary of China's ambitions. Their concern is China's economic clout. They are fretting that China will derive disproportionate benefits from the links. CPEC has stalled as the two sides are having trouble working out how to turn the proposals into concrete projects. In

---

[10] Farhan Bokhari, "China Urges Pakistan to Give Army Role in Silk Road Project," Financial Times, July 22, 2016, 5.

[11] It has been estimated that China's coal industry could have 3.3 billion tons of excess capacity within two years. Overcapacity within the aluminum, oil refining and chemicals industries poses a threat not only to China but also abroad. The output of China's overcapacity industries may send global prices plunging and hurt rivals in the global market. "Gluts for Punishment," The Economist, April 9, 2016.

[12] Don Weinland, "China to Tackle Corruption in Belt and Road Projects," Financial Times, July 19, 2019, available at www.ft.com/content/

[13] Alun John, *Europe Back on Chinese Investors' Radar, Says Official*, South China Morning Post, July 15, 2016, B1.

[14] Usman W. Chohan, "What Is One Belt One Road? A Surplus Recycling Mechanism Approach," in Julien Chaisse and Jędrzej Górshki, The Belt and Road Initiative – Law, Economics and Politics (Brill Nijhoff 2018) 205.

Pakistan, the internal debate is whether the government should take ownership of the Corridor projects.[15]

Chinese goods may flood their markets and drown their own nascent industries. In terms of China's foreign direct investment (FDI), it is rather well known that China places more emphasis on laying tarmac and iron rather than sharing technical know-how. The new trend is that China has outgrown its fixation with commodities and energy. Chinese investors are hungry for western brands and technology, and their demand for assets far afield remains quite robust. There has been a wave of China-led mergers and acquisitions that is sweeping over the world economy.[16] Chinese investors announced nearly $100 billion in cross-border M&A deals in 2016, almost double the 2015 value of $61 billion. China's shares of cross-border M&As has averaged roughly 6 percent over the past five years, and it accounts for nearly 15 percent of global GDP.[17] China's FDI is increasingly going along the Silk Road. FDI by China in OBOR countries rose twice as fast as the increase in total FDI in 2015, while 44% of China's new engineering projects were signed with OBOR countries in 2015.[18] A full quarter of China's outbound FDI in 2017 was poured into the Europe, showing the importance of the OBOR in China's cross-border investment activities.[19]

Although Chinese investment has been welcomed by other countries as a source of scarce capital after the recent global financial crisis, skepticism about rising Chinese investment flows has grown, largely because the majority of China's outbound FDI is executed by state-owned enterprises (SOEs) and Chinese investments in other countries mostly focus on energy and infrastructural sectors, often facing tough scrutiny or even backlash. The rumor that China had hacked into Australia's Bureau of Meteorology and stolen data in 2015 must also be factored into the Australian government's investment decisions. Australia's concerns come amid a wave of Chinese investment in

[15] Farhan Bokhari, *China Urges Pakistan to Give Army Role in Silk Road Project*, Financial Times, July 22, 2016, 5.
[16] Asia has nearly doubled the volume of mergers and acquisitions by companies based in the Americas into other regions. Don Weinland & Jennifer Hughes, *Asia Overtakes US in Value of Outbound Deals*, Financial Times, July 20, 2016, 16 (citing Dealogic's report).
[17] *Money Bags*, The Economist, April 2, 2016, 61.
[18] *Our Bulldozers, Our Rules*, The Economist, July 2, 2016, 29.
[19] Matt Ferchen, Frank N. Pieke, Frans-Paul van der Putten, Tianmu Hong and Jurriaan de Blécourt, "Assessing China's Influence in Europe through Investments in Technology and Infrastructure: Four Cases," 2018 Leiden Asia Centre, available at www.leidenasiacentre.nl

housing, agriculture and public infrastructure assets that caused the Australian government to tighten foreign investment rules, and more fundamentally, to introduce a new framework on infrastructure. Australia blocked State Grid Corporation and Hong Kong-based Cheung Kong Infrastructure from submitting AU$10bn-plus bids for electricity company Ausgrid. A Chinese consortium's plan to buy S Kidman & Co. (a cattle farm stretching across more than 1 percent of Australia's land mass) was also blocked.[20] The Australian government cited national interest and security concerns (instead of protectionism) as legitimate reasons for derailing these Chinese bids even though Chinese investors own less than 0.5 percent of Australia's agricultural land.[21] Some studies confirm a weak linkage between China's outbound investment in Europe and its influence in the region.[22]

The OBOR initiative was viewed as a response or even a challenge to the United States' efforts to promote new US-centric economic zones such as TTP and TTIP.[23] The United States is a focal point of two main trading blocs, one trans-Atlantic, the other trans-Pacific. Two regional trade deals, the TPP and TTIP, embody this approach. OBOR, instead, treats Asia and Europe as a single bloc of which China becomes the focal point. This is an institution-building strategy reshaping the focal point of global trade and investment, leading to a shared order between China and the US for the geopolitical future.[24] Due to the geopolitical concern, the United States' views over BRI have been rather negative and cautious – it is a deliberate attempt to economically, politically and even militarily marginalize the US for a Eurasian sphere of influence.[25]

---

[20] Although Australia historically relied on foreign investment to drive its economy, the Liberal–National coalition government, stepping into power in 2013, blocked three significant transactions; one of them was the proposed takeover of Australian agribusiness GrainCorps by Archer Daniels Midland of the United States.

[21] Jamie Smyth, *Australia Defends Moves to Block Chinese Bids*, Financial Times, October 19, 2016, available at www.ft.com/content/94bb61c4-91ab-11e6-a72e-b428cb934b78 (last accessed March 30, 2020).

[22] Matt Ferchen, Frank N. Pieke, Frans-Paul van der Putten, Tianmu Hong & Jurriaan de Blecourt, *Assessing China's Influence in Europe through Investments in Technology and Infrastructure: Four Cases*, Leiden Asia Centre 2018, available at www.leidenasiacentre.nl.

[23] PRC Ministry of Commerce, China FTA Network, *China's Free Trade Agreements*, available at http://fta.mofcom.gov.cn/english/fta_qianshu.shtml.

[24] Michael J. Mazarr, Timothy R. Heath and Astrid Stuth Cevallos, China and the International Order (AND Corp. 2018) 123.

[25] Alek Chance, "American Perspectives on the Belt and Road Initiatives: Sources of Concern and Possibilities for Cooperation", Institute for China-America Studies (2016) at 3.

Along with the OBOR initiative, China has been aggressively promoting its outbound investment. Meanwhile, harking back nostalgically to
the Silk Road, China envisages a web of bilateral agreements with the
beneficiaries of the OBOR's largesse. Part of this web of agreements is
China's eagerness to build up a network by concluding more bilateral
investment treaties (BIT), free trade agreements (FTAs) and megaregional investment pacts.

Apart from its 129 BITs, China has been an active player in negotiating
and concluding over a dozen free trade agreements (FTA). As of
January 2013, China had signed FTAs with eighteen countries and
regions and is in negotiations with numerous other countries including
Australia, the Gulf Cooperation Council, Norway and the Southern
African Customs Union. According to the figures of the Chinese
Ministry of Commerce, a quarter of the Chinese mainland's foreign
trade is with its FTA partners.[26] Furthermore, China has been proactive
in promoting multilateral efforts in regional integration by entering into
regional or multilateral free trade agreements and economic cooperation
agreements with regional organizations. The most recent of them include
an Agreement on Investment of the Framework Agreement on
Comprehensive Economic Cooperation[27] concluded on August 15,
2009, with the Association of South East Asian Nations (ASEAN) in
Bangkok, Thailand (the China–ASEAN Treaty) and the Agreement
among the Government of the Republic of Korea, the Government of
the People's Republic of China and the Government of Japan for the
Promotion, Facilitation and Protection of Investment (TIT), signed by
China, Korea and Japan on 13 May 2012 in Beijing. China's FTAs and
multilateral investment treaties such as the China–ASEAN Treaty and
TIT often include a chapter providing for investment protections. The
expropriation clauses in these FTAs are more detailed, if not more
advanced, than those in China's BITs.

This article advocates that China should take advantage of the OBOR
initiative to develop a megaregional investment agreement. This is
a sensible way for China to apply a lawfare approach to upgrading
collaboration at the regional level. An investment treaty covering all the

---

[26] *Deal Sealed with a Handshake and Fish*, China Daily, May 3, 2013 (last accessed May 20,
2014).
[27] Agreement on Investment of the Framework Agreement on Comprehensive Economic
Cooperation Between the Association of Southeast Asian Nations and the People's
Republic of China, available at www.aseansec.org/22974.pdf.

OBOR nations can help China solidify its leading role in the OBOR region and reshape its legalistic image on the international stage.

An OBOR-based investment treaty will also help China to counter the impact of the US-led TPP and TTIP. The facts that China's growing importance in outbound FDI activities, the United States' promotion of the Trans-Pacific Partnership Agreement (TPP, now CPTPP with 11 member states in Asia Pacific region) without involving China and the TPP's more preference margins than the BITs[28] creating more comparative advantages for member states, would further affect or even reshape China's strategy to negotiate and enter into BITs with its trading partners. The key goal of the United States' expansion of BITs, and particularly the TPP nowadays, is to entrench some protections of customary law so as to assure full protection and security, to dismantle public law regulations inimical to the market[29] and to protect the rights of the TPP countries to regulate in the public interest.[30] Apart from its economic, political and ideological importance, the TPP would help the United States reshape a newer FTA standard worldwide in the twenty-first century and a better investment environment for its trading partners.[31] Without tying itself to the TPP or a new wave of FTA standards influenced by the TPP, China may not maintain its competitiveness nor avoid marginalization in the global market. China's attitudes towards the TPP may imply its geopolitical concerns. However, it would be in China's great interest to upgrade its BIT standards and expand its FTA network to offset any impacts that the TPP may exert upon the Asia-Pacific region. The TPP covers a wide range of fields and includes investment,[32] which provides China with a new tool for furthering its internal structural reform and external institutional objectives. For instance, a negative list approach is being transplanted into China, in particular, Shanghai's free trade zone. Meanwhile, China is actively exploring the possibility of reaching a regional trade and investment pact in the framework of the Regional Comprehensive Economic Partnership (RCEP),

---

[28] It is usually the case that bilateral trade agreements offer more preference margins than multilateral ones. Donald Barry & Ronald Keith (eds), Regionalism, Multilateralism and the Politics of Global Trade (Vancouver: UBC Press 1999).

[29] Akira Kotera, *Regulatory Transparency*, in Peter Muchlinki et al. (eds.), The Oxford Handbook of International Investment Law 617, 623 (2008).

[30] Congyan Cai, *Trans-Pacific Partnership and the Multilateralization of International Investment Law*, 6 Journal of East Asia and International Law, 385, 400 (2013).

[31] Zhongwei Liu & Jiewen Shen, *The Review of Research Frontier and Frameworks of Trans-Pacific Partnership Agreement (TPP)*, 36 Journal of Contemporary Asia-Pacific Studies (in Chinese) 44–45 (2012).

[32] Chapter 12, P-4, available at www.fta.gov.sg/fta_tpfta.asp?hl=12.

involving the ten ASEAN member states and their FTA partners such as India, Australia, Japan, Korea and New Zealand.[33] In a larger context, China needs to reconsider and reengineer its policies and strategies in foreign investment protection by being more active in negotiating FTAs with proinvestment terms. The wider FTA network gives China a new opportunity to participate in shaping multilateral rules and the global administrative law order.[34] One strategy China may take is to upgrade its standards of review, and one core standard is compensation for expropriation. It may be fair and safe to predict that China is perhaps likely to move towards a more proinvestment protection stance in its further BIT/FTA/RCEP negotiations.

More substantially, an OBOR-based investment treaty can offer better protections to China's outbound investment. China is not only a major capital importer but also a significant capital exporter. China became the second largest investor in 2017 and 2018, right after the United States or Japan.[35] In terms of its foreign direct investment stock, China is one of the largest developing-country investors in Africa.[36] It is the top investing country in some least-developed countries such as Sudan, Nigeria, Zambia and Algeria.[37] Starting in 2001, China shifted its policy and has been steadily promoting outbound FDI in order to lessen the external surplus and secure access to natural resources in other developing countries. The Communist Party of China (CPC), China's ruling party, took the initiative in crafting the well-known "go global" strategy in 1998.[38] In embarking on this strategy, the State Council not only included it in the Tenth Five-Year Plan for National Economy and Social Development of

[33] UNCTAD, *World Investment Report 2014: Investing in the SDGs: An Action Plan*, xix.
[34] Gus Van Harten & Martin Loughlin, *Investment Treaty Arbitration as a Species of Global Administrative Law*, 17(1) *European Journal of International Law* 121–50 (2006) (claiming the emergence of global administrative law based on international investment arbitration).
[35] Xinhua, "China's Outbound Investment Second Only to Japan in 2018", September 6, 2019, China Daily, available at www.chinadaily.com.cn/a/201909/16/WS5d7f4a9ea310cf3e3556bb90.html; XinhuaNet, "China's Accumulated Outbound Direct Investment Ranks Second Worldwide in 2017", Xinhua, October 7, 2018, available at www.xinhuanet.com/english/2018-10/07/c_137516024.htm (last accessed March 30, 2020).
[36] UNCTAD, *World Investment Report 2013: Global Value Chains: Investment and Trade for Development*, xvi.
[37] *Id.*, 5.
[38] See http://finance.people.com.cn/GB/8215/126457/8313172.html (last visited April 29, 2010); see also Ministry of Commerce of the PRC – MOFCOM, available at http://njtb.mofcom.gov.cn/subject/zcq/index.shtml (in Chinese); see also Communist Party of China's Central Committee, *Improvement of the Social Economy Market*, available at http://news.xinhuanet.com/newscenter/2003-10/21/content_1135402.htm.

2001, but also set a clear objective of promoting up to fifty globally competitive "national champions" by 2010.[39] In playing a guiding role in the promotion of overseas expansion,[40] the State Council formulated regulations in 2004 replacing the substantial approval regime with the registration regime.[41] This regulatory and policy change may adequately explain why, after 2004, China's outbound FDI saw a sharp surge,[42] as indicated in Figure 6.1 below.

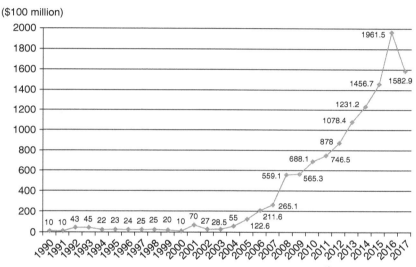

Figure 6.1   Growth of China's outbound investment (1990–2017)[43]

---

[39] See Usha C. V. Haley, *Hearing on China's World Trade Compliance: Industrial Subsidies and the Impact on U.S. and World Markets Statement before the U.S.–China Economic and Security Review Commission on April 4, 2006*, available at www.uscc.gov/hearings/2006hearings/written_testimonies/06_04_04wrts/06_04_04_haley.php.

[40] Florencia Jubany & Daniel Poon, *Recent Chinese Engagement in Latin America and the Caribbean: A Canadian Perspective*, FOCAL (Mar. 2006), available at www.focal.ca/pdf/China-Latin%20America_Jubany-Poon-FOCAL_Chinese%20Engagement%20Latin%20America%20Caribbean%20Canadian%20Perspective_March%202006.pdf.

[41] China's State Council, *Decision on Reforming the Investment System*, Parts II & III, available at http://news.xinhuanet.com/zhengfu/2004–07/26/content_1648074.htm (in Chinese).

[42] See *Editorial, China's Forex Reserve Overtakes the Total Amount of G7 Countries*, available at http://news.163.com/08/0603/02/4DFRH5E00001234J.html (in Chinese).

[43] *Statistical Bulletin of China's Outward Foreign Direct Investment* (2018), available at http://images.mofcom.gov.cn/fec/201810/20181029160824080.pdf (last visited on June 28, 2020).

Given China's massive foreign currency reserves and its continuous efforts to liberalize its foreign exchange controls,[44] Chinese companies desire to grow globally. Likely, this wave of outbound investment from China will continue to increase.[45] In the aftermath of the global financial crisis, Chinese players have yet to slow their expanding pace. Rather, more Chinese companies are finding their way to a heightened profile in a growing number of industries.[46] It appears inevitable that Chinese companies will become a major force in FDI in the global sphere. Meanwhile, Chinese investors are facing some challenges in the global market.

While China's growing economic dominance has been clear in central Asia, investment security may be one of the most pressing challenges. OBOR covers a large part of central Asia, which was historically a thoroughfare for Uighur militants who wish to join terrorist groups in Afghanistan and Pakistan. The Chinese government has previously condemned some violent attacks within China following the radicalization of China's Muslim Uighur minority by international militant groups. The Chinese embassy in Kyrgyzstan was hit by a suicide attack on August 30, 2016. This was a worrying development in a time when China is stepping up investments in central Asia under the OBOR initiative. Kyrgyzstan's economy increasingly relies on Chinese trade and investment, including some Chinese-backed infrastructure projects such as a railway network linking China to Uzbekistan running through the country. The attack's conscious targeting of a Chinese embassy[47] caused consternation in China as an early wave of protests broke out in 2016 across Kazakhstan on the back of fears that a new land code would allow Chinese investors to buy up Kazakh land.

Naturally, China has placed more emphasis on using BITs as legal instruments for the protection of Chinese investments overseas by signing new BITs with developing countries and updating old BITs with developed countries. Against this background, China's stance in BIT practice evolved from a restrictive to a balanced or even liberal stance. Starting with the Barbados–China BIT of 1998, China started to provide foreign investors with stronger and more comprehensive substantive and procedural

---

[44] Shen Hong, *Beijing Steps in to Tame Currency*, *Wall Street Journal*, October 16, 2013, C2.

[45] Daniel H. Rosen & Thilo Hanemann, *The Rise in Chinese Overseas Investment and What It Means for American Businesses*, available at www.chinabusinessreview.com/the-rise-in-chinese-overseas-investment-and-what-it-means-for-american-businesses/.

[46] Julie Jiang & Jonathan Sinton, *Overseas Investments by Chinese National Oil Companies*, Information Paper (February 2011).

[47] Christian Shepherd & Jack Farchy, *Chinese Embassy in Kyrgyzstan Hit by Suicide Bomb Attack*, Financial Times, August 30, 2016 (online) (citing Raffaello Pantucci, directory of international securities studies at the Royal United Services Institute).

protections, largely comparable to those of capital-exporting states.[48] This change made the China-Barbados BIT the starting point of the second-generation of Chinese BITs with stronger foreign investment protection standards, evidenced by the much relaxed investor-state dispute settlement provisions, which allow foreign investors to initiate investment arbitration against Chia more easily. The key element in this China-Barbados BIT is an expanded term of dispute without confining the arbitral dispute to the amount of compensation arising out of expropriation. In other words, under this BIT, the foreign investor can make a claim against the Chinese government not only over the expropriation but also the amount of compensation arising out of expropriation. This is a great step taken by the Chinese government towards a more liberal BIT regime. It is no coincidence that the change in Chinese BIT policy came contemporaneously with the launch of the "go global" strategy. China's increased confidence in providing sufficient protections to foreign investors, its increasing outbound FDI and its more sophisticated legal system well explain China's growing acceptance of modern BIT jurisprudence and related international investment law. Owing to the increasing number of disputes raised on the ground of indirect expropriation, recent BITs concluded by the United States and Canada have included more detailed provisions, and China appears to be following this trend in BIT jurisprudence and practice.

Political risks have been the major concern to foreign investors when they invest in OBOR countries. Some OBOR countries such as Central Asian countries present complex security challenges.[49] According to the Political Risk Services, eighteen of thirty-two countries covered by the OBOR initiative have much higher political risks than others. Figures 6.2 and 6.3 showcase the higher political risks of some OBOR countries exceeding the average level in such indexes as the World Justice Project Rule of Law Index[50] and the Regulatory

---

[48] Stephan W. Schill, *Tearing Down the Great Wall: The New Generation Investment Treaties of the People's Republic of China*, 15 *Cardozo J. Int'l & Comp. L.* 73, 73–118 (2007); Yuqing Zhang, *The Case of China, in Investor-State Arbitration – Lessons for Asia* 156 (Michael Moser ed., 2008).

[49] Thomas Zimmerman, "The New Silk Roads: China, the US, and the Future of Central Asia," (2015) New York University Center on International Cooperation Report.

[50] The World Justice Project Rule of Law Index® is the world's leading source for original, independent data on the rule of law. Covering 128 countries and jurisdictions, the Index relies on national surveys of more than 130,000 households and 4,000 legal practitioners and experts to measure how the rule of law is experienced and perceived worldwide. Available at https://worldjusticeproject.org/our-work/research-and-data/wjp-rule-law-index-2020.

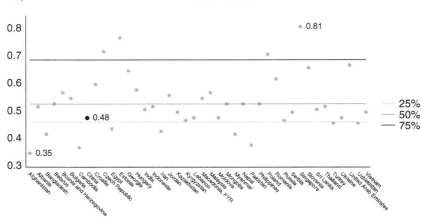

Figure 6.2   Rule of Law Index (WJP)

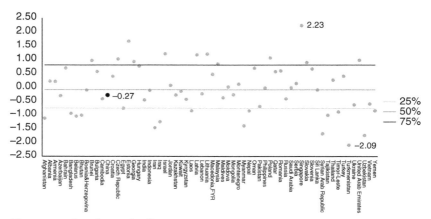

Figure 6.3   Regulatory Quality

Quality Index[51] respectively. Political risks in OBOR countries have been manifestly evidenced by a large number of international investment cases involving these countries as respondents. The Doing

---

[51] Regulatory Quality index is prepared by the World Bank in the frame of GovData360 to measure the ability of the government to formulate and implement sound policies and regulations that permit and promote private sector development, available at https://govdata360.worldbank.org/indicators/hf8a87aec?country=BRA&indicator=394&viz=line_chart&years=1996,2018

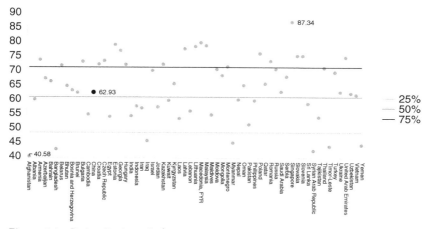

Figure 6.4   Doing Business Index

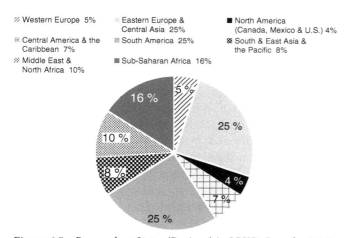

Figure 6.5   Respondent States (Regions) in ICSID Cases by 2017

Business Rankings,[52] as shown in Figure 6.4, also show the hardness to do business in the Belt and Road countries. Figure 6.5 below indicates that almost 42 percent of existing investment arbitration cases involve

---

[52] Doing Business provides objective measures of business regulations for local firms in 190 countries. The World Bank Doing Business, available at www.doingbusiness.org/en/doingbusiness

such countries that are covered by the One Belt One Road Initiative.[53] In 2017, over 55 percent of ICSID-filed investment arbitration cases involved OBOR countries. This high portion of investment arbitration cases also suggests the importance of BITs as well as FTAs in terms of protecting foreign investors from being expropriated when they invest along OBOR. Most of the sixty-five countries covered by the OBOR initiative have FTAs and BITs with China.

This chapter focuses on the expropriation clauses in these BITs and FTAs so as to formulate a picture showing the evolution of those clauses. The reason for focusing on the expropriation clauses in these BITs lies in the fact that most of the OBOR countries are developing countries and lack a strong legal infrastructure for property rights protection, which may damage China's interest in protecting its outbound investment. Given the lack of domestic legal infrastructure in these OBOR countries, reliance on BITs' higher protection standards (i.e., avoiding expropriation) is a natural tool for China's outbound investors when they enter these countries for investment.

This chapter focuses on the notion of expropriation and the related compensation standard by examining expropriation clauses in China's existing BITs. The underlying rationale of this focus is the correlation between expropriation, which is a most pressing risk in relation to outbound investment, and foreign investment protection. This is a highly relevant legal issue in relation to the security and soundness of China's outbound investment and foreign investors' inbound investment. In terms of China's outbound investment projects, uncertainty or instability is always present in the host country's policy of welcoming China's investment. A recent example came with the UK government's rethink on one of China's investments (a consortium participated in by CGN and CNNC) by delaying Hinkley Point plant, a part-finance but long-delayed €18 billion nuclear power plant to be built by French power utility EDF.[54]

The doctrine and case law on expropriation in international investment law is an unsettled area due to a variety of factors such as the diversity of interests between capital importing and exporting states, the

[53] ICSID, The ICSID Caseload-Statistics (Issue 2018-1), ICSID, available at, https://icsid .worldbank.org/en/Documents/resources/ICSID%20Web%20Stats%202018-1 (English).pdf

[54] Kiran Stacey, Kate Allen & Lucy Hornby, *UK Decision to Delay Hinkley Point Plant Catches China by Surprise*, Financial Times, July 29, 2016 (online).

divergence in legal, economic and cultural concepts of property rights, and more importantly, the regulatory role of the state in cross-border investment activities. Although China has been an active "treaty maker" in the universe of international investment arbitration, evidenced by its nearly 130 bilateral investment treaties (BITs), the notion of expropriation in these BITs is in a state of flux.

The origins of expropriation can be traced back to the international law standards for the protection of aliens. In modern international investment protection law, expropriation is permitted only if it is carried out on a nondiscriminatory basis, for a public purpose, in compliance with due process and the principle of payment of compensation. Bilateral investment treaties regulate the exercise of the state's power to expropriate investments. In fact, investors' chances to succeed in a claim against a state for expropriation are rather slim, in particular in such cases where the disputed expropriation is a regulatory one. Tribunals have always found it difficult to conclude either that the state's actions amount to an actual taking or that the accumulative effect of the state's act reaches the threshold of expropriation.

Expropriation is a critically important issue in Chinese BITs,[55] considering China's enormous amount of foreign capital, its history of nationalizing foreign investment soon after the founding of the PRC[56] and China's emerging "new state order" and "creeping renationalisation" to "attack private enterprises" by grabbing state land from privately owned coal mines and residents.[57] However, the utility of expropriation clauses in China's 129 BITs and free trade agreements, including the Peru–China Free Trade Agreement (the Peru–China FTA) entered into between China and Peru on April 28, 2009, is a mysterious arena given the fact that extremely few BIT arbitration cases brought before the ICSID have involved Chinese BITs.

---

[55] All the BITs cited herein are available at ita.law.uvic.ca/investmenttreaties.htm; www.unctadxi.org/templates/DocSearch_779.aspx; or www.kluwerarbitration.com/BITs-countries.aspx.

[56] Laurie A. Pinard, *United States Policy Regarding Nationalization of American Investments: The People's Republic of China's Nationalization Decree of 1950*, 14 *California Western International Law Journal* 148 (1984).

[57] Jamil Anderlini & Geoff Dyer, *Beijing Accused of Attacking Private Enterprise*; Geoff Dyer, *Crackdown on Coal Mines Ignites Fears of State Land Grab*, Financial Times, November 26, 2009, 3.

6.1   The Concept of "Indirect Expropriation": Scope and Content

Under the investment treaty jurisprudence, it is almost settled that, subject to the precise wording of the given BIT, expropriation extends to both direct and indirect measures as well as to "creeping expropriation."[58] However, investment treaties do not define expropriation, in particular, indirect expropriation, and leave the specific contours of the concept to customary international law.[59] This approach has also been recognized in BIT jurisprudence,[60] recent US BITs[61] and Chinese FTAs.[62] The lack of a uniform definition of indirect expropriation has become the greatest source of trouble not only for host governments but also investment arbitration tribunals.

Some Chinese BITs, such as the Germany–China BIT, touch upon indirect expropriation by stipulating that "investments by investors of either Contracting Party shall not directly or indirectly be expropriated, nationalised or subjected to any other measure the effects of which would be tantamount to expropriation or nationalization in the territory of the other Contracting Party."[63] The Mexico–China BIT expressly refers to expropriation being made directly or "indirectly through measures tantamount to expropriation or nationalization."[64] The term "tantamount to expropriation"[65] allows a number of tribunals to provide the broadest protection for the investments of foreign investors who may suffer harm

---

[58] International investment jurisprudence often equates direct expropriation to a forcible taking by the government of tangible or intangible property owned by individuals or companies through administrative or legislative actions, while placing emphasis on the effect of the measures taken by the host governments on the investment in adjudicating indirect expropriation even in the absence of formal transfer of title or outright seizure. The situation in which an investment may be affected by measures gradually but eventually resulting in expropriation is known as creeping expropriation. Campbell McLachlan, Laurence Shore & Matthew Weiniger, International Investment Arbitration: Substantive Principles (Oxford: Oxford University Press 2007) ch. 8.

[59] Jack Coe, Jr. & Noah Rubins, *Regulatory Expropriations and the TECMED Case: Context and Contributions, in* Todd Weiler (ed.), International Investment Law and Arbitration: Leading Cases from the ICSID, NAFTA, Bilateral Investment Treaties and Customary International Law (London, Cameron May 2005) 601.

[60] Saluka Investments BV v. Czech Republic, UNCITRAL Ad Hoc Arbitration, Partial Award, March 17, 2006, para. 261.

[61] US Model BIT 2004, *Annex B Expropriations*, at 38.

[62] New Zealand–China FTA, Article 143; Peru–China FTA, Article 132(2)(c).

[63] Germany–China BIT, Article 4(2); Jordan–China BIT, Article 5(1); Uganda–China BIT, Article 4(1).

[64] Mexico–China BIT, Article 7(1).

[65] Greece–China BIT, Article 4(1).

by being deprived of their fundamental investment rights.[66] For instance, in *Eureko* v. *Republic of Poland*, the tribunal concluded that "tantamount to deprivation" extends to the frustration of the benefits of an investor's contractual rights.[67]

A large number of Chinese BITs have other variations to similar effect. Examples are the Czech Republic–China BIT, Denmark–China BIT, Indonesia–China BIT and Iceland–China BIT with the phrase "having an effect equivalent to,"[68] the Greece–China BIT with the caveat of "tantamount to"[69] and the France–China BIT with the phrase "same effect." Based on the extensive jurisprudence, any of these formulations may be held by the tribunals to have the effect of bringing indirect expropriations into the ambit of a treaty,[70] as the state's actions or measures effectively "neutralise the benefit of the property of the foreign owner."[71] In line with general BIT practice,[72] the Peru–China BIT, like most Chinese BITs, contains in Article 4 a generic expropriation clause as follows:

> Neither Contracting Party shall expropriate, nationalize or take similar measure (hereinafter referred to as "expropriation") against investments of investors of the other Contracting Party in its territory, unless the following conditions are met:
>
> (a) for the public interest;
> (b) under domestic legal procedure;
> (c) without discrimination;
> (d) against compensation.[73]

---

[66] Pope & Talbot Inc v. Government of Canada (Merits, Phase 1) (June 26, 2000), para. 99; Waste Management Inc. v. United Mexican States (Merits), para. 143–45; GAMI Investments, Inc v. Government of the United Mexican States (Merits), para. 131; Tecnicas Medioambientales Tecmed, SA v United Mexican States (Merits), paras. 113–15 and 121; Compania del Desarrollo de Santa Elena, SA v Republic of Costa Rica (Merits), paras. 71–72 & 76.

[67] Eureko B.V. v Republic of Poland, Ad Hoc Arbitration, Partial Award, paras. 240–42 (involving the Netherlands–Poland BIT 1992).

[68] Indonesia–China BIT, Article 6(1).

[69] Greece–China BIT, Article 4(2).

[70] ADC Affiliate Limited and ADC & ADMC Management Limited v. Hungary, ICSID Case No. ARB/03/16, para. 426; Waste Management, Inc. v. Mexico (Number II), ICSID Case No. ARB(AF)/00/3, Final Award, April 20, 2004, para. 143.

[71] CME Czech Republic BV v. Czech Republic, UNCITRAL Partial Award September 13, 2001, paras. 604.

[72] Andrew Newcombe, *The Boundaries of Regulatory Expropriation in International Law,* ICSID Review – Foreign Investment Law Journal 8–9 (2005).

[73] Peru–China BIT, Article 4(1).

In line with general BIT practice,[74] most Chinese BITs contain a generic expropriation clause covering "nationalization," "expropriation" and any other "similar measures," without providing any detailed definitions of these terms.

In comparison with other Chinese BITs and the Peru-China FTA, the Peru-China BIT contains no rules on indirect expropriation through the reference to "other measures having similar effects",[75] which resembles the wording in NAFTA.[76] The Peru-China BIT's silence on "indirect expropriation" adds uncertainty to be faced by an investor when considering whether to bring a claim to investor–state arbitration. Nor does the Peru–China BIT, apart from the phrase of "other similar measures," contain a more functionalist definition of "indirect expropriation," which consequently may allow the tribunals to adopt a more expansive approach to cover indirect expropriation.[77] Due to the lack of guidance in the Peru–China BIT in applying the treaty standard to specific circumstances, the application of international law to relevant disputes seems to be an option.

What is noteworthy is the completeness contributed by the Peru–China FTA to the definition of indirect expropriation, which not only covers an "equivalent effect" scenario but also provides a two-pronged test of determining the existence of indirect expropriation, that is, the severity or an indefinite period of the expropriatory act and proportionality to the public interest.

International investment treaty jurisprudence makes a structural distinction between full or substantial deprivations and "regulatory takings," the latter referring to measures taken in the context of the modern regulatory state including strangulating taxation.[78] This distinction is not easily sustained,[79] but has been recognized as one of the

---

[74] Newcombe, *supra* note 72.
[75] China–Finland BIT 2006, Article 4(1); China–Germany BIT 2003, Article 4(2); China–Portugal BIT 1992, Article 4(1). China recognized the concept of indirect expropriation in its Model BIT adopted as early as in the 1980s. See Chinese Model BIT, reprinted in Wenhua Shan & Nora Gallagher, Chinese Investment Treaties, Policies and Practice (Oxford: Oxford University Press 2009) Appendix 4.
[76] NAFTA 1992, Article 1110, 107 Stat. 2057, 32 ILM 289.
[77] The Protocol to the TIT includes an identical definition of indirect expropriation, which details some key perspectives of "indirect expropriation". The Protocol to the TIT, Article 2a(ii).
[78] Stephan W. Schill, The Multilateralization of International Investment Law (Cambridge: Cambridge University Press 2009) 82.
[79] Rosalyn Higgins, *The Taking of Property by the State: Recent Developments in International Law*, 176 Recueil des Cours 331 (1982).

most contentious issues in international investment law[80] by both international legislative documents[81] and case law. The general rule is that a diminution in value remains uncompensated so long as rights of use, exclusion and alienation remain untouched.[82] Most tribunals follow this legal approach, while others integrate some economic elements. In the latter approach, economic elements are taken into account to assess questions of causation and damage. Some tribunals have favored the economic approach. The tribunal in *Telenor* required "a major adverse impact on the economic value of the investment,"[83] and in *Parkerings* "a substantial decrease of the value of the investment."[84] In *Tecmed*, the tribunal held that the deprivation analysis is focused on "economic use and enjoyment of its investments" as the rights related thereto – such as the income or benefits related to the expropriation – ha[d] ceased to exist.[85] Even though some tribunals favor the economic approach, when the question comes to the economic conception, they have not provided any conclusive answer to the threshold of a diminution in value, with some exceptions, such as *GAMI v. Mexico*.[86]

The Peru–China BIT does not specify the evidentiary requirement of a causal link between a measure of expropriation and subsequent damages. The Tribunal recognized that other tribunals had dealt with this based on general principles of international law.[87] In some cases, such as *LG&E Energy Corp et al.* v. *Argentinean Republic*, the decrease in the investment's capacity to maintain its activities or a loss of profit

[80] Thomas Walde & Abba Kolo, *Environmental Regulation, Investment Protection and "Regulatory Taking" in International Law*, 50 ICLQ 811, 814 (2001).

[81] The official commentary to the OECD Draft Convention of 1967 states that "the taking of property, within the meaning of the Article [3], must result in a loss of title or substance – otherwise a claim will not lie." OECD Draft Convention on the Protection of Property, Adopted by the Council in its 150th Meeting on October 12, 1967 (1968) 7 ILM 117, 126.

[82] Rosalyn Higgins, *The Taking of Property by the State: Recent Developments in International Law*, 176 Recueil des Cours. *Collected Courses of the Hague Academy of International Law, 1982-III* (The Hague: M. Nijhoff 1983) 271.

[83] Telenor Mobile Communications AS v. Republic of Hungary, ICSID Case No. ARB/04/15, Award, para. 64.

[84] Parkerings-Compagniet AS v. Lituania, ICSID Case No ARB/05/8, Award, 11 September 2007, para. 455.

[85] Tecmed, para. 115.

[86] Gami Investment, Incorporated v. The Government of the United Mexican States, Final Award (September 15, 2004) Ad Hoc Tribunal (UNCITRAL).

[87] *Id.*, para. 167.

margins is not sufficient, especially when the investment remains operational.

The Peru–China FTA sides with a more legalistic approach by providing that "The fact that an action or series of actions by a Party has an adverse effect on the economic value of an investment, standing alone, does not establish that an indirect expropriation has occurred."[88]

Investment treaty tribunals often follow a "sole effect" doctrine or "orthodox" approach, one of the dominant conceptions in international law,[89] by centering their assessments around the effects of government measures.[90] An expropriation is found to be in existence if the government measure's effect is a complete or substantial deprivation of an investment,[91] a material decline in the value of its assets or an impairment in the ability of the business to function,[92] which would require compensation.[93] The focus in this assessment is the degree of interference with an investment, measured by the severity of the economic impact, which is the decisive criterion.[94] Judicial practice confirms the magnitude or severity of this test in deciding whether an indirect expropriation actually takes place.[95] There emerged a tendency to equate indirect expropriation with "a measure that effectively neutralizes the

---

[88] Peru–China FTA, Annex 9, Article 4.

[89] Newcombe, *supra* note 72, at 10.

[90] Dolzer, *Indirect Expropriations: New Developments?*, 11 *New York University Environmental Law Journal* 64 (2002), at 64 & 78. *See also* J. Paulsson & Z. Douglas, *Indirect Expropriation in Investment Treaty Arbitrations*, in Arbitrating Foreign Investment Disputes 148 (N. Horn & S. Kroll eds., 2004).

[91] Pope & Talbot Inc. v. Government of Canada, Interim Award, paras. 96 & 102 (June 26, 2000) Ad Hoc Tribunal (UNICITRAL), available at http://opil.ouplaw.com/view/10.1093/law:iic/192–2000.case.1/IIC192(2000)D.pdf (last visited on October 9, 2014); Occidental Exploration & Production Company v. The Republic of Ecuador, L.C.I.A. Case No. UN3467 (July 1, 2004), *reprinted in* 43 I.L.M. 1248.

[92] P. Cameron, *Stabilisation in Investment Contracts and Changes of Rules in Host Countries: Tools for Oil & Gas Investors*, AIPN Research Paper Final Report (2006) 60. *See also* N. Rubins & S. Kinsella, International Investment, Political Risks and Dispute Resolution: A Practitioner's Guide 207 (2005).

[93] I. Brownlie, Principles of Public International Law 546 (5th ed. 1967).

[94] C. Schreuer, *The Concept of Expropriation under the ETC and Other Investment Protection Treaties*, 28–29, 81, available at www.univie.ac.at/intlaw/pdf/csunpublpaper_3.pdf (last visited September 22, 2014). *See also* A. Hoffmann, *Indirect Expropriation, in* Standards of Investment Protection (A. Reinisch ed., 2008).

[95] Metalclad Corp. v. United Mexican States, ICSID Additional Facility Case No. ARB(AF)/97/1, para. 103 (Aug. 30, 2000); *See also* LG&E Energy Corporation and Others v. the Republic of Argentina, ICSID Case No. ARB./02/1 (2007).

enjoyment of the property" even if the measure itself does not involve an overt taking.[96] Interferences constitute expropriation if they "approach total impairment,"[97] that is, "wiping out *all or almost all* the investor's investments."[98] This approach has been followed by some tribunals in various cases in deciding whether interference constitutes an expropriation.[99] In sum, a taking does not have to be complete but only "have the effect of depriving the owner, in whole or in significant part, of the use or reasonably-to-be-expected economic benefit of property even if not necessarily to the obvious benefit of the host State."[100]

There has been some doubt over the question whether the sole effect doctrine should be the only factor in determining whether a regulatory measure in the field of tax, environment, health, human rights and other welfare interests of the state affects a taking.[101] It has been argued that the purpose and context of the governmental measure should be taken into account. Peru's argument is reflective of a greatly narrow, restrictive and obsolete approach which required Tza to prove an expropriatory "purpose." This is a purpose-oriented approach focusing on the host state's intention or motivation to expropriate.[102]

Further clarity has been brought to China's newer BITs and FTAs. Both the Finland–China BIT and Netherlands–China BIT are even closer to the US approach[103] to expropriation.[104] The most sophisticated

---

[96]   *See* CME Czech Republic B.V. v. The Czech Republic, UNCITRAL Arb. Trib. para. 591 (2001).

[97]   J. Coe & N. Rubins, *Regulatory Expropriation and the Tecmed Case: Context and Contributions, in* International Investment Law and Arbitration: Leading Cases from the ICSID, NAFTA, Bilateral Treaties and Customary International Law 621 (T. Weiler ed., 2005).

[98]   LG&E Energy Corporation and ors. v. the Republic of Argentina, ICSID Case No. ARB/02/1, para. 191 (2007) (emphasis added).

[99]   Metalpar SA & BuenAire SA v. Argentina, Award on the Merits, ICSID Case No. ARB/03/5, para. 172–73 (June 6, 2008).

[100] Metalclad Corporation v. Mexico, Award, ICSID Case No. ARB(AF)/97/1, para. 103 (2000).

[101] Rudolf Dolzer, *supra* note 96, 79–80.

[102] Anne K. Hoffmann, *Indirect Expropriation, in* August Reinisch (ed.), Standards of Investment Protection (Oxford: Oxford University Press 2008) 156–58.

[103] The approach taken by the United States in negotiating its BITs is to ensure that the standards created by the takings clause of the Fifth Amendment to the US Constitution are also applied to the protection of investment. To this end, the term "expropriation" explicitly covers both direct and indirect expropriation. Accordingly, any expropriation is required to be consistent with the general absolute treatment standards such as fair and equitable treatment, full protection and security, and treatment in accordance with customary international law. Kenneth J. Vandevelde, U.S. International Investment Agreements (Oxford: Oxford University Press 2009) ch. 7.

[104] Finland–China BIT, Article 4; Netherlands–China BIT, Article 5.

definition of indirect expropriation, drawing on recent BIT case law, appears in the New Zealand–China FTA, under which it is confined to measures which are (a) equivalent to direct expropriation, in that "[they] deprive . . . the investor in substance of the use of the investor's property"; (b) either severe or indefinite; and (c) disproportionate to the public purpose.[105] Clear interpretative guidelines are provided on what actions constitute expropriation.

In the Protocol of the India–China BIT 2006, the criteria for indirect expropriation were stipulated in detail as follows:

(2) The determination of whether a measure or a series of measures of a Party in a specific situation, constitute measures as outlined in paragraph 1 above requires a case by case, fact based inquiry that considers, among other factors:

   (i)   the economic impact of the measure or a series of measures, although the fact that a measure or series of measures by a Party has an adverse effect on the economic value of an investment, standing alone, does not establish that expropriation or nationalization, has occurred;

   (ii) the extent to which the measures are discriminatory either in scope or in application with respect to a Party or an investor or an enterprise;

   (iii) the extent to which the measures or series of measures interfere with distinct, reasonable, investment-backed expectations;

   (iv) the character and intent of the measures or series of measures, whether they are bona fide public interest purposes or not and whether there is a reasonable nexus between them and the intention to expropriate.

(3) Except in rare circumstances, non-discriminatory regulatory measures adopted by a Contracting Party in pursuit of public interest, including measures pursuant to awards of general application rendered by judicial bodies, do not constitute indirect expropriation or nationalization.[106]

These largely copy the provisions from the US Model BIT 2004[107] and indicate China's intention to emulate the US approach on expropriation.

---

[105] New Zealand–China FTA, Annex 13.
[106] Protocol to India–China BIT, Article III, Ad Article 5.
[107] US Model BIT 2004, Annex B, Article 4.

Few BITs specify the treaty interpretative methodology. The Peru–China FTA calls for "a case-by-case, fact based inquiry."[108] This common law type of case-by-case method is also codified into other BITs including the Canadian Model BIT 2004.[109] This pragmatic and realist approach was adopted by the Tribunal in this particular case. The Tribunal echoed that the question of expropriation "cannot be answered in the abstract but only on the basis of particular circumstances and in the context of particular purposes."[110]

6.2   Lawful Grounds for Expropriation

Expropriation is not unlawful under international law as long as certain formalistic conditions are met.[111] Generally, a signatory state is able to expropriate, nationalize or take other similar measures against investments of investors of another Party if the action is: "(a) for the public purpose; (b) under domestic legal procedure; (c) without discrimination; and (d) against compensation."[112] Both the Peru–China BIT and the Peru–China FTA, in a fairly traditional manner, clone the Chinese investment treaty practice by imitating these four elements.

6.2.1   Public Purpose

In international law, the existence and validity of public interests have traditionally been accepted. A public purpose is germane to expropriation as the regulatory measure can be authorized by the government for diverse reasons. The requirement of public purpose for an act of expropriation is a widely accepted principle in customary international law as well as investment treaties.[113] However, the term "for a public purpose" has not been well defined. Nor has it been explained in a form of

---

[108] Peru–China FTA, Annex 9, Article 4. Identical terminology also appears in the Protocol to the TIT, Article 2b(1).
[109] Canadian Model BIT 2004, Annex B 13(1)(b).
[110] Jennings and Watts (eds.), Oppenheim's International Law (Longman 9th ed. 1992) 916–17.
[111] R. Dolzer & C. Schreuer, Principles of International Investment Law 91 (2008).
[112] Agreement on Investment of the Framework Agreement on Comprehensive Economic Cooperation, concluded by the Association of South East Asian Nations and China (Aug. 15, 2009), Article 8(1).
[113] Energy Charter Treaty, Article 13(1)(a); NAFTA, Article 1110(1).

illustrative grounds. Thus, the application of this criterion in the expropriation analysis leaves the tribunal with some discretion.

Variations on the phrase "for a public purpose" include "for the public interests" adopted by a large number of Chinese BITs such as the Cyprus–China BIT and Benin–China BIT, and "for public benefits," which appears in the Germany–China BIT. These terminologies do not indicate substantial differences. The formula of "public purpose, security or national interests" adopted by the Belgium–Luxembourg–China BIT makes this criterion more operative, even though the host state may be in a more advantageous position as such an operative criterion is easier to be satisfied. Other variations, such as "the need of social and public interest" and "national security and public interest" appearing in the Argentina–China BIT[114] and the Philippines–China BIT,[115] respectively, are less operative due to their wide or vague coverage. But these varied terms indicate the scope and nature of the "for a public purpose" criterion, and would entail consideration of detailed facts in the specific case.

Some Chinese BITs[116] contain a carve-out for the reasonable exercise of a state's "police powers," which is intended to offer a safe harbor for regulation that is reasonably justified in the public interest. Given the lack of a police powers carve-out in some BITs, the "for a public purpose" condition may function as a haven for expropriation regulations. "Public power" that refers to the authority of state governments to enact measures to protect public health, welfare and morals, serves the public purpose. As it may serve a local protectionist purpose, it is difficult to discern from an international perspective. The tribunals may then weigh heavily such elements as bad faith, arbitrariness or discrimination in determining whether a "public" but more domestic "purpose" is acceptable or not.

6.2.2   Due Process

Due process is a required element to satisfy the public interest exception. The tribunal in the case of *Methanex*, e.g., decided the taking question against the investor on more general terms as follows:

---

[114] Argentina–China BIT, Article 4(1).
[115] The Philippines–China BIT, Article 4(1).
[116] New Zealand–China FTA, Annex 13.

> As a matter of general international law, a non-discriminatory regulation for a public purpose, which is enacted in accordance with due process and, which affects, inter alia, a foreign investor or investment is not deemed expropriatory and compensable unless specific commitments had been given by the regulating government to the then putative foreign investor contemplating investment that the government would refrain from such regulation.[117]

Any defect in due process may lead a tribunal to invalidate an expropriation. For example, the tribunal in the case of *Metalclad* equated the fact that the "municipality acted outside its authority" to unlawful prevention of "the Claimant's operation of the landfill."[118] In *Middle East Cement*, the tribunal transformed a lawful seizure into an indirect expropriation because of a lack of due process (inter alia, a failure to properly notify the investor of the seizure and auction of its vessel Poseidon).[119] Both the Peru–China BIT and the Peru–China FTA adopt the term "under domestic legal procedure."[120] The reference to the "domestic law" provides the state with more flexibility and control over the process as the expropriation process will be subject to domestic laws of the expropriating state. In any event, this criterion should be relatively easy to be satisfied by the expropriating state where the domestic review procedure of the expropriatory act, fair hearing and impartial tribunals are available.[121]

The Peru–China BIT, unlike other Chinese BITs, only lists "under domestic legal procedure" rather than "due process of law"[122] as one of four conditions that must be fulfilled to justify the right to expropriate foreign property. Legally speaking, "domestic legal procedure" can be interpreted more narrowly than "due process," thereby bringing more local legal elements into play. Since the Peru–China BIT does not offer a functional definition of "under domestic legal procedure," the tribunal made reference to both international and domestic law. This again confirms the hybrid nature of the international investment

---

[117] Methanex Corporation v. US, UNCITRAL Arb. Trib. 7 (2005).
[118] Metalclad Corp., ICSID Case No. ARB(AF)/97/1, 79 (2000).
[119] Middle East Cement Shipping and Handling Co. S.A. v. Arab Republic of Egypt, ICSID Case No. ARB/99/6, 139–44 (2002).
[120] Peru–China BIT, Article 4(1)(b); *Supra* note 3, Article 133(1)(b).
[121] Dolzer & Schreuer, *supra* note 111.
[122] China–France BIT Article 4(3); China–Denmark BIT Article 4(1); China–Spain BIT Article 4(1). Most BITs China has signed with European countries adopt "due process of law" instead of "under domestic legal procedure".

arbitration jurisprudence composed of both international and municipal law.[123]

Under some Chinese BITs, the norm "due process of national laws" or "in accordance with its laws" is more operative as the investor is granted the right to a judicial review of a completed expropriation and of the amount of compensation due. The UK–China BIT, for example, provides that "the national or company affected have a right, under the law of the Contracting Party making the expropriation, to prompt review, by a judicial or other independent authority of that Party, of his or its case and of the valuation of his or its investment in accordance with the principles set out in this paragraph."[124] Similar rights are granted under other Chinese BITs such as the Germany–China BIT, according to which the investor may request that "the legality of any such expropriation and the amount of compensation shall be subject to review by national courts."[125] The ASEAN–China Treaty does not follow this route by providing the investors with the right for review. Accordingly, an investor may have to rely upon investor–state arbitration for a claim against expropriation.

6.2.3   Without Discrimination

Nondiscrimination in regard to the status and treatment of aliens and property is a well-established principle of customary international law,[126] treaty law and case law.[127] Breach of the nondiscrimination principle gives rise to international responsibility.[128] In practice, discrimination complaints are more likely to be raised with regard to due process and payment of compensation. However, the discriminatory factor, due to the lack of guidance and specificity, is "extremely difficult to prove in concrete cases."[129] Thus, the blanket exception for nondiscriminatory measures may create more complexity or a "gaping loophole in international protections against expropriation."[130]

---

[123] A. Newcombe & Luís Paradell, Law and Practice of Investment Treaties section 2.7 (2009).

[124] UK–China BIT, Article 5(1).

[125] Germany–China BIT.

[126] Alex Genin and Others v. Republic of Estonia, ICSID Case No. ARB/99/2, para. 368 (2001).

[127] BP v. Libya, *reprinted in* 53 I.L.R. 297, 329 (1979); Libya v. Libyan Am. Oil Co., *reprinted in* 20 I.L.M. 20, 58 (1981).

[128] I. Brownlie, System of the Law of Nations 81 (Clarendon Press 1983).

[129] M. Shaw, International Law 751 (5th ed. 2003).

[130] Pope & Talbot Inc. v. Canada, para. 99 (June 26, 2000).

Breach of the nondiscrimination principle gives rise to international responsibility.[131] The nondiscrimination requirement appears in many Chinese BITs and is only absent in a small number of BITs between China and Austria, Germany, Indonesia, Italy, Oman and the UK. This requirement adds more value to the investor protection if the BIT does not offer the national treatment protection.

6.3   Compensation

Payment of compensation is necessary in cases of expropriation.[132] It is difficult to reach consensus on an acceptable standard of compensation for lawful expropriation. While developed countries insist on full compensation according to the so-called Hull Formula, that is, "prompt, adequate, and effective compensation,"[133] developing countries prefer either "appropriate" compensation or no compensation at all.[134] The great majority of BITs adopt customary international law on lawful expropriation, including the Hull Formula, with some variations.[135]

6.3.1   Value

The investment treaty jurisprudence in this area has shown an increasing level of convergence that compensation needs to be equivalent to "fair market value."[136] The Peru–China BIT adopts the following compensation clause:

---

[131]   Brownlie, *supra* note 128.

[132]   Brownlie, *supra* note 93.

[133]   *See, e.g.,* Treaty between the United States of America and the Oriental Republic of Uruguay concerning the Encouragement and Reciprocal Protection of Investment, U.S.–Uruguay, Nov. 4, 2005, S. Treaty Doc. No. 109-9, Article 6(1)(c), *reprinted in* 44 I.L.M. 268. *See also* S. Corey, *But Is It Just? The Inability for Current Adjudicatory Standards to Provide "Just Compensation" for Creeping Expropriations,* 81 Fordham L. Rev. 989 (2012); T. Ginsburg, *International Substitutes for Domestic Institutions: Bilateral Investment Treaties and Governance* 6 (Ill. Law and Economics Working Paper No. LE06-027, 2006), *recited from* G. Hackworth, Digest of International Law 228, 655–65 (1942).

[134]   1974 Charter of Economic Rights and Duties of States, GA Res. 3281, U.N. GAOR, 29th Sess., Supp. No. 31, UN Doc.A/9631, 50 (1974). For details, *see* F. Francioni, *Compensation for Nationalization of Foreign Property: The Borderland between Law and Equity,* 24 Int'l & Comp. L. Q. 255–56 (1975).

[135]   *See Bilateral Investment Treaties 1995–2006: Trends in Investment Rulemaking,* available at http://unctad.org/en/docs/iteiia20065_en.pdf, para. 52, UNCTAD/ITE/IIT/2006/5 (2007) (last visited Sept. 22, 2014) (2007).

[136]   Newcombe, *supra* note 72.

> The compensation mentioned in Paragraph 1, (d) of this Article shall be equivalent to the value of the expropriated investment at the time when the expropriation is proclaimed, be convertible and freely transferrable. The compensation shall be paid without unreasonable delay.[137]

The Peru–China FTA adopts an identical but slightly different "compensation" clause as follows:

> The compensation mentioned in subparagraph 1(d) of this Article shall be equivalent to the fair market value of the expropriated investment immediately before the expropriation took place ("the date of expropriation"), convertible and freely transferrable. The compensation shall be paid without unreasonable delay.[138]

This provision reflects "adequate" and "prompt," respectively. The first sentence in the quoted clause connects the financial concept of fair market value to the abstract concept of adequate compensation as the market value of the taken property is supposed to be adequate to compensate the investor. The fair market value is the price reached between the buyer and seller acting "at arm's length in an open and unrestricted market when neither is under compulsion to buy or sell and when both have reasonable knowledge of the relevant facts."[139] However, BITs usually do not explicitly define the term "fair market value." Article 133(2) of the Peru–China FTA, for example, merely stipulates that "the compensation ... shall be equivalent to the fair market value of the expropriated investments immediately before the expropriation took place, convertible and freely transferable." This suggests that the compensation is not reflective of any change in value occurring because the intended expropriation had become known earlier. In other words, this is meant to curb the negative impact on the value of the taken property which may result from the public's advanced knowledge of the fact of expropriation. The China–Germany BIT, however, includes the following clause:

> The compensation shall be paid without delay and shall carry interest at the prevailing commercial rate until the time of payment; it shall be effectively realizable and freely transferrable.[140]

---

[137] Peru–China BIT, Article 4(2).
[138] Peru–China FTA, Article 133(2).
[139] National Grid plc v. The Argentine Republic, UNCITRAL Arb. Tri. (Nov. 3, 2008) para. 263.
[140] The Agreement between the Federal Republic of Germany and the People's Republic of China on the Encouragement and Reciprocal Protection of Investments, F.R.G.–P.R.C., Dec. 1, 2003, Article 4(2), *reprinted in* 42 I.L.M. 609 (2003).

Although each of these legal instruments are in line with the general "value" formulae, the differences are also obvious. The Peru–China FTA moves one step further by stipulating that "[compensation shall] be equivalent to the fair market value of the expropriated investment."[141] However, neither of these two value formulae are operative in a practical sense.

The adoption of more operative valuation methods and principles is recommended by the World Bank, incorporated by NAFTA and endorsed by some tribunals in order to increase the transparency of the valuation method.[142] Another concern is that it is not clear whether the wording in the Peru–China FTA compensation formula actually refers to the full market value. In this sense, the Peru–China FTA makes little substantial progress in clarifying the issue of how to evaluate an expropriated investment. Certainly, it may be argued that the Peru–China FTA approach gets closer to the Hull formula since the wording has absorbed some market-orientated factors.

6.3.2   Moral Damages

Few investors have sought moral damages under bilateral investment treaties. In fact, the case law granting moral damages in investment arbitration is scarce. There are recent signs of an increasing role for this category of damages. The concept of moral damages encompasses all compensatory but nonpecuniary and nonmaterial damages.[143] The Draft Articles on State Responsibility state that "the ... state is under an obligation to make full reparation for the injury caused by the internationally wrongful act. Injury includes any damage, whether material or moral, caused by the internationally wrongful act."[144] This suggests the

---

[141] Peru–China FTA Article 133(2).

[142] World Bank Guidelines on the Treatment of Foreign Direct Investment (1992) *reprinted in* 31 I.L.M. 1366, Article IV.5; NAFTA (listing a set of criteria that must be taken into account by the tribunal, *e.g.*, "going concern value, asset value including declared tax value of tangible property, and other criteria, as appropriate to determine fair market value.") *See also* CME, UNCITRAL Arb. Trib. 103 (March 2003) (recognizing that a discounted cash flow valuation is the most widely employed approach to the valuation of a going concern).

[143] S. Ripinsky & K. Williams, Damages in International Investment Law 307 (2008).

[144] Draft Articles on Responsibility of State for Internationally Wrongful Acts, with commentaries 2001, Article 31, *available at* http://legal.un.org/ilc/texts/instruments/english/commentaries/9_6_2001.pdf (last visited Sept. 23, 2014).

real importance of potential moral damages in providing a victim full compensation under international law.

6.3.3   Valuation Date

The appropriate date of expropriation is important in calculating interest.[145] The date is an integral part of the total compensation awarded by the tribunal for expropriation and can be the most keenly contested issue. Chinese BITs usually fix the valuation date by relying on one or two cut-off points, such as "immediately prior to the time when the expropriation became public"[146] or "immediately before the expropriation measures were taken."[147] The Greece–China BIT adopts both. It states that "such compensation shall amount to the value of the investments affected immediately before the measures … occurred or became public knowledge."[148] This level of clarity helps guarantee that the "value of the expropriated investment" will not depreciate once expropriation is known to the public. It may also guarantee the investor a full and adequate recovery in cases of creeping expropriation.

The Peru–China FTA uses "the date immediately before the expropriation took place" as the date of expropriation. While this may be beneficial to the aggrieved investor, it does not offer much clarity or practicality. The general practice is that the accrual of interest should begin at the time when the expropriation occurs and end on the date when the payment is made. The full compensation principle has led the tribunal to determine the interest due from the date of expropriation to the actual payment of compensation.[149]

6.3.4   Interest

Neither the Peru–China BIT nor the Peru–China FTA makes a reference to any specific interest rate. Both, however, require the compensation to

---

[145] However, it has been also suggested to distinguish the "moment of expropriation" from the "moment of valuation" as the former is related to the question of liability, while the latter goes to the question of damages. For details, *see* M. Reisman & R. Sloane, *Indirect Expropriation and Its Valuation in the BIT Generation*, 74 Brit. Y.B. Int'l L. 115 (2004).

[146] Austria–China BIT (1985), Article 4(1).

[147] The Netherlands–China BIT (2001), Article 5(1)(c); New Zealand–China FTA (2008), Article 145(2); Mexico–China BIT (2008), Article 7(2)(a).

[148] Greece–China BIT (1992), Article 4(2).

[149] Tza Yap Shum v. The Republic of Peru, ICSID Case No.ARB/07/6, 7 July 2011, paras. 286 and 292.

"be paid without unreasonable delay."[150] The ambiguity provides the prospective tribunal with some flexibility.

Interest shall be compounded semiannually according to well-established practice as the desirable method to recognize the realities of trade and to fully compensate the investor.[151] Compounding also counteracts somewhat the risk assumed by the investor against the accrual arising from this award and ideally is an incentive for its timely payment.[152] The final ruling on this point was that the interest rate on damages would be tied to the average monthly rate on ten-year US treasury bonds.[153]

6.3.5 Exchange Rate

More effective compensation should be made in a form usable by the investor. Therefore, the currency of payment must be freely usable or convertible into a freely usable currency.[154]

Some Chinese BITs adopt several formulas such as the "average of the daily exchange rates,"[155] the "official exchange rate" on the day of transfer[156] and the "exchange rate applicable for the payment of the compensation ... on the date used to determine the value of the investment,"[157] all of which are helpful in avoiding potential disputes in this regard. Unlike some other Chinese BITs, both the Peru–China BIT and the Peru–China FTA do not specify the way to determine the exchange rate between the local currency and the freely usable currency. However, both require compensation to "be convertible and freely transferrable."[158] Tza made his monetary claim in Peruvian Nuevos Soles, but the tribunal granted damages in US dollars.[159] Likely, the

---

[150] Peru–China BIT, Article 4(2); Peru–China FTA, Article 133(2).

[151] Metalclad Corp., ICSID Case No. ARB(AF)/97/1, §128 (2000). *See also supra* note 44, §440 (2001).

[152] Tza Yap Shum v. The Republic of Peru, ICSID Case No.ARB/07/6, 7 July 2011, para. 291.

[153] *Id.*, para. 290.

[154] World Bank Guidelines on the Treatment of Foreign Direct Investment, Article IV.7 (1992), *reprinted in* 31 I.L.M. 1366.

[155] Australia–China BIT (1988).

[156] Korea–China BIT (1992).

[157] Greece–China BIT (1992) Article 4(2).

[158] Peru–China BIT (1994) Article 4(2); Peru–China FTA (2008) Article 133(2).

[159] The Award, *supra* note 3, para. 266.

tribunal took into consideration the required elements of convertibility and free transferability.[160]

There has been no mechanically straightforward or uniform way of applying the expropriation clause in BIT arbitration. The methodology adopted by the tribunal in this instant case echoes the pragmatic approach advocated in the investment arbitration circle that "[the constitution of expropriation] cannot be answered in the abstract but only on the basis of particular circumstances and in the context of particular purposes."[161] No BIT has been comprehensively useful in outlining an exhaustive list of elements so that the tribunals can technically rely on them in deciding the occurrence of an expropriation. Nor is the Peru–China BIT. It does not provide much guidance on how to interpret or apply the expropriation clause.

At the two extremes of the spectrum are two treaty interpretive approaches to deal with the concept of indirect expropriation. One extreme is marked by a trend of tribunals to conceptualize or theorize the terminology of indirect expropriation with the aim of delineating between takings and police power.[162] At the other end of the spectrum is a focus on the semantic components of the concept of indirect expropriation.[163] Interestingly, the treaty interpretation methodology deployed by the tribunal in this case reflects a hybrid character, combining efforts not only to conceptualize, but also textualize the notion of expropriation. This hybrid enriches the conceptual framework of indirect expropriation by striking a balance between legalistic and economic elements of "destructive harms." It brought the expropriatory acts to investments, while relying on the textual dimensions of indirect expropriation by following the guidance given in the Peru–China FTA rather than the Peru–China BIT. Such a process may inevitably cause tension.[164] Compared to the Peru–China BIT, the Peru–China FTA outlines a more comprehensive decisional matrix to activate some key aspects of indirect expropriation, thereby transforming this

[160] Peru–China FTA, *supra* note 2, Article 133(2).
[161] *Oppenheim's International Law* 916–17 (R. Jennings & A. Watts eds., 9th ed. 1992).
[162] Wenhua Shan, The Legal Framework of EU-China Investment Relations: A Critical Appraisal, ch. 6 (2005).
[163] *Id.*
[164] S. Franck, *The Nature and Enforcement of Investor Rights Under Investment Treaties: Do Investment Treaties Have a Bright Future?* 12 U. C. Davis J. Int'l L. & Pol'y 47–99 (2005). *See also* A. Joubin-Bret, *BITs of the Last Decade: A Ticking Bomb for States?, in* The Future of Investment Arbitration 145–53 (C. Rogers & R. Alford eds., 2009).

ambiguous black-letter doctrinal concept into a more practical notion. The tribunal's teleological interpretation of the Peru–China BIT may reassure the sentiment to favor the protection of the investor and investment.[165]

To rely on the textual framework of a legal instrument is a safe and useful undertaking. However, it is only convincingly helpful if the legal instrument is clear and comprehensive. By contrast, conceptualizing the doctrine of indirect expropriation appears more important when all members of the international community are expected to normatively abide by publicly known and well-crafted limits. The real challenge facing international investment arbitration is to take a more consistent and institutionally coherent approach to the evaluation of indirect expropriation in investor–state arbitration proceedings.[166] Against this backdrop, the tribunal's hybrid route is a realist one; it combines the conceptual and textual methodologies to more comprehensively address current arbitral inconsistencies in the expropriation arena and to foster a predictable and clear jurisprudence of expropriation. In any event, the award rendered in this case is definitely not the end, but, perhaps, the end of the beginning in interpreting and applying substantive terms in Chinese BITs.

International investment law shares similarities with administrative law on the national level in terms of many factual instances of protection of rights or entitlements. Expropriation law and due process are common grounds of both international investment law and municipal legal orders. In this sense, international investment law constitutes the main body of global administrative law.[167] Both bilateral investment treaties and international investment law jurisprudence (composed of a large number of investment arbitration awards) form the main body of a growing system of international administrative law consisting of the key ingredients of foreign investment protection law and practice. While neither customary international law nor international investment law reveals a recognizable consensus on many expropriation-related rules, capital-exporting countries have long been in a process of shaping the international legal framework on the basis of idealized versions of

[165] SGS Societe Generale de Surveillance S.A. v. The Philippines, para. 116 (2004).
[166] S. Franck, *The Legitimacy Crisis in Investment Treaty Arbitration: Privatizing Public International Law Through Inconsistent Decisions*, 73 Fordham L. Rev. 1521–1625 (2005).
[167] R. Dolzer, *The Impact of International Investment Treaties on Domestic Administrative Law*, 37 N.Y.U. J. Intl L. &Pol'y 970 (2005).

their domestic legal doctrines[168] aiming at providing better legal standards for the protection of their outbound investments.

As a consequence, international investment law not only transfers bilateral legal doctrines to the multilateral level, but also cements a foundation for de facto heightened judicial review of national laws and regulations. Noncompliance with these often adjudicated ingredients may result in state responsibility under international law.[169] Naturally, internationally recognized rules including minimum standard of treatment, compensable takings and standard of compensation are expected to influence domestic laws[170] and proinvestment alternatives. This will be the case for China, which is in a transitional process leaning mostly towards global constitutionalism. Likely, legal norms and doctrines of foreign investment law will be applied and embedded locally, thereby reshaping property rights and the foreign investment protection regime in China.[171]

6.4   Tentative Conclusion

It is clear from the above discussion that China's BITs have been experiencing a generational evolution, meaning that the whole evolutionary process can be divided into several generations. In terms of expropriation standards, the cut-off point of China's BITs was 2006 when China signed a BIT with India, for the first time including the concept of indirect expropriation in the China–India BIT. Recognizing indirect expropriation and adopting better compensation to expropriation offers better legal protection to investors when they bring expropriation cases to the ICISD for international investment arbitration.

---

[168] D. Schneiderman, Constitutionalizing Economic Globalization – Investment Rules and Democracy's Promise 56 (2008).
[169] A. Afilalo, *Constitutionalization through the Back Door: A European Perspective on NAFTA's Investment Chapter*, 34 N.Y.U. J. Intl L. & Pol. 1 (2001).
[170] For an account of Latin America, *see* Schneiderman, *supra* note 168, at 59–61.
[171] Although China is an increasingly important capital-exporting state, it remains a major capital importing country. Differently from the United States, whose goal of using BITs is to entrench customary rights as well as to improve the general investment environment of BIT partners, China's use of BITs has a de facto domestic dimension, which is often overlooked by international investment lawyers. For an account of the American purposes of using BITs, *see* Akira Kotera, *Regulatory Transparency*, *in* The Oxford Handbook of International Investment Law 623 (P. Muchlinki et al. eds., 2008).

Nevertheless, most of the BITs between China and OBOR counterparties were signed before 2006. As we can see, there are in total 65 countries, and 8 of them did not sign BITs with China. In these 57 countries, only 28.7% of them signed BITs (or the new ones) BITs with China after 1998, which suggest that China merely has old-generation BITs with most of OBOR countries.

As a result, the expropriation (the key indicator of political risk for foreign investment) and compensation standards in these existing BITs were not up to higher standards for protecting China's outbound investment into these OBOR counterparties. A sensible approach to fill in this gap is to have a BIT network in the form of a megaregional investment treaty covering China and OBOR countries and applying the doctrines of indirect expropriation and the Hull Formula to compensate for expropriated investments. Similar proposal has been made to make some law reform efforts towards harmonized trade laws or other laws in the OBOR region to address the issue of diverse laws and legal systems[172] with the aim of achieving a sustainable legal and regulatory framework.[173] Some Chinese scholars even made a proposal to have a multilateral dispute settlement center to cover the OBOR countries so as to facilitate the investor-state dispute settlement in the field of cross-border investment.[174]

Chinese scholars highly praised the value of Belt and Road initiative and conceptualized it in a regional community of common destiny.[175] The Belt and Road initiative has been interpreted by some Western commentators as China's version of the Marshall Plan, an analogy to dramatize its dividing effect between two blocks in a geopolitical sense.[176] Both the Marshall Plan and the BRI share the commonality that both help to strengthen a particular region – the Marshall Plan focused on the Western

---

[172] Bruno Zeller, "One Belt One Road – One Law?" in Poomintr Sooksripaisarnkit and Sai Ramani Garimella (eds.), China's One Belt One Road Initiative and Private International Law (Routledge 2018) 145.

[173] Nicholas Morris, "Developing a Sustainable Legal System for the Belt and Road Initiative", in Wenhua Shan, Kmmo Nuotio and Kangle Zhang, Normative Readings of the Belt and Road Initiative: Road to New Paradigms (Springer 2018) 44.

[174] Beiping Chu, *The Construction of an OBOR Multiple Dispute Settlement Centre: Present and Future* (2017) 6 *China Legal Science* 72–90.

[175] Zeng Lingliang, *Conceptual Analysis of China's Belt and Road Initiative: A Road Towards a Regional Community of Common Destiny* (2016) 15 *Chinese Journal of International Law* 517–541.

[176] Marc Trachtenberg, *"The Marshall Plan as Tragedy"* (2005) 7(1) *Journal of Cold War Studies* 135–140.

Europe while the BRI extends China's influence along the Belt and Road countries. But the fundamental difference between these two schemes rests on the objective. BRI tries to achieve the prosperity of the region without a clear political agenda but the Marshall Plan made the US the leader of the world through a series of economic strategies and reforms, turning the US-Soviet Union relationship to a confrontation.[177] The alternative understanding of this initiative is to view it as one of the key pillars that counter the US-led Bretton Wood system along with the emergence of some new global governance structures such as the G20, a coordinating executive body.[178] This article advocates a megaregional solution to promote the cross-border investment in the Belt and Road countries by having an investment treaty, which can be used to solidify China's efforts to frame a global investment governance regime along with its aggressive stance in negotiating BITs with the United States and the EU, and regional investment treaties in Asia-Pacific. From a realistic perspective, deepening China's BIT network, in the form of a minilateral agreement or arrangement,[179] in the regions covered by the OBOR initiative is likely to be more critically important for expanding China's outbound investment in these regions compared with the RCEP and CPTPP.[180] This could be a meaningful response to the call for a formal mechanism or institution for cooperation on and coordination of the Belt and Road Initiative.[181]

[177] Scott D. Parrish and Mikhail M. Narinsky, "*New Evidence on the Soviet Rejection of the Marshall Plan, 1947: Two Reports*" (1994) Cold War International History Project Working Papers Series.

[178] Sungjoon Cho and Claire R. Kelly, "*Promises and Perils of New Global Governance: A Case of G20*" (2012) 12(2) *Chicago Journal of International Law* 491–562.

[179] See generally Chris Brummer, Minilateralism – How Trade Alliances, Soft Law, and Financial Engineering and Redefining Economic Statecraft (Cambridge University Press 2014).

[180] Tristan Kohl, *The Belt and Road Initiative's Effect on Supply-Chain Trade: Evidence from Structural Gravity Equations* (2019) 12(1) *Cambridge Journal of Regions, Economy and Society* 77–104.

[181] Simeon Djankov and Sean Miner, *China's Belt and Road Initiative: Motives, Scope, and Challenges* (2016) *Peterson Institute for International Economics PIIE Briefing* 16-2, p. 17.

7

Multilateral Reform of Investor–State Dispute Resolution Mechanism

A Balance between Public Legitimacy Management and Private Efficiency Refinement

PENG WANG[*]

Nowadays, states, irrespective of levels of development, all face common policy challenges associated with foreign direct investment (FDI) and its dispute settlement system, namely Investor–State Dispute Settlement (ISDS).[1] ISDS lies at the heart of international investment law and generates the bulk of its controversy as well as its appeal among business communities, legal practitioners and academia.[2] Increasing FDI from emerging economies appears to spur the demand of most developed states for balanced international investment agreements (IIAs) and ISDS.[3] No one denies the importance of balancing private property rights of investors with the regulatory policy space of contracting states in international investment law in general and ISDS in particular. However, the issue of how to turn the public–private balance theory into an operational policy action plan is still understudied.[4]

This chapter aims to propose a balanced design for investment dispute settlement mechanisms, namely Multilateral Investment Dispute

[*] The author would like to thank Professor Wenhua Shan for his insightful comments and suggestions on an early draft of this chapter. The research underlying this chapter benefited from financial support from a Chinese National Social Science Research Grant (18CFX084).

[1] J. E. Alvarez, *The Public International Law Regime Governing International Investment* (Martinus Nijhoff Publishers 2011) 209.
[2] S. Hidelang & M. Krajewski, "Towards a More Comprehensive Approach in International Investment Law" in S. Hindelang & M. Krajewski (eds.), *Shifting Paradigms in International Investment Law: More Balanced, Less Isolated, Increasingly Diversified* (Oxford University Press 2016) 13.
[3] Alvarez (n 1).
[4] UNCTAD, *UNCTAD's Reform Package for the International Investment Regime* (United Nations 2017).

Resolution (MIDR), to increase the input and output legitimacy of the ISDS system without destroying its private efficiency of party autonomy and mass protection. In light of the low, if any, feasibility of a comprehensive multilateral agreement on investment, this article focuses primarily on the procedural and institutional aspects of the ISDS system, especially the qualifications of arbitrators, the allocation of appointing authority and the decision-making process, rather than the substantive provisions of IIAs. This in no way denies the importance of the latter. On the contrary, I acknowledge that without including substantive rules, procedural reform alone is not sufficient to address all the legitimacy concerns of the ISDS system.

The unique ISDS system is probably the key to the success of the whole of international investment law[5] as well as the most significant source of public controversy.[6] Nevertheless, this chapter holds that an MIDR of public legitimacy management and private efficiency refinement could respond to most of the legitimacy concerns surrounding international investment law and contribute to further comprehensive reform of IIAs, including harmonization of substantive investment rules. In other words, the reform of ISDS toward MIDR is desirable as much as it is feasible, even though it might not kill all birds with one stone.

The ideal ISDS system is probably situated somewhere between a purely public court system and private commercial arbitration. However, the design of such an ideal ISDS system will be a work of art, and the evaluation of its desirability is nevertheless a subjective process. The EU's ICS proposal is a bold move and represents the choice of the European people. But in some eyes, the ICS proposal may go too far in the public direction, depriving the disputing party of all its autonomy and destroying the foundation of the whole system's efficiency. I will be quite satisfied if this chapter provided another possibility and contributed to the current search for a balanced ISDS system.

The rest of the chapter proceeds in six parts. Part I explores the hybrid nature of the ISDS system and develops the public-private debate in an operational legitimacy–efficiency balance framework. Part II restates the depoliticized emergence, efficiency-driven rise and legitimacy-led fall of the ISDS system. Part III proposes the establishment of an MIDR to

---

[5] Hidelang & Krajewski (n 2) 4.
[6] C. Olivet and P. Eberhardt, *Profiting from Injustice: How Law Firms, Arbitrators and Financiers Are Fuelling an Investment Arbitration Boom* (Transnational Institute 2012). T. McDonagh, *Unfair, Unsustainable and Under the Radar – How Corporations Use Global Investment Rules to Undermine a Sustainable Future* (The Democracy Center 2013).

respond to the legitimate efficiency design of a future ISDS system. Part IV focuses on the internal balance (desirability) of such a multilateral system to manage public legitimacy and refine private efficiency. Part V explores the external balance (feasibility) of a multilateral system to consider the key processes and key players. Part VI offers a brief conclusion.

7.1   Hybrid Nature of the ISDS System

Investment arbitration is a hybrid system adjudicating public law issues on the blueprint of commercial arbitration.[7] As stated by Thomas Walde in his Separate Opinion in *International Thunderbird Gaming Corporation* v. *Mexico*, "investment arbitration is in substance a special form of international quasi-judicial review of governmental conduct using as a default methods of commercial arbitration."[8]

The hybrid origins[9] of ISDS imply the inherent public and private dimensions of investment arbitration. The public-private debate[10] anchors on the balance of state and investor interests. The public side requires dispute settlement to exhibit certain characteristics of public law, that is, the element of legitimacy, while the private side requires that the resolution of an investment dispute should be final and affordable, that is, the element of efficiency. Therefore, the public-private debate[11]

---

[7] C. Brown, "Procedure in Investment Treaty Arbitration and the Relevance of Comparative Public Law" in Stephan W. Schill (ed.), *International Investment Law and Comparative Public Law* (Oxford University Press 2010) 659.

[8] *International Thunderbird Gaming Corp.* v. *Mexico*, UNCITRAL/NAFTA, Award, January 26, 2006, Separate Opinion of Thomas Walde, para. 129.

[9] Z. Douglas, "The Hybrid Foundations of Investment Treaty Arbitration" (2003) 74 *British Yearbook of International Law* 151. G. Sacerdoti, "Bilateral Investment Treaties and Multilateral Instruments on Investment Protection" (1997) 269 *Recueil des Courts* 251.

[10] Wenhua Shan, "From North-South Divide to Private-Public Debate: Revival of the Calvo Doctrine and the Changing Landscape in International Investment Law" (2007) 27 *Northwest Journal of International Law and Business* 631–64. Professor Shan points out that primary tension underlying IIAs shifted from strong states versus weak states, that is, the North–South divide, towards state sovereignty versus corporate sovereignty, that is, the private-public debate, and there should be a better chance to strike a sensible global deal on the protection, supervision, promotion and regulation of international investment for the general good of the world.

[11] Some scholars acknowledge the public-private dualities of international investment law but use the term in different meanings. For example, Alex Mills uses the term "public" to refer to the international community as a whole and the term "private" to quasicontractual arrangements between particular states or between states and investors. A. Mills, "The Public-Private Dualities of International Investment Law and Arbitration" in

could be further specified as the legitimacy–efficiency balance in terms of the design of an investment dispute settlement mechanism (IDSM).[12]

The legitimacy–efficiency balance[13] framework is compatible with other standards of evaluating ISDS reform. To date, most proposals emphasize the importance of public law characteristics. For example, five nonexclusive criteria have been summarized by Gus Van Harten to evaluate proposals for ISDS reform: fairness, independence, openness, balance and subsidiarity.[14]

Legitimacy and efficiency are among the most important characteristics of dispute settlement. As two distinct dimensions, legitimacy and efficiency might be mutually reinforcing, as a more efficient court might be perceived as legitimate by stakeholders.[15] However, legitimacy management and efficiency refinement measures might sometimes operate in a mutually undermining manner, as some legitimacy management measures would inevitably slow down the process of dispute resolution and vice versa.[16]

Legitimacy–efficiency balance implies an IDSM should lie at the right point between a public court and a private arbitration. Existing proposals primarily focus on the public law dimension, which is the right direction, but the private efficiency of ISDS as a dispute settlement mechanism should not be underestimated, if not overlooked already.

C. Brown & K. Miles (eds.), *Evolution in Investment Treaty Law and Arbitration* (Cambridge University Press 2011) 99.

[12] Y. Shany, "Stronger Together? Legitimacy and Effectiveness of International Courts as Mutually Reinforcing or Undermining Notions" in N. Grossman, H. G. Cohen, A. Follesdal & G. Ulfstein (eds.), *Legitimacy and International Courts* (CUP and Pluricourts 2016).

[13] The intertwined relation between legitimacy and effectiveness of the ISDS system has been acknowledged by some scholars. P. Sands, "Conflict and Conflicts in Investment Treaty Arbitration: Ethical Standards for Counsel" in Brown & Miles (n 11) 20.

[14] G. V. Harten, "Reforming the System of International Investment Dispute Settlement" in C. L. Lim (ed.), *Alternative Visions of the International Law on Foreign Investment* (Cambridge University Press 2016) 103–30, 111, 115–16. A short list of criteria of independence, openness and fairness was once used by Gus Van Harten to evaluate EU and UNCTAD reform agendas. See Gus Van Harten, "The EC and UNCTAD Reform Agendas: Do They Ensure Independence, Openness, and Fairness in Investment Treaty Arbitration?" in Hindelang and Krajewski (n 2).

[15] R. Vernon, "The Multilateral Enterprise: Power versus Sovereignty" (1971) 49 *Foreign Affairs* 736. B. S. Shimni, "The Past, Present and Future of International Law: A Critical Third World Approach" (2007) 8 *Michigan Journal of International Law* 499. Alvarez (n 1) 208.

[16] Shany (n 12) 1.

The dichotomy of legitimacy versus efficiency would be a powerful prism though which we could understand the tensions underlying the design and operation of the ISDS system stemming from its hybrid nature, and hopefully sheds light on the design of the next generation of the ISDS system. It should be emphasized that the legitimacy–efficiency distinction does not intend to imply that the concepts are, or can ever be, entirely distinguishable, and certainly not that such a distinction can be made objectively or without normative implications. The problematic character of public-private distinctions is well documented.[17] However, the legitimacy–efficiency balance stemming from the public-private debate is still a useful device for the current purpose of evaluating a new framework for a Permanent Court of Investment Arbitration, because it offers a method for characterizing and comparing competing perspectives.

7.2 Evolution of the ISDS System

The logics of legitimacy and efficiency are intertwined in the evolution of the ISDS system. At the early stage of development they operated in a mutually reinforcing manner, as a vibrant and strong ISDS system contributed to acceptance and proliferation among states. However, with the explosion of caseloads, the legitimacy of the entire ISDS system has attracted growing attention at both national and international levels. The tension between legitimacy and efficiency has become very evident. Efficient operation resulted in an irrational expansion of jurisdiction, which undermined the legitimacy of the whole system and has been followed by some states' denouncement of the ICSID Convention.[18]

7.2.1 Rise and Fall of ISDS: Driving Logic and Changing Contexts

7.2.1.1 Emergence

Functionally, at its emergence the ISDS was driven by the efficiency logic as a neutral, depoliticized and international settlement mechanism for investment disputes.

IIAs were designed to deal with a particular perceived problem: the salient fact that private investors have maximum leverage with respect to a host state only before deciding whether to invest, but that once they do

---

[17] Mills (n 11) 98.
[18] For example, Bolivia (2007), Ecuador (2009) and Venezuela (2012).

so, the investment becomes subject to an obsolescing bargain.[19] Once an investor has sunk capital into the host state, the host state gains enormous leverage over the investment, which is subject to the host state's regulatory or even expropriatory measures, and there is frequently little that an investor can do about it.[20] Therefore, an IIA affords "an instrument of control over abusive changes of national law by the host state."[21] As Thomas Walde put it, IIAs seek:

> to balance this pre-existing and inherent structural asymmetry in which foreign investors find themselves: to compensate them for exposure to the host State as contract party, regulator, sovereign and judge by having a forum for disputes that is not controlled by the host State. The apparent asymmetry of investment treaties is thus nothing but the reverse mirror image of investor exposure to host State adjudication.[22]

The whole premise of the investment regime had been, after all, that host states' national laws and national courts granted insufficient protections, and that both international guarantees and neutral third-party arbitrators were needed to protect those who had put millions of dollars in sunk costs at risk.[23] The United States' bilateral investment treaties (BITs), as well as those of leading European states with comparable BIT programs, were in these early years highly asymmetrical agreements. These asymmetries were intentional. The United States, like its European allies that had established BIT programs decades before, sought BITs only with least developing countries because these were the states that had caused the most problems to their investors for decades.[24]

The ICSID was designed to provide a neutral forum for the settlement of investment disputes[25] with the desired consequence of creating "an atmosphere of mutual confidence and thus stimulating a larger flow of private international capital into those countries which wish to attract it."[26]

---

[19] R. Vernon, *Sovereignty at Bay: The Multinational Spread of US Enterprise* (Basic Books 1971) 46.

[20] Alvarez (n 1) 277–78.

[21] T. Walde, "The Specific Nature of Investment Arbitration" in P. Kahn & T. Walde (eds.), *New Aspects of International Investment Law* (Martinus Nijhoff 2007) 55.

[22] Ibid.

[23] Alvarez (n 1) 438.

[24] Alvarez (n 1) 268.

[25] I. F. I. Shihata, *Towards a Greater De-politicization of Investment Disputes: The Roles of ICSID and MIGA* (ICSID 1993). A. Newcombe and L. Paradell, *Law and Practice of Investment Treatments: Standards of Treatment* (Kluwer Law International 2007) 27.

[26] Report of the Executive Directors of the International Bank for Reconstruction and Development on the Convention of the Settlement of Investment Disputes Between

Following the logic of depoliticization, ISDS emerged as a fast resolution mechanism of investment dispute. "Governments were enticed to become parties to ICISD Convention by its assurance that once ICSID jurisdiction was triggered, contacting states would be precluded from resorting to diplomatic espousal.[27] ICSID parties would no longer bear the brunt of angry and usually powerful home states of transnational corporations. ICSID arbitration promised the end of gunboat diplomacy and intended to enforce the rights of aliens."[28] As phrased by Ibrahim Shihata, the ICSID provides "a forum for conflict resolution in a framework that carefully balances the interests and requirements of all the parties involved, and attempts in particular to depoliticize the settlement of investment disputes."[29] "The investor's government inevitably would treat the resolution of the dispute as one factor in its overall political relationship with the host-home government. Claims, in other words, would be resolved only if it was politically expedient to do so. Providing a mechanism whereby claims could be submitted to binding arbitration without the involvement of the investor's own government depoliticized the dispute."[30]

However, depoliticization might just shift "the blame for the result from the political branches to the legal system." The benefits of IIAs are difficult to quantify, but arbitral awards adverse to the host state readily quantify at least some of their cost.[31] And arbitrators face the inherent conflicts all the time: on the one hand, they have to decide the case at hand in accordance with the precise terms used in the treaty before them (as is required by the ordinary rules of treaty interpretation that stress the singular importance of plain meaning);[32] on the other hand, they have to render the consistent or harmonious interpretations of international investment law that many assume are needed to best protect the stable and settled expectations of both investors and host states.[33]

States and Nationals of Other States, 1 ICSID Rep. 23 (Report of the Executive Directors on the Convention).

[27] ICSID Convention, Art. 27.

[28] Alvarez (n 1) 224–25.

[29] I. F. I. Shihata, "Towards a Greater De-politicization of Investment Disputes" (1986) 1 *ICSID Review* 1. I. F. I. Shihata became the Secretary General of the ICSID in 1983.

[30] K. J. Vandevelde, *Bilateral Investment Treaties: History, Policy and Interpretations* (Oxford University Press 2010) 432.

[31] Ibid.

[32] VCLT, Art. 31(1)(a).

[33] Alvarez (n 1) 217–18.

7.2.1.2   Proliferation

ISDS clauses did not become standard provisions in IIAs until the 1970s,[34] and peaked in terms of proliferation in the 1990s. The importance of investment protection to economic development was widely recognized during the 1990s, as was the ISDS system for investment protection. The investment regime is among the few international regimes in which states have implicitly delegated some of their regulatory authority to third parties that are not within their exclusive control.[35] Both the substance and procedure of the investment regime for interpretation and enforcement are structurally biased in favor of the ideology of the free market and privatization, elements associated with the Washington Consensus.[36] According to mainstream development thinkers of the time, all societies, rich or poor, needed to maximize their economic performance by enabling market players to transact with each other, nationally and internationally.[37]

It is easy to see the initiation of the US IIA programme in the mid-1980s and the explosion in the ratifications of IIAs after 1989 as a perfect storm inspired by the victory of the capitalist west over what was then its only rival, namely, the planned economies of socialist and communist regimes.[38] What US negotiators saw as a minimal commitment to liberal, free market principles was, in retrospect, a politically loaded treaty obligation that reflected the then-reigning Washington Consensus among US government departments, aid agencies and international financial institutions.[39]

The functional orientation of IIAs is changing from investment protection tool to "instruments of globalization, removing barriers to trade and investment, much in the same way that the FCNs of the eighteenth and nineteenth centuries sought to establish commercial relations between countries."[40] The initial expansion of ISDS did not yield substantial disadvantages because of the moderate caseload of the time.

---

[34] J. Pohl, K. Mashigo & A. Nohen, "Dispute Settlement Provisions in International Investment Agreements: A Large Sample Survey" (2012) 2 *OECD Working Papers on International Investment* 11.

[35] Alvarez (n 1) 211.

[36] Alvarez (n 1) 256.

[37] See, for example, D. Kennedy, "The Rule of Law Political Choices and Development Common Sense" in D. M. Trubek & A. Santos (eds.), *The New Law and Economic Development* (Cambridge University Press 2006) 129.

[38] Alvarez (n 1) 273.

[39] D. Rodrik, "Growth Strategies" in P. Aghion & D. Steven (eds.), *Handbook of Economic Growth* (Elsevier 2004).

[40] Vandevelde (n 30) 69.

7.2.1.3   Overexpansion

FDI projects are embedded in host states, and may bear unintended effects on other stakeholders beyond foreign investors.[41] "The permanent presence of a foreign controlled enterprise produces far more sociological, economic and cultural consequences for the home state of the enterprise and particularly for the host state in which that foreign enterprise is located. These effects can be positive or negative or in all likelihood both, but they are hard to ignore."[42] "Most countries are drawn into a web of economic interdependence and resulting cycles of boom and bust from which few can escape."[43]

The negative effects of FDI are increasingly manifested with the expansion of the ISDS system beyond the intended legal disputes into regulatory disputes. In discussions over the Draft ICSID Convention, the ICSID was (and still is) intended to cover investment disputes of a legal character:

> The phrase in question was the result of compromise between two positions, the first being that the reference need only be to investment disputes, and the second that there should be a precise definition of an investment dispute. The danger had been envisaged that a party might attempt to bring before the center disputes of a purely commercial or political nature. The words of a legal character were intended to cover cases involving a difference of view as to a legal right. That would exclude such cases as those, for example, of a company wishing to raise objections to a price control system, which involved question of fairness and not of legal right. It was perhaps advisable to make it clear that if no legal right were involved, the facilities of the Center would not be available. In that connection he referred to Article 36 of the Statute of the International Court of Justice[44] which defined legal disputes.[45]

Naturally, Article 25(1) of the final ICSID Convention reads: "The jurisdiction of the Centre shall extend to any legal dispute arising directly

---

[41] This is essentially the definition of foreign investment adopted by the OECD and IMF. See L. Sachs & K. P. Sauvant (eds.), *The Effect of Treaties on Foreign Direct Investment: Bilateral Investment Treaties, Double Taxation Treaties, and Investment Flows* (OUP 2009) xxxiii.

[42] Alvarez (n 1) 206.

[43] P. Muchlinski, "Policy Issues" in P. Muchlinski (ed.), *Oxford Handbook of International Investment Law* (OUP 2008) 11–12.

[44] Statute of the International Court of Justice, Art. 36.

[45] First Preliminary Draft of Convention on the Settlement of Investment Disputes between States and Nationals of Other States, Annotated Text, August 9, 1963, Introductory Note, History of ICSID vol. II-1, 328.

out of an investment."[46] Therefore, it is seemingly safe to conclude that the ICSID and other ISDS tribunals should confine themselves to legal disputes arising out of investments, and a regulatory dispute of a general policy character is not within the original scope of the ICSID Centre's jurisdiction.

However, the ISDS system has outgrown its origins.[47] Because of its success, some actors, especially investors, push ISDS to tackle issues beyond investment protection. And some tribunals have ventured beyond its advantageous zone of economic dispute,[48] and therefore magnified the inherent deficit of public legitimacy. Under the current ISDS system, it is hard, if not impossible, to distinguish and delineate protection against regulatory risk from the ordinary commercial risk of an adjustment of the regulatory environment in the host state, the latter to be borne by the investor.[49] The growing awareness of the general public in domestic discourse further fuels the legitimacy crisis of the ISDS and IIA system as a whole. The high-profile cases against industrialized countries such as *Vattenfall v. Germany*,[50] *Ping An v. Kingdom of Belgium*[51] or *Eli Lilly and Company v. Canada*[52] have led to some noticeable public opposition to ISDS.[53]

It is now generally recognized that "investment treaty arbitration involves not only the review of decisions that affect the claimant in a specific and discrete way. It extends to polycentric legislative, judicial, and executive decisions and often engages matters of general significance."[54] As has also been stated:

---

[46] ICSID Convention, Art. 25(1).

[47] Alvarez (n 1) 503.

[48] Alvarez (n 1) 228. For a review of some controversial cases, see J. E. Alvarez & K. Khamsi, "The Argentine Crisis and Foreign Investors" in K. P. Sauvant (ed.), *Yearbook of International Investment Law & Policy 2008–2009* (OUP 2009) 379.

[49] J. E. Vinuales, "The Environmental Regulation of Foreign Investment Schemes under International Law" in P. M. Dupuy & J. E. Vinuales (eds.), *Harnessing Foreign Investment to Promote Environmental Protection: Incentives and Safeguards* (Cambridge University Press 2013) 273–320.

[50] *Vattenfall AB and others v. Federal Republic of Germany*, ICSID Case No. Arb/12/12.

[51] *Ping An Life Insurance Company of China, Limited and Ping An Insurance (Group) Company of China, Limited v. Kingdom of Belgium*, ICSID Case No. ARB/12/29.

[52] *Eli Lilly and Company v. The Government of Canada*, UNCITRAL, ICSID Case No. UNCT/14/2.

[53] Hidelang & Krajewski (n 2) 2.

[54] G. V. Harten, "Investment Treaty Arbitration, Procedure Fairness, and the Rule of Law" in S. W. Schill (ed.), *International Investment Law and Comparative Law* (Oxford University Press 2010) 637.

No longer limited to merely technical questions, contemporary investment arbitrations frequently implicate general issues regarding the scope of the regulatory powers of the respondent states that reach well beyond traditional simple expropriations and nationalization. Instead, a much broader variety of regulatory as well as public-goods-providing contexts has come to be addressed through investment arbitration, ranging from the provision of basic public service, such as water and sanitation, to the maintenance of public order.[55]

Yet, unfortunately, some tribunals have still failed to "avoid intervening in matters that are appropriately left to decision-makers which are more representative, more expert, or otherwise more able than the courts."[56]

7.2.2 Surge against ISDS: Manifested Demand of Legitimacy

The regulation of FDI might cause economic, political and security concerns among the general public. For example, transnational enterprises will put local enterprises out of business, violate local laws or cultural norms, and control and compromise access to technology essentially for national security. For these reasons, FDI and its protection mechanisms, including ISDS, are often the first target of reform-minded new governments,[57] especially in times of economic downturn.[58] The ISDS practice is criticized in many aspects: for a lack of coherence and consistency, for a lack of transparency, for a lack of respect towards democratically elected governments implementing policies in the public interest,[59] and last but not least, for having created an oligopolistic dispute resolution industry.[60]

7.2.2.1 Procedural Defects

Democratic Deficit: Private Arbitration of Public Issues International arbitration is a fundamentally inapposite mechanism for deciding

---

[55] W. White & A. Staden, "The Need for Public Law Standards of Review in Investor-State Arbitration" in S. W. Schill (ed.), *International Investment Law and Comparative Public Law* (Oxford University Press 2010) 689.

[56] Harten (n 54) 639.

[57] Alvarez (n 1) 210.

[58] Alvarez (n 1) 246. The investment regime's legitimacy deficits can be characterized as vertical, horizontal, ideological and legal.

[59] S. Hindelang, "Study on Investment-State Dispute Settlement" in J. A. CanDuzer, P. Simons & G. Mayeda (eds.), *Integrating Sustainable Development into International Investment Agreements: A Guide for Developing Countries, Prepared for the Commonwealth Secretariat* (IISD August 2012).

[60] Sergio Puig, "Social Capital in the Arbitration Market" (2014) 25 *European Journal of International Law* 387–424.

weighty issues of public policy.[61] Composed of three arbitrators selected by the disputing parties, ISDS tribunals make final and binding decisions in secret and perhaps in parallel forums[62] on regulatory issues rather than purely commercial issues in the host state.[63] Public interest issues are usually regulated through democratic process by domestic authorities. And ISDS tribunals lack the democratic authority to address public interest issues.[64]

Legitimacy Deficit: Institutional and Perceived Bias of Arbitrators   The disputing parties are entitled to appoint the arbitrating tribunal. Institutionally, ISDS tribunals are inclined to arbitrate in favor of claimants who hold the triggers to initiate the process, and those actors "wield power over appointing authorities or the system as a whole."[65] In other words, ISDS arbitrators are institutionally biased in favor of investor claimants and perhaps the more powerful states as well.[66] In this sense, it does not matter whether an individual arbitrator is actually biased or not in a particular arbitration proceedings. The bias toward protecting investors' economic interests vis-à-vis host states is reinforced by the small group of dominant adjudicators in ISDS arbitration.[67] Such suspicions fuel speculation about why the United States, the ISDS defendant with the third-highest number of cases, has managed not to lose a single claim against it.[68]

[61] G. V. Harten, *Investment Treaty Arbitration and Public Law* (Oxford University Press 2007). S. Sassen, "De-Nationalized State Agendas and Privatized Norm-Making" in K. Ladeur (ed.), *Public Governance in the Age of Globalization* (Ashgate Publishing 2004).
[62] Alvarez (n 1) 256–59.
[63] W. White and A. Staden, "Private Litigation in a Public Law Sphere: The Standard of Review in Investor-State Arbitration" (2010) 35 *Yale Journal of International Law* 314–22.
[64] A. Chander, "Globalization and Distrust" (2005) 114 *Yale Law Journal* 1193.
[65] Harten (n 54) 627.
[66] That's why some scholars argue that the investment regime violates the principle of sovereign equality, despite that the regime was premised on putting all states on a "level playing field," at least as compared to the bad old days of gunboat diplomacy. Alvarez (n 1) 253–56. At a time when the investment regime is approaching universal participation, and with a considerable portion of capital flows going into wealthy western states while some emerging nations are coming into their own as capital exporters, the proliferation of investment treaties cannot be explained simply as variations of the one-sided capitulation agreements once concluded between colonial powers and the periphery. This is not to deny that some bilateral relationships concerning capital flows or some BITs may indeed be forms of neocolonialism. J. T. Gathii, "Foreign and Other Economic Rights upon Conquest and under Occupation: Iraq in Comparative and Historical Context" (2004) 25 *University of Pennsylvania Journal of International Economic Law* 491.
[67] Puig (n 60).
[68] Statement of Robert K. Stumberg, Professor of Law and Director of the Harrison Institute for Public Law, Georgetown University Law Center, in US House of Representatives,

7.2.2.2   Substantive Defects

Lack of Consistency   The large amount of inconsistent awards a in time of economic crisis fuels the movement against globalization, including against the liberal investment regime.[69] This is a natural consequence of an efficiency-oriented ad hoc arbitration system without a review mechanism. Meanwhile, the divergent backgrounds of arbitrators contribute to different and sometime even conflicting interpretations of core substantive and procedure issues. This output inconsistency undermines trust, and therefore the legitimacy of the ISDS system as a whole.[70]

Overexpansion of Jurisdiction   The trespass of ISDS into regulatory relations undermines the consent foundation of states to the whole system, as some states might consider the tribunals lack jurisdiction in the first place.[71] "The intrusive nature of many of these claims involving challenges to environmental regulations, to the way states conduct administrative proceedings at all levels of government, or to national measures taken to handle a financial crisis, is exacerbated by the unpredictability of the resulting awards."[72]

7.2.3   Various Proposals on ISDS

Despite the irrational reactions to globalization in general and rational revaluation of ISDS regime in particular, the current regime of international investment law is increasingly contested:[73] on one end of the

---

Committee on Ways and Means, Subcommittee on Trade, Hearing on Investment Protections in US Trade and Investment Agreements, Serial No.111-20, May 14, 2009, 40.

[69] According to Kenneth J. Vandevelde, the reaction against globalization in the 1990s partly resulted from the occurrence of financial crises. The openness of capital accounts was believed by some scholars to be the cause of these crises, and these perceptions resulted in questioning of the access principle. Vandevelde (n 30) 70–71.

[70] Alvarez (n 1) 259. A. Bjorklund, "Investment Treaty Arbitral Decisions As Jurisprudence Constante" in C. Picker et al. (eds.), *International Economic Law: The State and Future of the Discipline* (Hart Publishing 2008) 265.

[71] Vandevelde (n 30) 432 ("In time, the investor-state arbitral process may place more weight on the BIT system than it can bear and some states may look for ways to shrink their BIT programs, if not to abolish them entirely, or at least to diminish or eliminate resort to investor-state arbitration.")

[72] Alvarez (n 1) 233. White & Staden (n 55) 692 (holding that some ISDS arbitration "invalidate[s] exercises of regulatory power and, in extreme cases, may affect the fundamental rights of citizens within the state," and "may even transcend the public regulatory or administrative context and enter a quasi-constitutional realm.")

[73] Hidelang & Krajewski (n 2) 3.

Table 7.1 *Proposals for changes to the ISDS mechanism*

Prearbitration	Process of Arbitration	Postarbitration
Institutionalized bodies, e.g., ICS	Greater transparency	Joint interpretation
Changing the appointing authority for arbitrators	Narrow scope of claims	Expand the ability of annulment committee to overrule
Dismiss frivolous claims	Narrow discretion of arbitrators	Appellate process
More detailed substantive rules	Third-party participation	
Qualifications of arbitrators	Consolidate related claims	
Joint determination	Legal assistance to arbitrators	
	Code of conduct	

spectrum, some parties have proposed aggressive if not radical reform plans, such as the European Union and India; on the other end, some countries have not renewed or have even terminated existing BITs, such as South Africa, Indonesia and Ecuador;[74] between these two ends are some countries choosing to maintain the status quo or embark on minor reforms, such as the United States.

Recent developments highlight the policy consensus on a balanced ISDS system among scholars and international policymakers.[75] Such an approach is warranted as the EU (e.g., ICS proposals) and other major players (US 2012 Model BIT) are turning international investment law from a special regime predominantly aimed at countries with weak domestic rule of law into a more general and comprehensive

---

[74] S. Clarkson and S. Hindelang, "How Parallel Lines Intersect: Investor-State Dispute Settlement and Regional Social Policy" in A. C. Bianculli and A. R. Hoffmann (eds.), *Regional Organizations and Social Policy in Europe and Latin America: A Space for Social Citizenship* (Palgrave 2015) 25–45.

[75] UNCTAD, *Investment Policy Framework for Sustainable Development* (United Nations 2012). OECD, Improving the System of Investor-State Dispute Settlement: An Overview, Working Papers on International Investment No. 2006/1 (2006). J. A. Vanduzer, P. Simons & G. Mayeda (eds.), *Integrating Sustainable Development into International Investment Agreements: A Commonwealth Guide for Developing Country Negotiators* (Commonwealth Secretariat 2013).

system[76] of controlling and reviewing the exercise of governmental powers, balancing the private property rights of investors and public policy of host states, irrespective of the level of development of the domestic rule of law.

7.3   Desirability of a Balanced MIDR

7.3.1   Function and Malfunction of ISDS

Proposing a framework for evaluating the function and utility of ISDS is not an easy task. The costs and benefits of ISDS may vary across states and issues.[77]

7.3.1.1   Investment Protection

As the direct goal, investment protection lies at the core of the ISDS system. Protection of investments and investors' rights in arbitration is self-evident, if not overemphasized. If evaluated from this perspective the ISDS system remains a strong and efficient mechanism compared to the alternatives.

In terms of investment protection function, ISDS is necessary and justifiable. However, it requires ISDS to balance investment protection and other (competing) legitimate public interests in an appropriate manner.[78] This balancing process – or some may say the insufficiency or even lack thereof – is at the heart of much critique on the basic orientation of the current investment law regime.[79]

7.3.1.2   Investment Promotion

In terms of empirical evidence, impacts of ISDS on investment promotion are inconclusive. For some states, promotion of FDI is not even the explicit goal of IIAs. The US negotiators from its early period in the 1980s confirmed that this omission of promotion provisions was not inadvertent: the US government resisted investment promotion provisions as

---

[76] Hidelang & Krajewski (n 2) 5.

[77] L. G. Skovgaard Poulsen, J. Bonnitcha & J. W. Yackee, *Analytical Framework for Assessing Costs and Benefits of Investment Protection Treaties* (LSE Enterprise 2013).

[78] J. Zhan, "Investment Policies for Sustainable Development: Addressing Policy Challenges in a New Investment Landscape" in R. Echandi & P. Suave (eds.), *Prospects in International Investment Law and Policy* (Cambridge University Press 2013) 13, 22–24.

[79] Hidelang & Krajewski (n 2) 5.

a matter of policy.[80] Politically, IIAs with the effect of outsourcing of jobs are a hard sell in domestic politics.[81] Ideologically, the United States viewed IIAs as market facilitative devices, not tools to encourage government interference in the market.[82]

An IIA is a necessary rather than sufficient condition for inducement of FDI. After all, the flow of FDI follows the logic of expected profitable returns on investment. An IIA was and maybe still is considered as a signal[83] of the "bare first step in establishing a liberal investment regime along these lines but one which would not in and of itself guarantee an increase in FDI flows."[84] Concluding IIAs, after all, did not ensure that a country would be attractive to a foreign investor seeking particular natural resources, a labor pool with certain skills or a huge new consumer market for its goods. Nor did the conclusion ensure that the domestic rule of law was fully in place.

The primary, if not sole, function of ISDS is to provide a few non-onerous and uncontroversial investment protection mechanisms[85] and fast resolution of associated disputes. For example, the United States saw its new treaty as a limited tool that would provide only limited guarantees with respect to public authorities' interference in investors' rights. Further, the IIAs would ensure access to international arbitration only with respect to certain treaty disputes between foreign investors and host states, and would not frustrate a broad range of government actions, from those designed to protect nascent industries to tax incentives to particular investors, any of which may admittedly be ineffective, costly or counterproductive.[86]

---

[80] K. J. Vandevelde, "Of Politics and Markets: The Shifting Ideology of the BITs" (1993) 11 *International Tax & Business Lawyer* 159, 162.

[81] Alvarez (n 1) 264.

[82] K. J. Vandevelde, "The BIT Program: A Fifteen-Year Appraisal" (1992) 86 *ASIL Proceedings* 532, 535.

[83] K. J. Vandevelde, *United States Investment Treaties: Policy and Practice* (Kluwer Law and Taxation, 1992) 1–43. US BIT negotiators adopted a highly ideological and relatively inflexible bargaining position and considered BIT as an essential building block for nations that were intent on building free market economies based on rule of law. The United States argued that signing a US BIT would send a signal that a country had accepted the basic premises of liberal economic theory, namely that free markets, consistent with the insights of David Ricardo, would yield the most efficient use of resources and the greatest productivity.

[84] K. J. Vandevelde, "Investment Liberalization and Economic Development: The Role of Bilateral Investment Treaties" (1998) 36 *Columbia Journal of International Law* 501, 522–25.

[85] Alvarez (n 1) 272.

[86] Alvarez (n 1) 272.

7.3.1.3   Sustainable Development

Investment regulation is also at the heart of the contentious question about the meaning of rule of law and whether its promotion is a necessary component of modernization.[87] Some might argue that one of the main purposes of modern investment law is to promote the sustainable development of contracting states,[88] even though a potential contribution to such goals might be not automatic.[89] Contribution to sustainable development[90] might be seen as the ultimate goal of the investment law regime as a whole, either by investment promotion[91] or institutional improvement.[92]

However, the direct effects of ISDS on sustainable development are mixed and inconclusive. On the one hand, the positive effect, or direct contribution, of ISDS to sustainable development in host states should not be overestimated. First, the promotion effect of ISDS is inconclusive, although there seems to be a widespread political consensus that foreign investment is one of the key elements in furthering the development of

---

[87] World Bank, *World Development Report 2005: A Better Investment Climate for Everyone* (World Bank and Oxford University Press 2004) (identifying the rule of law as a key component of good governance and contending that investment treaties are part of it). Alvarez (n 1) 490.

[88] T. W. Walde, "Improving the Mechanisms for Treaty Negotiation and Investment Disputes: Competition and Choice as the Path to Quality and Legitimacy" in K. P. Sauvant (ed.) *Yearbook on International Investment Law & Policy 2008–2009* (Oxford University Press 2009) 583–84.

[89] M. Orellana, "Science, Risk and Uncertainty: Public Health Measures and Investment Disciplines" in P. Kahn & T. W. Walde (n 21) 789.

[90] Which could be understood broadly in the sense of a harmonious pursuit of a diverse set of economic, environmental, cultural and social interests without attributing a priori more weight to one or the other.

[91] US post-2004 BITs reflect what David Kennedy has characterized as a newly chastened form of neoliberalism. The United States has not given up on David Ricardo or the free market (Kennedy [n 37] 150). The 2004 US Model BIT still adheres to a capitalist conception of the role of the state vis-à-vis the market and still adheres to the threefold premises of the original US BIT outlined earlier: the state will protect bargains struck by private parties, defer to the market and intervene in the market only insofar as necessary. Alvarez (n 1) 308.

[92] The object and purpose of 2004 Model is less about the investor and more about the rule of law itself (Alvarez [n 1] 309). It emphasizes the need to establish stable rules of the road to guide both the investor and the state. It appears to presume that building the rule of law itself is the "essence of good governance, itself a pre-condition for long-term economic, social and civil development and an objective shared by host and parent state alike." T. Walde, "The Present State of Research Carried Out by the English-Speaking Section of the Centre for Studies and Research" in P. Kahn & T. Walde (n 21) 106–07, 113. Kennedy (n 37) 157.

states,[93] their economies and societies.[94] Second, ISDS might be not a perfect venue for reasons of public interest balance, and certainly not an ideal substitute or improvement for undeveloped local institutions.[95] On the other hand, ISDS might impose undue restrictions on regulatory measures of host states that otherwise ought to be the first best for maximization of local interests in host states. Differently put, ISDS curtails or even frustrates the sustainable development of host states. At the extreme, IIAs are depicted as hegemonic instruments, straitjackets preventing host states from taking much-needed measures.[96]

If we evaluate the efficiency of the ISDS system from a direct-goal approach, the ISDS system continues to function well. However, from an ultimate-goal perspective, the ISDS system is clearly in need of improvement. If viewed from a functional perspective, ISDS is still a desirable mechanism. Although the overall effect of ISDS on investment promotion and sustainable development remains inconclusive, the ISDS system has done a quite good job with investment protection, despite its defects and criticism leveled against it. If we consider that protection of investment is still the direct goal of ISDS, while contribution to sustainable development is the ultimate goal, the "imperfect but heavily used" ISDS system should be reformed from an efficiency-driven process into a legitimate-efficiency-driven process rather than replaced in its entirety.[97]

---

[93] Hidelang & Krajewski (n 2) 7.
[94] A. Newcombe, "Sustainable Development and Investment Treaty Law" (2008) 8 *Journal of World Investment and Trade* 357. United Nations, Monterrey Consensus of the International Conference on Financing for Development, Report of the International Conference on Financing for Development, Monterrey, Mexico, March 18–2, 2002 UN Doc. A/CONE. 198/11, chapter 1, resolution 1, annex (United Nations 2003). However, controversy has long existed around the question of precisely which qualities an investment should exhibit in order to fulfill its function without compromising competing public interests.
[95] Tom Ginsburg, "International Substitute for Domestic Institutions: Bilateral Investment Treaties and Governance" (2005) 25 *International Review of Law and Economics* 107–23.
[96] A. T. Guzman, "Why LDCs Sign Treaties that Hurt Them: Explaining the Popularity of BITs" (1998) 38 *Va JIL* 639. E. Benvinisti & G. W. Downs, "The Empire's New Clothes: Political Economy and the Fragmentation of International Law" (2007) 60 *Stan L. Review* 595, 611–16.
[97] Walde (n 88) 506–12 (categorizing ISDS as an unmitigated success that provides a legal foundation to help the current process of global economic integration run more smoothly marred by only minor flaws). Hidelang & Krajewski (n 2) 9 (warranting a more balanced approach, shifting away from a preoccupation with protection of private property interests towards sustainable development).

7.3.2   Tensions Underlying ISDS: From Efficient Remedy to Legitimately Efficient Remedy

7.3.2.1   Public Legitimacy Management

With regard to the diverse terms used, potential sources of legitimacy include[98] consent legitimacy, output legitimacy, exist legitimacy, rule of law legitimacy[99] and institution-building legitimacy. The above sources could be grouped into three main categories of legitimacy: the source of legal power, the process of exercising such legal power and the overall outcome produced.[100]

As a dispute settlement mechanism, the ISDS system should employ an independent and impartial process. In this sense, party autonomy in the resolution process should be maintained and perhaps refined. Therefore, legitimacy management should focus mainly on the *ex ante* and *ex post* process of investment dispute resolution, namely input legitimacy and output legitimacy.

Input Legitimacy: Appointment of Arbitrator and Public Code of Conduct To enhance democratic legitimacy, arbitrators adjudicating public law issues in investment arbitration should secure the consent of both disputing parties, namely the foreign investor and the host state, and all contracting states to the underlying treaty.[101] Therefore, the appointment procedure in arbitration should be redesigned to encompass the consent of both the disputing parties and contracting states. A state's appointed prearbitrator pool supplemented by the subsequent appointment by the disputing parties of specific tribunals seems to be the solution. Such an appointment mechanism would also serve to ameliorate the institutional and perceived bias of arbitrators. For the protection of all stakeholders affected by investment disputes, transparency of the process should be enhanced, perhaps by the participation of contracting states on behalf of the interested stakeholders.

---

[98] Santigao Montt, *State Liability in Investment Treaty Arbitration: Global Constitution and Administrative Law in the BIT Generation* (Hart Publishing 2009) 141–54.

[99] Judicial independence and procedural fairness are emphasized by Gus Van Harten (n 54) 634–42.

[100] Shany (n 12) 4.

[101] Limiting the jurisdiction of future ISDS tribunals is also helpful to recalibrate the system that has gone off-course; however, this suggestion, as well as the suggestion of concluding a MAI are more substantive rule-focused proposals, which is not the main focal point here.

Output Legitimacy: Consistency of Awards   A relatively small group of arbitrators from a state-appointed arbitrator pool could contribute to the consistent interpretation of investment rules *ex ante*, while review and annulment of awards should be available as an *ex post* internal scrutiny mechanism. Given that some different interpretations and applications could be attributed to the different wording of BITs, a detailed Multilateral Agreement on Investment (MAI) would be the ideal solution for the inconsistency puzzle.

7.3.2.2   Private Efficiency Refinement

Similar to evaluations of legitimacy, multiple approaches to the effectiveness of organizations, such as the rational system approach, open system approach and system source approach,[102] focus on different aspects of institutions respectively, that is, goals, impact, and resources and ability to sustain.[103] If we understand the goals of the ISDS system broadly, the direct goal, impacts, and capacity to sustain could converge into the direct and ultimate goal of the ISDS system.[104]

In terms of dispute settlement mechanisms, to settle a dispute in an autonomous and fast manner is always the golden standard. For the purpose of private efficiency refinement, party autonomy in a form conducive to reducing time and cost[105] would be the focus. "ISDS is no longer the speedy alternative to national court litigation that they were once touted to be."[106] Therefore, any meaningful reform proposal should carefully weigh up the possible increase of time and cost.

Party Autonomy: Disputing Parties' Rights to Appointment   Party autonomy is the cornerstone of arbitration as a neutral, independent and depoliticized dispute settlement mechanism. Procedurally, the disputing parties' appointment of tribunal members is one of the most important manifestations of party autonomy. Substantively, the

---

[102] See, for example, J. L. Price, "The Study of Organizational Effectiveness" (1972) 12 *Sociological Quarterly* 3–7. R. W. Scott & G. F. Davis, *Organizations and Organizing: Rational, Natural and Open Systems Perspectives* (Harlow 2007) 31.

[103] Yuval Shany, *Assessing the Effectiveness of International Courts* (Oxford University Press 2014).

[104] See, for example, Yuval Shany, "Assessing the Effectiveness of International Courts: A Goal-Based Approach" (2012) 106(2) *American Journal of International Law* 225–70.

[105] Resistance to many reform proposals usually stems from fears that they will make ISDS – which has already become more costly and time consuming – even more so. Alvarez (n 1) 475.

[106] Alvarez (n 1) 228.

disputing parties' right to appoint arbitrators is also arguably a prerequisite for enforcement of pertinent decisions as arbitration awards in the sense of the Convention on the Recognition and Enforcement of Foreign Arbitral Awards.[107]

Time and Cost Friendly: Limited Review As a fast resolution mechanism, the Investment DSM should offer an appeal procedure only for exceptional cases. However, in order to remedy incorrect awards within the system, a review mechanism seems necessary. As a compromise, a limited review and annulment procedure should be available. In order to minimize the cost of the resolution process as a whole, the design of the review mechanism should pay special attention to safeguards against the abuse of rights by both investors and states.

In light of the low feasibility of a comprehensive MAI, a permanent arbitral body would seem to be an ideal framework encompassing both public legitimacy and private efficiency.[108] The desirable as well as feasible combination of the aforementioned reform and refinement measures demands an institutionalized yet low-cost, moderated and controlled yet autonomous DSM with internal checks and balances, which this chapter refers to as Multilateral Investment Dispute Resolution (MIDR). Such MIDR could hopefully provide smooth settlement of investment disputes, respecting party autonomy and retaining the nature of international arbitration, as well as legitimate settlement of investment disputes, ensuring dual consent on arbitration appointment and equipping the contracting states with a controlled review and annulment procedure.

---

[107] Cf. Convention on the Recognition and Enforcement of Foreign Arbitral Awards, Article I(2): "The term 'arbitral awards' shall include not only awards made by arbitrators appointed for each case but also those made by permanent arbitral bodies to which the parties have submitted." Also, Article V(1)(b): "The party against whom the award is invoked was not given proper notice of the appointment of the arbitrator or of the arbitration proceedings or was otherwise unable to present his case."

[108] Gus Van Harten, "A Case for an International Investment Court" (June 30, 2008), Society of International Economic Law (SIEL) Inaugural Conference 2008 Paper, available at https://ssrn.com/abstract=1153424 or http://dx.doi.org/10.2139/ssrn.1153424. Gus Van Harten, "The European Commission's Push to Consolidate and Expand ISDS: An Assessment of the Proposed Canada-Europe CETA and Europe-Singapore FTA" (June 2, 2015), Osgoode Legal Studies Research Paper No. 23/2015, available at https://ssrn.com/abstract=2613544 or http://dx.doi.org/10.2139/ssrn.2613544.

7.4   Key Features of MIDR: Internal Balance

MIDR intends to balance the public legitimacy and private efficiency of investment dispute resolution. The institutional structure of MIDR should be one of internal balance between fast and fair resolution of investment disputes. Three tensions – between state and arbitrator, between investor and host state, and between state and Tribunal – need to be carefully balanced throughout the entire process of dispute resolution. These internal tensions delimit the institutional boundaries of MIDR.

7.4.1   Institutional Structure: Permanent Annulment Committee with Only One Hearing

In terms of institutional structure, MIDR is an institutionalized tribunal with only one hearing. First, the contracting states establish an investment committee under BITs or free trade agreements (FTAs) and appoint by positive consensus the chairperson and all panelists of the permanent annulment committee via the investment committee. The investment committee consists of representatives of the contracting states meeting periodically and upon special request of the contracting states. There should also be a minimum requirement for attendance (e.g., two-thirds of all contracting states) for each session. Second, the chairperson (and the vice chairperson in the absence of the chairperson) of the

Table 7.2 *The structure of MIDR*

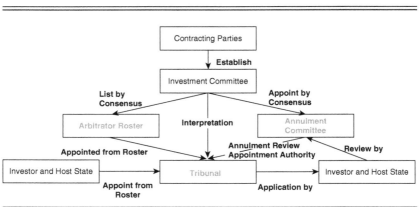

annulment committee is in charge of day-to-day operations of MIDR, with the assistance of a possible outsourcing secretariat (separately or under the auspices of the ICSID), and facilitates the establishment of a tribunal by the parties to a dispute, namely, the investor and the host state. Third, the tribunal actually hears and adjudicates the dispute with the assistance of the secretariat. There is no appellate body, and a tribunal's awards shall be final, unless reviewed and annulled by the permanent annulment committee.

An institutionalized tribunal can easily be controlled, and therefore ultimately accepted by states, while a single hearing is a cost-friendly structure. The considerations underlying a permanent yet less hierarchical structure are to strike a balance between fast and fair resolution in order to increase legitimacy while retaining the cost advantage of MIDR. Fast resolution of investment disputes is the inherent advantage of the ISDS system and should be retained in the new MIDR. Fair resolution is the emerging policy consideration. As investment disputes increasingly embed within local governance systems, the perceived legitimacy of ISDS awards at local level becomes increasingly demanding. Institutionalization provides a source of legitimacy for the ISDS system in the eyes of local stakeholders as states could retake control of the dispute resolution process. Also, a permanent annulment committee with a limited group of panelists appointed by the contracting states is arguably more likely to produce consistent awards.

Some might worry that institutionalization may entail additional costs, while one hearing may be not sufficient to produce consistency in awards. One hearing is insisted on for reasons of cost as investment arbitration should first and foremost constitute a fast resolution system. Some of the concerns are legitimate and thus the following mechanisms on arbitrator appointment, constitution of the tribunal and review of arbitral awards need to be carefully configured. These mechanisms are necessary tools for states to monitor and correct, if necessary, the ISDS system while keep the whole system running.

7.4.2 Compulsory Arbitrator Roster: State-Appointed Arbitrator Roster with Code of Conduct

The panelists of the annulment committee should be appointed by the contracting states through positive consensus of the investment committee for a fixed term of, say, six years, with the possibility of renewal. The

Table 7.3 *Selected aspects of reform proposals*

		EU ICS	US ISDS	The MIDR
Yes =				
Variant =	Limited Jurisdiction	Yes	Yes	Yes
No =	Permanent Institution	Yes	No	Yes
	Appellate Body	Yes	Variant	No
	Code of Conduct	Yes	Yes	Yes
	State-Appointed Arbitrator Pool	Yes	No	Variant
	Investor's Right to Appoint Division Member	No	Yes	Yes
	Review of Awards	Yes	Yes	Yes
	Private Enforcement of Awards	No	Yes	Yes

arbitrator roster consists of arbitrators nominated and confirmed by all contracting states, or in case of a BIT, two lists of nationals of both contracting states and a list of third-state nationals. In the case of a future multilateral system, each contracting state could nominate up to three candidates (its nationals or nationals of other states) to the roster, subject to confirmation by positive consensus of all contracting states present at a meeting of the investment committee.[109] Upon final expiry of tenure, a member should not accept new appointments from new tribunals, but could still sit as a member of already constituted tribunals before the date of expiry.[110] Arbitrators should possess high qualifications, no less than Judges of the ICJ or Members of the WTO Appellate Body, and follow a code of conduct upon appointment before, during and after any specific arbitration. The arbitrators on the roster shall be subject to restrictions on outside activities that would be incompatible with judicial independence and impartiality. The chairperson and vice chairperson should be selected by positive consensus of the investment committee from among the panelists of the annulment committee, and serve for

---

[109] As argued by Gus Van Harten, the security of tenure provides adjudicators with the legitimacy and the independence to proclaim coherent and unbiased investment law. Gus Van Harten, "A Case for an Investment Court," Society for International Economic Law, working paper no. 22/08 (2008).

[110] This is a measure aiming to maintain the effective function of MIDR tribunals in light of the relatively long duration of investment arbitration.

a term of two years. The remuneration for panelists, roster arbitrators and sitting tribunal members should be competitive.

Delineating the pool of "judges" for investment arbitration could enhance the input legitimacy of the ISDS system. First, all members of tribunals ultimately appointed by either investors or host states in a particular arbitration would be done so with the consent of all contracting states. Association of a public law background with a code of conduct would judicialize MIDR. The arbitrator roster would give *ex ante* control to states over arbitrators and could serve to strike a balance between those two groups. Second, the arbitrator roster would also be helpful to counteract the incentive for arbitrators to rule in favor of parties initiating arbitration, because their appointments ultimately depend on the dual consent of the disputing parties and all contracting states. Third, the scrutiny of states over all potential tribunal members would also serve to "support the confidence of the public and of those not represented directly in the adjudicative process but nevertheless affected by it."[111] Fourth, a relatively stable group of arbitrators could also provide greater continuity across cases involving the same or similar parties and facts, even more so with the assistance of an institutionalized secretariat.[112]

The distribution of members of the arbitrator roster could become problematic if MIDR becomes truly multilateral. First, the pool might be too small to be responsive, or might become too big to be consistently functional. Second, it would become increasingly difficult to choose the chairperson and panelists of the annulment committee as the number of member states increases.

7.4.3 Constitution of Tribunal with Dual Consent: Disputing Parties' Right to Appoint Tribunal Members

The tribunals that actually hear and adjudicate cases should be appointed by the disputing parties from the arbitrator roster agreed by the contracting states. The investor is entitled to appoint a member of the tribunal, which arguably maintains the arbitration nature of MIDR. In other words, it is the disputing parties that have the right to appoint the members of tribunal. In this case, the members of the tribunal will enjoy the consent of all contracting states in the process of compiling

---

[111] Harten (n 54) 637.
[112] Alvarez (n 1) 474.

the arbitrator roster, and that of the disputing parties in the process of selection of tribunal members.

The policy consideration for the investor's right to appoint tribunal members is to strike a balance between the investor and the host state. First, disputing parties appointing the adjudicating body is the predominate practice in international arbitration. Second, the independence of the tribunal could be guaranteed and trusted in by both disputing parties. Third, members of the tribunal appointed from the preset arbitrator roster adhere to a code of conduct and are of qualifications equivalent to those of judges of the home state. This dual consent in the selection of tribunal members could significantly increase the input legitimacy of MIDR. Forth, the investor's right to appoint is also compatible with the New York Convention[113] for purposes of enforcement of awards.

The investor's right of appointment could create some side effects. The (perceived) bias of a tribunal attributed to the investor's power to appoint is a major source of criticism regarding the legitimacy deficit. However, the investor's right in MIDR is different, as the member of the tribunal is selected from an arbitrator pool which has already been scrutinized by the contracting states on a consensus basis. Another concern is the possible delay in the constitution of the tribunal. However, this concern is twofold, as the host state's right to appoint may also cause this very delay. Nevertheless, a supplementary appointment power is vested in the annulment committee, which will appoint a member to the tribunal when the disputing parties fail to do so in time.

7.4.4   Annulment Committee's Restricted Review and Annulment of Awards

The award of the tribunal shall be final and binding on the disputing parties unless reviewed and annulled by the annulment committee upon application of either disputing party. The power to review and annul awards upon application of the disputing parties is vested in the annulment committee, which is the most powerful organ of MIDR. If the annulment committee is convinced that the tribunal erred in the inter-

---

[113] In particular, Convention on the Recognition and Enforcement of Foreign Arbitral Awards, Art. V.1(b): "The party against whom the award is invoked was not given proper notice of the appointment of the arbitrator or of the arbitration proceedings or was otherwise unable to present his case."

pretation of applicable law or failed to observe fundamental procedures, another tribunal should be constituted to rehear and issue another award on the dispute.

It should be noted that the review and annulment procedure is an extraordinary remedy for exceptional and important cases, dealing with legitimacy of process or decision rather than substantive correctives, and therefore not a routine appeal mode for the losing party.[114] The grounds for annulment stated by the annulment committee, particularly the general interpretation (rather than application in light of specific factual context) of key applicable rules, shall be binding on all subsequent tribunals.

Considerations for review and annulment are to increase the consistency of awards and enhance output legitimacy. Even a highly developed judicial system may go wrong, and the MIDR tribunal is no exception, especially in cases involving new issues or new provisions of BITs. In this sense, a review mechanism is required. However, the review procedure has to be moderated in favor of fast resolution. Therefore, review and subsequent annulment shall be exceptional and subjected to high thresholds. The grounds for review and annulment are limited to incorrect interpretation of applicable rules, manifestly exceeding tribunal's power, failure to state reasons and serious departure from a fundamental rule of procedure.[115]

The arguments against an institutional appellate body are twofold: cost increases and abuse of rights. First, an institutional appellate body will

---

[114] The review and annulment procedure of MIDR is similar to the ICSID annulment procedure, which excludes reconsiderations of merits. I. Marboe, "ICSID Annulment Decisions: Three Generations Revisited" in C. Binder, U. Kriebaum, A. Reinisch & S. Wittich (eds.), *International Investment Law for the 21st Century* (Oxford University Press 2012) 201.

[115] Another option is *rationale personae* control. For example, only disputing states, namely the host state and home state, are allowed to initiate the review procedure. Here is a rebuttable assumption that states would give consideration and care to the overall balance of the system as a whole and use the review right more cautiously. As the injured party, investors are inclined to exhaust all procedures within the limits of affordable costs and pay little, if any, attention to the policy impacts of the cases. Therefore, investors should have no direct right to review. But the investors are not left unattended. They could persuade the home state to espouse the appeal and initiate the review procedure. However, the political concerns of the home state may prevent the annulment committee from effective operation. The home state may refrain from participation in the review procedure out of worry over repoliticization of its relations with the host state. Additionally, the home state may also be reluctant because of its absence in the first tribunal procedure.

attract more applications than an annulment review mechanism,[116] as it opens the door for disagreements on factual issues. But extraordinary review rather than routine appeal might moderate increases in cost and time to some degree.[117] Second, in order to prevent abuse of process, a high hurdle for review has been set. The basis for review under MIDR is broader than ICSID annulment, as it covers the general interpretation of applicable rules in addition to other procedural issues under ICSID Article 52.[118] The annulment committee's restricted review of tribunal awards could adequately balance the power between the contracting states and the tribunals, because, after all, it is the tribunal that should hear and adjudicate disputes. This could maintain the nature of MIDR as an independent organ and also prevent it from adopting overly expansive or even aggressive interpretations.[119]

The institutionalization of MIDR inevitably entails further power delegation from states to a permanent body. However, in order to prevent MIDR from moving in the wrong direction, internal checks and balances need to be devised to evaluate MIDR if necessary. In this sense, the investment committee is established partly to prevent MIDR from changing into a legislative body rather than a dispute settlement body that ought to be neutral. Therefore, the investment committee enjoys the power to issue joint interpretations of IIA provisions that shall be binding on all subsequent tribunals and the annulment committee.

I propose establishing MIDR in order to enhance the public legitimacy of the ISDS system without destroying its private efficiency. Combining measures of public legitimacy management and private efficiency refinement, MIDR has four key features: its institutional structure features an investment committee, an annulment committee and a compulsory

---

[116] Alvarez (n 1) 228. The importance of the right to initiate should not be underestimated. Who is entitled to bring claims also matters a great deal with respect to the intensity with which issues may be pursued, the prospect of annulment or enforcement challenges or for settlement, and the likelihood that litigants will raise political or other extraneous issues in the course of adjudication.

[117] This can be seen from comparisons between cases of the WTO Appellate Body and ICSID Annulment Committee.

[118] Cf. ICSID, Art. 52.

[119] This would arguably prevent permanent bodies with tenured judges from proclaiming principles or rules that go beyond the limits of the relevant stakeholder of the regime (Alvarez [n 1] 475). After all, concluding an MAI or establishing a permanent multilateral court on recent arbitration awards might prove misguided, because they risk entrenching and legitimizing rather than correcting an investment regime that lacks fairness and balance. Osgoode Hall Statement, Public Statement on the International Investment Law Regime (August 31, 2010).

arbitrator roster, but without an appellate body; for the prearbitration stage, contracting states appoint members of the arbitrator roster; for the process of arbitration, party autonomy prevails and all members of the tribunal have the dual consent of both contracting states and disputing parties; for the postarbitration stage, the annulment committee may review the awards of the tribunal upon application of either disputing party, and the investment committee could issue joint interpretations, if necessary, binding on all subsequent tribunals and the annulment committee.

Compared to the ICS proposal by the EU and the insistence of the United States on traditional ISDS, we may find some similarities as well as differences. Like EU's ICS proposal, MIDR is an institutionalized bodies with an arbitrator pool appointed by states. However, MIDR is also designed to remain efficient and cost friendly: MIDR respects the party autonomy of disputing parties, especially the right of investors to appoint members of tribunals; it avoids additional costs associated with institutionalization yet without compromising the goal of consistency of awards. Like the US 2012 Model BIT, MIDR is consistent with the nature of international arbitration. However, MIDR is also designed to enhance legitimacy: MIDR could secure dual consent for members of a tribunal, while institutionalized review is better for securing consistency of awards.

MIDR aims to provide a balanced, more efficient and more pragmatic reform plan. We have attempted to adhere to the nature of arbitration in MIDR, as investors still have the right to appoint tribunal members even from a small arbitrator pool. We have attempted to address the legitimacy concerns of ISDS in a cost-friendly manner in order to maintain its efficiency advantages.

7.5   Feasibility of MIDR: External Balance

This part explores the external balance (feasibility) of such MIDR and considers three questions relating to the process of and key players in the multilateralization of such a proposal.

7.5.1   *Procedure before Substance: Is MIDR without a Substantive MAI Feasible?*

Without a comprehensive and detailed multilateral treaty, could we really mitigate the inconsistency of investment arbitration awards at all? This very question involves the relation, or balance, between procedure and substance in the investment regime. Given the evident fact that BITs differ, sometimes substantially, and that significant changes are sometimes made even to a single country's preferred negotiating text over relatively short periods of time, there is a serious question over whether investment law is truly coalescing into wholly coherent definitions of substantive investment guarantees or residual exceptions for governmental regulatory power.[120]

7.5.1.1   Historic Experience of Procedure before Substance

In times of substantive disagreement, procedure before substance is a way out, such as the ICSID in the late 1960s.[121] In 1961, Aron Broches, General Counsel of the World Bank, emphasized the importance of creation of "a mechanism for the impartial settlement of international investment disputes"[122] in light of the divided opinion of states on substantive standards revealed in discussion at the United Nations.[123]

Potential tensions between procedure and substance for contracting states are well framed by Santiago Montt:

> Once the decision of adopting open-ended substantive provisions of investment treaties had been made, treaty-negotiators confronted the following two alternative institutional designs. They could choose *ad hoc* arbitral panels – as they ultimately did – and risk a lack of coherence in the system, or choose an appellate body or international investment court, and risk coherence in the wrong direction. By the latter risk I mean, what in this work has been previously referred to as the bad case or BITs-as-gunboat-arbitration: a situation corresponding to a Lochnerian jurisprudence that overprotects investment and property rights. Negotiators, then, faced a clear trade-off of risks: lack of coherence v coherence in the wrong direction.[124]

Following this logic, Santiago Montt argues that "premature establishment of an appellate body or international investment court could prove

---

[120]   Alvarez (n 1) 316.

[121]   Alvarez (n 1) 224. At the time the ICSID Convention was concluded in 1966, it was assumed that consent to arbitration would occur through an ad hoc submission to arbitration contained in agreements between host states and investors as a particular dispute between then had arisen or because of a clause providing advance consent to arbitration contained in an investment contract between an investor and a host state. The rise of BITs and FTAs containing advance consent to ISDS has vastly expanded the universe of potential investor–state claims.

[122]   E. Lauterpacht, "Foreword" in C. Schreuer, L. Malintoppi, A. Reinisch & A. Sinclair, *The ICSID Convention: A Commentary* (Cambridge University Press 2009) xi.

[123]   Shihata (n 25).

[124]   Montt (n 98) 157.

disastrous for the system's legitimacy" unless "countries are able to sit at the table to produce an extensive and detailed treaty, which reduces the adjudicative discretion available to arbitrators under the current overly broad investment treaty standards."[125]

7.5.1.2 Coordination between Procedure and Substance

There are areas in which the line between procedure and substance is difficult to draw. A substantive MAI is important. For the present purpose, the emphasis is on the procedural and institutional design of MIDR. However, due to their intertwined nature, procedure and substance should be coordinated at least in order to fully address the legitimacy concerns weighing on the ISDS system.

The procedure before substance approach in case of MIDR is of enough policy consensus. Most observers believe that another attempt to negotiate a multilateral investment treaty, presumably outside the OECD, is not likely in the near term.[126] This does not mean that forward movement on multilateral rules regarding some aspects of investment is not possible.[127] Procedure before substance could work as a second-best in a time of low feasibility of a comprehensive MAI.

A patching substantive rule is necessary as pure MIDR is not sufficient to resolve all the sources of legitimacy deficit. After all, the differences in the wording of the BITs matter for adjudications. In the short term, the scope of MIDR jurisdiction should be carefully calculated. In the long term, MIDR plus MAI should constitute a complete set. MIDR could work as the first step towards a comprehensive MAI.

7.5.2 The Road to Rome: Standalone Process or Existing Institutions?

The second question involves the relationships between MIDR and existing institutions. There are two broad possibilities: a standalone process, or cooperation with existing international mechanisms.[128]

---

[125] Montt (n 98) 159.
[126] Alvarez (n 1) 478.
[127] P. Sauve, "Multilateral Rules on Investment: Is Forward Movement Possible" (2006) 9(2) *Journal of International Economic Law* 325–55 (advocating WTO-affiliated MAI initiatives). On a de facto multilateral agreement to emerge through the network of BITs and FTAs or multilateral bilateralism, see E. Chalamish, "The Future of Bilateral Investment Treaties: A De Facto Multilateral Agreement" (2009) 34(2) *Brooklyn Journal of International Law* 303.
[128] W. Shan, "Toward a Multilateral or Plurilateral Framework on Investment," E15 Task Force on Investment Policy, November 2015, 11.

7.5.2.1   Standalone Process

A standalone process may be feasible and appealing given multiple attempts at MAI. However, two conditions for successful initiatives are worth mentioning. First, there must be at least one leading state to initiate the process. Second, there must be a consensus among the great powers on the design of MIDR. Given the similarities between the EU's ICS and MIDR, it would be desirable if, for example, the EU and China could work together to promote the institutionalization of ISDS mechanisms[129] under the auspices of UNCITRAL discussions, and to persuade other states, especially the United States, to follow this course.

7.5.2.2   MIDR with Existing Institutions

Given the functional similarities, the ICSID would be the first choice for the MIDR process under the framework or with the support of existing institutions. The ICSID is an institutionally experienced organization of well-trained personnel for investment dispute resolution.

MIDR is different from the ICSID in terms of arbitrator appointment, annulment review and interpretation of an investment committee. The process of MIDR under the auspices of the ICSID would therefore require considerable changes to the ICSID, maybe in cooperation with its Appeal Facility Project.[130] As a member-driven organization, ICSID reform needs the political will of member states, especially the powerful ones.[131] In any event, the ICSID could at least provide secretariat service to MIDR. Similar issues exist also with regard to other institutions like the WTO, IMF, ECT or AIIB.[132]

---

[129] There is, however, considerable skepticism regarding the feasibility of an investment court system. Until a well-designed investment court becomes a realistic possibility, attention should be focused on a number of areas, including ensuring that the ethical rules for arbitrator conduct are appropriately designed to cater for the unique features of the investment treaty system. Hidelang & Krajewski (n 2) 13.

[130] Such an upgrade will inevitably need the support of powerful states. Otherwise, the chances for such a proposal are small. D. A. Gantz, "An Appellate Mechanism for Review of Arbitral Decisions in Investor-State Dispute: Prospects and Challenges" (2006) 39 *Vanderbilt Journal of Transnational Law* 39, 39. See also D. McRae, "The WTO Appellate Body: A Model for an ICSID Appeals Facility?" (2010) 1 *Journal of International Dispute Settlement* 371–387.

[131] J. Pauwelyn, R. A. Wessel & J. Wouters, "When Structures Become Shackles: Stagnation and Dynamics in International Lawmaking" (2014) 25(3) *European Journal of International Law* 733–63.

[132] For more analysis, see Shan (n 128) 11–13.

7.5.3   Balance of Rights and Balance of Powers: What Role for the Great Powers?

The third question is on the role of great powers, or to be exact, the role of the European Union, the United States and China in the process of establishing MIDR. Any supposedly multilateral endeavor without these "Big Three" is incomplete nowadays. The United States is seemingly becoming more inward-looking. What rules could be devised to attract the cooperation of the great powers? And could the EU and China advance such course and attract the cooperation of the United States in the process?

7.5.3.1   Key Rules

In the design of MIDR, rules of high distributive effects should be calculated for balance among potential leading states. Among others, the decision-making procedure of the investment committee and allocation of annulment committee panelists are of greatest significance.

For the decision-making procedure of the investment committee, different types can be pursued. For annulment decisions, a negative consensus procedure is necessary for the sake of smooth operation of MIDR. For other matters concerning joint interpretations, amendments to MIDR rules and the appointment of chairpersons and panelists to the annulment committee as well as all arbitrators of the roster, a positive consensus procedure is necessary to make sure all rules are arrived at by consensus of the contracting states.

For allocation of panelists of the annulment committee, procedures should be subject to similar selection rules for those of ICJ Judges,[133] representing the main forms of civilization and the principal legal systems of the world.

7.5.3.2   Key Players

When considering potential leading states, it is necessary to encompass the Big Three, namely the United States, the European Union and China, if the MIDR aims to become a truly multilateral initiative. But it is not an

---

[133] The International Court of Justice is composed of fifteen judges elected to nine-year terms of office by the United Nations General Assembly and the Security Council. These organs vote simultaneously but separately. In order to be elected, a candidate must receive an absolute majority of the votes in both bodies. This sometimes makes it necessary for a number of rounds of voting to be carried out. See more at ICJ website, www.icj-cij.org/court/index.php?p1=1&p2=2.

easy job nowadays to have the Big Three on board despite the fact that present-day investment flows are not unidirectional.[134] In most years since World War II, the United States has been the largest recipient of FDI as well as the leading capital exporter.[135] The United States shares this duality with others, such as Brazil, Russia, India and China, all leading recipients and exporters of capital. Transnational corporations from emerging markets are now important players in the investment regime.[136] The bilateral negotiations among China, the United States and EU respectively may succeed as a platform for the process of establishing MIDR.[137] The positions taken in some recent IIAs, particularly those concluded by China, the United States and the European Union, appear to be converging on key points and might exert a multilateral influence in favor of MIDR.

The debate on ISDS reform also concerns the kind of globalization and international economic order we prefer to endorse and defend.[138] "Many of proposed reforms for investment regime reflect a belated recognition of the continued significance of maintaining political support for that regime among all its stakeholders, and not only potential investor claimants."[139] "That both investment treaties and arbitral interpretations of them are now coming to reflect the changing views of states and others concerning economic globalization and how best to achieve development should not surprise anyone."[140] "The regime may be like globalization itself a site of continued contestation and struggle."[141]

7.6   Concluding Remarks

In this chapter, we hope to contribute to the discussion of ISDS reform by proposing a more balanced, pragmatic and legitimately efficiency-driven

[134] Alvarez (n 1) 296–97.
[135] C. Cai, "China–US BIT Negotiations and the Future of Investment Treaty Regime: A Grand Bargain with Multilateral Implications" (2009) 12 *Journal of International Economic Law* 457, 462.
[136] D. Aykut & D. Ratha, "South–South FDI Flows: How Big Are They?" (2003) 13 *Transnational Corporation* 149. K. Davies, "While Global FDI Falls, China's Outward FDI Doubles" (2009) 5 *Columbia FDI Perspectives* 1.
[137] W. Shan & L. Wang, "The China–EU BIT and the Emerging Global BIT 2.0" (2015) 30(1) *ICSID Review* 260–67.
[138] Alvarez (n 1) 491.
[139] Ibid., 492.
[140] Ibid.
[141] Ibid., 494.

Multilateral Investment Dispute Resolution system. Recent years have witnessed renewed pressure for protectionist policy. Forces against globalization seem to be catching wind in their sails in most developed countries, and some may wonder whether it is the right time to advance reforms to the ISDS regime in this brave new world. These worries seem understandable but misplaced. Countries question the desirability of a liberal IIA regime in times of economic crisis but not the dispute resolution system, especially not a balanced tribunal.

This chapter briefly introduces the theoretical framework of legitimacy–efficiency balance stemming from the public-private nature of ISDS, and primarily focuses on the design of a legitimate efficiency-driven MIDR as well as the challenges we might encounter in the process of establishing MIDR. The ISDS system is a hybrid system, adjudicating public law issues on the blueprint of commercial arbitration. This hybrid nature implies an inherent public-private dimension of investment arbitration. It is important that we bear in mind such a duality when evaluating the ISDS system. The public-private debate applies to both substantive and procedural issues. This chapter places this public-private debate in the context of the legitimacy–efficiency balance to specifically address the legitimacy crisis of the ISDS system. This chapter uses the legitimacy–efficiency balance framework to restate the evolution of the ISDS system and highlight the shift in the driving logic underlying the ISDS system from functional efficiency to legitimate efficiency. The ISDS system's success is attributed to its efficiency as a neutral, independent and depoliticized DSM. However, the ISDS system is a victim of its own success. Some actors push ISDS to tackle issues beyond investment protection. The inherent deficit of public legitimacy is therefore increasingly manifested.

How to reform an ISDS system oriented on fast resolution to make it a fair resolution system is the core challenge. Various measures have been proposed and even implemented to reform the ISDS system. Most notably, the EU launched its proposal for an International Court System, attempting to address both procedural and substantive defects of the ISDS system. Other actors, like the United States, took a more moderate (or perhaps conservative in the case of the USMCA) approach to repair the ISDS on a case-by-case basis. If viewed from a functional perspective, ISDS is still a desirable mechanism. Although the overall effect of ISDS on investment promotion and sustainable development remains inconclusive, the ISDS system has done a quite good job on investment protection. If we consider that protection of investment is still, by and large, the primary goal of ISDS, while contribution to sustainable development is the ultimate goal, the "imperfect but heavily used" ISDS system should be reformed rather than replaced in order to be a legitimate efficiency-driven process.[142] In other words, the decisive tension underlying the design of ISDS has become the relation between public legitimacy and private efficiency. These two factors need to be carefully balanced in order to establish a legitimately efficient mechanism. Accordingly, we try to enhance the public legitimacy of the ISDS system without destroying its private efficiency. For public legitimacy enhancement, we consider how to increase input and output legitimacy, adopting measures like establishing a state-appointed arbitrator roster and increasing the consistency of awards. For the private efficiency requirement, we consider how to preserve party autonomy in the dispute resolution process in a manner conducive to controlling time and costs, such as keeping the disputing parties' right to appoint tribunal members and limiting the right to review.

Combining measures for public legitimacy management and private efficiency refinement, we propose to establish MIDR: it has an institutionalized structure with an investment committee, a permanent annulment committee and an arbitrator roster; for the prearbitration stage, contracting states appoint the members of the arbitrator roster; for the process of arbitration, party autonomy prevails and all members of the tribunal have the dual consent of all contracting states and disputing parties; for the postarbitration stage, the annulment committee could review the awards of the tribunal upon application of either disputing party. MIDR aims to provide a balanced, more efficient and more pragmatic reform plan. We try to keep the nature of MIDR as one of arbitration while addressing the legitimacy concerns of ISDS in a cost-friendly manner. We also preliminarily explore the feasibility of MIDR and argue that the process of establishing MIDR should be one of external balances, moderating tensions between the procedure and the substance of MIDR, between MIDR and existing institutions, and between the legal rights of MIDR stakeholders and the political will of leading states.

---

[142] Walde (n 88) 506–12 (categorizing ISDS as an unmitigated success that provides a legal foundation to help the current process of global economic integration run more smoothly, marred by only minor flaws).

Energy Dispute Resolution along the Belt and Road

Should China Accede to the Energy Charter Treaty?

ANATOLE BOUTE

8.1 Introduction

Energy cooperation is at the center of China's ambitious Belt and Road Initiative.[1] Building on its experience with the development of cross-border energy projects, China is intensifying its efforts to interconnect foreign energy reserves with its domestic energy infrastructure.[2] This interconnectivity strategy covers most aspects of the energy industry: coal, oil, gas, hydropower, nuclear, wind and solar power. A key objective of the energy interconnection policy is to increase China's energy imports to fuel its economic growth. Given depleting domestic gas reserves and growing demand for gas to replace coal, China realizes the importance of international cooperation to fuel its resource-intensive economy.[3] Foreign energy investments along the Belt and Road play a strategic role in ensuring the availability of Chinese external energy supplies.[4] In addition to these investments in the upstream energy infrastructure, Chinese energy companies are increasingly active in the making of investments in downstream energy, including renewable

---

[1] National Development and Reform Commission, Ministry of Foreign Affairs and Ministry of Commerce of the People's Republic of China, *Vision and Actions on Jointly Building Silk Road Economic Belt and 21st Century Maritime Silk Road Affairs* (first ed., March 2015) 4–5, http://en.ndrc.gov.cn/newsrelease/201503/t20150330_669367.html (accessed on June 25, 2018).

[2] International Energy Agency, *World Energy Outlook 2017* (OECD/IEA, 2017), 486–87.

[3] R. Sutter, *Chinese Foreign Relations: Power and Policy Since the Cold War* (fourth ed. Rowman & Littlefield 2016) 66.

[4] Institute of Quantitative & Technical Economics in Chinese Academy of Social Sciences, "The 'One Belt, One Road' Strategy: Interconnection, Interoperability and Common Development – Building Energy Infrastructure and Integrating Asia-Pacific Regional Energy Markets," (2015) 23(8) *Intl. Petroleum Economics* 15, 17.

energy and electricity networks. The EU, Central Asian and Russian energy sector are important destinations for Chinese investments under China's energy interconnectivity strategy.[5]

Many Belt and Road countries are characterized by challenging investment conditions. In particular, regulatory and political risks are high in Russia and the Central Asian states. These countries are China's strategic energy partners, but perform relatively poorly on the World Bank ranking of countries in which to "Do Business In," with respect to such issues as the independence of the national judiciary and the enforcement of contracts.[6] Foreign energy investors in these countries have been affected by state interference with their investments and have brought disputes to investment arbitration following the deterioration of investor–state relations.[7]

Regulatory and political risks are not limited to energy investments in countries characterized by weaker institutional conditions. In the European Union, sudden changes to the support of renewable energy investments took the business community by surprise, undermining the trust of investors in this sector.[8] Investors reacted to retroactive changes to renewable energy subsidies by instituting arbitral proceedings against host states (e.g. Spain, Italy and the Czech Republic) before international investment tribunals.[9]

---

[5] B. Conrad & G. Kostka, "Chinese Investments in Europe's Energy Sector: Risks and Opportunities?," (2017) 101 *Energy Policy* 644–48.

[6] See, for example, World Bank Group, "Doing Business 2018, Reforming to Create Jobs, Economy Profile Kazakhstan," www.doingbusiness.org/~/media/WBG/DoingBusiness/Documents/Profiles/Country/KAZ.pdf (accessed on June 25, 2018); World Economic Forum, "The Global Competitiveness Report 2017–2018," www.weforum.org/reports/the-global-competitiveness-report-2017–2018 (accessed on June 25, 2018).

[7] See, for example, *AES Corporation and TAU Power B.V.* v. *Kazakhstan*, ICSID Case No. ARB/10/16, Award (November 1, 2013); *Caratube International Oil Company LLP and Mr. Devincci Salah Hourani* v. *Kazakhstan*, ICSID Case No. ARB/13/13, Award (September 27, 2017); *Yukos Universal Limited (Isle of Man)* v. *The Russian Federation*, PCA Case No AA 227, Award (July 18, 2014).

[8] See, for example, House of Commons Energy and Climate Change Committee, "Investor Confidence in the UK Energy Sector, Third Report of Session 2015–16," www.publications.parliament.uk/pa/cm201516/cmselect/cmenergy/542/542.pdf (accessed on June 25, 2018).

[9] *Blusun S.A., Jean-Pierre Lecorcier and Michael Stein* v. *Italian Republic*, ICSID Case No. ARB/14/3, Award (December 27, 2016); *Eiser Infrastructure Limited and Energia Solar Luxembourg S.A.R.I.* v. *Spain*, ICSID Case No. ARB/13/36, Award (May 4, 2017); *Jürgen Wirtgen, Stefan Wirtgen, Gisela Wirtgen, JSW Solar (zwei) GmbH & Co. KG* v. *The Czech Republic*, PCA Case No. 2014/03, Award (October 11, 2017).

Taking into account the capital intensity and long-term nature of energy investments, the risk of government interference increases the cost of capital of these investments and deters market players from making sufficient investments.[10] In the energy sector, regulatory and political risk can jeopardize energy security if the necessary investments in the energy infrastructure are not made on time.[11]

Minimizing noncommercial risks associated with energy sector investments in order to achieve energy security is the objective pursued by the Energy Charter Treaty (ECT) – the only energy-specific multilateral trade and investment agreement in the world. The ECT is the result of an EU initiative directed at improving external energy security by stimulating foreign energy investments by the energy partners of the EU.[12] More specifically, the ECT is based on the reasoning that:

> The perceived degree of political risks in the host country considerably affects the decision of foreign companies whether to make an investment in the first place or not, and what level of return it would require. The higher the perceived risk, the higher the return that the foreign investors demand. Vice versa, the lower the perceived risk, the more capital is likely to be invested and the more potential revenue the host country will gain.[13]

The ECT seeks to reduce regulatory and political risk by establishing substantive protection standards that shield foreign energy investors from illegitimate state interference with their investments.[14] By creating a stable and predictable environment, the ECT aims to "boost investor

---

[10] See, for example, M. Desai, "Capital Structure with Risky Foreign Investment," (2008) 88 (3) *Journal of Financial Economics* 534–53; UNCTAD, *World Investment Report 2008: Transnational Corporations and the Infrastructure Challenge* (United Nations Publications, Geneva 2008), 85, 162; and M. Bergara, W. Henisz & P. Spiller, "Political Institutions and Electric Utility Investment: A Cross-Nation Analysis," (1997) *POWER* 1–27, at 1.

[11] This argument builds on A. Boute, "Challenging the Re-regulation of Liberalized Electricity Prices under Investment Arbitration" (2011) 32 *Energy Law Journal*, 497–439. See also M. Bergara, W. Henisz & P. Spiller (n 10); G. Brunekreeft & T. McDaniel, "Policy Uncertainty and Supply Adequacy in Electricity Power Markets," (2005) 21(1) *Oxford Review of Economic Policy*, 111–27, at 113.

[12] See Energy Charter Secretariat, "An Introduction to the Energy Charter Treaty," in *The Energy Charter Treaty and Related Documents*, 14, www.ena.lt/pdfai/Treaty.pdf (accessed June 18, 2018).

[13] Energy Charter Secretariat, "The Energy Charter Treaty: A Reader's Guide," (Energy Charter Treaty, Brussels 2002), 19, available at www.encharter.org/fileadmin/user_up load/Publications/ECT_Guide_ENG.pdf (accessed on June 25, 2018).

[14] Energy Charter Secretariat, "Frequently Asked Questions," available at www .encharter.org/index.php?id=18&L=0 (accessed on June 25, 2018). See also, Title II, Point 4, Concluding Document to the Hague Conference on the European Energy

confidence and to contribute to an increase in international investment flows."[15] Many investment arbitration cases against Russia and Central Asian countries, as well as against EU Member States (renewable energy disputes), were brought on the basis of the ECT investor–state dispute resolution regime.[16]

China adheres to the 2015 International Energy Charter Declaration – a nonbinding statement of principles of international energy governance that complements the Energy Charter Treaty. However, China has so far not decided whether it will accede to the Energy Charter Treaty.[17]

This chapter discusses the added value that the Energy Charter Treaty can potentially offer to Chinese external energy security by protecting Chinese outbound investments in countries along the Belt and Road. All Central Asian countries are contracting parties to the ECT, as is the EU and its Member States.[18] With the notable exception of the Russian Federation, which decided to withdraw from the treaty,[19] the

Charter (December 17, 1991), https://energycharter.org/fileadmin/DocumentsMedia/Legal/1991_European_Energy_Charter.pdf (accessed on June 25, 2018).

[15] Energy Charter Secretariat, "Investment: Overview," https://energycharter.org/what-we-do/investment/overview/ (last updated April 9, 2015) (accessed on June 25, 2018).

[16] Energy Charter Secretariat, "List of All Dispute Settlement Cases," https://energycharter.org/what-we-do/dispute-settlement/all-investment-dispute-settlement-cases/ (last updated June 4, 2018).

[17] On the debate on China's accession to the ECT, see, for example, S. Zhang, "The Energy Charter Treaty and China: Member or Bystander?," (2012) 13 *Journal of World Investment and Trade* 597, 609–10; Z. Wang, "Securing Energy Flows from Central Asia to China and the Relevance of the Energy Charter Treaty to China" (Energy Charter Secretariat 2015) 41, www.energycharter.org/fileadmin/DocumentsMedia/Thematic/China_and_the_ECT_2015_en.pd%0Af (accessed on June 25, 2018); N. Yodogawa & A. M. Peterson, "An Opportunity for Progress: China, Central Asia, and the Energy Charter Treaty" (2012) 8 (1) *Texas J. Oil, Gas & Energy L.* 111, 133–34; Z. Bai & Y. Pan, "Advantages and Disadvantages of China's Accession to the Energy Charter Treaty" (2010) 10 *Ecological Economy* 75; W. Shan, P. Wang & H. Wang, "'One Belt, One Road' Construction and China's Accession to the Energy Charter Treaty: A Cost-Benefit Analysis," (2016) *Intl. L. Research* 39, 43. More generally on the protection of Chinese foreign energy investments, see W. Shan, *International Law Protection for China's Overseas Energy Investment: The Research of Regulations Based on Field Research and Research in Different Regions* (Qing Hua University Press 2014).

[18] Energy Charter Secretariat, "Energy Charter Treaty Signatory and Contracting Parties," https://energycharter.org/process/energy-charter-treaty-1994/energy-charter-treaty/signatories-contracting-parties/ (last updated June 5, 2015).

[19] Rasporiazhenie Pravitel'stva RF July 30, 2009 no. 1055-r "O namerenii Rossiiskoi Federatsii ne stanovit'sia uchastnikom Dogovora k Energeticheskoi Khartii, a takzhe Protokola k Energeticheskoi Khartii po voprosam energeticheskoi effektivnosti i sootvetstvuiushchim ekologicheskim aspektam," Sobranie zakonodatel'stva RF, (August 10, 2009) No. 32 4053. See also Konoplianik, "Vykhod Rossii iz vremennogo

geographical scope of the ECT to a large extent covers China's main energy partners along the Silk Road Economic Belt. Taking into account the existing web of bilateral investment treaties,[20] what would the ECT offer to Chinese outbound energy investors in the resolution of disputes with Belt and Road countries?

The analysis starts by examining how the ECT can contribute to facilitate the access of Chinese outbound energy investors to arbitration (investor–state dispute settlement) (Section 2), before assessing the added value of the ECT substantive investment protection standards (Section 3). The analysis focuses on investment treaty arbitration, and not on the resolution of disputes concerning energy trade and transit.[21]

8.2 Access to Arbitration

Access of foreign investors to arbitration depends, among other things, on whether these investors and their investments fall within the scope of application of the applicable investment treaty. In the context of the Belt and Road energy strategy, an important challenge for the access of Chinese investors to arbitration relates to the application of investment treaties to state-owned entities (SOEs) and their strategic investments (Section 2.1). Furthermore, the ability of foreign investors to successfully launch an investor–state dispute settlement procedure depends on the scope of the arbitration clause of the applicable investment treaty. For Chinese investors in key energy destinations along the Belt and Road (e.g., Kazakhstan and Turkmenistan), an important obstacle to arbitration concerns the narrow definition of the dispute resolution clause in the applicable "first-generation" Chinese BITs (Section 2.2).

Accession to the ECT can help address the jurisdictional obstacle resulting from a narrow dispute settlement clause. However, the ECT does not establish a special regime for SOEs and their strategic investments.

---

primeneniia DEKh i 'delo Iukosa': kommentarii po itogam protsedurnogo resheniia arbitrazhnogo suda v Gaage," 8 *Neft', Gaz i Pravo* (2010).

[20] The full text of BITs entered into by China can be found at the Ministry of Commerce website, http://tfs.mofcom.gov.cn/aarticle/h/at/200212/20021200058387.html (accessed on June 25, 2018). On China's BIT policy, see, for example, A. Berger, "The Politics of China's Investment Treaty-Making Program," in T. Broude, A. Porges, M. Busch (eds.), *The Politics of International Economic Law* (Cambridge University Press 2011) 162–85.

[21] On the ECT trade and transit regime, see, for example, L. Ehring & Y. Selivanova, "Energy Transit," in Y. Selivanova (ed.), *Regulation of Energy in International Trade Law – WTO, NAFTA and Energy Charter* (Alphen aan den Rijn, Kluwer 2012) 49–107.

8.2.1   Strategic Energy SOEs and the Definition of "Investors"

SOEs play an important role in China's external energy security strategy and the implementation of the energy objectives of the Belt and Road Initiative.[22] The literature on foreign investments by Chinese SOEs highlights the special nature of these investments.[23] By contrast to commercially driven energy companies, the pursuit of profit is not always central to the making of outbound investments by the Chinese energy SOEs. Instead, the strategic objective of securing the availability of external energy supply to the Chinese market and, in some cases, the objective of exercising strategic influence can be the determining motive of these projects. According to the 2017 World Energy Outlook of the International Energy Agency:

> Initially as part of the government's "Going Abroad" strategy, and since 2013 in the context of the Belt and Road Initiative, the activity of Chinese-owned energy companies abroad has become a major and important element of international flows of investment and technology. The drive for international investment has been underpinned in part by a strategic desire to strengthen regional connectivity and to build new supply chains, given China's growing dependence on imported energy resources.[24]

Fitch Rating's 2017 report on the initiative considers that "genuine infrastructure needs and commercial logic might be secondary to political motivations. [The 'Belt and Road'] . . . is a component of China's efforts to expand its strategic international influence."[25] According to

---

[22] This section builds on A. Boute, "Economic Statecraft and Investment Arbitration" (2019) 40 *University of Pennsylvania Journal of International Law*, 383–418; and A. Boute, "China's External Energy Security: Energy Trade and Investment Along the 'Belt and Road'" (2019) 20 *Journal of World Investment & Trade* 195–220. On the globalization of Chinese energy SOEs, see e.g. B. Kong & K. Gallagher, "The Globalization of Chinese Energy Companies: The Role of State Finance," (2016) Boston Economic Governance Initiative at 11–13, www.bu.edu/pardeeschool/files/2016/06/Globalization.Final_.pdf (accessed on June 25, 2018).
[23] See, for example, Ø. Tunsjø, *Security and Profit in China's Energy Policy: Hedging Against Risk* (Columbia University Press 2013); M. Laruelle & S. Peyrouse, *The Chinese Question in Central Asia: Domestic Order, Social Change, and the Chinese Factor* (London, Hurst Publishers 2012); T. Miller, *China's Asian Dream: Empire Building along the New Silk Road* (London, Zed Books 2017); W. Norris, *Chinese Economic Statecraft: Commercial Actors, Grand Strategy, and State Control* (Ithaca, Cornell University Press 2016).
[24] International Energy Agency, *World Energy Outlook 2017* (OECD/IEA 2017), 486–87.
[25] Fitch Ratings, "China's One Belt, One Road Initiative Brings Risks," January 25, 2017, www.fitchratings.com/site/pr/1018144.

Laruelle and Peyrouse, Chinese investments in Central Asia "are legitimised by much larger political and geopolitical rationales."[26]

The state control and strategic nature of Chinese foreign energy investments pose a challenge to investment arbitration.[27] Investment arbitration was developed to depoliticize the resolution of investor–state disputes by removing the home state from the resolution of investment disputes.[28] Can Chinese SOEs have access to this dispute resolution mechanism taking into account the role of the home state in the making of these investments and the strategic objectives pursued?[29]

8.2.1.1 Strategic SOEs under China's BITs

With the exception of the China–Uzbekistan BIT that explicitly covers state-owned enterprises,[30] China's investment treaties with Russia and the Central Asian countries leave open the form of ownership of the investors covered by the treaty.[31] According to arbitral practice, the absence of an explicit reference to state ownership and control does not exclude SOEs from the scope of investment treaties.[32]

---

[26] M. Laruelle & S. Peyrouse, *The Chinese Question in Central Asia: Domestic Order, Social Change, and the Chinese Factor* (London, Hurst Publishers 2012), at 79.

[27] See more generally, P. Blyshak, "State-Owned Enterprises and International Investment Treaties: When Are State-Owned Entities and Their Investments Protected?," (2011) 6 *Journal of International Law and International Relations* 1, 14; UNCTAD, *The Protection of National Security in IIAs* (UN 2009) 1, 30–32, http://unctad.org/en/docs/dia eia20085_en.pdf (accessed on June 25, 2018).

[28] The core objective of investor–state dispute resolution is to insulate investors' claims "from political and diplomatic relations between states" and remove the home state from the arbitration process: Separate Opinion of A. Lowenfeld, in *Corn Products International, Inc.* v. *United Mexican States*, ICSID Case No. ARB (AF)/04/1, Award (2008) para. 1. See also S. Poulsen, "States as Foreign Investors: Diplomatic Disputes and Legal Fictions," (2016) 31 *ICSID Review – Foreign Investment Law Journal* 12; M. Paparinskis, "Limits of Depoliticisation in Contemporary Investor-State Arbitration," in J. Crawford & S. Nouwen (eds.) *Select Proceedings of the European Society of International Law* (Hart Publishing 2012).

[29] The following analysis builds on A. Boute, "Economic Statecraft and Investment Arbitration," (2019) 40 *University of Pennsylvania Journal of International Law* 383.

[30] Signed April 19, 2011, entry into force September 1, 2011.

[31] D. Labin, *Mezhdunarodnoe pravo po zashchite i pooshchreniiu inostrannykh investitsii* (Wolters Kluwer, Moscow 2008); N. Gallagher & W. Shan, *Chinese Investment Treaties: Policies and Practice* (Oxford University Press 2009).

[32] According to Cour d'Appel de Paris, *Etat d'Ukraine* v. *Société PAO TATNEFT*, Arrêt (November 29, 2016), Affaire No. 14/17964, para. 15, treaties that do not explicitly include the requirement of private ownership in the definition of investors cannot be limited in scope to "private investors." See also C. Annacker, "Protection and Admission of Sovereign Investment under Investment Treaties," (2011) 10 *Chinese Journal of International Law* 531, at 539.

The Uzbek–China BIT explicitly includes SOEs in the definition of "investors," but narrows the definition of "investments" by requiring "the expectation of gain or profit."[33] This definition opens the question of whether investments made for strategic purposes – and thus not necessarily in the pursuit of profit – fall within the scope of application of the BIT.

It is difficult to assess the real motivation of an investor when making a foreign investment. According to the *Saluka* v. *Czech Republic* tribunal, "even if it were possible to know an investor's true motivation in making its investment, nothing ... makes the investor's motivation part of the definition of an 'investment.'"[34] Along the same lines, Annacker argues that investment treaties do not "exclude investments because the assets invested are ... invested in furtherance of State policies or purposes."[35]

However, in *China Heilongjiang* v. *Mongolia,* the arbitral tribunal accepted to examine whether the claimants acted as "quasi-instrumentalities of the Chinese government."[36] In particular, the tribunal assessed whether the Chinese state-owned enterprises acted under the Chinese government's "express instruction to invest abroad in order to serve China's foreign policy goals," and concluded that they did not.[37] Similarly, in the 2017 *Beijing Urban Construction Group* v. *Yemen* award, the tribunal assessed whether the Chinese state-owned enterprise functioned as an agent of the state.[38] The tribunal focused on the functions of the enterprise "in the particular instance" of its investment activity, and again ruled that the SOE did not make the investment concerned as a state agent.

Following the purpose-based interpretative approach endorsed by the *China Heilongjiang* and *Beijing Urban Construction Group* tribunals, an arbitral tribunal can in principle refuse jurisdiction if there is evidence that the foreign investment was made in the pursuit of the home state's strategic interest, based on express instructions by the home state government. In principle, strategic energy investments along the Belt and Road could thus be excluded from arbitration if the respondent can

[33] Article 1, China–Uzbek BIT.
[34] *Saluka Investments BV* v. *Czech Republic,* UNCITRAL, Partial Award (March 17, 2006), para. 209.
[35] Annacker (n 32), at 543–44.
[36] *China Heilongjiang International Economic & Technical Cooperative Corp., & Ors* v. *Mongolia*, UNCITRAL, PCA, June 30, 2017, para. 418.
[37] Ibid, para. 418.
[38] *Beijing Urban Construction Group* v. *Yemen*, ICSID Case No ARB/14/30, Award (May 31, 2017) para. 42.

successfully prove that these investments were made on the basis of express government orders to realize these projects as part of China's foreign policy. Taking into account that many Chinese outbound energy investments along the Belt and Road are made in the pursuit of China's external energy security policy objectives, this obstacle to arbitration presents a real risk for Chinese energy companies.

8.2.2.2   Strategic SOEs under the ECT

Accession to the ECT is unlikely to address this jurisdictional risk. The ECT explicitly limits the concept of "investment" to an "Economic Activity in the Energy Sector."[39] Although the ECT falls short of explicitly requiring the pursuit of gain or profit, the reference to an "economic activity" could potentially be interpreted as excluding projects that are made for purely strategic purposes, if gain or profit is considered to be part of an "economic activity."

The ECT refers to SOEs, but only in relation to the attribution of actions of these enterprises to the host state, not in relation to the control of these enterprises by the home state. The reference to SOEs in the ECT is thus irrelevant for claims by Chinese SOEs against other states.

8.2.2   Dispute Resolution Clause

8.2.2.1   Narrow Dispute Resolution Clauses

An important procedural obstacle for claims by Chinese energy investors against states along the Belt and Road is the restrictive formulation of the dispute resolution clause in first-generation Chinese BITs. China renegotiated its BITs with Russia and Uzbekistan, and included in the new BITs a broad dispute resolution clause opening access to arbitration to all legal disputes arising under the treaty. However, the BITs with key energy partners such as Kazakhstan and Turkmenistan limit access to

---

[39] For example, Article 1(6) ECT, 1994 O.J. L 380/25. "Economic Activity in the Energy Sector," as defined elsewhere in Article 1(5) of the ECT, is "economic activity concerning the exploration, extraction, refining, production, storage, land transport, transmission, distribution, trade, marketing, or sale of energy materials and products." See also A. Turinov, "'Investment' and 'Investor' in Energy Charter Treaty Arbitration: Uncertain Jurisdiction," (2009) 26(1) *Journal of International Arbitration*, 1–24; E. Gaillard, "Investments and Investors Covered by the Energy Charter Treaty," in G. Coop & C. Ribeiro (eds.), *Investment Protection and the Energy Charter Treaty* (JurisNet, Huntington, NY 2008), 54–72.

arbitration to "disputes concerning the amount of compensation in case of expropriation."[40]

In one of the first cases on the interpretation of "narrow" dispute resolution clauses,[41] the *Berschader* v. *Russia* tribunal ruled that the dispute resolution clause excludes disputes concerning whether or not an act of expropriation actually occurred, taking into account the "ordinary meaning" of the dispute resolution clause.[42] Similarly, a restrictive interpretation was followed by the tribunal in *Sanum Investments Limited* v. *Laos* based on the China–Laos BIT – a decision that was later annulled by the Singapore Court of Appeals.[43]

However, the tribunal in *Tza Yap Shum* v. *Peru* – the first publicly available investment treaty arbitration decision on a claim brought by a Chinese investor – followed a broad approach to the interpretation of the narrow dispute resolution clause:

> in order to give meaning to all elements of the Article [dispute resolution clause], the words "involving the amount of compensation for expropriation" must be interpreted to include not only the mere determination of the amount but also other issues that are normally inherent in an expropriation, including whether the property was actually expropriated.[44]

In *Beijing Urban Construction Group* v. *Yemen*, the tribunal focused on the investment promotion objective and purpose of the China–Yemen BIT to support a broad interpretation of the dispute resolution clause:

> The Respondent's "narrow" interpretation would undermine achievement of the BIT's object and purpose. The lack of investor protection would discourage investment. The BIT would be seen as a trap for unwary

---

[40] Article 9, Kazakh–China BIT, signed August 10, 1992, entry into force August 13, 1994, http://investmentpolicyhub.unctad.org/IIA/CountryBits/107; Turkmen–China BIT, signed November 21, 1992, entry into force July 4, 1994, http://investmentpolicyhub .unctad.org/IIA/CountryBits/42 (accessed on June 25, 2018).

[41] For an overview of relevant arbitral practice, see A. Reinisch, "How Narrow are Narrow Dispute Settlement Clauses in Investment Treaties?," (2011) 2(1) *Journal of International Dispute Settlement*, 115–74.

[42] Paragraph 153 SCC Case 080/2004 *Vladimir Berschader and Moïse Berschader* v. *Russia* (Award of April 21, 2006). See also para. 114 2007 SCC Case V079/2005 *RosInvest UK Ltd.* v. *Russia* (Award on Jurisdiction of October 1, 2007).

[43] *Sanum Investments Limited* v. *Lao People's Democratic Republic*, UNCITRAL, PCA Case No. 2013-13 (December 13, 2013); Judgment of the Court of Appeals of Singapore of September 29, 2016.

[44] ICSID Case No ARB/07/6 *Señor Tza Yap Shum* v. *Peru* (Decision on Jurisdiction and Competence of June 19, 2009), para. 188 ibid (quoted in para. 103, ICSID Case No. ARB/ 07/6 *Señor Tza Yap Shum* v. *Peru* (Decision on Annulment of February 12, 2015).

investors instead of an incentive for them to invest in "the other Contracting Party."[45]

This approach opens the door for investor claims regarding the occurrence of expropriation (not just for claims regarding the amount and method of payment in case of expropriation). However, claims regarding other investment protection standards cannot be brought before arbitration on this basis.

8.2.2.2 Access to Arbitration Based on the Most Favored Nation Clause

China's first-generation BITs generally contain most favored nation clauses, that is, clauses requiring the host state to treat investments from the other contracting party no less favorably than the treatment it accords to investments from third states.[46] However, investors are unlikely to be successful in invoking the most favored nation clause to broaden access to arbitration based on first-generation BITs. Although certain arbitral tribunals have recognized that most favored nation clauses enable an investor to invoke the more generous substantive guarantees of other investment agreements (Section 3.1), with few exceptions, arbitral tribunals are reluctant to import more generous jurisdictional guarantees.[47]

In *Tza Yap Shum* v. *Peru*, the tribunal found that the specific wording of the narrow dispute resolution clause should prevail over the general wording of the most favored nation clause.[48] Similarly, in a case involving a relatively broadly formulated most favored nation clause applying to "all matters covered by the present Treaty," the *Berschader* v. *Russia* tribunal concluded that "not even seemingly clear language like this

---

[45] Paragraph 90, *Beijing Urban Construction Group Co. Ltd* v. *Republic of Yemen*, Award, ICSID ARB/14/30. Similarly, see para. 56 *Renta 4 S.V.S.A and Others* v. *The Russian Federation* SCC Case 24/2007 (Award on Preliminary Objections of March 20, 2009).

[46] See, for example, Article 3, Kazakh–China BIT.

[47] See, for example, J. Wong, "The Application of Most-Favored-Nation Clauses to Dispute-Resolution Provisions in Bilateral Investment Treaties," (2008) 3(1) *Asian Journal of WTO and International Health Law and Policy*, 171–98, at 173; M. Valenti, "The Most-Favored-Nation Clause in BITs as a Basis for Jurisdiction in Foreign Investor-Host State Arbitration," (2008) 24(3) *Arbitration International*, 447–66; S. Vesel, "Clearing a Path Through a Tangled Jurisprudence: Most-Favored-Nation Clauses and Dispute Settlement Provisions in Bilateral Investment Treaties," (2007) 32 (1) *The Yale Journal of International Law*, 125–90.

[48] Paragraph 216 *Tza Yap Shum* Award (Decision on Jurisdiction and Competence).

can be considered to have an unambiguous meaning in the context of an MFN clause."[49]

By contrast, the *RosInvest* v. *Russia* tribunal accepted jurisdiction based on the most favored nation clause of the 1989 UK–Soviet BIT by ruling that:

> If this effect is generally accepted in the context of substantive protection, the Tribunal sees no reason not to accept it in the context of procedural clauses such as arbitration clauses. Quite the contrary, it could be argued that, if it applies to substantive protection, then it should apply even more to "only" procedural protection.[50]

8.2.2.3   Access to Arbitration on the Basis of the ECT

In theory, the extensive interpretation of narrow dispute resolution clauses by certain arbitral tribunals provides Chinese energy investors that are covered by first-generation BITs with jurisdictional relief. Nevertheless, there is a significant risk for Chinese investors that arbitral tribunals will stick to the "ordinary" meaning of the narrow dispute resolution clause and refuse arbitration in cases that do not concern the amount and method of payment in case of expropriation. To broaden the scope of dispute resolution, China can either renegotiate its first-generation BITs with strategic energy partners (as it did with Russia and Uzbekistan) or accede to the ECT.

In stark contrast to the first-generation Chinese BITs, the ECT contains a broad investor–state dispute resolution clause (Article 26). It applies to "disputes between a Contracting Party and an Investor of another Contracting Party relating to an Investment of the later in the Area of the former which concern an alleged breach of an obligation of the former under Part III [investment promotion and protection]."[51] According to the *Plama* v. *Bulgaria* tribunal, the dispute resolution clause of the ECT:

---

[49] *Berschader* Award para. 184. This negative outcome is in line with the following awards: para. 102ff. *Salini* Decision on Jurisdiction; *Telenor Mobile Communications A. S.* v. *Hungary* ICSID Case No. ARB/04/15 (Award of September 13, 2006) para. 81ff.; *Plama Consortium Limited* v. *Republic of Bulgaria* ICSID Case ARB/03/24 (Decision on Jurisdiction of February 8, 2005) para. 183ff.

[50] *RosInvest* Award on Jurisdiction para. 132. See K. Hobér, "MFN Clauses and Dispute Resolution in Investment Treaties: Have We Reached the End of the Road?," in C. Binder et al. (eds.), *International Investment Law for the 21st Century: Essays in Honor of Christoph Schreuer* (Oxford University Press, Oxford 2009), 31–41.

[51] Article 26, ECT. See P. Pinsolle, "The Dispute-Resolution Provisions of the Energy Charter Treaty," (2007) 10(3) *International Arbitration Law Review*, 74–81, at 82.

provides to a covered investor an almost unprecedented remedy for its claims against a host state … By any standards, Article 26 is a very important feature of the ECT which is itself a very significant treaty for investors, marking another step in their transition from objects to subjects of international law.[52]

Taking into account the overlap between the ECT contracting parties and key Belt and Road energy partners (e.g., in Central Asia), accession to the ECT would avoid the renegotiation of BITs with a large number of countries.

8.3 Substantive Protection

By joining the ECT, China can help protect its foreign energy investments based on the relatively strict substantive investment protection standards of the ECT (Section 3.1). While these standards of protection can also be extended to Chinese investors on the basis of the most favored nation clause in China's existing BITs with Belt and Road countries, the ECT presents the advantage of a relatively consistent practice on the resolution of energy disputes (Section 3.2). However, a bias in favor of the EU (resulting from the European origins of the ECT) distorts the level playing field that the ECT is supposed to create (Section 3.3).

8.3.1   The ECT Investment Protection Standards

In general, the Chinese BITs with Belt and Road countries include the substantive investment protection standards that are found in most investment treaties, including the ECT.[53] Chinese investors abroad are protected against illegitimate expropriation, unfair and inequitable treatment and discriminatory and arbitrary measures. However, national treatment clauses are often narrowly formulated, by excluding "applicable laws and regulations" in the host state from the scope of application of these provisions. The same investment protection guarantees under the ECT are drafted in a relatively investor-friendly way, which can help reinforce the protection of Chinese energy investors abroad.[54] For

---

[52] *Plama Consortium Limited* v. *Republic of Bulgaria* ICSID Case ARB/03/24 (Decision on Jurisdiction of February 8, 2005) para. 141.

[53] See, for example, N. Gallagher & W. Shan, *Chinese Investment Treaties: Policies and Practice* (2009).

[54] On the ECT substantive investment protection standards, see, for example, K. Hober, "Arbitration of Energy Disputes under the Energy Charter Treaty: Added Value for the

instance, the fair and equitable treatment clause of the ECT commits the contracting parties to:

> encourag[ing] and creat[ing] stable, equitable, favorable and transparent conditions for Investors of other Contracting Parties to Make Investments in Its Area. Such conditions shall include a commitment to accord at all times to Investment of Investors of other Contracting Parties fair and equitable treatment … In no case shall such Investments be accorded treatment less favorable than that required by international law, including treaty obligations.[55]

The reference to stability confirms the objective of the ECT regarding the stabilization of investment conditions, which can trigger the responsibility of the host state in case of significant changes to the regulatory framework on the basis of which energy investments were made.[56] In addition, the ECT possesses an umbrella clause according to which "each Contracting Party shall observe any obligations it has entered into with an Investor or an Investment of an Investor of any other Contracting Party."[57] On this basis, violations of obligations which the host state has assumed vis-à-vis foreign investors can amount to a violation of the investment treaty.[58]

However, on its own, the protection offered by these clauses is unlikely to be seen as a sufficient argument in favor of China's accession to the ECT. Indeed, Chinese energy investments along the Belt and Road could benefit from the generous ECT substantive investment standards, even without China's accession to the ECT. Based on the most favorable

Belt and Road Initiative," *Journal of World Investment and Trade* (forthcoming). See also A. Konoplyanik & T. Wälde, "Energy Charter Treaty and its Role in International Energy," (2006) 24(4) *Journal of Energy and Natural Resources Law*, 523–58.

[55] See Art. 10(1) Energy Charter Treaty.
[56] See more generally, R. Dolzer, "Fair and Equitable Treatment: A Key Standard in Investment Treaties," (2005) 39(1) *International Lawyer*, 87–106; M. Potestà, "Legitimate Expectations in Investment Treaty Law: Understanding the Roots and the Limits of a Controversial Concept," (2013) 28(1) *ICSID Review – Foreign Investment Law Journal*, 88–122.
[57] See last sentence of Art. 10(1) Energy Charter Treaty. In accordance with Art.26(3)(c) of the ECT, contracting parties may enter a reservation with respect to the arbitration of claims on the basis of this umbrella clause.
[58] K. Yannaca-Small, *Interpretation of the Umbrella Clause in Investment Agreements* (OECD, Paris 2006), 3; C. Schreuer, "Investment Treaty Arbitration and Jurisdiction over Contract Claims: The *Vivendi I* Case Considered," in T. Weiler (ed.) *International Investment Law and Arbitration: Leading Cases from the ICSID, NAFTA and Bilateral Treaties and Customary International Law* (Cameron May, London 2005), 281–323, at 299.

nation clause in the applicable BIT, Chinese investors in Belt and Road countries that are contracting parties to the ECT could invoke its investment protection disciplines. Indeed, by contrast to access to arbitration, arbitral tribunals have more readily accepted that most favored nation clauses enable an investor to invoke the more generous substantive guarantees of other investment agreements.[59]

8.3.2 The ECT Energy Jurisprudence

The ECT is not only relevant for Chinese energy investments along the Belt and Road because it provides broad substantive protection standards, but also because it specifically applies to the energy sector. The substantive protection standards of the ECT are drafted in an investor-friendly way but do not significantly differ from the traditional standards of protection that can be found in most other BITs. The ECT investment disciplines are not specifically tailored to the special characteristics of energy investments and to the special political and regulatory risks that can affect these investments. However, an energy-specific arbitral practice has been developed on the basis of the ECT investment protection standards.[60] By interpreting and applying the ECT standards to energy disputes, arbitral tribunals provided guidance on the meaning of these standards for energy investors and the protection that these standards offer against certain risks.[61]

An example of energy-specific arbitral practice developed on the basis of the ECT is the arbitration of renewable energy disputes in the EU.

---

[59] A. Ziegler, "Most-Favored-Nation (MFN) Treatment," in A. Reinisch (ed.) *Standards of Investment Protection* (Oxford University Press, Oxford 2008), 59–86, at 60; P. Acconci, "Most-Favored Nation Treatment and International Law on Foreign Investment," in P. Muchlinski, F. Ortino & C. Schreuer (eds.), *The Oxford Handbook of International Investment Law* (Oxford University Press, Oxford 2008), 363–406, at 365.

[60] Hobér (n 54). It must be noted that there is no doctrine of precedent under international investment law. In accordance with Art. 53(1) of the International Convention for the Settlement of Investment Disputes (International Center for Settlement of Investment Disputes, ICSID Convention, Regulations and Rules), an award is binding on the parties. Future arbitral tribunals can interpret the Treaty differently and apply it to the specific facts of the case according to their own appreciation, https://icsid.worldbank.org/ICSID/ StaticFiles/basicdoc/CRR_English-final.pdf (accessed on June 25, 2018). See also C. Schreuer, "Diversity and Harmonization of Treaty Interpretation in Investment Arbitration" (2006), 10–15, www.univie.ac.at/intlaw/pdf/cspubl_85.pdf (accessed on June 25, 2018).

[61] See, for example, K. Hober, "Overview of ECT Cases," in Maxi Scherer (ed.), *International Arbitration in the Energy Sector* (Oxford University Press 2018).

Foreign investors made use of the ECT to oppose the changes to renewable energy subsidies that affected the financial performance of their investments. Although the interpretation and application of the ECT standards to renewable energy investments has not always been consistent, existing arbitral practice to some extent provides guidance on the protection that the ECT can provide (or not provide) in case of a sudden reduction of the amount or duration of an energy subsidy.[62]

8.3.3   A European Treaty?

The ECT results from a European initiative aimed at protecting European investments in the energy sector of the former Soviet Union and, on this basis, ensuring the security of energy supplies to the EU. To secure these investments, the ECT aims to ensure the creation of a "level playing field" for energy investments throughout the Charter's constituency, and in particular reduce the political and regulatory risks that can affect these investments.[63] However, the European roots of the ECT undermine the "level playing field" that the ECT is supposed to create for energy investors and, by doing so, affects the level of protection that this treaty could provide to Chinese energy investors in the EU.[64]

8.3.3.1   The EU Roots of the ECT

The perception of the ECT as a European treaty is an obstacle to the further deployment of this international legal instrument and its endorsement by other countries as a tool to achieve energy security. Most notably, Russia has criticized the EU-centered nature of the

---

[62] A. Boute, "Regulatory Stability and Renewable Energy Investment" (2020) 121 *Renewable and Sustainable Energy Reviews*, https://doi.org/10.1016/j.rser.2019.109673. On the risk of inconsistency of investment arbitration practice for renewable energy investments, see A. Boute, "Combating Climate Change through Investment Arbitration" (2012) 35 *Fordham International Law Journal*, 613–664.

[63] Energy Charter Secretariat, "An Introduction to the Energy Charter Treaty," in Energy Charter Secretariat, *The Energy Charter Treaty and Related Documents – A Legal Framework for International Energy Cooperation*, 2004, at 14, available online at www.encharter.org.

[64] The following analysis builds on A. Boute, "The Protection of Russian Investments in the EU Energy Market: A Case in Support of Russia's Ratification of the Energy Charter Treaty," (2014) 29(3) *ICSID Review- Foreign Investment Law Journal* 525–47; A. Boute, "Energy Trade and Investment Law: International Limits to EU Energy Law and Policy", in M. Roggenkamp et al. (eds.), *Energy Law in Europe*, third edition (Oxford: Oxford University Press, 2016), 137–185.

ECT.[65] Russia's perception of this treaty as a legal instrument primarily directed at guaranteeing the security of the energy supply within Europe is often invoked as one of the main reasons for Russia's refusal to ratify it.[66] This perception of the ECT as a European treaty finds support in its origins.

In 1991, following an initiative by the former prime minister of the Netherlands, states under the leadership of the European Community (later Union) signed the European Energy Charter Declaration, a nonbinding text setting out general principles of energy governance. The Energy Charter is thus a European initiative, which originated from the perceived opportunities to invest in the energy sector of the former Soviet Union following its collapse.[67] Indeed, the underlying reasoning of the Energy Charter was that "Russia and many of its neighbours were rich in energy resources but needed major investments to ensure their development, whilst the states of Western Europe had a strategic interest in diversifying their sources of energy supplies."[68] According to the late Thomas Wälde:

[65] See, for example, N. G. Doronina and N. G. Semilyutina, *Mezhdunarodnoe chastnoe pravo i investitsii* (Moscow: Institut zakonodatel'stva i svravnitel'nogo pravovedeniia pri Pravitel'stve RF 2012), at 74; E. P. Gubin, "Zashchita prav inostrannykh investorov po zakonodatel'stvu Rossiiskoi Federatsii," (2013) 1 *Predprinimatel'skoe pravo* 1–5, at 2, accessed via Konsul'tantPlius.

[66] For an analysis of the Russian position on the ECT and reasons underlying Russia's decision not to ratify the Treaty, see, for example, A. Belyi, "A Russian Perspective on the Energy Charter Treaty" (Real Instituto Elcano, 2009) www.realinstitutoelcano.org/wps/wcm/connect/e6e3e5004f018b7db7c6f73170baead1/ARI98-2009_Belyi_Russian_Perspective_Energy_Charter_Treaty.pdf?MOD=AJPERES&CACHEID=e6e3e5004f018b7db7c6f73170baead1 (accessed on June 25, 2018); S. Seliverstov, "Proekt Konventsii po obespecheniiu mezhdunarodnoi energeticheskoi bezopasnosti – novyi energeticheskii miroporiadok?," (2011) 11 *Iurist* 31–38; I. Gudkov, "Rossiiskii kontseptual'nyi podkhod i Dogovor k Energeticheskoi Khartii,"(2007) 1 *Neft', Gaz i Pravo* 17–30; D. Doe, S. Nappert, A. Popov, "Rossiia i Dogovor k Energeticheskoi Khartii: obshchie interesy ili neprimirimye protivorechiia?," (2006) 5 *Neft', Gaz i Pravo* 9–12; A. Belyi, "Russia's Position on the Energy Charter," Meeting Summary: Russia and Eurasia Programme (April 27, 2012) www.chathamhouse.org/sites/default/files/public/Research/Russia%20and%20Eurasia/270412summary.pdf (accessed on June 25, 2018); S. Handke & J. de Jong, *Energy as a Bond: Relations with Russia in the European and Dutch Context* (Clingendael International Energy Program, The Hague 2007) 51–60 http://clingendael.info/publications/2007/20070900_ciep_energy_handke.pdf (accessed on June 25, 2018). See also Speech of State Duma Delegate V. Yazeyev on the Occasion of the Anniversary Session of the Energy Charter Conference (Brussels, December 17, 2001).

[67] On the history of ECT, see T. Wälde (ed.), *The Energy Charter Treaty – An East-West Gateway for Investment and Trade* (Kluwer International Law 1996) 156–78. See also K. Hobér, "Russian Energy Policy and Dispute Settlement," in Martha Roggenkamp & Ulf Hammer (eds.), *European Energy Law Report VII* (Intersentia, Mortsel 2010), 235–66.

[68] See "An Introduction to the Energy Charter Treaty," in Energy Charter Secretariat, *The Energy Charter Treaty and Related Documents – A Legal Framework for International*

The ECT is largely a product of EU external political, economic and energy policy. ... it is intended to promote EU investment in these countries and energy flows from these countries to the EU.[69]

8.3.3.2   An "Unlevelled Playing Field"

In reaction to the criticism of the EU-centered nature of the ECT, the proponents of the ECT refer to the reciprocal application of its investment and dispute resolution regime.[70] The ECT also protects investments by companies from producer countries against political and regulatory risks in downstream energy markets.[71]

However, arbitral practice on the application of the ECT in disputes against EU Member States highlights a potential bias of the ECT in favor of the EU.[72] A potentially determining obstacle to the success of arbitration claims by Chinese energy investors against EU Member States concerns the specific nature of EU energy law and the specific interaction of EU energy law with the ECT. In particular, EU Member States can seek to justify interference with Chinese energy investors (foreign energy investors in general) by invoking the necessity to comply with EU energy law as a supranational legal regime. Confronted with potential claims by EU energy investors, China will not have the possibility to justify state interference with foreign investments on this basis, taking into account that a state may not invoke its domestic law as an excuse for alleged breaches of its international obligations. If, under the ECT, EU Member States can invoke defenses that China cannot invoke, the ECT can be

---

Energy Cooperation (2004) 14, www.encharter.org/fileadmin/user_upload/document/EN
.pdf (accessed on June 25, 2018).

[69] T. Wälde, "Arbitration in the Oil, Gas and Energy Field: Emerging Energy Charter Treaty Practice," (May 1, 2004) *Transnational Dispute Management*, 4, quoted in *Electrabel S. A. v. Hungary*, ICSID Case No. ARB/07/19, Award (November 30, 2012), para. 4.132.

[70] See Art. 2 ECT that establishes the "complementarities and mutual benefits" of the Treaty for all Contracting Parties. See however R. Dolzer & C. Schreuer, *Principles of International Investment Law* (second ed., Oxford University Press, 2012) 20, for a critical discussion of the existence of a principle of reciprocity in international investment law.

[71] Speech delivered at the Fourth IEF Energy Lecture at the Secretariat of the International Energy Forum (Riyadh, March 2007). See also Y. Selivanova, "The Energy Charter and the International Energy Governance," in Y Selivanova (ed.), *Regulation of Energy in International Trade Law: WTO, NAFTA and Energy Charter* (Alphen aan den Rijn: Kluwer Law International 2001), 373, at 392 and 403, providing counter-arguments to the criticism of the unbalanced character of the ECT.

[72] See more generally G. Coop, "Energy Charter Treaty and the European Union: Is Conflict Inevitable?," (2009) 27 *Journal of Energy and Natural Resources Law*, 416.

considered to distort the level playing field for foreign investors from the EU and China.

The interrelation between EU law and the ECT was raised in the *AES v. Hungary* and *Electrabel* v. *Hungary* cases.[73] Both cases concern interference by Hungary with long-term energy purchase agreements in the context of Hungary's accession to the EU, and thus touch upon Hungary's obligation to comply with EU competition law.[74] In the *AES* case, the arbitral tribunal highlighted the "dual nature" of EU law as an international law regime and as part of the national law of the member states. Taking into account the international law nature of EU law, the tribunal recognized that the need to comply with EU law can be considered when determining the rational, reasonable, arbitrary and transparent nature of state measures affecting investments.[75] In a comparable way to the *AES* tribunal, the tribunal in *Electrabel* recognized the dual nature of EU law (international and national) and considered EU law, being part of the respondent's national law, as a "fact relevant to the Parties' dispute."[76]

The *Electrabel* tribunal went further than the *AES* tribunal by establishing "a presumption that no contradiction exists between the ECT and EU law" and ruled that, where possible, the ECT should be interpreted in harmony with EU law.[77] The EU "played from the outset a leading role" in the ECT: "as a matter of legal, political and economic history, the EU was the determining actor in the creation of the ECT."[78] It would thus have made no sense for the EU to conclude the ECT "if that had meant entering into obligations inconsistent with EU law."[79, 80]

In *Electrabel*, the tribunal considered that there was no inconsistency between the ECT and the enforcement by Hungary of a competition law decision of the EU Commission.[81] The tribunal considered *obiter dicta*

---

[73] *AES Summit Generation Limited and AES-Tisza Erömü Kft v. The Republic of Hungary,* ICSID Case No. ARB/07/22; *Electrabel S.A. v. Hungary,* ICSID Case No. ARB/07/19, Award (November 30, 2012).

[74] Both cases concern "intra-EU" investment relations (i.e., the claim of an EU investor against an EU Member State), but are to a large extent relevant for "extra-EU" investment issues (including claims by Chinese energy investors against an EU Member State), as will be seen from the statements below.

[75] Ibid.

[76] *Electrabel S.A. v. Hungary* para. 4.119.

[77] Ibid, para. 4.134, 4.130.

[78] Ibid, para. 4.131, 4.92.

[79] *Electrabel S.A. v. Hungary* para. 4.133.

[80] Ibid, para. 4.142.

[81] Ibid, para. 4.169.

that, even in case of inconsistency between the ECT and EU law, "EU law would prevail over the ECT's substantive protections."[82]

This conclusion is problematic for China because the special status of EU energy law under the ECT negatively affects the prospect for successful claims by Chinese investors to be brought in respect of EU norms and their implementation by Member States. Arbitral tribunals are unlikely to grant similar status to Chinese law. The special interrelation between EU law and the ECT potentially penalizes Chinese energy investors in the EU in comparison to EU energy investors in China.

8.4   Conclusion

By acceding to the ECT, China can help increase the protection of its foreign energy investments against political and regulatory risks in strategic energy destinations along the Belt and Road. The broad dispute resolution clause of the ECT helps overcome the obstacle of limited access to arbitration in first-generation Chinese BITs, without having to renegotiate the BITs with all countries with which China concluded first-generation BITs. Moreover, the broad substantive standards of the ECT provide guarantees of protection to Chinese foreign energy investments, such as against breaches of contracts entered by the host state as a sovereign. Although Chinese investors could possibly be able to rely on these clauses even in the absence of China's accession to the ECT (based on the most favored nation clause of the applicable BIT), the ECT provides the advantage of an increasing practice of dispute resolution in the energy sector (e.g. changes to renewable energy subsidies).

However, accession to the ECT would not help mitigate the potential jurisdictional obstacle relating to the strategic nature of the Belt and Road Initiative. Following the purpose-based interpretation in *China Heilongjiang* v. *Mongolia* and *Beijing Urban Construction Group* v. *Yemen,* there is a risk that arbitral tribunals could refuse jurisdiction in cases concerning investments that are made based on an explicit mandate by the Chinese government in the pursuit of the foreign policy objective of securing external energy supplies. Taking into account the strategic dimension of the Belt and Road energy infrastructure policy, this jurisdictional risk is a potential limitation to the added value of the ECT for China.

---

[82] Ibid, para. 4.189–91.

More fundamentally, the special status of EU law, as recognized in the *Electrabel* v. *Hungary* decision, can distort the level playing field that the ECT is supposed to create regarding the protection of foreign energy investments. The EU-centered interpretation of the ECT by an independent arbitral tribunal sends a negative signal to China regarding the nature of the ECT and raises fundamental questions concerning the interests that the Energy Charter process represents. Recognizing a special status for EU energy and competition law under the ECT limits the potential of success of claims by Chinese energy investors against EU Member States under the ECT, and thus reduces the added value of the ECT for the protection of Chinese energy companies investing in the EU internal energy market.

The ongoing modernization of the Energy Charter offers a unique opportunity to address the deficiencies of the ECT from a Chinese perspective. The 2015 International Energy Charter Declaration is a first step in moving away from the original European focus of the Energy Charter (as reflected in the 1991 European Energy Charter Declaration). In addition, participating in the modernization of the ECT could help China shape the treaty to reflect the special characteristics of its foreign energy investments and adjust this mechanism to the benefit of China's increasing energy activities in the large number of Belt and Road countries that are also contracting parties to the ECT.

PART IV

China, BRI and Resolution of Maritime Disputes

The Belt and Road Initiative and the Potential for Dispute Settlement under the UN Convention on the Law of the Sea

NATALIE KLEIN*

9.1 Introduction

The strategy of the Belt and Road Initiative (BRI) entails a vast re-imagining of trade routes and trade linkages between China and countries across Asia to the borders of the European Union. It has been described as 'creat[ing] the world's largest platform for economic cooperation, including policy coordination, trade and financing collaboration, and social and cultural cooperation'.[1] As the foreign policy and economic strategy of one of the world's great powers, the significance of this initiative cannot be easily dismissed.[2] As one commentator has noted:

> The result will be to channel Eurasian economic transactions toward China to deepen interdependence between individual countries of Eurasia on the one hand, and the massive Chinese economy on the other. This economic interdependence will give China superior leverage over any other Eurasian country in a one-on-one negotiation, and will

---

* Parts of this chapter draw on Natalie Klein, *Maritime Security and the Law of the Sea* (OUP, 2011).
[1] Tian Jinchen, *'One Belt and One Road': Connecting China and the World, McKinsey Report*, July 2016, available at www.mckinsey.com/industries/capital-projects-and-infrastructure /our-insights/one-belt-and-one-road-connecting-china-and-the-world.
[2] 'The Belt and Road project is undoubtedly the most important international project that China has embarked on in the last few decades.' European Parliament Directorate-General for External Policies, Policy Department, *Challenges to freedom of the seas and maritime rivalry in Asia*, 14 March 2017, available at www.europarl.europa.eu/RegData/etudes/IDAN/ 2017/578014/EXPO_IDA(2017)578014_EN.pdf (hereinafter European Parliament). As the economic belt could encompass three billion people, it would constitute the biggest trade market globally. Ibid, 10.

give China a leadership position in any Eurasian multilateral economic policy setting.[3]

The BRI comprises land and maritime dimensions, with the 21st Century Maritime Silk Road reflecting the maritime initiative. A 2015 policy document, 'Vision and Actions on Jointly Building Silk Road Economic Belt and 21st-Century Maritime Silk Road', reflects the implementation of the BRI and describes the purpose of the maritime component as achieving 'interconnection and intercommunication' between countries that are along this Maritime Silk Road.[4]

The maritime aspects of the BRI predominantly entail developing ports and ensuring unimpeded access along key trade routes identified through maritime regions of southeast Asia, south Asia, the Middle East, east Africa and the Mediterranean. While the initial focus is on southeast Asia, trade routes are also to be developed across the Indian Ocean to the Persian Gulf and east Africa, as well as through the Red Sea into the Mediterranean.[5] A sea route is also envisaged into the south Pacific.[6] Concerns may arise about how navigational and port access rights will be enforced in the future.[7] Further questions may also arise as to the extent that commercial interests and economic development also further military and strategic goals in the maritime arena (and beyond).

To the extent that conflict between states may arise in light of the BRI strategy, it is worth considering what options may exist to resolve those disputes peacefully. Some disputes will be focused on trade and may be referred to the World Trade Organisation regime;[8] others may relate to investors who have protection under bilateral investment treaties or regional trade agreements, or other treaty relationships may be implicated. Some disputes may be commercial in nature and engage the terms

---

[3] David Arase, 'China's Two Silk Road Initiatives: What it Means for Southeast Asia' (2015) *South East Asian Affairs* 25, 33.

[4] Cited in Guobin Zhang & Yu Long, 'Connectivity and International Law in the 21st Century Maritime Silk Road' in Maximilian Meyer (ed.) *Rethinking the Silk Road and Emerging Eurasian Relations* (Springer Singapore, 2018) 57, 57–58.

[5] Arase, above n 3, 35.

[6] Chen Jia, *'Belt and Road' Takes New Route*, 15 April 2015, *China Daily*, available at www .chinadaily.com.cn/bizchina/2015–04/15/content_20435585.htm.

[7] Arase has noted, 'The difference in economic scale between China and its neighbours means that deepening economic interdependence gives China more bilateral leverage, and military superiority gives China additional leverage.' Arase, above n 3, 32–33.

[8] Under the 1994 Dispute Settlement Understanding. Understanding on Rules and Procedures Governing the Settlement of Disputes, Annex 2, World Trade Organisation Agreement, 1869 UNTS 401; 33 ILM 1226 (1994).

of particular contracts, which will be resolved through commercial arbitration or in national courts. For disputes relating to the maritime dimensions of the BRI, the UN Convention on the Law of the Sea (UNCLOS) may further provide a mechanism for states to resolve disputes.[9]

Every state that becomes a party to UNCLOS, as nearly 170 states have done,[10] agrees to be bound by the rights and obligations enshrined in that treaty and to the possibility of disputes relating to those rights and obligations being referred to arbitration or adjudication. UNCLOS is similar in this regard to the World Trade Organisation dispute settlement regime, but has been used much less frequently. Nonetheless, there is clear potential for states to invoke this dispute settlement regime, especially in situations where a poorer or less powerful state is seeking ways to recalibrate the dynamics of the dispute to enhance its position.

This chapter therefore explores the potential use of the UNCLOS dispute settlement regime in relation to certain aspects of the BRI. The importance of this dimension has been recognised in the following terms:

> According to most Chinese scholars' view, in the process of converting ideas into action, [the Maritime Silk Road] needs to be guided, promoted, and safeguarded by international law. In turn, some argue that to eventually build the [Maritime Silk Road] greatly depends on the ability of China to shape, formulate, and implement cooperation based on international law. Therefore, China should carefully study the international law relevant to [the Maritime Silk Road] in order to resolve the actual challenges of 'maritime connectivity'.[11]

In light of the relevance of international law to China and the opportunities and obstacles presented by its dispute settlement mechanism, this chapter proceeds as follows. It first provides an overview of the UNCLOS dispute settlement procedures and then considers their application in relation to possible disputes relating to three subjects that may arise pursuant to the BRI: ports, navigation and military activities.

The chapter concludes in observing that there is undoubtedly an important role for judges or arbitrators to play in ensuring that the

---

[9] United Nations Convention on the Law of the Sea, opened for signature 10 December 1982, 1833 UNTS 3 (entered into force 16 November 1994) (hereinafter UNCLOS).

[10] See *Chronological lists of ratifications of, accessions and successions to the Convention and the related Agreements*, last updated 6 November 2017, available at www.un.org/depts/los/reference_files/chronological_lists_of_ratifications.htm.

[11] Zhang & Long, above n 4, 58.

implementation of the BRI remains consistent with the rights and obligations agreed under UNCLOS. How successfully this role is played will ultimately depend on the precise details of any dispute and the final decisions of a particular court or tribunal, including the enforcement of those decisions. Courts or tribunals will likely see themselves as having a critical position in ensuring that the balance of interests agreed in UNCLOS is not jeopardised by the national strategies or priorities of any one state party.

9.2   Overview of UNCLOS Dispute Settlement

Part XV of UNCLOS is divided into three Sections that operationalise dispute settlement processes for controversies that may arise in relation to the rights and obligations owed under that treaty. At the outset, it is important to note that the UNCLOS dispute settlement regime is not available for each and every maritime dispute. Instead, the regime is designed for legal disputes relating to the interpretation or application of provisions of UNCLOS.[12] Although the jurisdictional scope has been challenged in different decisions,[13] the UNCLOS dispute settlement regime will not necessarily be available for all differences of opinions that may arise in the implementation of the BRI. This section of the paper provides an overview of the dispute settlement procedure, indicating its limitations, before turning to a more detailed discussion on the potential resolution of disputes relating to specific aspects of BRI in the following sections.

Section 1 of Part XV sets out initial requirements to resolve any disputes that may arise in relation to the interpretation or application of UNCLOS. Consistent with the UN Charter,[14] states are to seek

[12] UNCLOS, Art. 288. A point emphasised in *M/V Louisa*. The M/V 'Louisa' Case (*Saint Vincent and the Grenadines* v. *Kingdom of Spain*), ITLOS Case No. 18, Judgment of 28 May 2013, para. 99 and para. 151.
[13] See, e.g., The South China Sea Arbitration (*Philippines* v. *China*), Award on Jurisdiction and Admissibility, Oct. 25, 2015, PCA Case No. 2013–19, www.pcacases.com/web/view/7; Chagos Marine Protected Area Arbitration (*Mauritius* v. *United Kingdom*), Award of 18 March 2015, PCA Case No. 2011-03, www.pcacases.com/web/view/11 (hereinafter Chagos Archipelago). For discussion, see Natalie Klein, 'The Vicissitudes of Dispute Settlement under the Law of the Sea Convention' (2017) 32 *International Journal of Marine and Coastal Law* 332; Kate Parlett, 'Beyond the Four Corners of the Convention: Expanding the Scope of Jurisdiction of Law of the Sea Tribunals' (2017) 48 *Ocean Development and International Law* 284, available at http://dx.doi.org/10.1080/00908320 .2017.1327289.
[14] UN Charter, Art. 2(3).

peaceful means for the resolution of their disputes and may engage in a diversity of dispute settlement methods, ranging from negotiation, mediation, and conciliation through to arbitration or adjudication.[15] States are allowed to choose their own means to resolve disputes,[16] and in some instances another dispute settlement process may prevail over those available under UNCLOS.[17] States are required to proceed to an exchange of views as to the means of dispute settlement in accordance with Article 283 of UNCLOS.[18]

In relation to a dispute settlement procedure prevailing over that in UNCLOS, Article 281 of UNCLOS anticipates that if states have agreed in another treaty to a method of dispute settlement, that process must be used unless no settlement is reached and the agreement does not exclude any further dispute settlement procedure. The other agreement must be a legally binding agreement,[19] but tribunals have differed as to whether UNCLOS dispute settlement procedures must be explicitly excluded or whether such an exclusion may be implied.[20] States rarely exclude UNCLOS dispute settlement in express terms in their treaties that also address other ocean affairs, and if such a benchmark is maintained, it is unlikely that Article 281 will prevent recourse to UNCLOS compulsory procedures even where other dispute settlement methods may have been available under an alternative ocean-related treaty.[21] Article 282 similarly prioritises dispute settlement procedures that produce binding results under a general, regional or bilateral agreement or otherwise over the UNCLOS dispute settlement mechanism.[22]

---

[15] UN Charter, Art. 33 and UNCLOS, Art. 279.

[16] UNCLOS, Art. 280.

[17] UNCLOS, Art. 281 and Art. 282.

[18] The parameters of Article 283 were discussed in *Chagos Archipelago*. See *Chagos Archipelago*, paras. 378–85.

[19] *A Conciliation Commission Constituted under Annex V to the 1982 United Nations Convention on the Law of the Sea between the Democratic Republic of Timor-Leste and the Commonwealth of Australia (Timor-Leste v. Australia), Decision on Australia's Objections to Competence*, 19 September 2016, available at www.pcacases.com/web/sendAttach/1921, para. 56.

[20] Contrasting views on this position may be seen in *Southern Bluefin Tuna* and the *South China Sea* arbitrations. See discussion in Klein, 'Vicissitudes', above n 13, 336–38.

[21] See ibid, 339–40.

[22] In *Somalia* v. *Kenya*, both states were parties to UNCLOS but proceedings were instituted before the ICJ based on their mutual acceptance of compulsory jurisdiction under Article 36(2) of the Court's Statute. This situation prompted consideration of the role of Article 282 of UNCLOS and which dispute settlement procedure would prevail. The ICJ emphasized that Article 282 applied to the alternative dispute settlement procedures applying in lieu of the UNCLOS procedures. Moreover, acceptances of the Court's jurisdiction under

Once states in dispute have exchanged views in accordance with Article 283 and there is no alternative dispute settlement option available under Articles 281 or 282, state parties may refer the dispute to any court or tribunal having jurisdiction under UNCLOS.[23] As to which court or tribunal may have jurisdiction, state parties to UNCLOS have an option of choosing between the International Court of Justice (ICJ), the International Tribunal for the Law of the Sea (ITLOS), an ad hoc arbitral tribunal constituted under Annex VII or a special arbitral tribunal constituted under Annex VIII to focus on fisheries, marine environment, marine scientific research or navigation.[24] States are able to declare their preferred forum when becoming parties to UNCLOS or at any time thereafter. If a state party fails to make a declaration, or states select different fora, arbitration under Annex VII is deemed the preferred option.[25] To date, no state has resorted to a special arbitral tribunal under Annex VIII for resolution of a dispute under UNCLOS nor referred a dispute to the ICJ on the basis of the UNCLOS compromissory clause. Any law of the sea dispute is thus most likely to be resolved by ITLOS or ad hoc arbitration if referred to compulsory procedures entailing binding decisions.

When a state institutes compulsory proceedings under UNCLOS, it has the option of seeking an order of provisional measures. Such measures may be needed for urgent matters where the state's rights may be irreparably prejudiced or serious harm to the marine environment may be caused prior to the rendering of a final award.[26] If a state is concerned that the institution of proceedings is an abuse of legal process or that prima facie the case is not well founded, a preliminary proceeding may occur to determine such a claim.[27] Such an option is only available in relation to disputes that concern those listed under Article 297 of UNCLOS.

Article 36(2) of its Statute still apply in lieu of compulsory procedures under UNCLOS where those acceptances include reservations comparable to those of Kenya's in the case before it. See *Maritime Delimitation in the Indian Ocean* (*Somalia* v. *Kenya*), Preliminary Objections (2017) ICJ Reports, Judgment of 2 February 2017, paras. 125–30.

[23] UNCLOS, Art. 286.
[24] UNCLOS, Art. 287.
[25] UNCLOS, Art. 287(3) and (5).
[26] UNCLOS, Art. 290(1). Under Article 290(5), ITLOS may make an order on provisional measures pending the constitution of an ad hoc arbitral tribunal depending on the urgency of the matter.
[27] UNCLOS, Art 294.

Article 297 of UNCLOS identifies the disputes that may be submitted to arbitration or adjudication in relation to a coastal state's exercise of sovereign rights or jurisdiction recognised under UNCLOS. Most particularly, Article 297 identifies when compulsory procedures entailing binding decisions are not available, and thereby reflects a limitation on what disputes may be referred to arbitration or adjudication.[28] Similarly, Article 298 sets out disputes that states may optionally exclude from arbitration or adjudication by declaration either at the time of becoming a party to UNCLOS or anytime thereafter.[29] The possible exclusions under Article 298 concern disputes relating to the delimitation of maritime boundaries under Articles 15, 74 or 83 of UNCLOS, or involving historic bays or titles;[30] disputes concerning military activities as well as certain law enforcement activities over fishing and marine scientific research in the EEZ;[31] and disputes over which the Security Council is exercising its functions.[32]

The UNCLOS dispute settlement regime thus provides a certain amount of deference to the preferences of the parties in selecting means for resolving differences concerning the interpretation or application of UNCLOS. The parties have choices as to what form of dispute settlement to use, as to which court or tribunal is preferred and as to whether to exclude certain categories of disputes. Where there is a lack of choice is in the event that a state institutes compulsory procedures over a matter that falls within the subject matter jurisdiction of a court or tribunal constituted under UNCLOS. A state is fully entitled to challenge the jurisdiction of any court or tribunal resolving a dispute under UNCLOS, but it is that court or tribunal that has the authority to resolve those questions relating to its jurisdiction, and any such decision will be final and binding on the parties.[33]

It is in this context, where a state party may institute compulsory arbitration or adjudication under UNCLOS, that it is important to

---

[28] *Chagos Archipelago* discusses that it limits disputes and leaves all others in as a 'jurisdiction-affirming' provision. *Chagos Archipelago*, paras. 308–17. See also Stefan Talmon, 'The Chagos Marine Protected Area Arbitration: Expansion of the Jurisdiction of UNCLOS Part XV Courts and Tribunals' (2016) 65 *International and Comparative Law Quarterly* 927, 942–943; Natalie Klein, *Dispute Settlement in the UN Convention on the Law of the Sea* 141–42.

[29] UNCLOS, Art. 298.

[30] UNCLOS, Art. 298(1)(a).

[31] UNCLOS, Art. 298(1)(b).

[32] UNCLOS, Art. 298(1)(c).

[33] UNCLOS, Art. 288(2); UNCLOS, Art. 296(1).

examine dispute settlement in relation to aspects of the BRI. If a state party considers that the implementation of the BRI impinges on rights granted under UNCLOS, that state party may ultimately seek to resolve the dispute through arbitration or adjudication. Such a case will proceed to a decision on the merits if it falls within the jurisdiction of the court or tribunal constituted under UNCLOS. The following sections examine what particular disputes might arise under the BRI that will also constitute disputes relating to the interpretation or application of UNCLOS. The analysis considers possible outcomes of resolving jurisdictional disputes through the UNCLOS dispute settlement procedures.

9.3 Potential Disputes over Ports

An important element of the BRI has been investment in a series of ports along the principal sea lanes of communication that are instrumental for China's trade with other participants in the BRI.[34] One of the priorities articulated in the Vision and Actions document is to 'push forward port infrastructure construction, build smooth land-water transportation channels, and advance port cooperation; increase sea routes and the number of voyages, and enhance information technology cooperation in maritime logistics'.[35] With the BRI emphasis on trade development, the smooth transition of ships (and goods) in and out of ports will be critical to the overall success of the strategy.[36]

China has already entered into agreements with states in relation to particular ports, or Chinese entities have assumed ownership rights over those ports. A striking example in the latter regard is the purchase of the Piraeus Container Terminal, which was already half-owned and managed by the Chinese state-owned shipping company COSCO.[37] Port investments have extended across at least another dozen countries.[38]

---

[34] The chain of ports in the Indian Ocean is referred to as the 'string of pearls'. European Parliament, above n 2, 8.

[35] Cited in Hu Zhang, 'The 21st Century Maritime Silk Road and the Leading Function of the Shipping Industry' in Maximilian Mayer, *Rethinking the Silk Road: China's Belt and Road Initiative and Emerging Eurasian Relations* (Springer Singapore, 2017), 43, 46.

[36] Zhang & Long, above n 4, observe that the Visions and Actions policy document notes that maritime connectivity refers to 'jointly building a free, safe and efficient channel with key ports as the node'. 58.

[37] Arase, above n 3, 26.

[38] As of January 2015, investments had been made in Bangladesh, Djibouti, Egypt, Greece, Indonesia, Kenya, Malaysia, Myanmar, Pakistan, Sri Lanka, Sudan and Tanzania. Arase, 36. Australia and Oman could also be added to this list. See Geoff Wade, 'China's "One

Ports are critical for the Maritime Silk Road both for the economies of the countries in which ports are developed and for enhancing interconnectivity along the route.[39]

Establishing authority over or creating ownership interests in a series of ports is essential for China to guarantee access of its ships into those ports. Ports are largely unregulated under UNCLOS, with the exception of indicating the relevance of ports for the purposes of delimiting the territorial sea,[40] and providing for the exercise of port state jurisdiction for the purposes of enforcing requirements relating to the protection and preservation of the marine environment.[41] Article 11 of UNCLOS does not specifically define ports, but to the extent they are to be utilized for maritime delimitation, ports are considered as 'permanent harbour works' and are regarded as forming part of the coast. As part of the coast, states have sovereignty over ports located within their territory[42] and may control what vessels enter their ports and under what conditions.

Access to ports is largely a matter of customary international law, or is otherwise regulated by separate agreement. Article V of the General Agreement on Tariffs and Trade (GATT) guarantees freedom of transit.[43] McDorman has noted that Article V is 'silent on the issue of vessel access to ports, although the denial of a right of access may amount to a trade barrier inconsistent with GATT'.[44] While a dispute may thus emerge within the international trade law system, it is not possible to point to a comparable provision within UNCLOS that guarantees any such access,[45] and thus could be the subject of dispute settlement proceedings under Part XV of UNCLOS.

Belt, One Road" initiative', *Parliamentary Library Briefing Book* available at www .aph.gov.au/About_Parliament/Parliamentary_Departments/Parliamentary_Library/ pubs/BriefingBook45p/ChinasRoad.

[39] See Zhang, above n 35, 49.

[40] UNCLOS, Art. 11.

[41] UNCLOS, Art. 218 and 211(3). Article 98(1)(c) refers to ports in the context of the duty to render assistance and provision of information as to the journey of a ship involved in a collision.

[42] Robin R. Churchill & A. Vaughn Lowe, *The Law of the Sea* (3rd ed., 1999) 61.

[43] General Agreement on Tariffs and Trade, Oct. 30, 1947, 61 Stat. A-11, 55 U.N.T.S. 194, Art V.

[44] Ted L. McDorman, 'Port State Enforcement: A Comment on Article 218 of the 1982 Law of the Sea Convention' (1997) 28 *Journal of Maritime Law and Commerce* 305, 310–11.

[45] Except for access and transit rights that may be granted to land-locked states under the requirements of Article 125 of UNCLOS.

In prescribing conditions for entry, states are entitled to regulate their ports consistent with their national interests. For example, the International Ship and Port Facility Security (ISPS) Code allows states to put in place notice requirements regarding the entry of a vessel into port as part of a suite of measures to reduce the likelihood of a terrorist attack against a port.[46] The Port State Measures Agreement allows states to set requirements and restrictions on fishing vessels seeking entry into port so as to prevent, deter and eliminate illegal, unregulated or unreported fishing.[47]

If access of a vessel is restricted because of environmental risks associated with that vessel, different treaties adopted under the auspices of the International Maritime Organisation (IMO), such as MARPOL,[48] may be at issue, but Article 211(3) of UNCLOS may also be invoked. This provision anticipates that states will 'establish particular requirements for the prevention, reduction and control of pollution of the marine environment as a condition for the entry of foreign vessels into their ports or internal waters or for a call at their off-shore terminals'. In doing so, a state is required to give due publicity to any such requirements and communicate them to the IMO, as the relevant competent intergovernmental organisation.[49] A state that considers itself prejudiced through denial of access on environmental grounds may challenge the port state's adherence to these procedural requirements under Article 211(3). A failure to provide appropriate notice would not, however, equate with requiring a state to grant access to its ports and on its own would seem to lack sufficient importance for the core issue of maintaining the flow of trade between various ports.

Ultimately, states engaging in the BRI have an incentive to ensure that conditions of access are consistent with international standards so that

[46] See Natalie Klein, *Maritime Security and the Law of the Sea* (OUP, 2011), 158–62 (discussing the ISPS Code).
[47] Agreement on Port State Measures to Prevent, Deter, and Eliminate Illegal, Unreported and Unregulated Fishing, signed 22 November 2009, entered into force 5 June 2016, UNTS Registration No. I-54133. See discussion in Klein, *Maritime Security*, above n 46, 72.
[48] See Convention on the Prevention of Marine Pollution by Dumping of Wastes and Other Matter (Concluded 29 December 1972, entered into force 30 August 1975) 1046 UNTS 120, Art 5(3). See also Convention for the Prevention of Pollution of the Sea by Oil, May 12, 1954, 327 UNTS 3, Art VI. A series of regional memoranda of understanding on port state control have been adopted to prevent the operation of substandard ships. See Ted L. McDorman, 'Regional Port State Control Agreements: Some Issues of International Law' (2000) 5 *Ocean and Coastal Law Journal* 207.
[49] UNCLOS, Art. 211(3).

their ports are commercially viable and business is not re-directed to another, less demanding, port.[50] The economic incentives associated with the BRI port investments may prompt bilateral agreements between China and the port state that guarantee access rights. These bilateral agreements may have their own dispute settlement procedures that would potentially prevail over the UNCLOS procedures if express provision is included to that effect.

In relation to the rights and obligations that a state may exercise over any vessels in its ports, this legal authority is also governed by customary international law and treaties other than UNCLOS. To this end, McDougal and Burke have noted:

> It is universally acknowledged that once a ship voluntarily enters port it becomes fully subject to the laws and regulations prescribed by the officials of that territory for events relating to such use and that all types of vessels, military and other, are in common expectation obliged to comply with the coastal regulations about proper procedures to be employed and permissible activities within internal waters.[51]

Exceptions to this authority apply in relation to vessels that have entered the port in distress,[52] vessels subject to sovereign immunity,[53] and in relation to the inapplicability of local labour laws.[54]

Inspections and other related law enforcement activities may be possible in port under the terms of particular multilateral treaties, including the Port State Measures Agreement[55] and the Fish Stocks Agreement.[56] Security restrictions in relation to ports are identified in the ISPS Code, which is included as part of the Safety of Life at Sea Convention.[57] An UNCLOS dispute may arise in relation to Article 218 of UNCLOS, which permits the exercise of port state jurisdiction over polluting vessels. However, if the dispute concerns commercial terms and conditions, or is otherwise unrelated to environmental concerns, it is much less likely that a dispute relating to the interpretation or application of UNCLOS

---

[50] See McDorman, 'Regional Port State', above n 48, 207–08, 218.
[51] Myres S. McDougal & William T. Burke, *The Public Order of the Oceans* (1962) 156.
[52] Stuart Kaye, 'The Proliferation Security Initiative in the Maritime Domain' (2005) 35 *Israel Yearbook of Human Rights* 205, 210–11.
[53] See UNCLOS, Art. 32 and Art. 95.
[54] Kaye, above n 52, 210–11.
[55] Port State Measures Agreement, Arts. 12–19.
[56] Fish Stocks Agreement, Arts. 21–22.
[57] International Convention for the Safety of Life At Sea, 1 November 1974 (entered into force 25 May 1980), 1184 UNTS 3, Chapter XI-2. For discussion, see Klein, *Maritime Security*, above n 46, 160–62.

will arise in relation to a state's assertion of authority over foreign-flagged vessels in its ports.

A central reason for ensuring that a series of ports is available for the BRI is to counteract the right of a coastal state to close a port to foreign shipping. This right is a corollary of the principle of state sovereignty,[58] and ports may be closed to safeguard good order on shore, to signal political displeasure or to defend 'vital interests'.[59] In practice, de La Fayette has observed that ports have been closed:

> for various reasons related to the protection of public health and safety; to ships carrying explosives; to ships carrying passengers with contagious diseases; to ships carrying dangerous cargoes, such as hazardous wastes; for general coastal pollution protection; to substandard ships; and to ships presenting hazards to maritime navigation.[60]

Unless the closure of the port is linked to other violations, particularly in relation to the freedom of navigation, it may be difficult to base a dispute concerning access or regulation of ports under the terms of UNCLOS.

Jurisprudence under UNCLOS has thus far addressed the situation of vessels detained in port and arguments that such detention violates the vessel's freedom of the high seas or its immunities if a warship. For example, in the *M/V Louisa* case, it was argued that a vessel in detention was permitted to leave a port because of the freedom of the high seas enshrined in Article 87 of UNCLOS. However, ITLOS determined that Article 87 could not be interpreted so as to encapsulate 'a right to leave the port and gain access to the high seas notwithstanding its detention in the context of legal proceedings against it'[61] where the vessel was arrested for activities conducted in the territorial sea. Yet a vessel arrested in port for activities on the high seas does render consideration of Article 87 relevant, as determined in the *M/V Norstar* decision on jurisdiction.[62] At

---

[58] Justin S. C. Mellor, 'Missing the Boat: The Legal and Practical Problems of the Prevention of Maritime Terrorism' (2002) 18 *American University International Law Review* 341, 393. See also A. V. Lowe, 'The Right of Entry into Maritime Ports in International Law' (1977) 14 *San Diego Law Review* 597, 607.

[59] See Klein, *Maritime Security*, above n 46, 67.

[60] Louise de La Fayette, 'Access to Ports in International Law' (1996) 11 *International Journal of Marine and Coastal Law* 1, 6.

[61] *M/V Louisa*, para. 109.

[62] The *M/V 'Norstar' Case, Panama v. Italy*, Preliminary Objections, ITLOS Case No 25, 4 November 2016, para. 122. But see ibid, Joint Separate Opinion of Judges Wolfrum and Attard, para. 5 and paras. 35–41, criticising the standard of appreciation used by the Tribunal to establish jurisdiction and the application of Article 87 in this context. See also ibid, Dissenting Opinion of Judge ad hoc Treves, paras. 12–16.

the merits stage of *M/V Norstar*, the Tribunal confirmed that the freedom of the high seas does not include the right to voyage towards the high seas.[63] Argentina had also argued that the detention of one of its warships in port in Ghana was a violation of the freedom of navigation under Article 87 in the *ARA Libertad* provisional measures case.[64] Yet the Tribunal rejected the view that the freedom of navigation related to the immunity of warships in port for the purposes of establishing prima facie jurisdiction.[65]

It may be argued that whether or not a dispute relates to particular UNCLOS provisions is sufficient to bring it within the jurisdiction of a court or tribunal constituted under UNCLOS. The Philippines pursued this view in asserting that China could not justify the use of its nine-dash line within the South China Sea based on historic rights.[66] In characterising China's claim as based on historic rights, the Philippines had to face the argument that historic rights are not explicitly addressed within UNCLOS. If UNCLOS does not have provisions dealing with historic rights at sea, is the claim one relating to the interpretation or application of UNCLOS for the purposes of exercising jurisdiction?

In resolving this issue, the *South China Sea* Tribunal determined:

> A dispute concerning the interaction of the Convention with another instrument or body of law, including the question of whether rights arising under another body of law were or were not preserved by the Convention, is unequivocally a dispute concerning the interpretation and application of the Convention.[67]

On this view, there is scope to incorporate other legal regimes that touch on matters also covered by UNCLOS but that are not strictly part of UNCLOS. Issues relating to access to ports and closure of ports may fall within this query of whether port rights were or were not preserved by the

---

[63] *The M/V 'Norstar' Case, Panama v. Italy*, Judgment, ITLOS Case No 25, 10 April 2019, para. 221.

[64] *'ARA Libertad' Case, Argentina v. Ghana*, Order, Provisional Measures, ITLOS Case No 20, [2012] ITLOS Rep 21, para. 43.

[65] ARA Libertad, para. 61. The Tribunal instead considered that Article 32, addressing the immunities of a warship, may instead form a basis of jurisdiction as the parties differed on the scope of application of that provision and whether it applied to more than the territorial sea. See ibid, para. 65.

[66] See *The South China Sea Arbitration (Philippines v. China)*, Award of 12 July 2016, PCA Case No. 2013-19, www.pcacases.com/web/view/7, paras. 169–278.

[67] *South China Sea* (Jurisdiction), para. 168.

Convention. In this scenario, a state may argue that port access or the regulation of ports 'interacts' with UNCLOS and hence should fall within jurisdiction. It may ultimately depend on how widely any court or tribunal is willing to interpret its jurisdictional remit. It is difficult to predict fully such a claim and how it might be resolved in the absence of specific facts.

9.4   Potential Disputes over Navigation

Facilitating the free movement of cargo vessels is an important dimension of the BRI and is thus dependent on the full recognition of navigational rights accorded under UNCLOS. China's interests in this regard should align with other states, like the United States, that share strong interests in maintaining the freedom of navigation. However, what should be rights accorded equally to all states appear to have been sought as exclusive rights in China's maritime engagements and have entailed Chinese efforts to control maritime areas to the exclusion of other commercial, fishing and military vessels.[68] The US Pentagon has referred to this Chinese strategy as 'Anti-Access/Area Denial'.[69] Yet China's policy in this regard appears to focus on asserting rights associated with China's territorial sovereignty claims over small islands in the South China and East China Seas.[70] As mentioned, China has also asserted historic rights over most of the South China Sea using a nine-dash line, but the *South China Sea* arbitral tribunal denied the legality of this claim.[71] If China seeks to assert sovereignty and exclusive authority over maritime areas with the effect of denying other states' navigational rights recognised in UNCLOS, it is very likely that disputes will arise.

Disputes concerning navigation may generally arise in relation to the passage of commercial vessels depending on the control or authority that a coastal state is exerting over its maritime areas.[72] A coastal state exercises sovereignty over the territorial sea, a band of water extending up to twelve miles from that state's baselines.[73] A coastal state's sovereignty over the territorial sea is subject to the right of innocent passage

---

[68] European Parliament, above n 2, 8.
[69] Arase, above n 3, 29.
[70] See Yen-Chiang Chang, 'The "21st Century Maritime Silk Road Initiative" and Naval Diplomacy in China' (2018) 153 *Ocean and Coastal Management* 148, 152 and 153.
[71] *South China Sea* (Award), para. 278.
[72] The passage of military vessels is addressed in the next section.
[73] UNCLOS, Art. 2.

enjoyed by foreign flagged vessels for traversing the waters of the coastal state. The right of innocent passage involves continuous and expeditious passage where the vessel does not enter the internal waters or ports of the coastal state.[74] To be innocent, the passage must not prejudice the peace, good order or security of the coastal state,[75] and UNCLOS identifies a list of inclusive activities that may be considered prejudicial, including the loading or offloading of any commodity, fishing activities or any research or survey activities.[76] The coastal state is authorized to take steps to prevent any passage that is not innocent.[77]

In this context, if a coastal state sought to hinder the passage of a vessel through its territorial sea that was engaged in international trade as part of the BRI, the flag state of the vessel concerned could potentially challenge those actions under the UNCLOS dispute settlement regime. The coastal state is allowed to introduce some regulations over the passage of vessels, including traffic separation schemes,[78] and must usually ensure that regulations relating to navigation align with international agreements or standards.[79] Any interference with passage would have to be consistent with the requirements of UNCLOS, and the international agreements alluded to in its provisions, to prevent a claim against the coastal state being upheld in arbitration or adjudication.

Outside the territorial sea, foreign-flagged vessels may exercise the freedom of navigation throughout the EEZ of a coastal state,[80] subject only to showing due regard for the rights and duties of the coastal state in that maritime area.[81] Compulsory dispute settlement is available 'when it is alleged that a coastal State has acted in contravention of [UNCLOS] in regard to the freedoms and rights of navigation, overflight or the laying of submarine cables and pipelines, or in regard to other internationally lawful uses of the sea specified in article 58'.[82] Consequently, if the BRI was thwarted by interference with the freedom of navigation in the EEZ of a coastal state, a flag state could utilise the UNCLOS dispute settlement regime to resolve this dispute if necessary. If a coastal state considered that the passage of vessels further to the BRI strategy was inconsistent

---

[74] UNCLOS, Art. 18.
[75] UNCLOS, Art. 19(1).
[76] UNCLOS, Art. 19(2).
[77] UNCLOS, Art. 25(1).
[78] See UNCLOS, Art. 22.
[79] UNCLOS, Art. 21.
[80] UNCLOS, Art. 58(1).
[81] UNCLOS, Art. 58(3).
[82] UNCLOS, Art. 297(1)(a).

with its rights under UNCLOS in the EEZ, it equally could resort to compulsory procedures in line with Part XV of UNCLOS.[83]

Freedom of navigation is also exercised on the high seas,[84] and it is most typically only the flag states of vessels on the high seas that have the right to regulate and enforce laws against those vessels.[85] The navy or policing vessels of one state may not visit or enforce laws against a foreign-flagged vessel on the high seas unless the flag state consents, either on an ad hoc basis or by treaty.[86] Flag states are required to 'effectively exercise ... jurisdiction and control in administrative, technical and social matters' over their ships.[87] If a flag state fails to take reasonable steps to exercise control over its vessels, a court or tribunal may find it responsible for its lack of due diligence in dispute settlement proceedings.[88]

To the extent that the BRI does not impinge on existing navigational rights that are enshrined and protected under UNCLOS, it should not be expected that the UNCLOS dispute settlement regime would be needed to uphold navigational rights. If, however, the BRI anticipates greater exclusivity in the exercise of navigational rights, rather than allowing the free, unhindered passage of commercial vessels across the varied maritime zones, flag states could challenge such restrictions through compulsory arbitration or adjudication. A central dynamic in the negotiation of UNCLOS was ensuring protection for the rights of navigation even in the face of increasing coastal state claims over greater expanses of ocean space. A court or tribunal faced with a dispute in relation to the implementation of the BRI would likely strive to ensure that the balance achieved at the time UNCLOS was adopted was maintained in future ocean use.

A further threat to navigation may eventuate if the safety of navigation routes is (or is perceived to be) threatened by maritime crime (notably, terrorism and piracy). In that situation, coastal states and other

---

[83] UNCLOS, Art. 297(1)(b).
[84] UNCLOS, Art. 90.
[85] UNCLOS, Art. 94.
[86] For example, the right of visit is granted under UNCLOS for a limited range of activities. See UNCLOS, Art. 110.
[87] UNCLOS, Art. 94(1).
[88] This possibility was discussed in relation to flag state responsibilities over fishing vessels that conduct unlawful fishing. See *Request for an Advisory Opinion submitted by the Sub-Regional Fisheries Commission* (SRFC) [2015] ITLOS Case No. 21, 2 April 2015, paras 110–40, available at www.itlos.org/fileadmin/itlos/documents/cases/case_no.21/advisory_opinion_published/2015_21-advop-E.pdf.

participants in the BRI, including China, may consider that joint law enforcement efforts may be required. China has recognised the importance of ensuring maritime safety for international shipping against terrorism and piracy threats.[89] Such law enforcement efforts may be considered as hampering the freedom of navigation depending on where (that is, in what maritime zones) and how (that is, authorised by the relevant coastal state or an international organisation including the UN Security Council) it is undertaken. A flag state may wish to challenge these law enforcement actions and may potentially turn to the dispute settlement procedures under Part XV of UNCLOS.[90]

Where the exercise of the freedom of navigation may further prove controversial is where there are different viewpoints as to which maritime zone a vessel may be traversing. In some instances, states will object to how a coastal state has drawn its baselines, or closing lines across bays, and those states will then hold a different view as to where the outer limits of the territorial sea may lie for a particular coastal state.[91] In the South China Sea, the United States has recently challenged China's declaration of territorial seas off artificial islands that have been constructed on fully submerged reefs.[92] If the reefs were never above water, they would not be entitled to a territorial sea. Similarly, states may dispute whether a particular feature is a rock or an island under Article 121 of UNCLOS, and hence what maritime zones may be claimed by the coastal state depending on the status of the feature as a rock or island.[93] This issue was of particular controversy in the *South China Sea* arbitration, which addressed the status of a variety of features in the South China Sea.[94] The validity of baselines, rights associated with artificial islands and the status of islands, rocks, low-tide elevations and reefs could all be assessed in the context of UNCLOS dispute settlement proceedings if

---

[89] See Zhang, above n 35, 50–51.

[90] It must be noted that a coastal state's law enforcement activities with respect to fisheries and some aspects of marine scientific research within its EEZ may be optionally excluded from compulsory arbitration or adjudication under Art 298(1)(b) of UNCLOS.

[91] See further Chang, above n 69, 153.

[92] See Preeti Nalwa, 'Beijing Remains "Undeterred" in the South China Sea', *The National Interest*, 10 January 2016, available at http://nationalinterest.org/blog/the-buzz/beijing-remains-%E2%80%98undeterred%E2%80%99-the-south-china-sea-14863; Franz-Stefan Gady, 'South China Sea: US Navy Conducts Freedom of Navigation Operation', *The Diplomat*, 10 August 2017, available at https://thediplomat.com/2017/08/south-china-sea-us-navy-conducts-freedom-of-navigation-operation/.

[93] UNCLOS, Art. 121(3).

[94] It found that none of the features in dispute were 'islands' under Article 121 of UNCLOS but at most were rocks, entitled only to a territorial sea.

necessary. However, where the sovereignty (or ownership) of a particular island or rock is also contested, it is unlikely that a territorial sovereignty question could be resolved by a court or tribunal with jurisdiction under UNCLOS.[95]

9.5 Potential Disputes over Military Activities

The military and strategic dimensions of the BRI have been the cause of speculation among commentators.[96] One assertion has contemplated that the string of ports and efforts to ensure open sea lanes of communication equally benefit the passage of military vessels.[97] For China's ever-growing navy, it shares an interest with the United States, as noted above, in ensuring that its naval vessels are able to move into different areas to assert a military presence in times of controversy or even in times of armed conflict.[98] To a large extent, military vessels share the freedoms of navigation enjoyed by commercial vessels as discussed in Section IV. However, there are some important differences that may trigger disputes concerning the interpretation or application of UNCLOS.

In relation to passage through the territorial sea, one unresolved issue has been whether prior notice or authorization is required for warships or other naval vessels. UNCLOS does not address this question specifically and state practice has varied on this point.[99] If a warship violates its right of innocent passage, the coastal state is limited in its responses because of the warship's immunity.[100] At most, it may request that the warship leave its territorial sea.[101] In this situation, it may also be open to the coastal state to challenge the actions of the warship through the dispute settlement procedures in UNCLOS.

---

[95] See *Chagos Archipelago*, paras. 217–19. The scope of jurisdiction to consider territorial disputes has been controversial. See Irina Buga, 'Territorial Sovereignty Issues in Maritime Disputes: A Jurisdictional Dilemma for Law of the Sea Tribunals' (2012) 27 *International Journal of Marine and Coastal Law* 65, 90.

[96] See Arase, above n 3, 40. See also Anoush Ehteshami, 'China's New Silk Road Is All Part of Its Grand Strategy for Global Influence', 6 January 2017, *The Conversation*, available at https://theconversation.com/chinas-new-silk-road-is-all-part-of-its-grand-strategy-for-global-influence-70862; Wade, above n 38; European Parliament, above n 2, 14.

[97] While China has built up 'commercial access points along its sea lanes . . . only a few ports can be used as military bases'. European Parliament, above n 2, 10. See also ibid, 24.

[98] For discussion of China's naval diplomacy, see generally Chang, above n 69.

[99] See discussion in Klein, *Maritime Security*, above n 46, 38–39.

[100] UNCLOS, Art. 32.

[101] UNCLOS, Art. 30.

Beyond navigating from one port to the next, naval vessels will also typically engage in military exercises and surveillance activities as part of their training and missions. Such activities are considered prejudicial to the peace, good order and security of a coastal state if conducted in the territorial sea of that coastal state.[102] However, outside the territorial sea, states like the United States have argued that such military activities fall within the freedom of navigation and other internationally lawful uses of the sea related to this freedom and have protested state actions contrary to this view.[103] China has disagreed with this view of third-state rights within the EEZ,[104] and has actively opposed US surveillance missions within China's EEZ.[105] One basis for this view is an interpretation of Article 58 of UNCLOS that focuses on the listing of the specific freedoms, and that not all military activities are related to the specified freedoms.[106]

Article 58 of UNCLOS provides that all states (including land-locked states) enjoy within the EEZ 'the freedoms referred to in Article 87 of navigation . . . and other internationally lawful uses of the sea related to these freedoms'.[107] In this respect, it must be borne in mind that the rights of navigation are qualified in various ways by Article 58. These qualifications include reference to 'relevant provisions' of UNCLOS, demanding 'due regard to the rights and duties of the coastal State' and require compliance with 'the laws and regulations adopted by the coastal State in accordance with the provisions of this Convention and other rules of international law in so far as they are not incompatible with this Part'.[108]

Yet the right of a coastal state to prevent or control military activities within its EEZ remains controversial.[109] Coastal states have objected to third states' military activities based on possible interference with its economic activities in the EEZ.[110] Thus, to the extent that coastal states

---

[102] UNCLOS, Art. 19(2).

[103] See Donald R. Rothwell & Tim Stephens, *The International Law of the Sea* (2nd ed., 2016) 296.

[104] As do other developing states, such as Bangladesh, Brazil, Cape Verde, India, Malaysia, Pakistan and Uruguay. See Chang, above n 69, 150.

[105] See Rothwell and Stephens, above n 102, 297.

[106] Klein, *Maritime Security*, above n 46, 48.

[107] Other high seas freedoms are incorporated into the EEZ provided that they are not incompatible with the EEZ regime in Part V of the Convention. UNCLOS, Art 58(2).

[108] See, e.g., Ren Ziafeng & Cheng Xizhong, 'A Chinese Perspective' (2005) 29 *Marine Policy* 139, 140.

[109] Klein, *Maritime Security*, above n 46, 47.

[110] See Jon M. Van Dyke, 'Military Ships and Planes Operating in the Exclusive Economic Zone of Another Country' (2004) 28 *Marine Policy* 29, 31.

have the right to prevent interference with its economic interests,[111] this right arguably extends to limiting what military activities are undertaken by third states.[112]

A further aspect of this debate relates to the meaning of Article 88 of UNCLOS, which provides that 'the high seas shall be reserved for peaceful purposes'. Some scholars argue that the navigation activities of warships must therefore be limited to align with this requirement.[113] However, an alternative view would allow the operation of military vessels in the EEZ of coastal states provided those activities do not breach the requirements of Article 2(4) of the UN Charter as a threat or use of force against the territorial integrity or political independence of any state, as indicated in Article 301 of UNCLOS. This debate may need to be resolved within the context of dispute settlement procedures considering the interpretation or application of these particular provisions.

As UNCLOS does not definitely settle what military activities may be permissible within the EEZ of a coastal state, any dispute might ultimately come down to a question of due regard. Have the military exercises or activities failed to show sufficient due regard to the rights of other vessels seeking to deliver goods pursuant to the BRI? There is no order of priorities between coastal states' rights and third states' rights in the EEZ established in UNCLOS.[114] A balance must instead be struck.[115] Much will ultimately depend on the particular activity in question and what influence it has on the rights and duties of the other user.

As UNCLOS does not have specific rules on military exercises outside the territorial sea, questions that relate to whether military operations fall within the freedom of navigation under Article 58 of UNCLOS or are for peaceful purposes under Article 88 could potentially be referred to compulsory arbitration or adjudication. However, an outstanding issue with any referral of a dispute under the UNCLOS dispute settlement procedures is the possibility that a state has issued a declaration under Article 298, as China has done, excluding from jurisdiction 'disputes

---

[111] Francisco Orrego Vicuna, *The Exclusive Economic Zone* (Cambridge University Press, 1989) 114.

[112] Klein, *Maritime Security*, above n 46, 47.

[113] See, e.g., Zhang and Long, above n 4, 63.

[114] D. J. Attard, *The Exclusive Economic Zone in International Law* (Clarendon Press, 1987) 64, 66.

[115] Bernard H. Oxman, 'The Third United Nations Conference on the Law of the Sea: The 1976 New York Session' (1977) 71 *AJIL* 247, 260–61 ('It can be anticipated that these balanced duties will provide the juridical basis for resolving many practical problems of competing uses.')

concerning military activities'. The precise parameters of this exception are unclear but have been considered in recent cases instituted under the UNCLOS dispute settlement regime.

In the *South China Sea* arbitration, the Tribunal indicated that where a state disavows that its activities are military in nature, this characterization is of distinct relevance. Hence, China's consistent claims that its land reclamation activities and creation of artificial islands were for civilian purposes meant that the military activities exception could not preclude examination of potential environmental violations in the course of that reclamation work.[116]

The military activities exception was also assessed in this arbitration in response to the Philippines' claims that China unlawfully aggravated the dispute in its actions subsequent to the commencement of the arbitration. Contrary to the view of the Philippines that the military activities exception did not apply because it had never been invoked by China, the Tribunal considered that such an explicit claim was not necessary.[117] Rather, the Tribunal emphasized 'the relevant question to be whether the dispute itself concerns military activities, rather than whether a party has employed its military in some manner in relation to the dispute'.[118] The facts before the Tribunal relating to certain incidents at Second Thomas Shoal were deemed to be a 'quintessentially military situation' and hence covered by the exception to jurisdiction enshrined in Article 298(1)(b).[119]

Questions relating to the passage of military vessels could potentially be viewed as questions of navigation, particularly if the status of the vessel as a military vessel is not decisive in the coastal state actions taken against the foreign vessel. This position was taken by ITLOS in *Detention of Three Ukrainian Naval Vessels* where Russia was considered to be undertaking law enforcement activities rather than military activities.[120] A court or tribunal may instead view an interpretation of Articles 56 and 58 as defining a state's rights in a particular maritime area and determining what falls within the 'freedom of navigation' and 'other internationally lawful uses of the sea related to these freedoms'.

---

[116] *South China Sea* (Award), paras. 893 and 934ff. See further ibid, paras. 1012 and 1028 in relation to Mischief Reef.
[117] Ibid, para. 1156.
[118] Ibid, para. 1158.
[119] Ibid, para. 1161.
[120] Case concerning the detention of three Ukrainian naval vessels (Ukraine v. Russian Federation), Provisional Measures, ITLOS Case No. 26, 25 May 2019, paras 64–74.

A dispute focused on the interpretation or application of those provisions of UNCLOS would likely fall within the subject matter jurisdiction of a court or tribunal constituted under UNCLOS. As such, the military activities exception would not necessarily apply.

While a court or tribunal has not yet had the opportunity to assess whether military exercises or surveillance activities by military vessels fall within the jurisdictional exception under Article 298, it could be anticipated that a strong argument as to the quintessential military nature of such activities could be successfully mounted. One tribunal has noted that the 'mere involvement or presence of military vessels is in and by itself' insufficient to bar the exercise of jurisdiction.[121] If a warship is not engaged in actual hostilities, its other key responsibilities are preparing for such hostilities through training activities or surveillance. If an interpretation of Article 58 has to be applied to these types of military activities then arguably the dispute 'concerns' military activities. The counterpoint to this argument is that the current trend in tribunals constituted under UNCLOS is to read grants of jurisdiction broadly and exceptions narrowly, so it cannot be too readily assumed that a more inclusive perspective on 'military activities' would necessarily be adopted in the context of an UNCLOS arbitration or adjudication.

9.6   Concluding Remarks

Given the overall scale of the BRI, the legal rights and duties associated with the maritime dimensions of the strategy are a relatively small component. Any dispute that may arise in relation to the BRI may well be multifaceted and implicate a variety of obligations under international law, as well as posing economic, social or diplomatic problems. A dispute arising under UNCLOS may thus be a small factor or potentially just one part of a much bigger dispute. Arguably, the *South China Sea* arbitration instituted by the Philippines against China under UNCLOS concerned some limited dimensions of a much bigger controversy concerning competing claims and entitlements in the South China Sea. The relevance of UNCLOS dispute settlement to the BRI may therefore be relatively contained.

A further lesson learned from the *South China Sea* arbitration is that China will not necessarily engage with international dispute settlement

---

[121] *Dispute Concerning Coastal State Rights in the Black Sea, Sea of Azov, and Kerch Strait (Ukraine* v. *the Russian Federation)*, Award on Preliminary Objections, PCA Case No 2017-06, para. 334

processes involving compulsory arbitration or adjudication. China advised at the outset of the arbitration that it would not participate.[122] The failure of China to appear did not prevent the arbitral tribunal from determining its jurisdiction and resolving the claims before it.[123] China instead issued various statements and policy papers to indicate its views without engaging fully and properly in analysis or defence of key legal positions.[124] When the decision was rendered largely in favour of the Philippines, China denounced it as null and void.[125]

China's response to the ruling of the *South China Sea* arbitral tribunal reflects disregard for the rule of law and international legal processes. The European Union considers China's reaction as 'open[ing] the way to other contests and put[ting] the law at risk'.[126] Instead, the European Union's Global Strategy anticipates engagement with and support for the international law of the sea and the use of mechanisms available for the peaceful resolution of disputes, including arbitration.[127] Such engagement will not be forthcoming from the United States, as it has not yet become a party to UNCLOS and may therefore not assert rights guaranteed only under that treaty nor rely on its processes to resolve law of the sea disputes falling within its terms. Other states may be dissuaded from pursuing dispute settlement options under UNCLOS in light of China's reaction to the *South China Sea* arbitration.

Yet it may be possible that China itself will wish to rely on the guaranteed rights within UNCLOS and potentially utilise the dispute settlement procedures to its own advantage. In this regard, one commentator has observed:

> What one sees is China deploying its growing military and civilian power in intimidating ways to get neighbours to cede their maritime territorial

---

[122] *South China Sea* (Jurisdiction), para. 111.

[123] UNCLOS, Annex VII, Art. 9.

[124] See, e.g., *South China Sea* (Jurisdiction), paras. 121–22.

[125] Statement of the Ministry of Foreign Affairs of the People's Republic of China on the Award of 12 July 2016 of the Arbitral Tribunal in the South China Sea Arbitration Established at the Request of the Republic of the Philippines, 12 July 2016, available at www.fmprc.gov.cn/nanhai/eng/snhwtlcwj_1/t1379492.htm; Chinese Society of International Law, 'The Tribunal's Award in the "South China Sea Arbitration" Initiated by the Philippines Is Null and Void', 10 June 2016, available at www.csil.cn/News/Detail.aspx?AId=201.

[126] European Parliament, above n 2, 22.

[127] 'In East and Southeast Asia, we (the EU) will uphold freedom of navigation, stand firm on the respect for international law, including the Law of the Sea and its arbitration procedures, and encourage the peaceful settlement of maritime disputes.' European Union Global Strategy, June 2016, 38, cited in European Parliament, above n 2, 19.

rights granted under [UNCLOS], which China has signed. It is possible
that China may decide to embrace the international rule of law and rely on
UNCLOS dispute resolution provisions at some point in future, but if it
does not, neighbours both large and small will face difficult choices. It is
already apparent that few, if any, of China's neighbours are willing to see
China govern the region single-handedly.[128]

As arbitration and adjudication hand responsibility to a small and select
group of individuals to decide legal questions and make determinations
that are legally binding on the states concerned, China may well perceive
this form of dispute settlement as too removed from its control and
influence. Yet China's neighbours that are also party to UNCLOS do
not need to rely on China's consent if they wish to institute proceedings
under UNCLOS. The *South China Sea* arbitration instead reflects that
a less powerful state may have a useful means available to influence
discussions and world perceptions in seeking to uphold maritime rights
and obligations protected under UNCLOS.

The full implementation of the BRI is by no means guaranteed and
there is no shortage of events that might be imagined that could re-shape
the strategy in the years ahead. If China's BRI vision is ultimately fulfilled,
the potential global impact may be tremendous:

> If any single state were to establish hegemony over the whole of the
> Eurasian land mass, the scale of resources and the geo-strategic advan-
> tages available to that state would allow it to dominate the entire world.[129]

The UNCLOS dispute settlement procedures are not able to prevent
world domination, but they count as one of many tools to be used to
moderate state behaviour as the BRI progresses. Most importantly, the
UNCLOS dispute settlement regime may prove vital if the freedom of
navigation for the benefit of all states is to be preserved.

---

[128] Arase, above n 3, 41.
[129] Ibid, 40.

Peaceful Resolution of Maritime Disputes and the UN Convention on the Law of the Sea

KEYUAN ZOU

10.1 Introduction

International disputes are not uncommon in the world community. In international law, there are a number of mechanisms for the settlement of such disputes, including such political means as negotiation and consultation, mediation and good offices, conciliation, investigation, and such judicial means as arbitration and international adjudication as listed in the Charter of the United Nations.[1] In addition, international organizations, whether universal or regional, have played an active role in dispute settlement.

10.2 Dispute Settlement Mechanisms under the UN Convention on the Law of the Sea

The International Court of Justice (ICJ) is defined as "the principal judicial organ of the United Nations."[2] According to the ICJ Statute, "the jurisdiction of the Court comprises all cases which the parties refer to it and all matters specially provided for in the Charter of the United Nations or in treaties and conventions in force."[3] Any UN member can declare at any time that it recognizes the Court's compulsory jurisdiction in all legal disputes concerning "the interpretation of a treaty; any question of international law; the existence of any fact which, if established, would constitute a breach of an international obligation; the nature or extent of the reparation to be made for the breach of an

---

[1] Article 33(1) of the UN Charter.
[2] Article 92 of the UN Charter, available at www.icj-cij.org/icjwww/ibasicdocuments/ibasic text/ibasicunchart.htm#Chapter14.
[3] Article 36 of the ICJ Statute, available at www.icj-cij.org/icjwww/ibasicdocuments/ibasic text/ibasicstatute.htm#CHAPTER_II.

international obligation."[4] In the event of a dispute as to whether the Court has jurisdiction, the matter should be settled by the decision of the Court.[5]

Acceptance of the Court's compulsory jurisdiction can facilitate the adjudication and more effective functioning of the ICJ. However, the comparable number of States which have accepted such jurisdiction has declined significantly with the increase of UN members, and they only account for one-third of the total 192 current members. In east Asia only three countries have done so (see Table 10.2). The causes under-lying this are complicated, and one of them may be attributed to the proliferation of international tribunals. Even after having accepted the compulsory jurisdiction of the ICJ, an accepting State may change its decision any time as it wishes following the procedure of the ICJ Statute. For example, Canada has twice withdrawn its acceptance of compulsory jurisdiction, first in the case of its 1969 legislation to protect its Arctic environment in areas beyond those recognized by the then applicable international law, and the second time to preserve straddling fish stocks off its east coast exclusive economic zone.[6] Some countries exclude law of the sea disputes from the Court's compulsory jurisdiction, such as Australia, which excluded disputes concerning natural resources of the seabed and subsoil of its continental shelf and/or within the meaning of its Pearl Fisheries Acts.[7] The Philippines' declaration excludes disputes "in respect of the natural resources, including living organisms belong-ing to sedentary species, of the seabed and subsoil of the continental shelf of the Philippines, or its analogue in an archipelago."[8] Perhaps the primary consideration behind such exclusions as made by these coun-tries is the preservation of their sovereign rights over marine resources rather than refusing dispute settlement. Nonetheless, they have in practice generated some negative effects on the settlement of law of the sea disputes.

[4] *Ibid.*
[5] *Ibid.*
[6] See Comments of Robert Hage, Minister, Permanent Mission of Canada to the European Union, Brussels, at the round table, "Comment apprécier la nouveller Cour?" in Lucius Caflisch (ed.), *The Peaceful Settlement of Disputes between States: Universal and European Perspectives* (The Hague: Kluwer Law International, 1998), at 100. It is interest-ing to note that the controversial Canadian legislation might led to the first case of a marine environmental dispute before the ICJ if Canada had not withdrawn its declaration.
[7] Declaration of February 6, 1954, 186 UNTS 77.
[8] Declaration of January 18, 1972, para. e.I, ICJ Yearbook 1994–1995, at 109.

The second main international judicial organ handling law of the sea disputes is the Permanent Court of Arbitration (PCA), which was established in 1899 in accordance with the 1899 Convention for the Pacific Settlement of International Disputes concluded during the first Hague Peace Conference, and revised in 1907. As of 2008, the PCA had 104 member States and "provides services for the resolution of disputes involving various combinations of states, state entities, intergovernmental organizations, and private parties."[9] Its secretariat serves as a registry for arbitral tribunals and commissions. While the scope of its involvement in dispute resolution is very broad, the PCA has competence to deal with law of the sea disputes. This competence was reinforced after the entry into force of the LOSC, as the latter has created four categories of dispute settlement mechanisms for States parties to choose, one of which is arbitration. Pursuant to Article 287(3) of the LOSC, arbitration under Annex VII is the default means of dispute settlement if a State has not expressed any preference with respect to the means of dispute resolution available under Article 287(1) of the Convention. Since the LOSC came into force in 1994, five cases have been arbitrated under Annex VII of that Convention. The PCA has acted as registry in four of those cases, including (1) *Ireland* v. *United Kingdom* (the "MOX Plant case"), which was instituted in November 2001 and terminated on June 8, 2008 with an Order to formalize the withdrawal of Ireland's claim against the United Kingdom; (2) *Malaysia* v. *Singapore*, which was instituted in July 2003 and terminated by an award on agreed terms rendered on September 1, 2005; (3) *Barbados* v. *Trinidad and Tobago*, which was instituted in February 2004 and decided by a final award rendered on April 11, 2006; and (4) *Guyana* v. *Suriname*, which was instituted in February 2004 and decided by a final award rendered on September 17, 2007.[10] Meanwhile, a cooperative relationship between the PCA and the International Tribunal for the Law of the Sea (ITLOS) has been established through an exchange of letters with respect to relevant legal and administrative matters.

Arbitration as a legal means of dispute settlement is more flexible than adjudication. The parties to a dispute can choose arbiters to form an arbitral tribunal. The PCA actually possesses a list of arbiter candidates for countries to select for their arbitral tribunals. It does not have the

---

[9] "About us," available at www.pca-cpa.org/showpage.asp?pag_id=1027.

[10] See "*Ad Hoc* Arbitration under Annex VII of the United Nations Convention on the Law of the Sea," available at www.pca-cpa.org/showpage.asp?pag_id=1288.

same organizational structure as the ICJ or ITLOS. Judges sitting in the
ICJ or ITLOS can also be chosen as arbiters. Though arbitration is one of
the legal means for dispute settlement, there is a difference between
arbitration and adjudication. The LOSC also allows States parties to
make recourse to special arbitration for disputes concerning (a) fisheries;
(b) protection and preservation of the marine environment; (c) marine
scientific research; and (d) navigation, including pollution from vessels
and by dumping.[11]

It is admitted that there are various institutions which can serve as
a venue to resolve law of the sea disputes. However, the ITLOS is
a specialized judicial organ designed only to handle law of the sea
disputes. Therefore, this chapter will limit itself mainly to its procedure
and practices, while some comparisons will be made between the above
judicial institutions and the ITLOS. Finally, east Asian States' attitudes
towards and practices in the judicial settlement of their disputes will be
examined through a number of recent cases.

10.3   Law of the Sea Disputes and ITLOS

The ITLOS was established in October 1996 in Hamburg, Germany,
under the general framework of the LOSC. The LOSC provides a set of
comprehensive compulsory procedures for dispute settlement, since
management (i.e. avoidance, reduction and settlement) of conflict is
one of the five specific goals to maintain a favorable marine legal
order.[12] If the parties to a dispute fail to reach settlement by peaceful
means of their own choice, they are obliged to choose one or more of the
following to settle their disputes: ITLOS, ICJ, arbitral tribunal and special
arbitral tribunal when they sign, ratify or accede to the Convention.[13]
When a State does not make a choice upon its ratification of the
Convention, it is deemed to have accepted the compulsory procedure
of arbitration.[14] This deemed acceptance does not affect the right of the

---

[11] See Annex VIII to the LOSC.
[12] See John Warren Kindt, "Dispute Settlement in International Environmental Issues: The
     Model Provided by the 1982 Convention on the Law of the Sea," *Vanderbilt Journal
     of Transnational Law* 22, (1989), 1107. The other four goals include security, promotion
     of efficiency and fair access in ocean use, protection of the environment and promotion of
     ocean knowledge.
[13] See Article 287 of the LOSC.
[14] See Article 298 of the LOSC.

State concerned to choose other procedures any time afterwards including the resort to the ITLOS.

The ITLOS can establish its jurisdiction over any law of the sea dispute that is submitted to it concerning the interpretation or application of the LOSC and the Agreement relating to the Implementation of Part XI of the Convention. In addition, it can adjudicate cases submitted by parties to other international treaties if such treaties allow it to do so.[15] The ITLOS has established the Seabed Disputes Chamber, which consists of eleven judges selected from within the ITLOS, and under this chamber some ad hoc chambers can be established when the need arises. In addition, the Tribunal has established five special chambers including the Chamber of Summary Procedure, which consists of five judges and two alternates; the Chamber for Fisheries Disputes, which consists of seven judges and is available to deal with disputes concerning the conservation and management of marine living resources; the Chamber for Marine Environment Disputes, which also consists of seven judges and is available to deal with disputes relating to the protection and preservation of the marine environment. Another important special chamber is the Chamber for Maritime Delimitation Disputes, which was created in March 2007, consisting of eight judges. Finally, the Tribunal can create chambers under article 15(2) of its Statute to deal with a particular dispute if the parties so request. In practice, such a special chamber was established in December 2000 to deal with the *Case concerning the Conservation and Sustainable Exploitation of Swordfish Stocks in the South-Eastern Pacific Ocean* (Chile/European Community). This was the first time that a case had been submitted to a special chamber of the Tribunal.[16] From its establishment in 1996 up to August 2008, ITLOS had received and dealt with fifteen cases (with one still pending). Among them, nine cases concern the prompt release of vessels and crews, while four cases concern requests by States parties for provisional measures from the Tribunal (see Table 6). These two areas have constituted the majority of the judicial activities of the Tribunal and are worth further scrutiny.

A related question concerns the choice of procedures to be made by States parties in accordance with Article 287 of the LOSC, which provides as follows:

---

[15] See Articles 21–22 of the Statute of the ITLOS.
[16] See "Chambers," available at www.itlos.org/start2_en.html.

> When signing, ratifying or acceding to this Convention or at any time thereafter, a State shall be free to choose, by means of a written declaration, one or more of the following means for the settlement of disputes concerning the interpretation or application of this Convention: (a) the International Tribunal for the Law of the Sea established in accordance with Annex VI; (b) the International Court of Justice; (c) an arbitral tribunal constituted in accordance with Annex VII; (d) a special arbitral tribunal constituted in accordance with Annex VIII for one or more of the categories of disputes specified therein.

As of June 2018, altogether sixty-one States parties had made statements on the choice of procedures. From the list prepared by the UN Office for Ocean Affairs and the Law of the Sea, it can be seen that twenty-seven States selected the ITLOS as the first choice for the settlement of law of the sea disputes when arising, while others selected the ICJ (including Denmark, Honduras, Nicaragua, Norway, Sweden and the United Kingdom) or arbitration as the first choice. Some States (including Australia, Belgium, Estonia, Finland, Italy, Latvia, Lithuania, Mexico, Oman, Portugal and Spain) listed the ITLOS and ICJ in parallel without order of preference.[17] This indicates that despite the fact that the ITLOS is designated as the first dispute settlement mechanism under the LOSC, there are a few countries which favor its jurisdiction. In east Asia, no country has ever made such declarations, and thus it is assumed that they have accepted arbitration in accordance with Article 287(3) of the LOSC.

The second constraint is also from the LOSC, which allows States parties to exclude certain disputes from the compulsory dispute settlement mechanisms established under the Convention. Article 298(1) of the LOSC provides that a State may declare not to accept the following categories of disputes: (a) disputes concerning the interpretation or application of Articles 15, 74 and 83 relating to sea boundary delimitations, or those involving historic bays or titles; (b) disputes concerning military activities, including military activities by government vessels and aircraft engaged in non-commercial service, and disputes concerning law enforcement activities in regard to the exercise of sovereign rights or jurisdiction excluded from the jurisdiction of a court or tribunal under Article 297(2) or (3); and (c) disputes in respect of which the United Nations Security Council is exercising the functions assigned to it by the Charter of the United Nations, unless the Security Council decides to remove the matter from its agenda or calls upon the parties to settle it by

---

[17] For details, see "Settlement of disputes mechanism: recapitulative tables," available at www.un.org/depts/los/settlement_of_disputes/choice_procedure.htm.

the means provided for in the Convention. As of June 2018, thirty-eight States parties had made such declarations.[18] Among them, some exclude all listed in the above provision (e.g. China and the Republic of Korea) and some exclude one or two of them (e.g. the United Kingdom and Italy). The effect of such exclusion is clear that disputes concerning the above matters are most likely to be resolved by political means, such as bilateral negotiation and consultation. Furthermore, it should be noted that the number of the above States include four permanent UN Security Council members, that is, China, France, Russia and the UK. It is almost certain that the United States upon ratifying the LOSC will make an exclusion statement as well. This can be seen from the recent draft declarations in a resolution passed by the US Senate Foreign Relations Committee for advice and consent of the full Senate, which will exclude all the items allowed by Article 298(1) of the LOSC.[19] The fact that all five permanent members of the UN Security Council exclude maritime disputes from compulsory dispute settlement mechanisms will no doubt discourage other States from using more of such mechanisms, which is detrimental to the rule of law at the international level.

Finally, it is worthwhile to look briefly at the issue of the fragmentation of international law, which could be caused by the proliferation of international judicial organs. Proliferation of international courts/tribunals has triggered doubts as to the necessity and efficiency of their establishment. For example, the International Criminal Tribunal for Rwanda (ICTR) only completed eight trials in its first eight years of operation. Second, such proliferation may also bring inconsistency in international jurisprudence as well as overlapping jurisdiction. The judicial practices concerning the *Southern Bluefin Tuna* case indicate there is a suspicion of conflicting international jurisprudence between the ITLOS and the Annex VII Arbitral Tribunal that revoked the provisional measures granted by the former. It is recalled that Judge Gilbert Guillaume, former President of the ICJ, once criticized such proliferation and brought his concerns to the United Nations.[20] Concerns in this respect

---

[18] For details, see *ibid.*

[19] Relevant materials are annexed to John A. Duff, "A Note on the United States and the Law of the Sea: Looking Back and Moving Forward," *Ocean Development and International Law*, 35(3), (2004), 214–15.

[20] See "Address by H.E. Judge Gilbert Guillaume, President of the International Court of Justice, to the United Nations General Assembly," October 26, 2000, available at www.icj-cij.org/icjwww/ipresscom/SPEECHES/iSpeechPresident_Guillaume_GA55_20001026 .htm. In the address, Guillaume gave an example of jurisprudential inconsistency by the ICTY in ruling on the merits in the *Tadic* case:

are also voiced by Asian countries. As a Chinese Delegate to the 6th Committee of the UN General Assembly stated, "with the ever increase of international judicial organs, how to ensure uniform application of international law so as to reduce the negative impact of the fragmentation of international law while these organs properly fulfill their judicial functions is a question that deserves the attention of the international community."[21] Therefore, the most efficient and effective way is to maximize the use of existing international courts, instead of establishing more such courts. On the other hand, there is a need for reform of the existing courts so as to meet the expectations of the world community.

10.4   Asian Experiences

10.4.1   Negotiations

On the other hand, there are a number of bilateral fishery agreements signed between east Asian States. Such agreements, in most cases, only provide a mechanism for direct negotiation between the parties to resolve any dispute. The question arises as to what kind of third-party mechanism they have to resort to when direct negotiation has failed. Could one of the parties submit the dispute to the ITLOS or other third-party settlement organs? The LOSC allows States parties to opt for a compulsory mechanism for disputes that are related to their sovereign rights to living resources in exclusive economic zones (EEZ).[22] That means coastal States may have the right to refuse the use of the compulsory mechanism, including the ITLOS. However, the recent bilateral fishery agreements signed in east Asia have established joint and/or common fishery management zones within their EEZs, which consist of shared zones between the two relevant countries. Even some of these zones retain the de facto status of the high

> The International Criminal Tribunal for the former Yugoslavia recently disregarded case-law formulated by the International Court of Justice in the dispute between Nicaragua and the United States of America. The Court had found that the United States could not be held responsible for acts committed by the contras in Nicaragua unless it had had "effective control" over them. After criticizing the view taken by the Court, the Tribunal adopted a less strict standard for Yugoslavia's actions in Bosnia and Herzegovina and replaced the notion of "effective control" with that of "overall control," thereby broadening the range of circumstances in which a State's responsibility may be engaged on account of its actions on foreign territory.

[21] Duan Jielong, "Statement on the Rule of Law at the National and International Levels," *Chinese Journal of International Law*, 6, (2007), at 187.
[22] See Article 297(3) of the LOSC.

seas, such as the Intermediate Zone established in the East China Sea based on the 1997 Sino-Japanese Fishery Agreement.[23] Although it is not clear whether a party to a dispute over the implementation of a bilateral fishery agreement, particularly concerning fishery management in shared zones, is eligible to resort to a compulsory mechanism under the LOSC, the window of possibility for ITLOS intervention could always remain open.

Regarding the management of marine nonliving resources, the legal concept of "joint development" has been applied to east Asian seas. Joint development refers to "an agreement between two States to develop so as to share jointly in agreed proportions by inter-State cooperation and national measures the offshore oil and gas in a designated zone of the seabed and subsoil of the continental shelf to which both or either of the participating States are entitled in international law."[24] It contains several characteristics: (a) it is an arrangement between two countries; (b) it concerns an overlapping boundary maritime area; (c) it is a provisional arrangement pending the settlement of the boundary delimitation disputes between the countries concerned; (d) it is designed to jointly develop the mineral resources in the disputed area. In east Asia, joint development agreements include, inter alia, the Japan–South Korea arrangement in the Sea of Japan and the East China Sea in the 1970s, the Malaysia–Thailand joint development area in the Gulf of Thailand and the Australian–Indonesia joint development zone for the Timor Gap.

The Japan-South Korea joint development arrangement was the first of its kind in east Asia. It was based on several agreements signed between the two countries. The arrangement is significant in State practice since it represents the first application of the idea of joint development of offshore oil where the parties failed to agree on boundary delimitation.[25] Under the agreement, concessionaires who are authorized by the two respective governments have an undivided interest with respect to each of the nine defined subzones, and one operator is chosen from among the concessionaires so authorized for a particular subzone.[26]

---

[23] See Zou Keyuan, "Sino-Japanese Joint Fishery Management in the East China Sea," *Marine Policy*, 27(2), (2003), at 134.

[24] British Institute of International and Comparative Law, *Joint Development of Offshore Oil and Gas: A Model Agreement for States for Joint Development with Explanatory Commentary* (London: British Institute of International and Comparative Law, 1989), at 45.

[25] Masahiro Miyoshi, "The Joint Development of Offshore Oil and Gas in Relation to Maritime Boundary Delimitation," *Maritime Briefing*, 2(5), (1999), at 1.

[26] *Ibid.*, at 12.

The agreement establishes a Joint Commission as a consultative body to implement the agreement.

What is more significant is the joint arrangement made by three countries – Malaysia, Thailand and Vietnam – in the Gulf of Thailand for their overlapping claimed sea areas, consisting of two separate but associated bilateral agreements either between Malaysia and Thailand or between Malaysia and Vietnam. In 1979, Malaysia and Thailand signed a Memorandum of Understanding (MOU) to establish, on an interim basis of fifty years, a Malaysia–Thailand Joint Authority "for the purpose of the exploration and exploitation of the non-living natural resources of the seabed and subsoil in the overlapping area."[27] More than ten years later, the two countries worked out the Constitution and other matters relating to the establishment of such an authority, which provides details of operations in the joint zone.[28] There are two striking characteristics in this joint development scheme: a powerful joint authority with the power to decide on the plan of operation and the work program, to permit operations and conclude transactions or contracts, to approve and extend the period of exploration and exploitation, to approve the work program and budgets of contractors, and to inspect and audit an operator's books and accounts;[29] and the introduction of a production sharing system that includes such terms and conditions as the duration of the contract not exceeding thirty-five years, the payment of 10 percent of gross production of petroleum by the contractor to the Joint Authority as royalty, 50 percent of gross production to be applied by the contractor for the recovery of costs, the remainder of gross production to be profit and divided equally between the Joint Authority and the contractor, all costs of operations to be borne by the contractor and any dispute arising out of the contract to be referred to arbitration unless settled amicably.[30]

In the same vein, Malaysia and Vietnam also signed an MOU in 1992 for joint development in the Gulf of Thailand. Accordingly, Petronas and Petrovietnam are assigned to undertake petroleum exploration and exploitation, respectively, in the "defined area." The arrangement between the two State-owned oil companies made in August 1993 established an eight-member coordination committee to issue policy guidelines for the management of petroleum operations. This is different from

---

[27] Text is reprinted in Jonathan I. Charney & Lewis M. Alexander (eds.), *International Maritime Boundaries* (Dordrecht: Martinus Nijhoff Publishers, 1993), vol. 1, 1099–1123.
[28] See *ibid.*
[29] See Article 7 of the 1990 Agreement.
[30] See Article 8 of the 1990 Agreement.

the Thai-Malaysian model in which the Joint Authority is appointed directly by the governments. After the conclusion of the commercial arrangement in July 1997, extraction began of oil from the Bunga Kekwa field.[31] Based on the bilateral arrangements, a tripartite mechanism has been evolving gradually for an overlapping maritime area.

There are a number of bilateral agreements concerning maritime boundary delimitation in east Asia. One recent one is the agreement between China and Vietnam regarding the Gulf of Tonkin. The size of the gulf, as agreed by the two countries, is more than 126,000 square kilometers,[32] with abundant marine living and nonliving resources. With the pace of the new law of the sea developments, China and Vietnam realized the importance and necessity of establishing a maritime boundary in the Gulf of Tonkin. The whole negotiation process was comprised of three stages: brief negotiations in 1974 as initiated by Vietnam; negotiations during the period between October 1977 and June 1978; and negotiations from 1992 to 2000.[33] On December 25, 2000, the two sides completed the negotiation process and signed the Agreement on the Delimitation of the Territorial Seas, Exclusive Economic Zones and Continental Shelves in the Beibu Gulf (the Sino-Vietnamese Boundary Agreement)[34] and the Agreement on Fishery Cooperation in the Beibu Gulf (the Sino-Vietnamese Fishery Agreement).[35] Both agreements came into effect from July 1, 2004, after ratification by the two countries concerned. A new marine legal order based on the LOSC has been, therefore, established in the Gulf of Tonkin.

The Sino-Vietnamese Boundary Agreement contains eleven clauses. Article 1 defines the area of the Gulf of Tonkin for the purpose of

[31] See Nguyen Hong Thao, "Vietnam and Joint Development in the Gulf of Thailand," *Asian Yearbook of International Law*, 8, (2003), at 145.
[32] The figure that Vietnam refers to is 126,250 square kilometers, while the Chinese figure is 128,000 square kilometers. See respectively "Interview by Foreign Minister Nguyen Dy Nien about Tonkin Gulf Delimitation Agreement," July 1, 2004, available at www.vnagency .com.vn/newsa.asp?LANGUAGE_ID=2&CATEGORY_ID=29&NEWS_ID=106778 and "Introduction to the Sino-Vietnamese Beibu Gulf Delimitation Agreement," July 30, 2004, available at www.fmprc.gov.cn/chn/zxxx/t145558.htm.
[33] See "Interview by Foreign Minister Nguyen Dy Nien about Tonkin Gulf Delimitation Agreement," *ibid.*
[34] An unofficial English text of the Boundary Agreement is attached to Zou Keyuan "Sino-Vietnamese Agreement on the Maritime Boundary Delimitation in the Gulf of Tonkin," *Ocean Development and International Law*, 36, (2005), 22–24.
[35] An unofficial English text of the Fishery Agreement is attached to Zou Keyuan "Sino-Vietnamese Fishery Agreement for the Gulf of Tonkin," *International Journal of Marine and Coastal Law*, 17(1), (2002), 127–48.

delimiting the territorial seas, exclusive economic zones (EEZs) and continental shelves of the two countries. Article 2 uses twenty-one geographic points to draw the maritime boundary in the Gulf of Tonkin. In the use of the coordinates, the line connecting Point 1 to Point 9 is the line to divide the territorial seas of the two countries, whereas the line connecting Point 9 to Point 21 is the line to delimit the EEZs and continental shelves of the two countries in the Gulf of Tonkin.

The Sino-Vietnamese Boundary Agreement has produced the first maritime boundary that China has ever agreed to share with its neighboring countries. As China still has maritime delimitation problems with eight countries (i.e. Brunei, Indonesia, Japan, Malaysia, North Korea, the Philippines, South Korea and Vietnam), the success of the delimitation in the Gulf of Tonkin is an invaluable experience for China in its future negotiations with other countries. The practice of using one single maritime boundary line to delimit three different maritime zones (territorial sea, EEZ and continental shelf) indicates that China may follow this practice in future negotiations with other neighboring countries, bearing in mind that China has used the doctrine of natural prolongation in its claim to the continental shelf in the East China Sea,[36] which would create two different maritime boundary lines in the event that China's claim were accepted by Japan. For Vietnam, though the Boundary Agreement is the second of the three agreements it has signed with its neighboring countries (with Thailand in 1997 and Indonesia 2003), Vietnam has admitted that this agreement is "the first most comprehensive of its kind."[37]

10.4.2   Regional Institutions

There is, however, a positive sign: all the claimants to the Spratly Islands have pledged to resolve their disputes in a peaceful manner and in accordance with international law, including the LOSC. The Association of Southeast Asian Nations (ASEAN) countries together with China have held several rounds of discussion to formulate a Code

---

[36] The doctrine of natural prolongation is embodied in the LOSC, which provides that "the continental margin comprises the submerged prolongation of the land mass of the coastal State, and consists of the sea-bed and subsoil of the shelf, the slope and the rise" (Article 76).

[37] See "Interview by Foreign Minister Nguyen Dy Nien about Tonkin Gulf Delimitation Agreement," (n 32).

of Conduct for the South China Sea.[38] On November 4, 2002, China and all the ASEAN member States signed the Declaration on the Conduct of the Parties in the South China Sea (the 2002 Declaration) in Phnom Penh, Cambodia.[39] It is the most remarkable document ever signed between China and ASEAN countries. The 2002 Declaration is designed to consolidate and develop the friendship and cooperation existing between China and ASEAN, to promote a peaceful, friendly and harmonious environment in the South China Sea and to enhance the principles and objectives of the 1997 Joint Statement of the Meeting of the Heads of State/Government of the Member States of ASEAN and President of the People's Republic of China.

The Declaration reaffirms the parties' commitment to the use of international law, in particular the LOSC, to conduct confidence building and cooperation. The parties ensure the freedom of navigation in and overflight above the South China Sea. They promise to resolve their territorial and jurisdictional disputes by peaceful means, without resorting to the threat or use of force. They intend to cooperate in the following matters: (a) marine environmental protection; (b) marine scientific research; (c) safety of navigation and communication at sea; (d) search and rescue operation; and (e) combating transnational crime, including but not limited to trafficking in illicit drugs, piracy and armed robbery at sea, and illegal traffic in arms. The parties will continue their dialogues on the South China Sea and restrain themselves from taking any provocative actions in the area. The Declaration absorbed many elements from the previous Chinese proposal, including, but not limited to, cooperative matters. China's signature can be regarded as a good gesture to show its willingness to resolve the South China Sea issue by peaceful means. It can be well perceived that there will be no major conflicts in the South China Sea in the near future. On the other hand, the parties still face a series of tasks to be accomplished in accordance with the 2002 Declaration. The Declaration itself, though being a first step, is not a code of conduct, and the parties concerned will have to work on its adoption in the years to come.

---

[38] The drafts of the Code of Conduct both from ASEAN and China are reprinted in Hainan Research Institute for the South China Sea (ed.), *Collection of Selected Foreign and Chinese Papers on the South China Sea* (Hainan: Haikou, 2002) (in Chinese), 180–83.

[39] The whole text is available on the ASEAN website: http://asean.org/?static_post=declaration-on-the-conduct-of-parties-in-the-south-china-sea-2.

10.4.3   Third-Party Settlement

The reluctance of east Asian countries to use international adjudication for dispute settlement may be rooted in Asian cultures and legal traditions. In China, Legalism was long replaced by Confucianism, which emphasizes rule by virtue rather than rule by law. For everyday people in the past, the use of law courts for dispute settlement was regarded as unfriendly and confrontational, and a loss of face. They tended to seek a solution by negotiations and/or third-party mediation. Although things have changed dramatically over time, such an unfavorable mentality towards law courts may still exist, and this has been reflected in China's attitude toward international adjudication.

However, in recent years, it seems that there is an increasing tendency to resort to international courts in east Asia. There are two significant cases submitted by east Asian States to the ICJ, including the case of *Sovereignty over Pulau Litigan and Pulau Sipadan* (Malaysia/Indonesia) (1998–2002) and the case on *Sovereignty over Pedra Branca, Middle Rocks and South Ledge* (Malaysia/Singapore) (2003–08). Both cases concern territorial disputes over small islands in the seas. In the first case, the ICJ granted the disputed islands to Malaysia, while in the second, the Court granted one to Malaysia and one to Singapore so as to reach a "win-win" solution.[40]

On January 22, 2013, the Philippines, by a *note verbale* with the Notification and Statement of Claim on West Philippine Sea (i.e. South China Sea), instituted the compulsory arbitration procedures stipulated in the LOSC against China, asking the Arbitral Tribunal to: (1) declare that China's rights in regard to maritime areas in the South China Sea, like the rights of the Philippines, are those that are established by UNCLOS, and consist of its rights to a Territorial Sea and Contiguous Zone under Part II of the Convention, to an Exclusive Economic Zone under Part V, and to a Continental Shelf under Part VI; and (2) declare that China's maritime claims in the South China Sea based on its so-called nine dash line (U-shaped line) are contrary to UNCLOS and invalid.[41] On March 30, 2014, the Philippines officially submitted its Memorial to the Arbitral Tribunal, which reiterated its statements regarding the U-shaped

---

[40] For details about the two cases, see the ICJ website: www.icj-cij.org/icjwww/idocket/ iinma/iinmajudgment/iinma_ijudgment_20021217.PDF and www.icj-cij.org/docket/ files/130/14492.pdf?PHPSESSID=a4740e3448ea1887e19ce0a89525d037.

[41] The diplomatic note and Philippines' "Notification and Statement of Claim" are available at www.gov.ph/downloads/2013/01jan/20130122-Notification-and-Statement-of-Claim-on-West-Philippine-Sea.pdf.

Table 10.1 *Contracting parties to the LOSC in east Asia and their maritime claims*

States	Date of ratification (d/m/y)	Territorial sea	Contiguo- us zone	EEZ	Continent- al shelf
Brunei	05/11/1996	12		200	
Cambodia		12	24	200	200(58)
China	07/06/1996	12	24	200	200/CM
Japan	20/06/1996	3/12	24	200	200/CM
S. Korea	29/01/1996	3/12	24	200	
N. Korea		12		200	
Laos	05/06/1998				
Malaysia	14/10/1996	12		200	200 m/ Exp(58)
Mongolia	13/08/1996				
Myanmar	21/05/1996	12	24	200	200/CM
Philippines	08/05/1985			200	Exp
Russia	12/03/1997	12		200	200/ CM(58)
Singapore	17/11/1994	3			
Thailand		12	24	200	200 m/ EXP(58)
Vietnam	25/07/1994	12	24	200	200/CM
(Chinese Taipei)		12	24	200	200/ CM(58)

N.B.:

• The date here is the date when the depository (the United Nations) received the instrument of ratification.
• Taiwan is not a member of the United Nations and not qualified to be a signatory of the LOSC.
• (58): Contracting Party to the 1958 Convention on Continental Shelf.
• CM: continental margin; Exp: exploitability; 200: 200 nm; 200 m: 200 meters.
• The Philippine territorial sea is rectangular in accordance with the so-called Treaty Limits.
• The three-mile limit, for South Korea, applies to the Korean Strait area, while for Japan it applies to the Soya Strait, the Tsugaru Strait, the eastern and western channels of the Tsushima Strait and the Osumi Straits only.

Source: Prepared by the author

Table 10.2 *Bilateral maritime agreements in east Asia*

Agreement between the Government of Malaysia and the Government of
Indonesia on the delimitation of the continental shelves between the two
countries, October 27, 1969

Treaty between the Republic of Indonesia and Malaysia relating to the delimitation of
the Territorial Seas of the Two Countries in the Strait of Malacca, March 17, 1970

Agreement between the Government of the Kingdom of Thailand and the
Government of the Republic of Indonesia relating to the delimitation of
a continental shelf boundary between the two countries in the northern part of
the Straits of Malacca and in the Andaman Sea, December 17, 1971

Agreement between the Government of the Republic of Indonesia, the
Government of Malaysia and the Government of the Kingdom of Thailand
relating to the delimitation of the Continental Shelf Boundaries in the Northern
Part of the Strait of Malacca, December 21, 1971

Agreement Stipulating the Territorial Sea Boundary Lines between Indonesia and
the Republic of Singapore in the Strait of Singapore, May 25, 1973

Agreement between the Republic of Korea and Japan concerning the establishment
of Boundary in the Northern Part of the Continental Shelf Adjacent to the Two
Countries, January 30, 1974

Agreement between the Republic of Korea and Japan concerning Joint
Development of the Southern Part of Continental Shelf Adjacent to the Two
Countries, January 30, 1974

Agreement between the Government of the Kingdom of Thailand and the
Government of the Republic of Indonesia relating to the delimitation of the seabed boundary between the two countries in the Andaman Sea, December 11, 1975

Treaty between the Kingdom of Thailand and Malaysia relating to the delimitation
of the territorial seas of the two countries, October 24, 1979

Memorandum of Understanding between the Kingdom of Thailand and Malaysia
on the delimitation of the continental shelf boundary between the two countries
in the Gulf of Thailand, October 24, 1979

Agreement between the Government of the Kingdom of Thailand and the
Government of the Socialist Republic of the Union of Burma on the delimita-
tion of the maritime boundary between the two countries in the Andaman Sea,
July 25, 1980

Agreement between the Union of the Soviet Socialist Republics and the
Democratic People's Republic of Korea on the Delimitation of the Soviet-
Korean National Border, April 17, 1985

Agreement between the Union of Soviet Socialist Republics and the Democratic
People's Republic of Korea on the Delimitation of the Economic Zone and the
Continental Shelf, January 22, 1986

Table 10.2 (*cont.*)

Agreement on Fishery Cooperation between the People's Republic of China and
the Union of the Soviet Socialist Republics, October 4, 1988

Agreement between the Government of the Union of Soviet Socialist Republics and
the Government of the Democratic People's Republic of Korea concerning the
Regime of the Soviet-Korean State Frontier, September 3, 1990

Agreement on Fisheries between the People's Republic of China and Japan,
November 11, 1997

Agreement on Fisheries between the Republic of Korea and Japan, November 28,
1998

Agreement on Fisheries between the People's Republic of China and the Republic
of Korea, August 3, 2000

Agreement on Fishery Cooperation in the Gulf of Tonkin between the People's
Republic of China and the People's Republic of Socialist Vietnam, December 25,
2000

Agreement on Maritime Boundary Delimitation in the Gulf of Tonkin between the
People's Republic of China and the People's Republic of Socialist Vietnam,
December 25, 2000

Source: Compiled by the author

line contained in its Statement of Claims. Regarding the arbitration case
initiated by the Philippines, China stated that it would not participate in
the arbitration and accused the Philippines of complicating the issue.[42]
China accused the Philippines of distorting "the basic facts underlying the
disputes between China and the Philippines. In so doing, the Philippines
attempts to deny China's territorial sovereignty and clothes its illegal
occupation of China's islands and reefs with a cloak of 'legality.'"[43] China
asked the Philippines to resume the proper track of negotiation and
consultation to settle the disputes so as to avoid further damage to bilateral
relations between the two countries.[44] On July 12, 2016 the ad hoc Arbitral
Tribunal rendered its Award, overwhelmingly favoring the Philippines.

---

[42] See "China: No to UN arbitration on sea row," available at www.abs-cbnnews.com
/nation/02/01/13/china-no-un-arbitration-sea-row.

[43] "Foreign Ministry Spokesperson Hua Chunying's Remarks on the Philippines' Efforts in
Pushing for the Establishment of the Arbitral Tribunal in Relation to the Disputes
between China and the Philippines in the South China Sea," April 26, 2013, available at
www.fmprc.gov.cn/eng/xwfw/s2510/2535/t1035577.shtml.

[44] "Answers from the Foreign Ministry to the questions at a press conference on the search
of the disappearing passenger airplane of the Malaysian Airlines and the issue of the South

This case has opened a Pandora's Box of "lawfare" in the South China Sea. The disputes over the Spratly Islands are very complicated, involving five countries and six parties including China, Chinese Taipei, Brunei, Malaysia, the Philippines and Vietnam. Such disputes can be defined as territorial disputes and/or maritime boundary disputes. However, the legal team of the Philippines packaged a case of territorial/maritime boundary disputes as a dispute of maritime entitlement, and strangely, the Tribunal, consisting of four Europeans and one European permanent resident, accepted the Philippine submissions and established its jurisdiction over the case. People may wonder why Asians could not solve their disputes through their own judicial bodies.

10.5   Conclusion

Sir Robert Jennings once wrote that "the primary task of a court of justice is not to 'develop' the law, but to dispose, in accordance with the law, of that particular dispute between the particular parties before it."[45] If there is no case for an international court to handle so as to fulfill such a primary task, that court may lose its legitimacy of existence. Unlike Europe or America, the Asian cultures (Confucianism, Islam, Buddhism, Christianity, etc.) and legal systems (continental law, common law, Islamic law, socialist law, etc.) are quite divergent. Such divergence has different impacts on the attitudes and policies of Asian countries toward the settlement of disputes. It may also be an obstacle to the regional integration of effective control of disputes as well as to the general acceptance of international judicial bodies whose foundations are essentially based on western legal systems. The questions about "the efficacy of future global initiatives that are perceived to be Western in origin and orientation, and how they can be amenably incorporated into the legal systems and cultures of non-Western countries"[46] should be timely and properly answered.

China Sea," March 26, 2014, available at http://world.people.com.cn/n/2014/0326/c1002-24745397.html.

[45] Robert Jennings, "Role of the International Court of Justice," *British Yearbook of International Law*, 68, (1997), at 41.

[46] See Douglas M. Johnston, "Environmental Law as 'Sacred Text': Western Values and Southeast Asian Prospects," in Douglas M. Johnston & Gerry Ferguson (eds.), *Asia-Pacific Legal Development* (Vancouver: UBC Press, 1998), at 416.

11

Unsaid Rules of UNCLOS

Essential Elements for its Proper Interpretation?

BINGBING JIA[*]

11.1   Unsaid Rules of a Treaty?

As part of the common theme for this collection of essays, the Belt and Road Initiative (BRI), dispute settlement in the maritime sphere plays an indispensable role for the building of the 21st Century Maritime Silk Road, given that the Silk Road connects Chinese and foreign ports lying along the coast of, among others, the South China Sea through to the Indian Ocean.[1] As far as ocean affairs are concerned, the United Nations Convention on the Law of the Sea (UNCLOS or "Convention") dominates them in all aspects, and will impact on any measures taken in furtherance of the BRI in the oceans. This paper examines the issue of treaty interpretation arising from a moment's reflection on the dispute settlement mechanisms established in UNCLOS. Those mechanisms, with primarily the International Tribunal for the Law of the Sea and Arbitral Tribunals established under Annex VII of the Convention making waves in recent times, are designed solely to deal with disputes concerning the interpretation or application of the Convention. Any dispute that may eventually seize those mechanisms for solution will be primarily related to treaty interpretation. Besides, while hugely

---

[*]   This chapter was originally written as a paper for, and subsequently delivered at, the 2017 *Colloquium on International Law: Common Future in Asia*, convened jointly by the Asian Academy of International law and the Chinese Society of International Law in July 2017. Necessary changes have been made to this text.

[1]   The National Development and Reform Commission and the State Oceanic Administration, People's Republic of China, "Vision for Maritime Cooperation under the Belt and Road Initiative," at: https://eng.yidaiyilu.gov.cn/zchj/qwfb/16639.htm (accessed March 5, 2018). This Vision paper was released on June 20, 2017, and included "shelving differences" as one of the principles. For international response to the BRI, see, for instance, UN S/RES/2344 (2017) of March 17, 2017, para. 34.

important, UNCLOS does not provide for all matters in the oceans.[2] If it is silent on matters indispensable for proper interpretation of some of its rules, what should be done in interpreting those rules? The object for this study is in the form of two rules unwritten in the Convention, which, it is thought, are indispensable for a proper interpretation of the provisions of dispute settlement in its Part XV.

A preliminary thought centres on the rules of interpretation as laid down in Articles 31 and 32 of the Vienna Convention on the Law of Treaties ("Vienna Convention"), which have been established as part of customary law.[3] Those rules are essential for a study on treaty interpretation. The immediate question to be addressed is why this article tackles rules *absent* from UNCLOS. The basic approach to treaty interpretation is, as will be discussed later, textual. If a word or phrase is not written into the text of a treaty, it is presumed not to be included in the intention of the negotiating parties. A treaty, from the preamble to the miscellaneous part, is supposed to reflect that type of intention throughout. Anything unwritten is not part of the authentic text of the treaty. The textual approach would be without an object in regard to unwritten words. However, can UNCLOS be so designed, in comparison with other treaties, that even rules unwritten may be critical for its proper interpretation and, consequently, application? This article suggests that it can. This may be illustrated by the silence of the Convention in respect of two matters.

In particular, the silence in question manifests itself in the form of gaps in the Convention, whose existence is attributable to various causes present during the negotiating process. It may be attributed to informal understandings sounded at the Third United Nations Conference on the Law of the Sea ("Third Conference") that some matters should simply be kept outside of the Convention, even though there will always be the possibility that those matters could be dragged into a dispute concerning the interpretation or application of the Convention. Such an understanding, while not reflected in any agreement or instrument in the sense of

---

[2] The preamble makes this point amply clear: "Affirming that matters not regulated by this Convention continue to be governed by the rules and principles of general international law."

[3] *Alleged Violations of Sovereign Rights and Maritime Spaces in the Caribbean Sea (Nicaragua v. Colombia)*, Preliminary Objections, Judgment of March 17, 2016, para. 35. Also see C. Schreuer, Diversity and Harmonization of Treaty Interpretation in Investment Arbitration, in M. Fitzmaurice, O. Elias, P. Merkouris (eds.), *Treaty Interpretation and the Vienna Convention on the Law of Treaties: 30 Years On* (Leiden/Boston, Martinus Nijhoff, 2010), 129 at 129–34.

Article 31(2) Vienna Convention,[4] does not fit in the category of a "subsequent agreement" or practice in terms of Article 31(3) Vienna Convention either.[5] To constitute a practice relevant to Article 31(3), it would have to be "a concordant subsequent practice common to all the parties" to the Convention.[6] In addition, Article 31(3) only requires interpreters to "take into account" subsequent agreements or practice, with the margin of appreciation firmly in the control of the interpreters.[7] Article 31 may thus provide little assistance to account for such an informal understanding, which, given its purported significance as suggested by this study, should be such that it commands a general support among States parties.

Be that as it may, it is, however, entirely possible that this type of unsaid rule may be hard to find on a reading of the *travaux*, as the latter offers no evidence of a common understanding attained at the Third Conference by the participating countries. So those States were simply made known of a possible limiting rule that was, however, left unaccounted for, that is, without being integrated as an understanding in the official record of the conference.

[4] This provides that "the context for the purpose of the interpretation of a treaty shall comprise, in addition to the text, including its preamble and annexes: (a) any agreement relating to the treaty which was made between all the parties in connection with the conclusion of the treaty; (b) any instrument which was made by one or more parties in connection with the conclusion of the treaty and accepted by the other parties as an instrument related to the treaty." Cf. Sir Ian Sinclair, *The Vienna Convention on the Law of Treaties* (Manchester, MUP, 2nd edn., 1983), at 119 (referring to "documents"). Also see International Criminal Court, Assembly of States Parties, Review Conference, *The Crime of Aggression*, ICC Res. RC/Res. 6, June 11, 2010 (adopting by consensus the "Amendments to the Rome Statute of the International Criminal Court on the crime of aggression" contained in the resolution's Appendix I), with Annex III of the resolution including the "Understandings regarding the amendments to the Rome Statute of the International Criminal Court on the crime of aggression".

[5] The provision provides that "there shall be taken into account, together with the context: (a) any subsequent agreement between the parties regarding the interpretation of the treaty or the application of its provisions; (b) any subsequent practice in the application of the treaty which establishes the agreement of the parties regarding its interpretation; (c) any relevant rules of international law applicable in the relations between the parties." Cf. *Kasikili/Sedudu Island (Botswana/Namibia)*, Judgment of December 13, 1999, ICJ Rep. (1999) 1045, paras. 78–79. Also see G. Nolte, "Report 1. Jurisprudence of the International Court of Justice and Arbitral Tribunals of Ad Hoc Jurisdiction Relating to Subsequent Agreements and Subsequent Practice," in G. Nolte (ed.), *Treaties and Subsequent Practice* (Oxford: OUP, 2013), 169, at 173–74.

[6] Sinclair, *supra* note 4, at 138.

[7] J. Crawford, "A Consensualist Interpretation of Article 31 (3) of the Vienna Convention on the Law of Treaties, " in G. Nolte (ed.), *Treaties and Subsequent Practice* (Oxford: OUP, 2013), 29, at 29–30.

The silence of UNCLOS may be shown in a second type of gap/unsaid rule, whose presence is attributed to the fact that the negotiating countries at the Third Conference refrained from establishing any rule, for whatever reason.

There is a subtle distinction between the two types of gap. A rule of the first type, while unwritten in the Convention, may exist as a matter of background knowledge at the Third Conference, and, subject to some debate about its relevance to the interpretation or application of the Convention, limits the applicability of the latter's provisions. For illustrative purposes, the category of territorial disputes is a prime example. The unsaid rule would be that those disputes are not open for a court or tribunal listed under Article 287 UNCLOS to decide on the basis of the Convention, subject to the limited exception of its regimes of the territorial sea and archipelagic States.[8] This rule, as will be shown, looms large in the interpretation of the provisions of UNCLOS regarding compulsory procedures of dispute settlement.

With regard to the second type, unlike the first type mentioned above, there is no trace of it in the record of negotiation. One particular aspect of the provision of Article 121(3) UNCLOS provides an example. To wit, the paragraph obviously lacks a legal criterion for assessing the necessary level of human habitation that qualifies a rock as an island. The term "human habitation" is not unambiguous in meaning. But a rule (or a criterion) is not laid down – thus unsaid – in the Convention. Yet, the significance of this term for a proper interpretation of Article 121(3) is clear. For, under the Convention, this ambiguity can stop a court or tribunal from reaching a decision on the legal status of a maritime feature,

---

[8] Cf. Art. 2 UNCLOS:

1. The sovereignty of a coastal State extends, beyond its land territory and internal waters and, in the case of an archipelagic State, its archipelagic waters, to an adjacent belt of sea, described as the territorial sea.
2. This sovereignty extends to the air space over the territorial sea as well as to its bed and subsoil.
3. The sovereignty over the territorial sea is exercised subject to this Convention and to other rules of international law.

And Art. 49, which reads: "The sovereignty of an archipelagic State extends to the waters enclosed by the archipelagic baselines drawn in accordance with article 47, described as archipelagic waters ... This sovereignty is exercised subject to this of Art 49 (3).. The regime of archipelagic sea lanes passage established in this Part shall not in other respects affect the status of the archipelagic waters, including the sea lanes, or the exercise by the archipelagic State of its sovereignty over such waters and their air space, bed and subsoil, and the resources contained therein."

as it leaves the question of human habitation wide open so that evidence proffered by different stakeholders may potentially engender several inter-pretations of the term. The consequences are either that, because of the existence of a *non liquet*, no conclusion can be drawn in respect of the requisite level of human habitation on the maritime feature in question, unless law is created, or that, given a general and less radical interpretation, the feature can reasonably qualify as a juridical island, generating a continental shelf and an exclusive economic zone (EEZ). In a case in which the legal status of a maritime feature is singled out for decision by a court or tribunal, the consequences described above would either compel the court or tribunal to abandon the approach that treats features com-prising an archipelago in an isolated fashion, due to the impossibility to decide, in a uniform fashion, the level of human habitation for each and every feature, or lead to a finding necessarily entailing exercises in mari-time delimitation in the case, thus likely triggering the exclusionary effect of Article 298(1)(a)(i) if a declaration has been filed by a State party to the proceeding, pursuant to the provision.[9] Having explained the conse-quences, it may be pointed out that the problem this case study seeks to address is the extent to which a court or tribunal may create law in a proceeding involving the interpretation of Article 121(3).

It is arguable that the two types of unwritten rule mentioned above may, for the sake of legitimacy, be anchored in the *travaux préparatoires* of the Third Conference so as "to *determine* the meaning when the interpretation according to article 31: (a) leaves the meaning ambiguous or obscure; or (b) leads to a result which is manifestly absurd or unreasonable."[10] Conscious of the uncertainties surrounding recourse to *travaux*,[11] it is felt that Article 32 imbues these materials with

---

[9] Article 298(1)(a)(i) provides, in part, that "when signing, ratifying or acceding to this Convention or at any time thereafter, a State may, without prejudice to the obligations arising under section 1, declare in writing that it does not accept any one or more of the procedures provided for in section 2 with respect to one or more of the following categories of dispute disputes concerning the interpretation or application of articles 15, 74 and 83 relating to sea boundary delimitations, or those involving historic bays or titles."

[10] Article 32 Vienna Convention (italics added). Similar views are expressed by Sinclair, *supra* note 4, 138 (citing, with approval, M. Yasseen, "L'interprétation des traités d'après la Convention de Vienne sur le Droit des Traités," 151 *Recueil des Cours* [176–III] 1, at 52).

[11] Especially (1) where the negotiating parties were deliberate in avoiding to give too much precision to a provision so that no clear commitment could be shown in future cases, and (2) a party involved in a case requiring treaty interpretation did not participate in the negotiation of the provision (for instance, it was not a participant of the informal consultations that resulted in the adoption of the provision): Sinclair, *supra* note 4, at 142, and 142–46.

a measure of potent power of determination, where the methods referred to in Article 31 fail to produce a clear and reasonable meaning. Its title, "Supplementary Means of Interpretation," may not be decisive as to its true potential. Here, determination flows from a decision by a court or tribunal, which in any event may become a rule. On a general level, the provision of Article 32 of the Vienna Convention is applied to clarify or determine "the meaning resulting from the application of Article 31," and Article 31 refers to the meaning "given to the terms of the treaty." The requirement for applying Article 31 is thus that a treaty subject to that provision contains terms whose interpretation may be aided by application of Article 32. What if the treaty does not contain certain terms or rules at all? This shows that the unsaid rules to be discussed here are difficult to categorize in the existing law of treaties.

The two types of gap may perhaps be categorized as instances of *non liquet*, although one term or another existent in the text of the Convention may imply their presence in the minds of the drafters. As will be shown later in this chapter, the terms implying the existence of the unsaid rules are neither defined in the Convention nor explained in an agreement or instrument as referred to in Article 31(2) of the Vienna Convention. For the purposes of effective interpretation of UNCLOS, the unsaid rules must somehow exist, even independently of the Convention, and function like rules of the Convention. Otherwise, the oversight of those unsaid rules could result in a *non liquet* or manifestly erroneous finding by a court or tribunal listed in Article 287 UNCLOS.

The precise meaning and implications of such unsaid rules are a matter of interpretation, which the court or tribunal listed in Article 287 UNCLOS is competent to carry out in accordance with the provisions of Part XV of the Convention. The problem remains as to how to produce by such process of interpretation an ordinary sense that is authoritative and appropriate. It is argued that the unsaid rules, just as any provision of the Convention, requires a basic, general, textual interpretation, reflective of a truly ordinary sense of the text and of relevant State practice outside the Convention. The requirement to reflect State practice is to minimise the effect of any overbroad judicial lawmaking exercise.

Ultimately, those unsaid rules have the capability to divest a court or tribunal listed under Article 287 UNCLOS of the compulsory jurisdiction it could have assumed under section 2, Part XV of the Convention. Alternatively, after jurisdiction has been assumed by the court or tribunal, it may have interpreted the rules wrongly in a judicial or arbitral proceeding initiated under the Convention by failing to heed the unsaid rules. In both situations, what results may not be a development of the rules of the Convention by interpretation, but an *ultra vires* decision. An act of judicial lawmaking, if deliberately undertaken in these circumstances, should be attempted with great caution, for the obvious reason that the legal terrace is uncharted under the Convention. In the meantime, the States parties to UNCLOS should closely monitor and assess the accumulative impact of such exercises.

11.2 Territorial Disputes and UNCLOS

The premise is that the matter of territorial disputes is of such a nature that it can forestall the exercise of compulsory jurisdiction by a court or tribunal listed under Article 287 UNCLOS. In a way, it is a matter preliminary to a determination of the jurisdiction as contemplated under Article 288(1),[12] because it is related to the nature of the dispute that an applicant State seeks to be brought under that jurisdiction. After the nature of the dispute is determined to be related to territorial sovereignty, it will follow that the compulsory jurisdiction recognized in section 2, Part XV UNCLOS is nonexistent over the dispute.

A recent arbitration case has expressly supported this unwritten rule. In the *Chagos* arbitration, in which the parties to the case argued this point at length, the tribunal held that:

> The negotiating records of the Convention provide no explicit answer regarding jurisdiction over territorial sovereignty. The Tribunal considers that the simple explanation for the lack of attention to this question is that none of the Conference participants expected that a long-standing dispute over territorial sovereignty would ever be considered to be a dispute "concerning the interpretation or application of the Convention."[13]

The tribunal concluded that "had the drafters intended that such claims could be presented as disputes 'concerning the interpretation or application of the Convention,' the Convention would have included an opt-out facility for States not wishing their sovereignty claims to be adjudicated, just as one sees in Article 298(1)(a)(i) in relation to maritime delimitation disputes."[14] Accordingly, jurisdiction over territorial disputes was not

---

[12] The provision provides: "A court or tribunal referred to in article 287 shall have jurisdiction over any dispute concerning the interpretation or application of this Convention which is submitted to it in accordance with this Part."
[13] *The Chagos Marine Protected Area Arbitration (Mauritius v. UK)*, Award of March 18, 2015 ("Chagos Arbitration"), para. 215.
[14] Ibid. para. 217.

considered by the tribunal to have been granted under the Convention, although that decision was carried by a vote of three against two among the arbitrators.[15] Is this another way to say that the participating States reached an agreement on this point? The answer is open. What could be said is that this understanding among the States existed at the Third Conference, but not in the form of an instrument or agreement as envisaged in Article 31(2) Vienna Convention.

In the *South China Sea* arbitration, the view of the tribunal was somewhat vague in this respect. Consider the following statement:

> The Tribunal is fully conscious of the limits on the claims submitted to it and, to the extent that it reaches the merits of any of the Philippines' Submissions, intends to ensure that its decision neither advances nor detracts from either Party's claims to land sovereignty in the South China Sea.[16]

What kinds of limits were in the mind of the arbitrators? The context in which this statement was made was, however, clear, as it focused on the nature of the dispute the Philippines sought to portray as its case.[17] The statement was made specifically in response to China's Position Paper of December 7, 2014, which emphasized the nature of the dispute as one of territorial sovereignty.[18] The implications are therefore that "the limits" referred to in the tribunal's statement were those imposed by, in particular, territorial disputes.

This presumed rule is probably extant on account of both case law and the *travaux préparatoires* of the Third Conference.[19] It can derail

---

[15] *Dissenting and Concurring Opinion* by J. J. Kateka and Wolfrum, paras. 38–45.

[16] PCA Case No. 2013–19, *The South China Sea Arbitration (Philippines v. China), Award on Jurisdiction and Admissibility*, October 29, 2015 ("Award on Jurisdiction and Admissibility"), para. 152. Also see ibid., para. 8 (sitting in the introduction to the award, it might give rise to a surmise that the tribunal implicitly adopted the view of the Philippines that the Convention was "not concerned with territorial disputes.")

[17] To be found in Ch. V, entitled "Identification and Characterisation of the Dispute," 45–70.

[18] At www.fmprc.gov.cn/nanhai/eng/snhwtlcwj_1/t1368895.htm (accessed June 30, 2017), para 3.

[19] M. Nordquist, S. Rosenne & L. Sohn (eds.), *United Nations Convention on the Law of the Sea 1982: A Commentary*, vol. V (Dordrecht, Martinus Nijhoff, 1989), at 88, MN 297.1 (referring to Ambassador Galindo Pohl's statement at the second session of the Third Conference in 1974). For a short summary of the negotiations, *see* I. Buga, "Territorial Sovereignty Issues in Maritime Disputes: A Jurisdictional Dilemma for Law of the Sea Tribunals," 27 *The International Journal of Marine and Coastal Law* (2012) 59, 69–71. *Also see* L. Sohn, "Peaceful Settlement of the Disputes in Ocean Conflicts: Does UNCLOS III Point the Way?," 46 *Law and Contemporary Problems* (1983) 195, 198 (where he noted the subdivision of Art. 298(1)(a)(i) that excluded territorial disputes "totally ... from

attempts to establish the compulsory jurisdiction of a court or tribunal under UNCLOS. But the preceding analysis could be enriched by the following observation.

As a matter of fact, the Convention partly recognizes this rule in the form of Article 298(1)(a)(i), which expressly allows for a State party to exclude by declaration disputes involving historic titles from the compulsory jurisdiction provided in section 2 of Part XV of the Convention. Accepting, for sake of argument, the term "historic titles" as interpreted by the *Award on the Merits*,[20] two points are clear: (A) The partial recognition in the Convention of the taboo of territorial disputes is confined to those related to the term "historic title." The term pertains to one of the means of acquisition of territorial sovereignty, and must be claimed by a State party by declaration under Article 298(1)(a)(i) to become a bar to the compulsory jurisdiction as granted by the Convention. The extent of recognition is very limited indeed. The reason for inclusion of this term may have to do with the controversial nature of the doctrine and limited practice of historic title.[21] A recent work on the topic of historic waters makes this point still clearer;[22] (B) There exists an *a contrario* interpretation of Article 298(1)(a)(i), to the effect that, if a declaration is not filed under the provision, the provision could be construed to include within the compulsory jurisdiction such territorial disputes as are excluded expressly by the part of the provision

---

dispute settlement under the Convention." He did not distinguish the procedure of conciliation from other means of settlement in this respect.)

[20] *The South China Sea Arbitration*, Award of July 12, 2016 ("Award on the Merits"), para. 225 ("Historic rights may include sovereignty, but may equally include more limited rights, such as fishing rights or rights of access, that fall well short of a claim of sovereignty. 'Historic title', in contrast, is used specifically to refer to historic sovereignty to land or maritime areas.")

[21] UN Secretariat, "Juridical Regime of Historic Waters Including Historic Bays," A/CN, 4/143 *Yearbook of the International Law Commission* (1962), vol. II, March 9, 1962, at para. 33 ("when it comes to a more precise definition of this title, its relation to the rules of international law for the delimitation of the maritime territory of a State or the question of the circumstances in which the historic title may arise, agreement is far from complete.")

[22] C. Symmons, *Historic Waters in the Law of the Sea: A Modern Re-Appraisal* (Leiden/Boston, Martinus Nijhoff, 2008), 8–10 (where, in his view, the legal sources of the alleged rules on historic waters "must inevitably be found within international customary law because of the lack of treaty law on the doctrine.") More interestingly, the uncertainty of legal rules in this respect is not helped by the work of commentators, including the UN Secretariat's Study of 1957, which faces the problem of the repetition and reiteration among themselves: ibid. 10–15. The observation of the use of writers' views in litigation is also illustrative of the difficulty for this academic practice to be counted as State practice.

regarding conciliation.[23] Both points could have been resolved by invoking the unsaid rule suggested here, which is envisaged as a comprehensive bar to the compulsory procedures of settlement laid down in section 2, Part XV of the Convention.

This narrative in support of the unsaid rule may not, however, be free from controversy in relation to point (A). If there is an unsaid and comprehensive rule blocking compulsory jurisdiction, how to square it with the reference to historic title-related disputes in the provision, which is only optional? If filing a declaration under this provision is necessary to exclude such disputes, what would be the situation with those States parties which have not filed one?

The controversy, if any, could perhaps be addressed in this way. Historic title, as a controversial topic in doctrine and practice, is construed in this context to mean sovereignty over maritime areas under Article 298(1)(a)(i).[24] It does not therefore concern territorial disputes over areas of land surrounded or divided by sea, which is covered by the unsaid rule. Furthermore, territorial sovereignty may be acquired by means other than that of historic title, and the first three lines of the provision clearly contain nothing on territorial disputes arising from claims based on, say, discovery, occupation or accretion.

But in one area of sea, the provision and the unsaid rule may overlap. This is where a dispute is concerned with an archipelago, where the sea and the land are historically inseparable, but which lies outside the scope of Part IV UNCLOS regarding "Archipelagic States." This is a dual-nature dispute, both territorial and maritime. If a dispute has such a dual nature, it would be an erroneous finding that "China does not claim historic title to the waters of [the] South China Sea."[25] On this error, a brief word of explanation is given below.

It is common knowledge that China has long claimed sovereignty over the Nansha Islands as an archipelago, including the islands and other features and the water areas in between. Based on existing evidence, there is a good case of a historic title to make for this claim. While China's claim in the South China Sea is first based on discovery and symbolic

[23] *Chagos Arbitration*, Award, paras. 218–19.
[24] *Award on the Merits*, para. 226. Cf. Y. Z. Blum, "Historic Rights," in 2 *Encyclopedia of Public International Law* (The Max Planck institute for Comparative Public Law and International Law, 1995), 710.
[25] *Award on the Merits*, para. 229.

annexation,[26] and its activities, including those of management, inspection, exploration and exploitation, can amount to a title even under the rubric of occupation,[27] it is, more importantly for present purposes, also open for China to claim sovereignty over the islands and relevant areas of sea on historic title, which is the only one that comes close to a title from time immemorial.[28] The evidence of Chinese activities is greater than that accumulated by other neighboring countries.[29] Even supposing Chinese claims arose towards the end of the nineteenth century, the competing claims by Vietnam and the Philippines were made public only some seventy years later in the early 1970s.[30] The *Award on the Merits* acknowledges that the disputes between relevant countries in the South China Sea involve both claims to sovereignty and claims to specific kinds of maritime jurisdiction.[31] It follows that the dispute between the Philippines and China could meet the requirement of Article 298(1)(a)(i) UNCLOS relating to historic titles. Such a historic claim of sovereignty as pertains to the Nansha Islands as a whole falls squarely within the scope of the term "historic title." Indeed, the Chinese claim can meet both the unsaid rule and the historic title condition of Article 298(1)(a)(i), with the latter, subject to the requirement that a declaration including it is filed by a State party, covered by the former.

In relation to point (B), it is submitted that the unsaid rule always remains a bar to compulsory jurisdiction, regardless of the *a contrario* interpretation of Article 298(1)(a)(i). Even if a declaration is not made by a State party under the provision to expressly cover "any unsettled dispute concerning sovereignty or other rights over continental or insular land territory," a qualification to be found towards the end of the provision, the unsaid rule remains in the way of compulsory jurisdiction in Part XV of the Convention. From this qualification, it may also be seen that historic title in this provision must have a very limited scope in terms

---

[26] *Island of Palmas (Netherlands/US)*, Award of April 4, 1928, II *Reports of International Arbitral Awards*, 829, 869.

[27] Z. G. Gao and B. B. Jia, "The Nine-Dash Line in the South China Sea: History, Status, and Implications," 107 *American Journal of International Law* (2013) 98, at 113.

[28] Cf. *Eritrea* v. *Yemen*, Phase One: Territorial Sovereignty And Scope of the Dispute, Award of October 9, 1998, 114 *International Law Reports* 2.

[29] J. M. Shen, "China's Sovereignty over the South China Sea Islands: A Historical Perspective," 1 *Chinese Journal of International Law* (2002) 94, 155–56.

[30] M. Samuels, *Contest for the South China Sea* (New York and London, Methuen, 1982), 99.

[31] *Award on Jurisdiction and Admissibility*, para. 152 ("There is no question that there exists a dispute between the Parties concerning land sovereignty over certain maritime features in the South China Sea.")

of disputes that it may exclude from the compulsory jurisdiction of Part XV. The term is concerned with maritime areas, as previously mentioned. Additionally, the exclusionary effect of the qualification mentioned above is restricted to disputes arising after the entry into force of the Convention, according to Article 298(1)(a)(i). So it may be said that the reference to historic title in Article 298(1)(a)(i) complements the unsaid rule to the extent that, within that limited range of disputes, it can be invoked in place of the unsaid rule, but its invocation depends on the filing of a declaration under Article 298(1)(a)(i).

The preceding argument would be sufficient to trigger the exclusionary effect of a declaration filed by a State party pursuant to Article 298(1)(a), such as the one filed by China with the UN Secretary-General in 2006.[32] The consequence of successfully invoking such a declaration should have resulted in a decline of jurisdiction by the tribunal seized of the *South China Sea Arbitration*.

The legal error of the *Award on the Merits* is thus twofold. On the one hand, there is the legal (and factual) error of inaccurately defining the real dispute between the two countries,[33] which ultimately rests on the Chinese claim of sovereignty over an archipelago and the presumed opposition thereto by the Philippines.[34] On the other, while the tribunal had a vague view on the impact of territorial disputes upon the compulsory jurisdiction recognized in Part XV UNCLOS, its interpretation of the term "historic title" should have included both maritime areas and land areas within them – an off-lying archipelago like the Nansha Islands. This would have resulted in a dismissal of the arbitration case brought by the Philippines.

---

[32] www.un.org/depts/los/convention_agreements/convention_declarations.htm#China%20Upon%20ratification (accessed June 7, 2017).

[33] S. Talmon, "The South China Sea Arbitration: Is there a Case to Answer?," in S. Talmon & B. B. Jia (eds.), *The South China Sea Arbitration: A Chinese Perspective* (Oxford and Portland, Hart Publishing, 2014) 15, at 43 and 63.

[34] This may be inferred from the Philippine argument that "no significance follows from the Philippines' focus on specific features. For the Philippines, this is *merely pragmatic* in light of the large number of maritime features in the Spratlys, and 'if the largest of the Spratly features is incapable of generating an EEZ and continental shelf entitlement, then it is most unlikely that any of the other 750 features will be able to do so,'" *Award on Jurisdiction and Admissibility*, para. 144(b). The truth is that the characterization by the tribunal of the dispute according to each feature selected by the Philippines, made without considering the Chinese claim to Nansha Islands as an archipelago, decidedly tipped the balance in this proceeding in favor of the Philippine case: ibid. para. 154. Once this was done, the tribunal's statement dismissing the existence of a practice concerning off-lying archipelagos would read almost like an aside, *Award on the Merits*, para. 576.

For any other country in a similar situation as China, reliance may be placed on both the unsaid rule and the reference in Article 298(1)(a)(i) to historic title, in order to defeat the arguments intended to found compulsory jurisdiction under UNCLOS.

11.3   A Non-Liquet in Article 121?

The single article that comprises Part VIII of UNCLOS establishing the regime of islands reads as follows:

Article 121
Regime of Islands
1. An island is a naturally formed area of land, surrounded by water, which is above water at high tide.
2. Except as provided for in paragraph 3, the territorial sea, the contiguous zone, the exclusive economic zone and the continental shelf of an island are determined in accordance with the provisions of this Convention applicable to other land territory.
3. Rocks which cannot sustain human habitation or economic life of their own shall have no exclusive economic zone or continental shelf.

If a maritime feature fulfills the requirements of paragraph 1, it constitutes an island in a legal sense. Where it fails to satisfy the requirements of paragraph 3, it will be treated as a rock to which no area of EEZ or continental shelf can attach, regardless of whether a claim to those areas of jurisdiction has been made.

The International Court of Justice (ICJ or "Court") has settled the matter of the status of Article 121 in its recent judgment in *Nicaragua* v. *Colombia*. While citing *Qatar* v. *Bahrain* to reaffirm the customary law status of the first two paragraphs of the article,[35] the ICJ stated that:[36]

> The Judgment in the Qatar v. Bahrain case did not specifically address paragraph 3 of Article 121. The Court observes, however, that the entitlement to maritime rights accorded to an island by the provisions of paragraph 2 is expressly limited by reference to the provisions of paragraph 3. By denying an exclusive economic zone and a continental shelf to rocks which cannot sustain human habitation or economic life of their own, paragraph 3 provides an essential link between the long-established

---

[35] *Maritime Delimitation and Territorial Questions between Qatar and Bahrain (Qatar* v. *Bahrain)*, Merits, Judgment, ICJ Rep. (2001) 91, paras. 167, 185, and 195.
[36] *Territorial and Maritime Dispute (Nicaragua* v. *Colombia)*, Judgment of November 19, 2012, ICJ Rep. (2012) 624, at para. 139.

principle that "islands, regardless of their size, ... enjoy the same status, and therefore generate the same maritime rights, as other land territory" (ibid.) and the more extensive maritime entitlements recognized in UNCLOS and which the Court has found to have become part of customary international law. The Court therefore considers that the legal régime of islands set out in UNCLOS Article 121 forms an indivisible régime, all of which (as Colombia and Nicaragua recognize) has the status of customary international law.

One question that has been left unanswered by the Court is of the criteria for assessing the state of human habitation or economic life on a rock. Even though paragraph 3 is part of customary law, the fact remains that the Convention, customary law or case law has no ready answer with regard to the requisite degree of human habitation or economic life for purposes of establishing the existence of a juridical island. Various zones of maritime jurisdiction can only accrue to an island pursuant to Article 121(2), after the preceding question is answered. The significance of the two criteria of human habitation and economic life is plain to see. In the instant case, the ICJ did not define the two criteria, but simply accepted the agreement of the parties that QS32, of Quitasueño,[37] is a rock.[38] This led it to find Quitasueño as a rock in terms of Article 121(3).[39]

The silence of the Court in this regard, however, did not help the Arbitral Tribunal in the *South China Sea Arbitration* that commenced two months after the delivery of the ICJ judgment, and the interpretation of Article 121(3) was a critical issue in the arbitration.[40] Faced with this issue, the Arbitral Tribunal developed its analysis through interpretation in pursuance of Articles 31 and 32 of the Vienna Convention.[41] It dealt with "the text, its context, the object and purpose of the Convention, and the *travaux préparatoires*, before setting out the conclusions that, in the Tribunal's view, follow with respect to the meaning of the provision."[42] The means of textual interpretation was, and admittedly should be, preeminently placed.[43] After the textually interpretative exercise, the

---

[37] Ibid., para. 24 ("a large bank.")
[38] Ibid., para. 183.
[39] Ibid., para. 238.
[40] *Award on the Merits*, paras. 473–74.
[41] Ibid., para. 476.
[42] Ibid., para. 477.
[43] Ibid., para. 478. Also see M. Villiger, "The Rules on Interpretation: Misgivings, Misunderstandings, Miscarriage? The 'Crucible' Intended by the International Law Commission," in E. Cannizzaro (ed.), *The Law of Treaties Beyond the Vienna Convention* (Oxford, Oxford University Press, 2011), 105, at 114–17. He recalled that

rest of its narrative on the context, purpose or object of the Convention,[44] and the *travaux préparatoires*,[45] merely served to confirm the textual interpretation. But it is submitted that at places wrong interpretations have been drawn after the aforementioned exercises.

The text of Article 121(3) UNCLOS is admittedly open to different interpretations,[46] among which there has been the one given by the Arbitral Tribunal in the *South China Sea Arbitration*.[47] For present purposes, it is this Tribunal's interpretation of the term "human habitation" that merits a further word. But before saying the word, it must be pointed out that, with the case as a whole being considered, the presumption adopted by this article differs from that adopted by the Arbitral Tribunal. On the basis of the Philippine Submissions Nos. 3, 5 and 7, the tribunal presumed that the maritime features of the Nansha Islands or Spratlys mentioned by the Philippines could be dealt with separately of each other, with each being treated as an independent object.[48] The presumption adopted by this article is, however, that the Nansha Islands or the Spratlys constitutes a unit, an archipelago, which is always claimed as such by China.[49] This point was in fact acknowledged by the Arbitral Tribunal,[50] which, somewhat unexpectedly, drew only a few lines of comment from it.[51] Notwithstanding the nonappearance of China in the proceedings, the tribunal should still have been obliged to consider China's claim in its true form, if only to have an accurate grasp of the dispute that gave rise to the arbitration. It is one thing to say that, after due examination, the claim may appear to stand on slippery ground, but quite another to hold, as the tribunal did, that

---

the approach of the International Law Commission was to state a general rule without "laying down a hierarchy of norms for the interpretation of treaties," ibid., at 114.

[44] *Award on the Merits*, para. 520.

[45] This is expected under Article 32 Vienna Convention, which sees *travaux* as something that may be considered, for one thing, to "confirm the meaning resulting from the application of article 31."

[46] R. Churchill and A. V. Lowe, *The Law of the Sea* (Manchester, MUP, 3rd edn., 1999), 50.

[47] *Award on the Merits*, footnote 519, which lists a few.

[48] Ibid., para. 473.

[49] For instance, upon filing its instrument of ratification of UNCLOS on June 7, 1996, the Chinese government stated that "The People's Republic of China reaffirms its sovereignty over all its *archipelagos* and islands as listed in article 2 of the Law of the People's Republic of China on the territorial sea and the contiguous zone, which was promulgated on 25 February 1992," www.un.org/Depts/los/convention_agreements/convention_declara tions.htm#China%20Upon%20ratification (accessed June 10, 2017).

[50] *Award on the Merits*, paras. 448–49.

[51] Ibid., paras. 573–76.

the claim is simply dismissed on account of certain rules of UNCLOS. For the problem with this latter approach is that none of the UNCLOS rules referred to in the *Award on the Merits* have ever been relied on for the Chinese claim.[52] Additionally, no analysis of relevant practice outside the Convention was attempted with regard to off-lying or mid-ocean archipelagos possessed by continental countries.[53] This brushing aside of a major aspect of the Chinese claim in just a few paragraphs is questionable. To do so without analysis certainly exacerbates the problem.

Whether any of the maritime features, including Taiping Island, in the Nansha Islands is an island or rock is a question that need not be answered under the preceding premise.[54] Even if the question has some-times been addressed by China,[55] relevant statements should have been understood by the tribunal in the light of the general claim of China over the whole archipelago.[56] Engagement with the preceding question alone has no impact upon the general claim, which has been long asserted and acted upon by China. The dismissal of this claim by the tribunal,[57] unpersuasive for overlooking the basis of the Chinese claim, was instrumental for the recognition by the tribunal of the applicability of Article 121(3) UNCLOS in the arbitration, and ultimately, conducive to the final outcome in the part of the case that concerns the status of certain features of the Nansha Islands. But the general claim of China over the archipelago should not concern us further on this occasion.

---

[52] Ibid., paras. 573–75.

[53] Ibid., para. 576.

[54] The Nansha Islands may be compared with the case of Minquiers and Ecrehos, both of which were defined by the ICJ as "groups" which "consist each of two or three habitable islets, many smaller islets and a great number of rocks." The Court was asked by the parties to "decide in general to which Party sovereignty over each group as a whole belongs, without determining in detail the facts relating to the particular units of which the groups consist," ICJ, *The Minquiers and Erechos Case (France/UK)*, Judgment of November 17, 1953, ICJ Rep. (1953) 47, at 53. No attempt was made by the parties or the Court to distinguish one feature from another in either group.

[55] *Award on the Merits*, paras. 466–67 (citing official statements by the Chinese Foreign Ministry in 2016).

[56] Ministry of Foreign Affairs, People's Republic of China, Foreign Ministry Spokesperson Hua Chunying's Regular Press Conference (March 24, 2016), at www.fmprc.gov.cn /mfa_eng/xwfw_665399/s2510_665401/2511_665403/t1350552.shtml (accessed June 1, 2017) ("The Nansha Islands including Taiping Dao have been China's territory since ancient times . . . China is firmly against attempts of the Philippines to unilaterally deny China's territorial sovereignty and maritime rights and interests in the South China Sea through arbitration.")

[57] *Award on the Merits*, paras. 573–75.

The proposition here is that the term "human habitation" is not one of legal terminology, and the point of *non liquet* suggested at the beginning of this chapter arises with regard to the juridical meaning of this term, if any. The rationale for raising this point is the consideration as to whether judicial interpretation can fill every gap in a treaty or customary law. Where the parties to a dispute agree to this way of interpretation by conferring jurisdiction on a court or tribunal, such interpretation can of course be justified. Where, however, the agreement of the parties is not forthcoming, the resultant interpretation, pursued on a presumptive ground of jurisdiction, may not be accepted by the dissenting party on the ground of excess of jurisdiction on the part of the interpreting court or tribunal. In other words, an *ultra vires* interpretative exercise naturally prompts noncompliance by the dissenter. Before taking a closer look at the interpretation of the term "human habitation" as given by the tribunal, two preliminary points should be made.

It is first recalled that the International Law Commission once thought that the very essence of the textual approach was that "the parties are to be presumed to have that intention which appears from the ordinary meaning of the terms used by them."[58] However, the Commission gave no indication as to whether terms of a treaty are capable of being interpreted in an ordinary sense and in *which* ordinary sense. The natural presumption is that the ordinary sense is one in legal terms. A sense in other than legal terms will be beyond the competence of a lawyer.[59]

Second, there is one aspect to the term "ordinary meaning" that is noteworthy but often overlooked. An authority in the law of treaties once echoed another by stating that "the ordinary meaning of a treaty provision should in principle be the meaning which would be attributed to it at the time of the conclusion of the treaty."[60] This raises yet another question about the method of interpretation employed in the *Award on the Merits*. For, prima facie, the reference to the *Shorter Oxford English Dictionary* in its 2002 edition may not be the best to reflect a meaning intended in 1982 when UNCLOS was adopted; nor can be an entry in a dictionary yet to be fully updated since its first publication in 1898.[61] Were this argument not convincing, it would fall for the tribunal to explain why the ordinary sense should be the one derived from the two

---

[58] *Yearbook of the International Law Commission* (1966), vol. ii, at 221, para. 12.
[59] Cf. *Legality of the Threat or Use of Nuclear Weapons*, Advisory Opinion of July 8, 1996, ICJ Rep. (1996) 226, para. 55.
[60] Sinclair, *supra* note 4, at 124 (referring to Fitzmaurice).
[61] *Award on the Merits*, para. 488, footnotes 531 (referring to Annex 815) and 532.

dictionaries. This point is raised because, as will be shown shortly afterwards, the *travaux* of the Third Conference reveals nothing about the way in which the negotiating countries chose the term "human habitation" and by which connotation. The literal or textual interpretation in light of relevant State practice would be the best solution in these circumstances.[62] The *Award on the Merits* seems to have failed on this count.

According to the *Award on the Merits*, the term "habitation" "implies a non-transient presence of persons who have chosen to stay and reside on the feature in a settled manner."[63] From a literal interpretation of the term "habitation" by reference to dictionary,[64] the tribunal's interpretation of the term "human habitation" ended with an "at a minimum" criterion, that "a feature be able to support, maintain, and provide food, drink, and shelter to some humans to enable them to reside there permanently or habitually over an extended period of time."[65]

The question must be asked whether this is *the* ordinary meaning of the term. For it is immediately clear that the term, when interpreted literally, contains nothing on the status of the persons composing the community; nor does it necessarily entail the finding that the feature *itself* must provide food, water and shelter, as opposed to an alternative interpretation that the amenities can be provided *on* the feature; nor does it provide any indication as to the length of habitation. It is felt that the term itself is descriptive at best. The ordinary meaning should be that, prima facie, humans can live, or have lived, on the feature.[66] A textual interpretation of the term does not necessarily lead to the one given by the Arbitral Tribunal. But there are several more questions.

On what basis may we say that one interpretation should be preferred to others? Is it because it has a more "ordinary" sense than the others? Or

---

[62] *Legality of the Threat or Use of Nuclear Weapons*, Advisory Opinion of 8 July 1996, ICJ Rep. (1996) 226, para. 55 ("The Court will observe that the Regulations annexed to the Hague Convention IV do not define what is to be understood by 'poison or poisoned weapons' and that different interpretations exist on the issue ... The terms have been understood, *in the practice of States*, in their ordinary sense as covering weapons whose prime, or even exclusive, effect is to poison or asphyxiate.") (italics added).

[63] *Award on the Merits*, para. 489.

[64] Ibid., para. 488.

[65] Ibid., para. 490.

[66] R. Kolb, "l'interprétation de l'article 121, paragraphe 3, de la convention de Montego Bay sur le droit de la mer: les 'rochers qui ne se prêtent pas à l'habilitation ou à une vie économique proper ... '" *Annuaire françqis de droit international* (1994) 876, at 907.

simply more frequently used in speech and writing? When inquiry boils down to this level, the focus is no longer on a juridical answer, but on a habitual usage of language.

Besides, questions of a substantive nature also arise with the Award's interpretation. For it has failed to define the following elements: the requisite length of the period of stay, the minimum number of residents, the way the persons become residents and what constitutes habitual living. Devoid of definitive answers to these substantive questions, the ordinary meaning given in the Award would become too anemic to be applicable.

Moreover, it may be asked what else could be added, as the Award seems to suggest, to the minimum criterion it chose. For a minimum standard signifies a necessary condition, but does not address the sufficiency *vel non* of that condition. In other words, the criterion might be useful for disqualifying a feature as an island, but insufficient to prove that a rock is in fact a juridical island.

Lastly, while the interpretation in question might be deemed ordinary by the Arbitral Tribunal, is it still so regarded in, for instance, scientific studies of human habitation conducted by anthropologists or urban planners, which may be closer to truth?[67]

It is clear, therefore, that the literal interpretation of the term given in the *Award on the Merits*, with a view to revealing its ordinary sense, begs more questions than it was intended to resolve. But the situation got worse when it came to evidence of State practice.

No analysis of the basis for this "at a minimum" criterion was attempted in the Award in reference to State practice, except for a recollection of the record of negotiations at the Third Conference which even the tribunal itself recognized as "imperfect."[68] The problem with that brief survey of the *travaux* is that the effort drew a blank in the search for anything that might shed light on the term "human habitation," among others. There was also a mingling of the word "sustain" in this interpretation,[69] whose ordinary sense is that of keeping in existence or alive or maintaining.[70] In its conclusion, however, the tribunal still found that the term stands for "the inhabitation of the feature by a stable

---

[67] The ordinary meaning of the term "rocks," as understood by geographers, is unsuitable for legal purposes under Art. 121: B. Kwiatkowska & A. Soons, "Entitlement to Maritime Areas of Rocks which cannot Sustain Human Habitation or Economic Life of Their Own," 21 *Netherlands Yearbook of International Law* (1990) 139, at 152–53.

[68] Ibid., para. 534, and paras. 526–33.

[69] Ibid., para. 486.

[70] Ibid. Cf. Kolb, *supra* note 66, at 905.

community of people for whom the feature constitutes a home and on which they can remain."[71]

With that conclusion, the tribunal was actually reading new words into the term "human habitation," and by producing forward-looking propositions through adding those new words, had performed an act of judicial lawmaking.[72] If so, support from State practice would be necessary, in that the rule to be created should have its elements based in an emerging trend of practice or, better still, established practice. If there is a shortage of evidence of practice, recourse should at least be had to general practice of international courts and tribunals.[73] Neither approach was pursued by the tribunal.

The validity of the tribunal's preferred interpretation may therefore have suffered from this act of lawmaking on four counts in relation to State practice.

First, existing practice in this regard knows no criterion that stipulates one or more forms of human habitation, which as a matter of fact "vary greatly."[74] UNCLOS or its *travaux* do not offer any guidance. Indeed, the references made by the tribunal to the *travaux* of the Third Conference clearly show that the intention behind the term "human habitation" could not be discernible by applying customary rules of interpretation. It would be fair to argue that it is unclear that the negotiating countries at the Third Conference meant to exclude from the term "human habitation" the form of habitation by soldiers or scientists. It would require some serious mental gymnastics to be persuaded by the view that a community centered around a military garrison is not a form of human habitation, and that such a community does not count for purposes of Article 121(3) even if it has domiciled on a feature continuously for long time. An example is the garrison stationed on Taiping Island for over sixty years prior to the start of the *South China Sea Arbitration*.[75] When the garrison was established on the island, it was

---

[71] *Awards on the Merits*, para. 542.

[72] *Fisheries Jurisdiction (UK v. Iceland)*, Merits, Judgment of July 25, 1974, ICJ Rep. (1974) 3, para. 40.

[73] It has been the position of the ICJ that "it is the duty of the Court to interpret the Treaties, not to revise them," *Interpretation of Peace Treaties* (Second Phase), Advisory Opinion of July 18, 1950, ICJ Rep. (1950) 221, at 229.

[74] *Award on the Merits*, para. 490.

[75] The building of the garrison on Taiping Island in 1956 and its maintenance subsequently, Samuels, *supra* note 31, at 85–86. About the decisiveness of the year 1956, S. Tønnesson, "The History of the Dispute," in T. Kivimäki (ed.), *War or Peace in the South China Sea?* (Copenhagen, NIAS, 2002), 6, at 13.

two years before the first UN conference on the law of the sea was convened in Geneva, and that, since 1956, the presence of the garrison has not attracted protest from any quarters.

Second, there is no requirement in international law that a community of persons living on an island or the like must be civilians in the strict sense, excluding soldiers, scientists and support/auxiliary personnel (who may well be civilians).[76] It is, in addition, difficult to be persuaded by the view that the purpose of human habitation is dominant for purposes of interpretation in this respect. Habitation means no more than that some humans live on the features in the Nansha Islands for some time, in the past or at present.[77] If humans lived on them in the past, this would satisfy the preference of the tribunal for historical evidence of human living.[78] If humans live on them when the dispute is submitted for adjudication, this fact would undoubtedly meet the ordinary meaning of the term "human habitation" as adopted by the *Award on the Merits*. Nothing can be drawn from the term itself to suggest that the humans in question must live on the feature voluntarily and for nongovernmental purposes. Volition in any case is subjective enough not to be counted as an element of a legal criterion in this context.

Third, contrary practice existed in parallel to the negotiations at the Third Conference.[79] In fact, existing practice also includes the damaging

---

[76] There are two further questions arising from this question. How to characterize a community of mainly solders living on a rock or island who have been there for decades? What if the civilian community is composed of former soldiers who, previously stationed on a rock or island, return, due to government subsidy, to live on it after decommissioning?

[77] *Award on the Merits*, para. 616:

> The principal features of the Spratly Islands are not barren rocks or sand cays, devoid of fresh water, that can be dismissed as uninhabitable ... At the same time, the features are not obviously habitable, and their capacity even to enable human survival appears to be distinctly limited. In these circumstances ... the Tribunal considers that the physical characteristics of the features do not definitively indicate the capacity of the features. Accordingly, the Tribunal is called upon to consider the historical evidence of human habitation ... on the Spratly Islands and the implications of such evidence for the natural capacity of the features.

[78] Ibid., para. 549. Cf. Y. Tanaka, *The International Law of the Sea* (Cambridge, Cambridge University Press, 2nd edn., 2015), at 67.

[79] The Jan Mayen Island, some 373 square kilometers in area, having around thirty to forty mainly meteorologists and crews navigation stations, under the authority of the Ministry of Defence, was not regarded as a rock under Art. 121(3), but an island by the Conciliation Commission established by Norway and Iceland, see the 1982 *Report and Recommendations*

type of uninhabited features that are treated by States in possession of them as islands entitled to, among others, an EEZ.[80] No protest has been recorded or maintained in these cases. Since the Second World War, for instance, Howland Island and Baker Island, both situated over 3,000 kilometers away from Honolulu, have been uninhabited, but the United States has claimed an EEZ for each, even though neither has "natural fresh water resources" or economic activity.[81] Likewise, the French Clipperton Island, uninhabited since 1945, had an EEZ established by the French Government in 1978, and the zone was extended in 1995 after French ratification of UNCLOS.[82] All three islands would compare poorly with Taiping Island in terms of the interpretation given by the *Award on the Merits* to the term "human habitation," but none has its status as an island questioned as much by other countries as Taiping Island.[83] The problem is not about the Award plunging for an interpretation unfavorable to the case of Taiping Island, but rather its oversight of a practice outside the Convention that clearly differs from what the tribunal thought to be the better interpretation of the term "human habitation."[84] Where the Convention and its *travaux* are silent on the connotation of the term, a better interpretation in the view of a tribunal is simply not a reason strong enough for it to attempt at lawmaking. The backing of States parties to the Convention is needed, and this can be conveniently found in practice. This approach is even more necessary if no subsequent practice based in the Convention is established. To reject or adopt this approach would require some word of explanation given by the tribunal in the instant case.

to the Governments of Iceland and Norway (the Conciliation Commission on the Continental Shelf Area between Iceland and Jan Mayen), International Legal Materials, vol. 20 (1981) 797, at 802, 803–04.

[80] Y. Tanaka, "Reflections on the Interpretation and Application of Article 121(3) in the South China Sea Arbitration (Merits)," *Ocean Development and International Law* (2017) (DOI: 10.1080/00908320.2017.1349529), 1, at 9–10.

[81] Y. H. Song, "The Application of Article 121 of the Law of the Sea Convention to the Selected Geographical Features Situated in the Pacific Ocean," 9 *Chinese Journal of International Law* (2010) 663, at 689–90.

[82] Ibid., at 691.

[83] There are other examples: A. Oude Elferink, "The South China Sea Arbitration's Interpretation of Article 121(3) of the LOSC: A Disquieting First" (September 7, 2016): http://site.uit.no/jclos/files/2016/09/The-South-China-Sea-Arbitrations-Interpretation-of-Article-1213-of-the-LOSC-A-Disquieting-First.pdf (accessed March 7, 2018).

[84] This practice is not limited to that subsequent to the adoption of UNCLOS in terms of Art. 31(3)(b) of the Vienna Convention, namely, "any subsequent practice in the application of the treaty which establishes the agreement of the parties regarding its interpretation."

Fourth, there was the curious approach of the tribunal insisting on historical records for assessing, in this contemporary case, the state of human habitation on a maritime feature. If the dispute in this arbitration arose in the 1930s or even 1950s, there might be some usefulness for a study of historical records, dated from the late nineteenth century,[85] of human activities on the features in question, because the facts contained in the records would be closer to the time when the dispute arose, thus being relatively contemporaneous.[86] However, the *South China Sea Arbitration* was initiated in 2013, with the great majority of incidents that might underpin the Philippine case involving the interpretation of Article 121(3) UNCLOS all arising within the preceding twenty years.[87] Should it not be natural for the tribunal to look at this part of the case with an emphasis on facts or incidents pertinent to that period? Why should the evidence of the state of habitation on the features be frozen to a period when the Philippines had yet to become a sovereign State and no dispute similar to those of the current arbitration could be anticipated to arise?

This method of reasoning by the tribunal may be contrasted with what the ICJ did in a territorial dispute case, where it stated:[88]

> In order to illuminate the meaning of words agreed upon in 1890, there is nothing that prevents the Court from taking into account the present day state of scientific knowledge, as reflected in the documentary material submitted to it by the Parties.

The Court employed current knowledge to inform its interpretation of the terms of an old treaty; whereas the *Award on the Merits* turned to old historical record to guide its interpretation of a modern treaty, even though contemporary evidence is abundant. There is no intention here

---

[85] *Award on the Merits*, para. 618, which did not deal with the records in detail. So reference might have to be made to paragraphs 597–600, in which records relating to the period 1868–1951 were quoted.

[86] The ICJ stated in a different context that "the issue which the Court has to decide is whether or not there exist at Quitasueño any naturally formed areas of land which are above water at high tide. It does not consider that surveys conducted many years (in some cases many decades) before the present proceedings are relevant in resolving that issue," ICJ, *Territorial and Maritime Dispute (Nicaragua* v. *Colombia)*, Judgment of November 19, 2012, ICJ Rep. (2012) 624, para. 35. The point made by the Court, that a current state of things at a geographical feature is far more relevant to a pending case than that when the surveys were conducted, remains valid for present purposes.

[87] The notable exception to this general comment is the part of the Philippine case regarding the "Nine-Dash Line" and China's claim to historic rights in the South China Sea.

[88] *Kasikili/Sedudu Island, supra* note 5, para. 20.

to embark on a long discussion of the doctrine of intertemporal law,[89] except for two comments.

On the one hand, while the juridical definition of an island came into being in 1958, with the adoption of the *Convention on the Territorial Sea and the Contiguous Zone*,[90] the rule on the status of rocks only emerged when UNCLOS was adopted in 1982. This fact should have discouraged a court or tribunal from relying on the pre-1930s practice to interpret the text of Article 121(3), had the court or tribunal taken it on itself to survey relevant State practice. It is recalled that Article 121(3), when adopted with UNCLOS, was not a codification of customary law,[91] and that its customary law status was only confirmed by the ICJ in 2012. In any event, the meaning of the term "human habitation" has yet to be decided by the Court.

On the other, while reliance on external supply is a factual question, even a heavy dependence, such as was suggested by the Award,[92] could not negate the fact of human habitation. For, plainly, Article 121(3) does not require a living to be eked out in sole reliance upon the natural conditions of a maritime feature as were first discovered by humans. In today's world, such a requirement would in any case give the term an unreasonable and static meaning unsupported by real life experiences.[93] If fresh water (not to mention fresh water of higher quality) is available only from outside supply, would that be sufficient to reduce an island to a rock? If higher quality foodstuffs consumed on an island, such as are sold commonly in a developed country, are dependent on external supply, could that fact turn the island to a rock? These are hardly legal questions, but, if they are given answers in legal terms, the answers must be based in State practice, rather than on a reasoning process that may throw up more than one answer to each question.

So, with regard to the term "human habitation," the *Award on the Merits* has failed to persuade by textual interpretation or analysis of State practice. A better course of action for the tribunal in such a situation

---

[89] The doctrine is important for treaty interpretation, see Sinclair, *supra* note 4, at 125.

[90] Article 10. Cf. United Nations, *The Law of the Sea: Regime of Islands, Legislative History of Part VIII (Article 121) of the United Nations Convention on the Law of the Sea* (New York, United Nations, 1988), paras. 9–11.

[91] H. Jayewardene, *The Regime of Islands in International Law* (Dordrecht, Martinus Nijhoff, 1990), p. 6.

[92] *Award on the Merits*, para. 547.

[93] Cf. *Maritime Delimitation in the Area between Greenland and Jan Mayen (Denmark v. Norway)*, Judgment of June 14, 1993, ICJ Rep. (1993) 38, in which Norway produced evidence on regular service by military aircraft for personnel transfers and light cargo deliveries to Jan Mayen (Counter-Memorial of Norway, May 11, 1990, paras. 78–101, cited in Tanaka, *supra* note 78, at 68).

would seem to stay with the descriptive interpretation Article 121(3) offers, without venturing into the more uncertain extralegal meanings of the term, about which it cannot claim expertise.

It is recognized that the ordinary sense given by a court or tribunal may prevail due to the provision of Article 288(4) UNCLOS.[94] But a problem immediately arises with that suggestion in relation to the *South China Sea Arbitration*, in which the very existence of the dispute that triggered it seems to be in doubt,[95] which, if substantiated, could forestall the compulsory procedure from the outset.[96] In addition, it is reasonably arguable that that provision and what follows from it can always be displaced by operation of Article 280 of the Convention,[97] when the parties to such a dispute as defined by the court or tribunal elect to settle that dispute or any part of it by their own choice of peaceful means, including negotiation. The resultant agreement between the parties would prevail over a decision rendered by the court or tribunal relying on Article 288(4).

In any case, an interpretation given judicial imprimatur may not conclude the present inquiry, because there is a possibility that the ordinary sense given by the tribunal in the *Award on the Merits* could in fact be erroneous, because it was given *ultra vires*. This is said in two senses. First, the interpretation was given on a wrongly assumed jurisdiction. Second, it was given by way of a judicial lawmaking action that not only found no support in the text of the Convention or its *travaux*, but strayed from existing State practice. Additionally, an error in interpretation may equally result in an error in application, as can be illustrated by the tribunal's application of its interpretation in the case of Taiping Island of the Nansha Islands.[98]

---

[94] "In the event of a dispute as to whether a court or tribunal has jurisdiction, the matter shall be settled by decision of that court or tribunal."

[95] The dispute between China and the Philippines has long been concerned with subject matter untouched by the Philippine claims raised for arbitration: B. B. Jia, "Four Legal Issues in relation to the South China Sea Arbitration," in M. Hibert, P. Nguyen & G. Polling (eds.), *Perspectives on the South China Sea* (Lanham, Rowman and Littlefield, 2014) 70, at 71. For a discussion of political issues and nonjusticiable disputes, see S. Koopmans, *Diplomatic Dispute Settlement* (TMS Asser Press, 2008), 15–19.

[96] B. B. Jia, "The Curious Case of Article 281: A 'Super' Provision within UNCLOS?," 46 *Ocean Development and International Law* (2015), 266–80.

[97] "Nothing in this Part impairs the right of any States Parties to agree at any time to settle a dispute between them concerning the interpretation or application of this Convention by any peaceful means of their own choice."

[98] A depiction of it was given in para. 401 of the *Award on the Merits*.

China's position with regard to the legal status of the island has been well known.[99] In the *South China Sea Arbitration*, the Philippines argued that it was a rock under Article 121(3).[100] The tribunal after some consideration endorsed the Philippine proposition in a twofold finding.

On the one hand, with regard to "the criterion of human habitation," the tribunal found, with Taiping Island in mind, that

> Taken as a whole, the Tribunal concludes that the Spratly Islands were historically used by small groups of fishermen. Based on the clear reference from 1868, the Tribunal also accepts that some of these individuals were present in the Spratlys for comparatively long periods of time, with an established network of trade and intermittent supply. At the same time, the overall number of individuals engaged in this livelihood appears to have been significantly constrained.[101]

With that, the tribunal found that "the record indicates a pattern of temporary residence on the features for economic purposes, with the fishermen remitting their profits, and ultimately returning, to the mainland."[102]

On the other hand, the Award included the composition of a local community in its criterion, as illustrated in the following statement in relation to Taiping Island and others:[103]

> The Tribunal does not consider that the military or other governmental personnel presently stationed on the features in the Spratly Islands by

[99] *Foreign Ministry Spokesperson Hua Chunying's Remarks on Relevant Issue about Taiping Dao*, June 3, 2016, available at www.fmprc.gov.cn/mfa_eng/xwfw_665399/s2510_665401/t1369189.shtml (accessed June 14, 2017):

> China has indisputable sovereignty over the Nansha Islands and its adjacent waters, including Taiping Dao. China has, based on the Nansha Islands as a whole, territorial sea, exclusive economic zone and continental shelf . . . The working and living practice of Chinese people on Taiping Dao fully proves that Taiping Dao is an 'island' which is completely capable of sustaining human habitation or economic life of its own. The Philippines' attempt to characterize Taiping Dao as a 'rock' exposed that its purpose of initiating the arbitration is to deny China's sovereignty over the Nansha Islands and relevant maritime rights and interests. This violates international law, and is totally unacceptable.

Also cited in *Award on the Merits*, para. 466.
[100] *Award on the Merits*, paras. 426 and 440.
[101] Ibid., para. 601.
[102] Ibid., para. 618.
[103] Ibid., para. 620.

one or another of the littoral States suffice to constitute "human habitation" for the purposes of Article 121(3). These groups are heavily dependent on outside supply, and it is difficult to see how their presence on any of the South China Sea features can fairly be said to be sustained by the feature itself, rather than by a continuous lifeline of supply and communication from the mainland. Military or other governmental personnel are deployed to the Spratly Islands in an effort to support the various claims to sovereignty that have been advanced. There is no evidence that they choose to inhabit there of their own volition, nor can it be expected that any would remain if the official need for their presence were to dissipate. Even where the current human presence in the Spratly Islands includes civilians, as is the case on at least Thitu and (very recently) Itu Aba, the Tribunal considers that their presence there is motivated by official considerations and would not have occurred, but for the disputed claims to sovereignty over these features.

Both findings beg questions in the light of the factual background of the island. But one major problem arises with the application in this case of the ordinary sense adopted by the tribunal. The conclusion of the tribunal set out above shows that Taiping Island has already met a basic and general interpretation of the term "human habitation," suggested by this chapter. Fishermen lived on the features for extended periods of time,[104] which in some cases ran into years.[105] On several features of the Nansha Islands, such as Taiping, Zhongye (Thitu), Nanwei (Spratly), Xiyue (West York) and Hongxiu (Namyit) Islands, there are relics of temples dedicated to worship the Chinese Earth God, apart from other indicators of settlement.[106] How long and how many people would it take to build and maintain a temple? Further, where the fishermen hailed from may be beside the point,[107] especially in a globalizing world where people move to and from a place without, however, being attached to it. The reason why they do so is, at any rate, an extralegal question. Taiping Island, viewed in this light, could well be a juridical island.

---

[104] Ibid., para. 601.
[105] Han Zhenhua et al. (ed.), *Collections of Historical Materials on Our Country's Islands in the South China Sea* (Beijing, Orient Press, 1988), at 118–19. There is the view that since *capacity* to sustain is the test under Art. 121(3), "it is not necessary that human habitation on an island is permanent," Tanaka, *supra* note 78, at 67.
[106] Ibid., at 119–21 (the materials came from a publication in 1975 titled *Documents on the Chinese Islands in the South China Sea*, vols. 8 [containing a memoir written in 1957 on the naval inspections of the Nansha Islands] and 9 [containing a record of the naval inspections of the Nansha Islands in 1956]).
[107] *Award on the Merits*, para. 618.

11.4   Concluding Remarks

Regarding the territorial dispute exception, it is curious that it is not expressly included in the Convention, although there is strong likelihood that it is taken for granted. With a broader scope than the historic title exception contained in Article 298(1)(a)(i), it is more of a rule independent of the text of the Convention. For better or worse, its existence is recognized by both tribunals and States appearing before them. The interpretation of Article 298(1)(a)(i), and of Article 288(1) in particular, still needs to consider this rule.

Regarding the question of Article 121(3), it is not suggested that every word of Article 121 needs a fresh and clear exposition by a court or tribunal. Many words of the article, such as those comprising paragraphs 1 and 2, need no further interpretation but speak clearly in an ordinary, legal sense. It could be part of the reason why the ICJ declared more than a decade ago in *Qatar* v. *Bahrain* that these two paragraphs represented rules of customary law. But the uncontroversial nature of the words of paragraphs 1 and 2 may not be reflected by those of paragraph 3. So a term like "human habitation" should be interpreted textually where possible; otherwise, it should be interpreted in the light of State practice. The basic, general sense of the term appears to be the better one to reflect an ordinary meaning what has not been controverted by State practice.

To conclude, interpretation may be the bread and butter of lawyers' work. What has been discussed here, however, shows that they can only do so much with their expertise in order to resolve disputes concerning the interpretation of the provisions of the Convention. Both types of gap discussed above seemingly amount to a case where *ratio verborum* and *ratio legis* could not easily match in producing a reasonably acceptable interpretation.[108] This is particularly true in the cases of the term "human habitation" and of the territorial dispute exception, where no legislative intention could be discerned from the *travaux* of the Third Conference. An unreasonable interpretation, in the sense of being legally erroneous, has little chance to become positive law. Furthermore, the customary rules of interpretation may just fail in a given case to engender one sense that is not only ordinary, but more ordinary than other interpretations.[109] This is true

---

[108]   C. Allen, *Law in the Making* (Oxford, Clarendon Press, 7th edn., 1964), 490.

[109]   J. M. Sorel and V. Boré Eveno, "Article 31, Convention of 1969," in O. Corten & P. Klein (eds.), *The Vienna Convention on the Law of Treaties: A Commentary*, vol. i (Oxford, Oxford University Press, 2011), 837 (referring to M. Rosenfeld, *Les interprétations justes* [LGDJ, Paris, 2001]: "all interpretations appear to be correct interpretations.")

in relation to the interpretation of such a term as "human habitation," which is not capable of being interpreted in legal terms, but only in the most basic, descriptive sense common to all dictionaries. An attempt at lawmaking exercises in these circumstances, without clear support from State practice, may easily produce an unreasonable interpretation such that it may push States to embrace the opposite interpretation. In view of all this, there is sense that such an interpretation would be unsafe to stand within or without the proceeding in which it was made. This will be more acute when it is attached to a term of a treaty that may affect fundamental interests of a State.

China and International Dispute Settlement

Implications of the South China Sea Arbitration

JIANGYU WANG

12.1 China's Evolving Approach to International Dispute Settlement

The attitude of the People's Republic of China (hereinafter PRC or China) toward international law serves as the basis for our understanding of China's approach to international dispute settlement. Sornarajah and Wang have argued that the contemporary Chinese approach to international law, "ambivalent and ambiguous as it is," may be the fusion of five influences, including China's appreciation of its position in the US-led international order, ancient/traditional Chinese thoughts on law and order, the Chinese nation's victimhood mentality as a result of the "century of humiliation," the determination to pursue power and influence on the global stage, and China's self-identification as a developing country.[1] Contemporary China, however, has a rather satisfactory record in complying with international law. As Ann Kent put it, "compliance research shows that . . . China has turned from a rebel with a cause in the 1960s into a reasonably good international citizen in the twenty first century that, for the most part, complies with its international obligations."[2]

China's participation in international dispute resolution, especially in international adjudication, seems to be somewhat an exception to its general approach to international law. In its Reform and Opening period,

[1] Muthucumaraswamy Sornarajah & Jiangyu Wang, "China, India and International Law: A Justice Based Vision between the Romantic and Realist Perceptions," *Asian Journal of International Law* 9 (2019) 217, 240.
[2] Ann Kent, "Compliance v Cooperation: China and International Law," *Australian International Law Journal* (2006), 19, 31.

China's reintegration into the world economy had driven its desire to pursuing a more active role in the international community, including the international legal order.[3] A landmark event was China's nomination of Professor Ni Zhengyu as the PRC's first Member of the International Court of Justice (ICJ), which ended China's complete separation from systems of international adjudication.[4] But, in general, China has been suspicious of binding dispute resolution at the international level:

> The Chinese government has tended to perceive international dispute settlement mechanisms involving independent adjudication by judges and arbitrators as Western-dominated, which has led to an instinctive distrust of him. Submitting to such processes involves a sacrifice of control, and thus sovereignty, which China is reluctant to cede.[5]

One may argue that the hesitation inherent in the Chinese approach to international adjudication appears to have an exception: international economic law. With respect to the world trading system, China has fully embraced the World Trade Organization (WTO) and is a regular participant in its unique dispute settlement system, which features compulsory jurisdiction.[6] China joined the Convention on the Settlement of Investment Disputes Between States and Nationals of Other States in February 1990, which has bound China to the arbitration procedures of the International Center for the Settlement of Investment Disputes (ICSID) as well as the obligation to accept and enforce ICSID awards.[7] In March 2017, the ICSID issued its first award involving China as the respondent state that proceeded to a substantive hearing and resulted in an award.[8] The award was clearly in favor of China, as the Arbitral Tribunal found the claim of the Korean investor Ansung Housing Co. to be "manifestly without legal merit." The PRC Ministry of Commerce

---

[3] Julian G. Ku, "China and the Future of International Adjudication," 27 *Md J Intl L.* (2012), 154, 161.

[4] *Id.*

[5] Harriet Moynihan, "China's Evolving Approach to International Dispute Settlement," *Chatham House*, March 29, 2017, at www.chathamhouse.org/sites/default/files/publica tions/research/2017-03-29-chinas-evolving-approach-international-dispute-settlement-moynihan-final.pdf (accessed December 2, 2018).

[6] As of this writing, China appeared as complainant in 20 cases, as respondent in 43 cases, and as third party in 163 cases. See "Dispute cases involving China," at www.wto.org /english/thewto_e/countries_e/china_e.htm (accessed December 2, 2018).

[7] Ku, *supra* note 3, 163.

[8] *Ansung Housing Co., Ltd.* v. *People's Republic of China*, ICSID Case No. ARB/14/25, March 9, 2017, award available at http://icsidfiles.worldbank.org/icsid/ICSIDBLOBS/ OnlineAwards/C3885/DC10053_En.pdf (accessed December 2, 2018).

praised the Tribunal and said China "welcomed the tribunal's treaty interpretation and the final award."[9]

China subscribed to the dispute settlement procedures under the United Nations Convention on the Law of the Sea (UNCLOS) when it joined the convention in 1996. In particular, as will be discussed later, by approving UNCLOS, China agreed to accept binding arbitration in case the parties have no agreement on the choice of procedures, subject to the declaration it made upon ratification of the convention.[10] In any event, China's accession to UNCLOS led to the observation that "China's pattern in the context UNCLOS is thus consistent: limit binding dispute resolution as much as possible and opt for arbitration over standing tribunals."[11] However, compared with China's rather adamant policy of nonappearance and nonparticipation in the *South China Sea* arbitration, the aforesaid observation looks rather optimistic in retrospect: after all, China not only totally rejected the arbitral tribunal's right to hear the case but also emotionally discredited the tribunal's legitimacy in this arbitration. However, on the other hand, it might be an overgeneralization to treat the *South China Sea* arbitration as "one litmus test" for China's approach to international dispute settlement,[12] given China's different compliance records in different areas of international law, as discussed above. That said, China's handling of the *South China Sea* proceedings does suggest several profound implications in its evolving approach to international dispute settlement.

This chapter aims to critically examine the different views, particularly Chinese perspectives, on the three major international law aspects of the *South China Sea* arbitration, including (1) the legitimacy of the Arbitral Tribunal (the Tribunal), (2) whether the Tribunal had jurisdiction over the case, and (3) whether the Tribunal erred in applying UNCLOS on certain important legal issues concerning the merits of the case, in light of the two awards (the SCS Jurisdiction Award and the Final Award) and the relevant rules and doctrines in international law. On this particular

---

[9] "Shangwubu Tiaoyue Falusi Fuzeren Jiu Ancheng Gongsi Su Zhongguo Zhengfu Touzi Zhengduan An Zhongfang Shengsu Fabiao Tanhua" ("Comment of the Head of the Department of Law and Treaty of the PRC Ministry of Commerce on China's Winning of the case *Ansung v. Chinese Government*"), March 10, 2017, at www.mofcom.gov.cn /article/ae/ag/201703/20170302531322.shtml (accessed December 2, 2018).

[10] See UN Division for Ocean Affairs and the Law of the Sea, "Declarations and Statements: China," at www.un.org/Depts/los/convention_agreements/convention_declarations.htm #China%20Upon%20ratification (accessed December 2, 2018).

[11] Ku, *supra* note 3, 167.

[12] Moynihan, *supra* note 5, 4.

case, it argues, while the tribunal's own legitimacy seems unquestionable, whether it actually had jurisdiction over the dispute is arguable. Most likely it did, but certain arguments made by China against its jurisdiction are worthy of discussion. However, the Final Award's interpretation and application of certain provisions of UNCLOS are problematic and possibly erroneous. Finally, the legal analysis suggests that China would have been in a much better position on the legal front had it formally participated in the case from the jurisdictional stage.

The chapter is organized as follows. After a brief introduction of the factual background of the case, it offers a general overview of the dispute settlement procedures of UNCLOS and its relevance to the South China Sea disputes. The limitations of UNCLOS will also be addressed. It then briefly describes the procedural history of the case and the key arguments and findings in the arbitral awards, followed by an examination of the legitimacy of the Tribunal by looking at its composition and the way it was established. The next two parts consider the jurisdiction of the Tribunal and assesses the decisions on the merits in the Final Award, especially those concerning historic rights, the "nine-dash line," and the definition of islands. The final part of the chapter looks at the implications of the case on the evolving Chinese approach to international dispute settlement and concludes.

12.2   The *South China Sea* Arbitration

The *South China Sea Arbitration* (*The Republic of Philippines v. The People's Republic of China*) is a landmark case in the history of both international law and international relations because of not only the geopolitical significance of the dispute but also the determination of the relevant tribunal in rendering a ruling to boldly define the rights, entitlements and obligations of the parties based on the UNCLOS .[13]

The arbitration brought to a historical level the longstanding disputes involving both territorial and maritime claims in the South China Sea, a vast body of semienclosed water in the south of continental Asia. Embracing an area of about 3.7 million square kilometers (which is roughly the size of Mexico), it is surrounded by mainland China, Taiwan, and several southeast Asian countries.[14] Chinese literature

[13] Information about this case from the Permanent Court of Arbitration can be found at www.pcacases.com/web/view/7 (accessed October 1, 2018).
[14] "South China Sea," *Encyclopedia Britannica*, at https://global.britannica.com/place/South-China-Sea (accessed September 18, 2018).

usually classifies the physical features in the South China Sea into three groups of islands and one submerged bank, which are named, in Chinese mandarin, Nansha Qundao (the Spratly Islands), Xisha Qundao (the Paracel Islands), Dongsha Qundao (the Pratas Islands), and Dongsha Qundao (the Macclesfield Bank).[15] While China and Vietnam have disputed the ownership of the Paracel Islands for decades, most of the disputes have arisen out of claims over the Spratly Islands, or Nansha Qundao, which contain more than 230 features including islands, shoals, reefs, and banks.[16] The claimant states are Brunei, the People's Republic of China (whose claims are identical to that of Taiwan), the Philippines, and Vietnam.

Although disputed claims over the islands and other geographic features in the South China Sea arguably date back to at least a century ago,[17] this was the first time in history that the disputes were brought to an international tribunal for adjudication by one of the claimants. On January 22, 2013, the Philippines initiated arbitration proceedings against China to seek the settlement of its disputes with China concerning the relevant claims in the South China Sea by an Arbitral Tribunal to be established in accordance with Annex VII of the UNCLOS. On October 29, 2015, the Tribunal issued its first award, ruling that it has jurisdiction over the case.[18] On July 12, 2016, the Tribunal rendered its second and final award on the merits of the case, which, in favor of the Philippines on almost all its claims, handed China a complete defeat in the case.[19]

China made it clear from the very beginning of the case that it would neither accept nor participate in the arbitral proceedings for both legal and political reasons. At least, as it stated in a *note verbale* in response to the Philippines' initiation of the case, the "core" of the disputes was about

---

[15]   See L. Zhao, *Haiyangfa Wenti Yanjiu [Study on Questions Concerning the Law of the Sea]* (Beijing: Peking University Press, 1996), 1–2. See also Wu Shicun, *Solving Disputes for Regional Cooperation and Development in the South China Sea: A Chinese Perspective* (Oxford: Chandos Publishing, 2013), 2–3.

[16]   J. Li, *Nanhai Zhengduan yu Guoji Haiyangfa [South China Sea Disputes and the International Law of the Sea]* (Beijing: Ocean Press, 2003), 1.

[17]   See Bill Hayton, *The South China Sea: The Struggle for Power in Asia* (New Haven: Yale University Press, 2014), chapters 2, 3 and 4. See also Li Jinming (2003), *supra* note 16, 5–6.

[18]   The South China Sea Arbitration Award on Jurisdiction and Admissibility (*The Republic of Philippines v. The People's Republic of China*), PCA Case No. 2013–19, October 29, 2015 (hereinafter "SCS Jurisdiction Award.")

[19]   The South China Sea Arbitration Award (*The Republic of Philippines v. The People's Republic of China*), PCA Case No. 2013-19, July 12, 2016 (hereinafter "SCS Merit Award.")

"territorial disputes over some islands and reefs of the Nansha Islands," a sovereignty-related issue which is beyond of the scope of UNCLOS.[20] In addition, since the arbitral procedure started, governmental and semiofficial agencies in China have issued numerous documents to defend China's nonparticipation position and repudiate, sometimes quite emotionally, the relevant criticisms. These documents include, most significantly, a Position Paper by the PRC Government,[21] a Statement of the Chinese Society of International Law,[22] and several statements and remarks by the PRC Ministry of Foreign Affairs and its Ministers.[23] Of course, none of these should "be regarded as China's acceptance of or its participation in the arbitration," according to China's official stance.[24]

The official statements, together with media comments and academic publications in China, offer a rudimentary framework of Chinese perspectives on the *South China Sea* arbitration case, which focus on three fronts insofar as international law is concerned.[25] First, China has

---

[20] *Note verbale* from the Embassy of the People's Republic in Manila to the Department of Foreign Affairs of the Republic of the Philippines, February 19, 2013, quoted in the SCS Jurisdiction Award, *supra* note 6, para. 27.

[21] Position Paper of the Government of the People's Republic of China on the Matter of Jurisdiction in the South China Sea Arbitration Initiated by the Republic of the Philippines, December 7, 2014, English version available at www.fmprc.gov.cn /mfa_eng/zxxx_662805/t1217147.shtml (accessed December 2, 2018) (hereinafter "PRC Position Paper.")

[22] "The Tribunal's Award in the 'South China Sea Arbitration' Initiated by the Philippines is Null and Void," statement of the Chinese Society of International Law, June 1, 2016, English version available at www.csil.cn/News/Detail.aspx?AId=201 (hereinafter "CSIL Statement.")

[23] See, for example, "Statement of the Ministry of Foreign Affairs of the People's Republic of China on the Award of 12 July 2016 of the Arbitral Tribunal in the South China Sea Arbitration Established at the Request of the Republic of the Philippines," July 12, 2016, English version available at www.fmprc.gov.cn/mfa_eng/zxxx_662805/t1379492.shtml (hereinafter "FMPRC Statement on SCS Final Award"); "Remarks by Chinese Foreign Minister Wang Yi on the Award of the So-called Arbitral Tribunal in the South China Sea Arbitration," PRC Ministry of Foreign Affairs, July 12, 2016, English version available at www.fmprc.gov.cn/mfa_eng/zxxx_662805/t1380003.shtml (hereinafter "Wang Yi Remarks on SCS Final Award"); and "Veil of the Arbitral Tribunal Must be Tore Down – Vice Foreign Minister Liu Zhenmin Answers Journalists' Questions on the So-called Binding Force of the Award Rendered by the Arbitral Tribunal of the South China Sea Arbitration Case," PRC Ministry of Foreign Affairs, July 13, 2016, English version available at www.fmprc.gov.cn/mfa_eng/wjbxw/t1381879.shtml (accessed 1 December 2018) (hereinafter "Liu Zhenmin's Remarks on SCS Final Award.")

[24] SCS Jurisdiction Award, para. 56.

[25] China has also argued that the arbitration "is completely a political farce staged under legal pretext," indicating that it was a maneuver by China's enemies. See Wang Yi Remarks on SCS Award, *supra* note 11.

consistently argued that the Arbitral Tribunal does not have jurisdiction over the case.[26] Second, China has attacked the legitimacy of the Tribunal as well as the neutrality of the arbitrators.[27] Third, Chinese officials and scholars have criticized the merits of the Final Award, which denied almost all of China's claims in the South China Sea, especially China's assertion of historic rights along the so-called nine-dash line and the legal status of the geographic features currently under Chinese occupation. In short, China has described the arbitral institution as a "law-abusing tribunal" that has issued an "ill-founded" award that "abuses international law [and] threatens world order."[28]

Outside China, the prevailing view is that what China did in the South China Sea showed deeply disrespectful attitudes toward international law,[29] and the SCS arbitral award rightly upholds justice in the international order. As *The Economist* has opined, "the ruling by the Permanent Court of Arbitration in The Hague … is firm, clear and everything China did not want to be."[30] China was advised to accept the ruling to comply with international law. "If, in its fury, China flouts the ruling … it will be elevating brute force over international law as the arbiter of disputes among nations."[31]

[26] See, for example, PRC Position Paper, *supra* note 9and CSIL Statement, *supra* note 10.
[27] See, for example, Liu Zhenmin's Remarks on SCS Award. See also Liu Zhen, "Questions of Neutrality: China Takes Aim at Judges in South China Sea Case," *South China Morning Post*, July 11, 2016, available at www.scmp.com/news/china/diplomacy-defence/article/1988119/questions-neutrality-china-takes-aim-judges-south-china (visited October 23, 2018; hereinafter "Questions of Neutrality.")
[28] See "Law-abusing Tribunal Issues Ill-founded Award on South China Sea Arbitration," Xinhua News Agency, July 12, 2016, available at http://news.xinhuanet.com/english/2016-07/12/c_135507651.htm (visited October 23, 2016) (hereinafter "Ill-Founded Award") and "OP-ED: South China Sea Arbitration Abuses International Law, Threatens World Order," *People's Daily*, June 29, 2016, available at http://en.people.cn/n3/2016/0629/c90000-9078797.html (accessed October 20, 2018) (hereinafter "Arbitration Abuses International Law.")
[29] Dean Cheng, "China's War against International law in the South China Sea," *National Interest*, May 19, 2015, at http://nationalinterest.org/feature/chinas-war-against-international-law-the-south-china-sea-12913?page=show (accessed December 1, 2018) (stating that China's land reclamation in the South China Sea "challenges an area of international laws" because it was "an attempt to alter facts on the ground [or in the water].")
[30] "The South China Sea: Come Back from the Brink, Beijing", *The Economist*, July 16, 2016, *available at* www.economist.com/news/leaders/21702194-why-china-should-accept-damning-international-ruling-come-back-brink-beijing (accessed December 2, 2018).
[31] *Id.*

But the Tribunal's bold ruling also surprised many observers. Although it was widely anticipated that the Tribunal would rule in favor of the Philippines,[32] the "court's rulings go further than expected in saying China is violating international law in the South China Sea."[33] The main concern has been geopolitical: the worry is that the ruling might push China into a corner to make it more provocative and aggressive, as "China's defeat was so crushing that it has left Beijing few ways to save face."[34] The legal aspect of the ruling seems to have been taken for granted, that is, the arbitral awards unquestionably represent good international law. It is important, however, to point out that although the Tribunal's decisions in the awards firmly clarify many relevant issues on the South China Sea disputes in international law, the awards contain, unfortunately, many blemishes in their legal reasoning concerning issues of both jurisdiction and merit. On the other hand, the fact that many of China's arguments against the jurisdiction of the Tribunal and critiques of the awards are flawed to various degrees does not necessarily mean that the awards are entirely correct in their views about the international legal issues concerned.

12.3   The General Scheme of Dispute Settlement under Unclos

The 307 articles and eleven annexes make UNCLOS one of the largest codes in international law. With the ambition "to settle, in a spirit of mutual understanding and cooperation, all issues relating to the law of the sea,"[35] it is not a surprise that "dispute settlement was one of the most

[32] See G. Allison, "Of Course China, Like All Great Powers, Will Ignore an International Legal Verdict," *The Diplomat*, July 11, 2016, at http://thediplomat.com/2016/07/of-course-china-like-all-great-powers-will-ignore-an-international-legal-verdict (accessed December 2, 2018) (stating, before the final award was issued, "There is not much suspense about what the tribunal will decide: it will almost certainly side with the Philippines.")

[33] Economist, "The Economist Explains: Why a Tribunal Has Ruled against China on the South China Sea," *The Economist*, July 13, 2016, at www.economist.com/blogs/econo mist-explains/2016/07/economist-explains-12 (accessed October 9, 2018). See also M. Rapp-Hooper, "Parting the South China Sea: How to Uphold the Rule of Law," 95 *Foreign Affairs* (September/October 2016), 76 (stating "Many observers had expected the tribunal to rule in Manila's favor . . . But few anticipated a ruling as definitive as the one ultimately handed down.")

[34] *Id.*, Rapp-Hooper, 76. See also Economist, *supra* note 33 (stating "the sweeping condemnation of [China's] activities by the court could raise tensions in the South China Sea further, embolden other countries to launch copy-cat court actions, and possibly lead China to react strongly.")

[35] UNCLOS, Preamble.

contentious issues" in the negotiations of the Convention.[36] But eventually, Part XV of the Convention, which establishes an elaborated system for the settlement of maritime disputes, became one of the main achievements of the Third United Nations Conference on the Law of the Sea.[37]

UNCLOS is premised on the basic principle that "States Parties shall settle any dispute between them concerning the interpretation or application of this Convention by peaceful means" in accordance with Article 2(3) of the United Nations Charter.[38] This is followed by the principle of party autonomy to allow the states that are parties to UNCLOS to agree at any time to settle their dispute by "any peaceful means of their own choice."[39]

What is most relevant to the *South China Sea* arbitration is UNCLOS' "principle of compulsory settlement" which applies "if the parties cannot agree upon a means of settlement, or if they choose a means which proves unsuccessful."[40] But it is first important to emphasize again that an agreement of settlement by the parties to a dispute has preemptive power. The system of dispute settlement under Part XV is thus a default system which would come into operation only when no settlement has been reached by the parties by recourse to means of their own choice and that "the agreement between the parties does not exclude any further procedure."[41]

Thus, Section 2 of Part XV of the Convention offers a set of compulsory procedures whereby a dispute can be submitted unilaterally by any party to a court or tribunal through one of the means prescribed in that Section, if the parties cannot reach settlement by their choice.[42] Being "compulsory," first of all, means they will generate binding decisions. The four means through which a signatory State of UNCLOS can exercise recourse to the compulsory procedures include the International Tribunal for the Law of the Sea (ITLOS), the International Court of Justice, an Arbitral Tribunal constituted in accordance with Annex VII of UNCLOS, and a special Arbitral Tribunal constituted in accordance

---

[36] J. G. Merrills, *International Dispute Settlement* (Cambridge University Press, 5th edn., 2011), 167.
[37] I. V. Karaman, *Dispute Resolution in the Law of the Sea* (Leiden: Martinus Nijhoff, 2012), 1.
[38] UNCLOS, Article 279.
[39] UNCLOS, Article 280.
[40] See Merrils, *supra* note 36, at 169.
[41] UNCLOS, Article 281(1).
[42] UNCLOS, Article 286.

with Annex VIII of UNCLOS.[43] Such a court or tribunal "shall have jurisdiction over any dispute concerning the interpretation or application" of UNCLOS regarding the dispute in question.[44] The Arbitral Tribunal in the *South China Sea* arbitration was one established under Annex VII of UNCLOS.

Understandably, the right of a party to refer a dispute unilaterally for binding settlement is subject to a number of exceptions, the most important of which is the written declaration of a State expressing that it does not accept any one or more of the compulsory procedures with respect to disputes relating to sea boundary delimitations or those involving historical bays or titles, disputes concerning military activities and certain kind of law enforcement activities in regard to the exercise of sovereign rights or jurisdiction in its Exclusive Economic Zone, or disputes in respect of the exercise of functions of the United Nations Security Council.[45] As will be discussed Part VI, one of the key issues in the *South China Sea* arbitration is about whether the Tribunal's jurisdiction is precluded by China's declaration under Article 298.

It is also important to point out the "sovereignty exception" to the compulsory dispute settlement of UNCLOS. That is, it is widely agreed that the Convention does not govern sovereignty-related issues. Accordingly, the questions of sovereignty and related rights over land territory are outside the subject matter of the UNCLOS court or tribunal.[46] This was confirmed in the *Chagos* arbitration,[47] in which the tribunal concluded that it is the intent of the UNCLOS negotiators to exclude issues concerning land sovereignty from the ambit of the Convention:

---

[43] UNCLOS, Article 287.

[44] UNCLOS, Article 288(1).

[45] UNCLOS, Article 298(1).

[46] S. Talmon, "The South China Sea Arbitration: Is There a Case to Answer?," in Stefan Talmon & Bing Bing Jia (eds.),*The South China Sea Arbitration: A Chinese Perspective* (Hart Publishing, 2014), 31 (stating "It is generally acknowledged that the Convention does not deal with questions of sovereignty and other rights over land territory, and that disputes concerning these questions are not subject to the jurisdiction *ratione materiae* of UNCLOS arbitral tribunals.") See also S. Pemmaraju, "The South China Sea Arbitration (The Philippines v. China): Assessment of the Award on Jurisdiction and Admissibility," 15 *Chinese Journal of International Law* (2016), paras. 18 and 19.

[47] *The Chagos Marine Protected Area Arbitration* (*Mauritius v. United Kingdom*), UNCLOS Annex VII Tribunal, Award, March 18, 2015, available at www.pcacases.com/pcadocs/MU-UK%2020150318%20Award.pdf (accessed December 2, 2018) (hereinafter "*Chagos* award").

In the Tribunal's view, had the drafters intended that such [sovereignty]
claims could be presented as disputes "concerning the interpretation or
application of the Convention", the Convention would have included an
opt-out facility for States not wishing their sovereignty to be adjudicated,
just as one sees in Article 298(1)(a)(i) in relation to maritime delimitation
disputes.[48]

12.4   The *South China Sea* Arbitration: Procedural History, Issues, and Key Findings

As noted previously, the Philippines commenced the arbitration proceedings in January 2013, seeking to establish an UNCLOS Annex VII
tribunal to adjudicate its disputes with China concerning maritime
entitlements in the South China Sea. Despite the objection to the arbitration in China's *note verbale* in February 2013, all five arbitrators were
appointed by June 2013, marking the establishment of the SCS Tribunal.
On July 11, 2013, the Tribunal formalized the appointment of the
Permanent Court of Arbitration (PCA) as Registry for Proceedings of
the *South China Sea* arbitration. The Rules of Procedure for the arbitration were adopted by the Tribunal on August 27, 2013.

In light of China's objection to the Tribunal's jurisdiction expressed
through its diplomatic notes, public statements, the Position Paper, and
letters to members of the Tribunal from the Chinese Ambassador to the
Netherlands, the Tribunal decided to bifurcate the proceedings and
convene a hearing on the matter of the Tribunal's jurisdiction and the
admissibility of the Philippines' submissions, which was conducted in
July 2015 (the Hearing on Jurisdiction).[49]

For the whole arbitration, the Philippines presented fifteen specific
final submissions, which were grouped by the Tribunal into four categories of interrelated matters. First, the Philippines sought a declaration
from the Tribunal that China's maritime entitlements in the South
China Sea may not extend beyond those permitted by UNCLOS. In
particular, China's claim to sovereign rights and jurisdiction, and to
historic rights within the nine-dash line marked on Chinese maps, are
without lawful effect to the extent that they exceed the entitlements that
China would be permitted by UNCLOS. Second, the Philippines
requested the Tribunal to determine that all of the features claimed by

---

[48] *Chagos* award, *supra* note 35, para. 217.
[49] SCS Jurisdiction Award, paras. 68 and 86.

both China and the Philippines in the Spratly Islands, as well as Scarborough Shoal, are either submerged banks or low-tide elevations incapable of generating an entitlement to an exclusive economic zone (EEZ) or to a continental shelf. Third, the Philippines asked the Tribunal to resolve a series of disputes between China and the Philippines concerning the lawfulness of China's actions in the South China Sea to interfere with the Philippines's exercise and enjoyment of the rights within and beyond its EEZ and continental shelf, as well as to inflict severe harm on the maritime environment by supporting Chinese fishermen's fishing activities and engaging in land reclamation. Fourth, the Tribunal was asked to find that certain actions by China aggravated and extended the disputes between the parties during the course of this arbitration.[50] Further, on jurisdiction alone, the Philippines requested the Tribunal to rule that the Philippines' claims "are entirely within its jurisdiction and are fully admissible."[51]

On October 29, 2015, the Tribunal issued a unanimous Award on Jurisdiction and Admissibility. Briefly, the Tribunal not only ruled that it was properly constituted under UNCLOS, but also rejected all of China's challenges to the Tribunal's jurisdictional authority to consider the case. The Tribunal concluded that the dispute in question concerned neither territorial sovereignty, nor maritime delimitation, which was supposed to be excluded by a declaration made by China in 2006. Further, the Tribunal rejected the argument that there was an agreement between China and the Philippines to select a means of their own choose. Largely on this basis, the Tribunal held that it did have jurisdiction with respect to the matters raised in seven of the Philippines' submissions.[52]

It would not be imprecise to describe China's response to the above award as furious. A day after the award was rendered, the PRC Ministry of Foreign Affairs issued a statement on the award, which said:

> Disregarding that the essence of this arbitration case is territorial sovereignty and maritime delimitation and related matters, maliciously evading the declaration on optional exceptions made by China in 2006 under Article 298 of the UNCLOS, and negating the consensus between China

---

[50] SCS Final Award, *supra* note 7, paras. 7–10. See also SCS Jurisdiction Award, paras. 4–6 (grouping the Philippines into three interrelated issues as the fourth one was not yet raised by the Philippines during the Hearing on Jurisdiction).
[51] "PCA Press Release: Arbitration between the Republic of the Philippines and the People's Republic of China," Permanent Court of Arbitration, The Hague, October 29, 2015, available at www.pcacases.com/web/view/7 (hereinafter "Seventh PCA Press Release.")
[52] See SCS Jurisdiction Award in general, and para. 413.

and the Philippines on resolving relevant disputes through negotiations and consultations, the Philippines and the Arbitral Tribunal have abused relevant procedures and obstinately forced ahead with the arbitration, and as a result, have severely violated the legitimate rights that China enjoys as a State Party to the UNCLOS, completely deviated from the purposes and objectives of the UNCLOS, and eroded the integrity and authority of the UNCLOS.[53]

In short, the statement reiterated that the SCS Jurisdiction Award "is null and void, and has no binding effect on China."[54]

The Tribunal nevertheless proceeded with the Hearing on Merits in November 2015.[55] On July 12, 2016, the Tribunal released the much anticipated Final Award, again a unanimous one, in which it rejected all of China's claims and ruled overwhelmingly in favor of the Philippines. On historic rights and the nine-dash line, the Tribunal decided that UNCLOS comprehensively allocates rights to maritime areas, irrespective of preexisting rights. For this reason, China's historic rights to resources in the South China Sea, if they ever existed, were extinguished to the extent they were incompatible with the EEZs provided for in the Convention. The Tribunal concluded that China's claims of historic rights to resources in the waters of the South China Sea based on the nine-dash line do not have legal basis under UNCLOS. On the legal status of features and entitlements to maritime areas, the Tribunal declared that none of the Spratly Islands, individually or collectively, are capable of generating extended maritime zones such as an EEZ or continental shelf (beyond a territorial sea of twelve nautical miles for some features). On this basis, the Tribunal concluded that certain sea areas claimed by China are within the EEZ of the Philippines. In terms of the lawfulness of Chinese actions, the Tribunal ruled that China had violated the sovereign rights of the Philippines in its EEZ by interfering with Philippine fishing and petroleum exploration, constructing artificial islands, and failing to prevent Chinese fishermen from fishing in the Philippines' EEZ. In addition, the Tribunal also declared that China had caused severe

---

[53] "State of the Ministry of Foreign Affairs of the People's Republic of China on the Award on Jurisdiction and Admissibility of the South China Sea Arbitration by the Arbitral Tribunal established at the Request of the Republic of the Philippines", PRC Ministry of Foreign Affairs, October 30, 2015, quoted in the SCS Jurisdiction Award, *supra* note 6, para. 61 (hereinafter the "FMPRC Statement on the Jurisdiction Award.")

[54] *Id.*

[55] SCS Final Award, para. 69.

harm to the maritime environment and had aggravated the dispute since the start of the arbitration procedure.[56]

China's response to the Final Award came as no surprise to anybody. A statement by the PRC Ministry of Foreign Affairs issued on the same day as the Award "solemnly declares that the award is null and void and has no binding force. China neither accepts nor recognizes it."[57] The statement, together with other remarks by senior Chinese officials, continued the Chinese practice of challenging both the legitimacy and jurisdiction of the Tribunal.

12.5   The Legitimacy of the Tribunal and the Neutrality of the Arbitrators

It is rather unusual in international dispute settlement that a State Party to a dispute would use very strong language to assault the credibility of the international tribunal that adjudicates the dispute as well as the neutrality of the members of the tribunal. In the *South China Sea* arbitration, China launched such attacks, and they should essentially be treated as another argument advanced by China against the authority of the Tribunal to handle this case, given the attacks were delivered by Chinese authorities through formal channels. A day after the Final Award was issued, Liu Zhenmin, a Vice Foreign Minister of the PRC, raised four points to call into question the legitimacy of the Tribunal and the arbitrators. In Liu's own words, "I mainly want to explain to you on whether the tribunal is a legitimate 'international court' in order to tear down the veil of the Arbitral Tribunal."[58]

First, Liu argued, the Tribunal was not to be given the weight of an "international court" as understood by many. The Tribunal did not have any relationship with the International Court of Justice (ICJ), was not part of the Hamburg-based International Tribunal for the Law of the Sea (ITLOS) established under UNCLOS, and was not in the system of the PCA. Thus, the Tribunal "is worth nothing" because it is not an "international court" as such.[59]

---

[56] See generally the SCS Final Award. For a summary of the Tribunal's findings see "Press Release: The South China Sea Arbitration", the Permanent Court of Arbitration, The Hague, 12 July 2016, available at www.pcacases.com/web/view/7 (hereinafter "11th PCA Press Release.")

[57] FMPRC Statement on the SCS Final Award, *supra* note 11.

[58] Liu Renmin's Remarks on SCS Final Award, *supra* note 11.

[59] *Id.*

Second, Liu accused the establishment of the Tribunal of being politi-
cized. In this regard, his fire was focused on the Japanese, who selected
most of the arbitrators:

> The establishment of the Arbitral Tribunal is in fact the result of political
> manipulation. The Arbitral Tribunal consists of five arbitrators. Apart
> from Professor Rüdiger Wolfrum from Germany, the arbitrator desig-
> nated by the Philippines, the other four arbitrators were appointed by the
> Japanese judge Shunji Yanai, who was the then ITLOS President. Who is
> Shunji Yanai? He is a judge of the ITLOS now and before as well as the
> Chairman of Advisory Panel on Reconstruction of the Legal Basis for
> Security set by the Shinzo Abe administration. He plays an important role
> in helping Shinzo Abe with the lifting of the ban on collective self-defense
> and challenging the international order after World War II. He was also
> former Japanese Ambassador to the US. Various sources prove that the
> composition of the Arbitral Tribunal was completely manipulated by him.
> Moreover, he also exerted his influence on the proceedings of the Arbitral
> Tribunal afterwards.[60]

Third, Liu criticized the composition of the panel for being Eurocentric
and unrepresentative. Liu pointed out that four of the five arbitrators
came from Europe, and the one from Ghana lived in Europe permanently. "So does a court like this have any representativeness? Do the
judges know well about Asian cultures? Do they know the South China
Sea issue well?"[61] In the eyes of China, "these factors matter to representativeness and fairness of an arbitral tribunal or court."[62]

Lastly, Liu emphasized the inconsistency in the views of some arbitrators and witnesses concerning the South China Sea disputes. In particular, he pointed out that one witness wrote that "at least 12 ocean terrains
can be classified as islands in Nansha Qundao, so 200 nautical miles of
exclusive economic zone can be claimed." "However, when stood as the
witness in the Arbitral Tribunal, he withdrew his previous view and said
'none of them are islands.'"

Despite the emotive language, certain points in Liu's remarks are
worth nuanced analysis. The first question is the nature of the Tribunal
itself. It is true that the Tribunal was temporarily established for the
special purpose of adjudicating the disputes between the Philippines and
China and is not a permanent establishment, but this nature per se does
not in any way undermine its legitimacy as a tribunal for dispute

[60] *Id.*
[61] *Id.*
[62] *Id.*

settlement, simply because this is how arbitration works in international dispute settlement. International arbitration has been defined as "a specially established mechanism for the final and binding determination of disputes ... by independent arbitrators, in accordance with procedures, structures and substantive legal or non-legal standards chosen directly or indirectly by the parties."[63] More significantly, the establishment of such an Arbitral Tribunal is one of the fora authorized by Article 287 of UNCLOS. Hence, there is no basis for a State Party to UNCLOS to claim that such a tribunal be "worth nothing," as long as the tribunal is established "in accordance with Annex VII" of the Convention.[64]

Is it problematic that four of the five arbitrators were appointed by Judge Shunji Yanai, a Japanese national? According to Article 3 of Annex VII, each party to the dispute shall appoint one member of the tribunal, who may be its national.[65] The other three members shall be appointed by agreement between the parties.[66] In case the parties cannot reach an agreement, "the President of the International Tribunal for the Law of the Sea shall make the necessary appointments."[67] That is, the President of the ITLOS has the duty to appoint other members if the parties to the dispute cannot agree on the appointments. In the *South China Sea* arbitration, the Philippines appointed Judge Rudiger Wolfrum as a member of the Tribunal when it initiated the arbitral proceedings.[68] Because China refused to participate in the proceedings, the Philippines requested Judge Shunji Yanai to appoint the other four members of the Tribunal, which he did in his official capacity as the President of the ITLOS.[69] Indeed, Yanai once served as chairman of a panel to advise the Japanese prime minister on his plan to revise Japan's postwar pacifist constitution to allow military action overseas, and for such reason he was described by Xinhua, China's national news agency, as a "typical rightist, hawkish figure."[70] However, Shunji Yanai acted *ex officio* in making the appointments. As one commentator observed, "Yanai's involvement could have been avoided. If China had decided to take part in the proceedings, it could have named one of the tribunal's arbitrators and

---

[63] J. D.M. Lew, L. A. Mistelis & S. M. Kroll, *Comparative International Commercial Arbitration* (The Hague: Kluwer Law International, 2003).
[64] UNCLOS, Article 287(1)(c).
[65] UNCLOS, Annex VII, Article 3(b).
[66] UNCLOS, Annex VII, Article 3(d).
[67] UNCLOS, Annex VII, Article 3(e).
[68] SCS Jurisdiction Award, para. 28.
[69] SCS Jurisdiction Award, paras. 29–31.
[70] "Question of Neutrality," *supra* note 15.

joint appointed three others in agreement with the Philippines."[71]
Nevertheless, the possibility for China to raise such an objection would
be lesser if Judge Yanai had excused himself from such a role "given the
territorial and maritime disputes between China and Japan in the East
China Sea, and Tokyo's attempts to involve itself in the South China Sea
issue," as suggested by Liu Zhenmin.[72] Needless to say, Yanai was not
legally required to refrain from involvement in the case.

The fact that all the members of the Tribunal have a strong European
background does not necessarily deprive it of its representativeness.
Legally, UNCLOS and Annex VII neither requires nor prohibits the
members of the tribunal to come from a particular region or regions.
Politically, given the complexities of political conflicts and security
clashes in Asia, it would not necessarily be in China's favor if the
arbitrators were from Asia. The result, it is submitted, might be the
opposite. Finally, the credibility of the arbitrators and witnesses concerning inconsistencies in their views before and after the arbitration was
initiated should have be questioned by China on the stand, had it taken
part in the arbitration. In short, as the Tribunal pointed out (on an issue
not related to its own legitimacy), "it is a general principle of international law that 'bad faith is not presumed,'" unless it is actually proven
to be.[73]

12.6   The Jurisdiction Issues Revisited

China's unyielding position of nonparticipation and nonacceptance was
predominately based on its objection to the jurisdiction of the Tribunal in
this dispute. China advanced three main arguments in this regard. First,
China asserted that "the subject-matter of the arbitration is the territorial
sovereignty over several maritime features in the South China Sea, which
is beyond the scope of the Convention."[74] Second, "China and the
Philippines have agreed, through bilateral instruments and the
Declaration on the Conduct of Parties in the South China Sea, to settle
their relevant disputes through negotiations."[75] Third, in any event, the
subject matter of the arbitration "would constitute an integral part of
maritime delimitation between the two countries, thus falling within the

[71] Id.
[72] Id.
[73] SCS Final Award, para. 1200.
[74] PRC Position Paper, supra note 9, para. 3.
[75] Id.

scope of the declaration filed by China in 2006 in accordance with the Convention, which excludes, inter alia, disputes concerning maritime delimitation from compulsory arbitration and other compulsory dispute settlement procedures."[76]

Both the Philippines and the Tribunal were aware of this. As recognized in the awards, the Philippines stated in its Notification and Statement of Claim that it "does not seek in this arbitration a determination of which Party enjoys sovereignty over the island ... Nor does it request a delimitation of any maritime boundaries."[77]

This section critically examines China's aforesaid arguments in light of the Tribunal's awards. As noted previously, the Tribunal rejected all China's arguments concerning jurisdiction and admissibility on the basis of the Philippines' submissions. It is, however, submitted that China's argument on territorial sovereignty is not entirely groundless, but the Tribunal might have been right in setting aside China's two other arguments.

Territorial Sovereignty

As noted previously, disputes concerning territorial sovereignty are excluded from the coverage of UNCLOS, on which China's first argument against the jurisdiction is premised. The Tribunal did not bother to offer lengthy reasoning, possibly because it believed it could be taken for granted that the Philippines' submissions were not related to sovereignty. The Tribunal invented a legal test to determine that sovereignty would be concerned "if it were convinced that either (a) the resolution of the Philippines's claims would require the Tribunal to first render a decision on sovereignty, either expressly or implicitly; or (b) the actual objective of the Philippine's claims was to advance its position in the Parties' dispute over sovereignty."[78] Applying the test to the disputes in question, the Tribunal simply concluded that "neither of these situations ... is the case" because it did not see that the Philippines was seeking a decision on the sovereignty of these maritime features.[79]

Clearly the Tribunal adopted a rather technical but unelaborated approach to reach this conclusion. This approach becomes unconvincing if the counterarguments about the sovereignty dimension of the disputes

---

[76] Id.
[77] SCS Jurisdiction Award, para. 26.
[78] SCS Jurisdiction Award, para. 153.
[79] Id.

are seriously taken into consideration. In this regard, there are at least two arguments that suggest that issues of sovereignty cannot be separated from the disputes.

First, one may argue that it is conceptually impossible to separate sovereignty issues from the determination of the status of maritime features as rocks or islands. Although it was submitted by the Philippines and accepted by the Tribunal that the SCS case is not about a "determination of which Party enjoys sovereignty over the islands claimed by both parties,"[80] any determination of the status of the features cannot be separated from determination of the sovereignty and sovereign rights of the claimant states in South China Sea. That is to say, the status of the features as "fully entitled islands" or "rocks" and their sovereign status are always determined simultaneously. Take Taiping Island or Itu Aba as an example. Taiping is currently occupied by Taiwan, officially known as the Republic of China (ROC), and Taiwan claims that it is "an island within the meaning of Article 121(1) of the UNCLOS" entitled to have both a territorial sea and an EEZ.[81] The determination of a tribunal that Taiping is not an island, but rather a rock, would automatically and instantaneously deprive Taiwan, which actually occupies Taiping, of its claimed sovereign rights with respect to an EEZ or continental shelf. The same logic applies to all the features currently occupied by China, and even other claimants than the Philippines.

Second, the Philippines directly challenged the validity of China's historic rights based on the nine-dash line. Although China has not fully clarified the nature of its claims in relation to the nine-dash line, there is little doubt the claims are related to sovereignty, at least per China's 2009 *notes verbales*, which states that "China has indisputable sovereignty over the islands in the South China Sea."[82] As such, "it is unclear how any finding on the validity of the nine-dash-line will not have the effect of prejudging the sovereignty claim that this may represent on the part of China," as observed by Antonios Tzanakopoulos.[83] True, the dispute was "packaged" by the Philippines as one concerning

---

[80] SCS Jurisdiction Award, para. 26.

[81] See *Amicus Curiae* Submission by the Chinese (Taiwan) Society of International Law for PCA Case No. 2013-19, Part C (hereinafter "Taiwan's *Amicus* Submission.")

[82] *Notes verbales* of the Permanent Mission of the People's Republic of China to the United Nations, May 7, 2009, CML/17/2009.

[83] A. Tzanakopoulos, "Resolving Disputes Over the South China Sea Under the Compulsory Dispute Settlement System of the UN Convention on the Law of the Sea," Oxford Legal Studies Research Paper No. 31/2016, available at SSRN: https://ssrn.com /abstract=2772659, at 7.

merely the technical interpretation of Article 121 of UNCLOS. However, it may be one directly involving sovereignty issues, as maintained by Sreenivasa Rao Pemmaraju, former Chairman of the International Law Commission and former President of the *Institut de Droit International*:

> China's case, as it repeatedly emphasized, is that it acquired historic rights over several of these maritime features through exercise of acts *á titre de souverain*. The Chinese case then cannot be disputed or disapproved merely by looking at the geological nature of the maritime features in question and the entitlements they can or cannot generate in terms of the relevant provisions of the UNCLOS. They can be assessed only be examining the nature of acts and functions of sovereignty China claims to have performed from times immemorial or through history.[84]

In short, the "dispute between the Philippines and China is obviously sovereignty over maritime features in the SCS, and only relatedly over maritime zones and the entitlements that the relevant features generate."[85] The Tribunal's lack of analysis on the sovereignty nature of the dispute alone made its jurisdiction over the case rather weak.

Settlement of the Dispute by Other Means

In response to China's argument that China and the Philippines had undertaken a mutual obligation to settlement their SCS disputes through "friendly consultations and negotiations" and thus "agreed to seek settlement of the dispute by a peaceful means of their own choice" in accordance with Article 281 of UNCLOS,[86] the Tribunal ruled that no such agreement existed to prevent the use of arbitration or other compulsory procedures. The Tribunal first examined the Declaration on the Conduct of Parties in the South China Sea in 2002 (DOC), which was asserted by China as one of the main documents that could establish an agreement between China and littoral states to settle their disputes through bilateral negotiations. Indeed, Article 4 of the DOC provides that "The Parties concerned *undertake* to resolve their disputes territorial and jurisdictional disputes by peaceful means, without resorting to the threat of force, through friendly consultations and negotiations by sovereignty states directly concerned, in accordance with universally recognized principles

---

[84] Pemmaraju, *supra* note 46, para. 52.
[85] Tzanakopoulos, *supra* note 83, at 6.
[86] PRC Position Paper, para. 31. See also SCS Jurisdiction Award, para. 202.

of international law, including the 1982 UN Convention on the Law of the Sea."[87]

To the extent it is accepted both by China and the Tribunal that a binding instrument requires the intention of both parties to establish rights and obligations between themselves,[88] China asserted that the use of the word "undertake" suggests "a clear intention to establish an obligation between the two countries in this regard."[89] It found support in an International Court of Justice (ICJ) judgement, *Bosnia and Herzegovina* v. *Serbia and Montenegro*, in which "undertake" was interpreted to mean committing to binding obligations.[90] It thus concluded in its Position Paper that "the relevant provisions in ... the DOC are mutually reinforcing and form an agreement between China and Philippines. On that basis, they have undertaken a mutual obligation to settle their relevant disputes through negotiations."[91]

It was not difficult for the Tribunal to refute the aforesaid argument made by China. The Tribunal easily distinguished the present SCS arbitration case from *Bosnia and Herzegovina* v. *Serbia and Montenegro* on the ground that, in the latter case, the court was operating clearly within a legally binding treaty.[92] while in the present case the Tribunal believed that "the DOC was not intended to create legal rights and obligations" by its drafters.[93] The Tribunal discovered numerous official statements made by drafters/negotiators of the DOC from China and other participants before and after the DOC was adopted. For example, in December 1999, the Chinese drafters pointed out that the DOC draft reflected the "consensus that the Code should be a political document of principle."[94] In August 2000, a spokesperson for the PRC Ministry of Foreign Affairs stated that the "Code of Conduct will be a political document to promote good neighborliness and regional stability instead of a legal document to solve specific disputes,"[95] which was affirmed by

---

[87] Emphasis added.
[88] See PRC Position Paper, paras. 30–56; SCS Jurisdiction Award, para. 213.
[89] PRC Position Paper, para. 38.
[90] ICJ Judgement of February 26, 2007, para. 162, cited also in PRC Position Paper.
[91] PRC Position Paper, para. 39.
[92] SCS Jurisdiction Award, para. 216.
[93] SCS Jurisdiction Award, para. 217.
[94] Memo of China's Position Regarding the Latest Draft Code of Conduct by the ASEAN, para. 2 (December 18, 1999), cited in SCS Jurisdiction Award, para. 217(a).
[95] Ministry of Foreign Affairs of the People's Republic of China, *Spokesperson's Comment on China–ASEAN Consultation*, 1 (August 30, 2000), cited in SCS Jurisdiction Award, para. 217(b).

an official meeting report of the DOC's Working Group on October 11, 2000.[96] Similar expressions can be found about other bilateral agreements between the Philippines and China, and the subsequent conduct of the parties to the DOC continues to demonstrate that the DOC has been treated as a political document rather than a legally binding instrument.[97]

In short, the finding that the DOC was not intended as a legally binding agreement is sufficient to exclude any prior agreement to bar the Tribunal's jurisdiction. China was clearly barred by estoppel to claim the legally binding effect of the DOC and other bilateral statements. Additionally, it was clear that the DOC and other bilateral statements do not exclude "any further procedure" rather than peaceful negotiation.

The 2006 Declaration to Exclude Certain Disputes

Article 298 of UNCLOS allows States to declare that they exclude the application of the compulsory binding procedures for the settlement of disputes under UNCLOS in respect of certain specified categories of disputes. China availed itself of this opportunity by making such a declaration in 2006, which excludes from the UNCLOS compulsory dispute settlement procedures "disputes concerning maritime delimitation, historic bays or titles, military and law enforcement activities, and disputes in respect of which the Security Council of the United Nations is exercising the functions assigned to it by the Charter of the United Nations."[98] That is, in China's view, even assuming the subject matter of the arbitration concerned the interpretation and application of UNCLOS, that subject matter would be excluded by China's 2006 Declaration because it formed an integral part of maritime delimitation.[99]

Interestingly, the Tribunal avoided directly addressing whether China's 2006 Declaration could effectively exclude the aforesaid issues,

---

[96] SCS Jurisdiction Award, para. 217(c).

[97] SCS Jurisdiction Award, para. 218. In its introduction to the DOC, the Ministry of Foreign Affairs of the People's Republic of China still says on its webpage that "the DOC is an important political document jointly signed by China and ASEAN countries, which demonstrates the political will of the Parities to promote stability, increase mutual-trust and pushing forward cooperation in the South China Sea." See Ministry of Foreign Affairs of China, "The Declaration on the Conduct of Parties in the South China Sea," available at www.fmprc.gov.cn/web/wjb_673085/zzjg_673183/yzs_673193/dqzz_673197/nanhai_673325/t848051.shtml.

[98] PRC Position Paper, para. 58. See also SCS Jurisdiction Award, para. 366.

[99] PRC Position Paper, Part IV.

especially maritime delimitation, from its jurisdiction. Instead, it characterized China's jurisdictional objection as one that does not "possess an
exclusively preliminary character."[100] That is to say, the Tribunal considered that the applicability of the limitations and exceptions under
Article 298 of UNCLOS might depend on certain aspects of the merits
of the Philippines' claims. As such, the Tribunal decided to go ahead with
the case so as to rule on such objections in conjunction with the merits
according to its own Rules of Procedure.[101]

Essentially, the Tribunal "decided not to decide" on whether the case
involved maritime boundary delimitation on the ground that it would
prejudge the merits of the dispute.[102] This approach was permitted under
the Tribunal's own Rules of Procedure, but looked to be a "disguised
replacement of concept" in the eyes of the Chinese government, which,
through a statement by the Chinese Society of International Law, argued,
largely sensibly, that "any determination of the status and maritime
entitlements of features will have an inevitable effect on the future
delimitation between China and the Philippines."[103]

What if China Attended the Proceedings on Jurisdiction?

It sounds pointless, as a practical matter, to ask what the result could have
been had China attended at least the proceedings on jurisdiction. It is,
however, a very meaningful question to ask because it concerns China's
general relations with international law. It is submitted that, by refusing
to participate in any way in the current South China Sea case, China has
lost at least two legal opportunities from the perspective of international
law. One opportunity is related to the constitution of the Arbitral
Tribunal. As noted previously, according to Article 3 of Annex VII to
the UN Convention on the Law of the Sea, from which the Tribunal
derived its legitimacy and procedural rules, each party to the dispute is
allowed to appoint at least one member of the Tribunal, "who may be its
national." The other three members shall be appointed by agreement
between the parties. In case the parties cannot reach an agreement, the
President of the International Tribunal for the Law of the Sea (ITLOS) is

---

[100] SCS Jurisdiction Award, paras. 380 and 390.
[101] SCS Jurisdiction Award, para. 390.
[102] Tzanakopoulos, *supra* note 83, at 11.
[103] Chinese Society of International Law, "The Tribunal's Award in the 'South China Sea
Arbitration' Initiated by the Philippines Is Null and Void," June 10, 2016, available at
www.csil.cn/News/Detail.aspx?AId=201 (accessed December 2, 2018).

authorized to make the appointments. If China had participated in the process – at least in the hearings concerning jurisdiction and admissibility of the claims – it would have been able to appoint at least one arbitrator and to block the appointment of the arbitrators that it believed to be unfriendly. Further, in accordance with the Rules of Procedure of the Tribunal, it can challenge any arbitrator for whom it has justifiable doubts about his/her impartiality or independence. Unfortunately, as can be seen, in the present case, all five arbitrators were appointed by the Philippines and the then ITLOS President, who, in China's eyes, is a rather suspicious Japanese national.

China's nonparticipation also led to the loss of its opportunity to present its own case before the Tribunal. A tribunal's decision is based on the legal arguments presented by the parties, supported by convincing interpretations of legal rules coupled with admissible evidence. In most cases, there could be more than one interpretation of the same legal rules as well as contradicting evidence about the same facts. To win a case or minimize the losses, a party must appear before the tribunal to present arguments and evidence. This is essential at least for counterbalancing the case of the other party and influencing the deliberations of the tribunal. This loss would look significantly regretful in light of the many good legal arguments raised not only in the PRC Position Paper, but also the lengthy statement of the state-controlled Chinese Society of International Law. Had China attended the proceedings on jurisdiction, the Tribunal would have had to seriously address the jurisdictional objections raised by China, many of which, as a matter of fact, were either avoided or not adequately taken up by the Tribunal in its Award on Jurisdiction and Admissibility.

It is important to stress that, based on established rules and practices in international law, participation in hearings on jurisdiction does not necessarily entail acceptance of the jurisdiction of the relevant international tribunal. Legally speaking, participation but nonacceptance is permissible under international law. If China had lost the case on jurisdiction issues, it still could have withdrawn from the case and refused to join the legal proceedings on the merits. Even when China was purposely absent in the second stage, it was still able to prepare the necessary legal arguments and evidence of the same quality – and quantity, if necessary – as the submissions made by a party that participates in the legal process to defend its position. In this sense, the PRC Position Paper should be celebrated, because it was the first document issued by China to elaborate its legal position on this case. It is a landmark document in the sense that it speaks the language of international law and roots China's own claims in international law, indicating that China has actually jumped on the bandwagon of using international law to protect its national interests. The Tribunal took note of some of the arguments in the Position Paper, but China apparently lost the opportunity to explain its legal positions.

12.7 The Merit Award: The Nine-Dash Line, Historic Rights, and Status of Features

The SCS Merit Award issued on July 12, 2016, marked China's complete defeat in the *South China Sea Arbitration*. This "final and binding" award,[104] unanimously adopted by the Tribunal, considered historic rights and the nine-dash line, entitlements to maritime areas and the status of features, lawfulness of Chinese actions, and harm to the marine environment in the South China Sea, in addition to whether China's actions since the commencement of the arbitration had aggravated the dispute between the parties. It essentially ruled that China has no legal basis to claim historic rights to the bulk of the South China Sea based on its nine-dash line claims. In this section, we critically examine the two major issues considered in the Merit Award, the nine-dash line and status of features (especially the Taiping island), which directly and substantially affect China's interests in the South China Sea.

12.7.1 Nine-Dash Line and Historic Rights

It has been said that China's claims to sovereign rights and the resources in the South China Sea are based on the so-called nine-dash line. Known also as the "dashed line" in Chinese literature, it first appeared as an eleven-dash line on an official map published by the Republic of China government in 1948.[105] Two dashes were removed in 1953, reportedly thanks to Chairman Mao Zedong's decision to hand over the Gulf of Tonkin to Vietnam in 1952, resulting in today's nine-dash line.[106]

---

[104] SCS Merit Award, para. 1172.
[105] See Zhao, *supra* note 15, at 37. See also (Y. Jia, "Zhongguo Zai Nanhai De Lishixing Quanli" ["China's Historic Rights in South China Sea"], 3 *Chinese Legal Science* 2015), 193–94.
[106] H. Beech, "Just Where Exactly Did China Get the South China Sea Nine-Dash Line From?," *Time*, July 19, 2016, at http://time.com/4412191/nine-dash-line-9-south-china-sea (accessed December 2, 2018).

Curiously, China has never officially clarified the legal basis or nature of its claims related to the nine-dash line. A *note verbales* communicated to the Commission on the Limits of the Continental Shelf of the United Nations on May 7, 2009, which includes a map that clearly shows the nine-dash line, stated China's official position as the following:

> China has indisputable sovereignty over the islands in the South China Sea and the adjacent waters, and enjoys sovereign rights and jurisdiction over the relevant waters as well as the seabed and subsoil thereof (see attached map). The above position is consistently held by the Chinese government, and is widely known by the international community.[107]

Obviously the aforesaid official position requires further clarification, which unfortunately has not been given by the Chinese government. It can, however, be concluded that China's position on land claims is clear: all lands within the nine-dash line are thus claimed to be part of Chinese territory. What is unclear are China's claims to water. Concepts like "the adjacent waters" and "sovereign rights and jurisdiction over the relevant waters" have been neither patently defined by China nor adequately understood in international law.

The United States Department of State, in a publication systematically analyzing China's maritime claims in the South China Sea, offers three possible interpretations about the nine-dash line. The first interpretation is that the nine-dash line aims only to indicate the lands over which China claims sovereignty, while the "adjacent waters" and "sovereign rights and jurisdiction over the relevant waters" shall be decided in accordance with the legal regimes of territorial sea, EEZ, and continental shelf under UNCLOS.[108] A bolder interpretation is that the nine-dash line is intended to be a national boundary between China and its neighbors.[109] The third interpretation is the nine-dash line is intended to indicate China's "historic" claim, the definition of which depends on the specific context.[110]

---

[107] *Notes verbales* CML/17/2009 and CML/18/2009 from the Permanent Mission of the People's Republic of China, May 7, 2009, available from the UN Division for Ocean Affairs and the Law of the Sea at www.un.org/depts/los/clcs_new/submissions_files/mysvnm33_09/chn_2009re_mys_vnm_e.pdf and www.un.org/depts/los/clcs_new/submissions_files/vnm37_09/chn_2009re_vnm.pdf.

[108] United States Department of State, "China: Maritime Claims in the South China Sea," *Limits in the Seas Series*, No. 143, December 5, 2014, at 11, available at www.state.gov/documents/organization/234936.pdf (accessed December 16, 2018).

[109] *Id.*, at 14.

[110] *Id.*, at 15.

Although, as previously mentioned, China has not clarified its position with respect to its claims associated with the nine-dash line, a reading of the official statements together with the writings of authors who are close to the Chinese government suggests that China does not have the intention to treat the line as national boundary. As observed by Jia Yu, the Deputy Director of the China Institute for Marine Affairs attached to the State Oceanic Administration:

> Either at the time when the Republic of China government published [the map] with the dashed lines, or in the years after 1949 when the People's Republic China [inherited] and continued the claims based on the dashed line, or when [the Chinese government] submitted the map with the dashed line to the United Nations to express China's objections to the submissions by Vietnam and Malaysia concerning the outer limits of the continental shelf beyond 200 nautical miles, every government in China has never defined the dashed line as a "national boundary" between China and its neighboring states, and never viewed the ocean space within the dashed line as China's internal waters or territorial waters, and never exercised sovereignty [over the aforesaid waters] as it does for China's land territories. The practice of all Chinese governments in the past has also never treated the dashed line as a national boundary and exercised [sovereignty] accordingly.[111]

Gao Zhiguo and Jia Bingbing, two eminent international law scholars in China, have also observed:

> The nine-dash line ... is not intended to assert a *historic* title of sovereignty over the sea areas, as enclosed by the lines, beyond what is allowed under international law. Chinese Note I, of 2009, explains this point clearly. That straight base lines drawn around the Xisha Island, promulgated by China in June 1996, further prove that point. The consistent in China's legislative and administrative practice is also matched by its maps.[112]

Thus, it is rather clear that the dashed line is not regarded as a national boundary even by China. But does China accept the first interpretation, that the dashed line is merely a line to embrace all the lands within? The answer is probably "no," as, according to Jia Yu, this interpretation "would in essence deny China's historic rights in the South China Sea" because that would make China's maritime entitlements decided under the relevant legal regimes of UNCLOS.[113] It can then be reasonably

---

[111] Jia, Y (2015), above note 105, at 198.
[112] Z. Gao & B. B. Jia, "The Nine-Dash Line in the South China Sea: History, Status, and Implications," 107 *American Journal of International Law* (2013), at 108–09.
[113] Jia Yu (2015), *supra* note 105, at 199.

concluded that the nine-dash line represents China's claims over all the lands within the line, plus "historic rights within the nine-dash line – under Article 14 of its 1998 law on the EEZ and the continental shelf – in respect of fishing, navigation, and exploration and exploitation of resources."[114]

The key question, then, is whether China can claim historic rights beyond those rights conferred upon it by UNCLOS. Clearly, the Tribunal totally denied China such rights. In the Merit Award, the Tribunal examined the history of UNCLOS and concluded that the Convention was adopted to comprehensively allocate the rights of states to maritime areas. Thus, "China's claim to historic rights to the living and non-living resources within the 'nine-dash line' is incompatible with the Convention to the extent that it exceeds the limits of China's maritime zones as provided for in the Convention."[115]

Having decided that China's historic rights do not go beyond UNCLOS, the Tribunal still examined the historical record to determine whether China actually had historic rights in the South China Sea prior to China's accession to UNCLOS. The Tribunal concluded that, although Chinese navigators and fishermen had historically used the islands in the South China Sea, this use was not exclusive, as they were also used by people of other countries for the same purposes. Moreover, since nearly all of the South China Sea formed part of the high seas, China's own navigation and trade in the South China Sea, as well as fishing beyond the territorial sea, represented the exercise of high seas freedoms.[116] Further, the Tribunal said it "is unable to identify any evidence that would suggest that China historically regulated or controlled fishing in the South China Sea, beyond the limit of the territorial sea."[117]

Indeed, compared with what China has lightly offered to justify its claim to historic rights, the Tribunal's analysis of this point looks more powerful and convincing in the sense that it sharply identified the fundamental weaknesses in China's argument about historic rights so far presented. This does not mean, however, that the Tribunal has destroyed the legal basis of China's claim to historic rights in the South China Sea. On this claim, there are at least three unsettled issues.

First, the Tribunal's analysis of China's claim to historic rights is not adequately conclusive, as it was not able to take into consideration

[114] Gao & Jia, *supra* note 112, at 109–10.
[115] SCS Merit Award, para. 261.
[116] SCS Merit Award, para. 269.
[117] SCS Merit Award, para. 270.

China's evidence to support its claim. The disagreement between China and the Tribunal (and the Philippines, whose view the Tribunal fully endorsed) is not about the legal test for establishing historic rights. Chinese literature seems to suggest that it subscribes to the prescribed "elements of title to historic waters'" by the International Law Commission in the 1962 Juridical Regime of Historic Waters Including Historic Bays.[118] The disagreement is about whether there is enough evidence to demonstrate "(1) the exercise of authority over the area by the State claiming the historic right; (2) the continuity of this exercise of authority; and (3) the attitude of foreign States."[119] In this regard, China believes it has acquired historic rights, in various degrees, to the waters and resources in the South China Sea through at least three means "in the course of history," which are discovery and use of the lands and resources by Chinese fishermen and navigators, administration of the region by local government authorities, and acquiescence by other countries.[120] China might have ample evidence to support such a claim, which, unfortunately, was neither presented to nor considered by the Tribunal, largely due to China's own absence during the arbitration proceedings.

Second, conceptually it is hard to say UNCLOS has entirely "superseded any historic rights or other sovereign rights or jurisdiction in excess of the limits imposed therein."[121] It is very clear that UNCLOS, as an international agreement, was never intended to provide for all the rights of States in an exhaustive way. Arguably, to the extent historic rights have their basis also in customary international law,[122] China may have a chance to justify its claim under customary international law, provided that it can present sufficient evidence to establish its historic rights, which is a task already difficult enough for China. And of course, it remains an open question whether such a right, even if it is based in

---

[118] See generally, Y. Jia, "Lun Lishi Quanli De Goucheng Yaojian" ["The Constituting Factors of Historic Rights"], 2 *Chinese Review of International Law* (2014), 33–48; Y. Jia (2015), *supra* note 105; Y. Huang & J. Huang, "Dui Meiguo Guowuyuan Baogao Zhiyi Zhongguo Nanhai Duanxuxian De Pingxi Yu Fanbo" ["A Commentary and Refutation of the US State Department's Report on China's Dashed Line in the South China Sea"], 3 *Chinese Review of International Law* (2015), 3–17.

[119] International Law Commission, Judicial Regime of Historic Waters, including Historic Bays, March 9, 1962, Document A/CN.4/143, para. 80.

[120] Y. Jia (2015), *supra* note 105, 201–03; Y. Huang & J. Huang, *supra* note 118, at 12–13.

[121] SCS Merit Award, para. 278.

[122] See, for example, SCS Jurisdiction Award, para. 407 (stating that traditional fishing rights may exist within the territorial waters of another State).

customary international law, can undermine the sovereignty or rights of the coastal states under UNCLOS.

Third, whenever the Tribunal considers the existence of historic rights, it falls back on the old jurisdictional question of whether territorial sovereignty is concerned. Obviously, if it can be found that China's claim to historic rights contain elements of sovereignty, then the issue should immediately be removed from the purview of the Tribunal. It seems, however, that the Tribunal considered the historic rights claim, including elements of sovereignty, and in that way prejudged the sovereignty of China's claims.

12.7.2   Status of Features Including the Taiping Island

Another fundamental issue decided by the Tribunal, which is considered as the "Tribunal's most important decision,"[123] is the status of features in the South China Sea and the entitlements to maritime areas that China could potentially claim pursuant to UNCLOS. It is the Tribunal's interpretation of Article 121(3) of UNCLOS that has most severely stricken China's claimed interest in the South China Sea.

As noted previously, in the UNCLOS legal regime, islands, rocks, and low-tide elevations are entitled to different maritime rights. A "fully entitled island" generates vast marine spaces including territorial sea, contiguous zone, exclusive economic zone, and even continental shelf. However, according to Article 121(3) of UNCLOS, "rocks which cannot sustain human habitation or economic life of their own shall have no exclusive economic zone or continental shelf." Rocks are, of course, islands according to Article 121(1) of UNCLOS, but they are not entitled to territorial seas.

The Tribunal ruled, largely along the lines of the submissions by the Philippines, that Scarborough Shoal (Huangyan Dao), Johnson Reef (Chigua Jiao), Cuarteron Reef (Huayang Jiao), and Fiery Cross Reef (Yongshu Jiao) are "high-tide features" (rocks) and that Subi Reef (Zhubi Jiao), Hughes Reef (Dongmen Jiao), Mischeif Reef (Meiji Jiao), and Second Thomas Shoal (Ren'ai Jiao) were submerged at high tide (low-tide elevations) in their natural

---

[123] R. Beckman and C. Sim, "Rule of Law in the South China Sea: Implications of the Philippines v China Decision on Jurisdiction and Admissibility," Centre for International Law, National University of Singapore, para. 89, at https://cil.nus.edu.sg/wp/wp-content/uploads/2016/06/Beckman-Sim-Hanoi-EU-DAV-16-June-2016.pdf (accessed December 2, 2018).

conditions.[124] The Tribunal concluded that *all* of the high-tide features in the Spratly Islands were "legally rocks for purpose of Article 121(3) and do not generate entitlements to an exclusive economic zone or continental shelf."[125] Therefore, no features occupied or claimed by China, including Taiping Island (known internationally as Itu Aba), are entitled to an EEZ or continental shelf, according to the Tribunal.

It is submitted that the Tribunal's legal reasoning with respect to the distinction between fully entitled islands and rocks is not entirely convincing, if not problematic. As provided in Article 121 of UNCLOS, a fully entitled island must not only possess the geological elements of being "a naturally formed area of land, surrounded by water, which is above water at high tide," but also not be a "rock" which "cannot sustain human habitation of economic life of [its] own."

The Tribunal interpreted the key terms in Article 121(3) including "rocks", "cannot", "sustain", "human habitation", "or", and "economic life of [its] own."[126] In the author's view, the Tribunal's interpretation of two of the terms is problematic, especially when applied to Taiping Island/Itu Aba. On "human habitation," the Tribunal suggested that it had to be habitation "by a group or community of persons."[127] It further explained that "no precise number of persons is specified in [Article 121], but providing the basic necessities for a sole individual would not typically fall within the ordinary understanding of human habitation: humans need company and community over sustained periods of time."[128] However, it is not clear what the legal basis is for requiring "a group or community of persons" to establish habitation, as one simply cannot infer any such requirement from the text of Article 121. Considering that the Tribunal admitted that both Article 121 and UNCLOS as a whole specified "no precise number of persons," the size of the "group" or "community" does not need to be large. If, clearly, one person does not make a group or community, will two or a few more do? Assuming it is true that "humans need company and community," it is highly possible that even two persons can form such company or community "over sustained periods of time."

---

[124] SCS Merit Award, paras. 554–640.
[125] SCS Merit Award, para. 646.
[126] SCS Merit Award, para. 478.
[127] SCS Merit Award, para. 491.
[128] SCS Merit Award, para. 491.

A high-tide feature can be a fully entitled island if it has "economic life of [its] own." In the view of the Tribunal, this meant the provision of material resources through local economic activity.[129] Further, the "of [its] own" component clearly required the feature "must have the ability to support an independent economic life, without relying predominantly on the infusion of outside resources or serving purely as an object for extractive activities, without the involvement of a local population."[130] In the words of the Tribunal, "for economic activity to constitute economic life of a feature, the resources around which the economic activity revolves must be local, not imported, as must be the benefits of such activity."[131]

One reservation has to be made about this interpretation. That is, the Tribunal's understanding of "economic life of [its] own" might be too narrow and restrictive. As a matter of fact, there are indeed many islands in the world which support an independent economic life through "relying predominantly on the infusion of outside resources," Singapore and Hong Kong being such examples. The *Jan Mayen* conciliation offers another example.[132] Jan Mayen belongs to Norway and was used by Norway for military and scientific research purposes through a meteorological station, a LORAN (long-range radio navigation) station, a coastal radio station, etc. "Between thirty and forty people live throughout the winter on the eastern coast in the central part of the island," which was where the stations and the airport were located.[133] The Conciliation Commission on the Continental Shelf Area between Iceland and Jan Mayen concluded Jan Mayen "must be considered as an island"[134] under Article 121 of the then Draft UNCLOS, which the Commission considered as reflecting "the present status of international law."[135] As observed by Tanaka, the "example of Jan Mayen seems to imply that the need for external supply does not deprive a marine formation of the legal status of an island."[136]

The flaws in the Tribunal's legal reasoning appear conspicuous when it was applied to Taiping Island/Itu Aba. First, on the evidence, the Tribunal almost entirely relied on the submissions of the Philippines, which in turn

---

[129] SCS Merit Award, para. 499.
[130] SCS Merit Award, para. 500.
[131] SCS Merit Award, para. 500.
[132] Report and Recommendations to the Governments of Iceland and Norway of the Conciliation Commission on the Continental Shelf Area between Iceland and Jan Mayen, 20 *I.L.M.* 797 (1981) (hereinafter "*Jan Mayen Report.*")
[133] See *Jan Mayen Report, supra* note 132, at 802.
[134] Ibid., at 802–03.
[135] Ibid., at 803.
[136] Y. Tanaka, *The International Law of the Sea* (Cambridge University Press, 2012), at 67.

almost solely relied on a 1994 scientific study on "The Flora of Taipingtao (Aba Itu Island)," which concluded that the water, soil, and vegetation demonstrated "the impossibility of sustaining human habitation" in Taiping Island,[137] plus the report of an expert who had not performed a field inspection of Taiping Island. It failed to analyze contrary evidence, like the ample documentary and other evidence submitted in the *amicus curiae* brief by the Chinese (Taiwan) Society of International Law.[138] Taiwan's *amicus curiae* brief, citing numerous books, reports, and other forms of empirical or scientific research, aimed to prove that Taiping Island not only had a "longstanding history of human habitation,"[139] but also "currently sustains the habitation of hundreds of people."[140] According to the *amicus curiae* brief, both empirical facts and scientific studies can establish that the island has a rich natural supply of fresh water which "is easily replenished by precipitation" and "averages 1800–2000 mm per year."[141] It was further presented that four ground-water wells provided up to 237,000 tons per year of water for drinking and cultivation.[142] The *amicus curiae* brief also presented evidence to prove that "the soil on Taiping Island has existed for more than a thousand years, and is capable of supporting indigenous vegetation and agricultural crops"[143] and that the "original and current vegetation of Taiping Island is capable of sustaining human habitation."[144]

This is not to say that the Tribunal should have instead relied on "contrary evidence" like that offered in Taiwan's *amicus curiae* filing. However, the Tribunal seemed to be almost totally unconcerned by the contrary evidence, or treated it rather carelessly. Nevertheless, the Tribunal still admitted that "the principal high-tide features in the Spratly Islands are capable of enabling the survival of small groups of people."[145] That is to say, the Tribunal actually recognized that some features, especially Taiping Island/Itu Aba, have the capacity to sustain human habitation. Still, the

---

[137] SCS Merit Award, para. 428.
[138] Chinese (Taiwan) Society of International Law, "*Amicus Curiae* Submission on the Issue of the Feature of Taiping Island (Itu Aba) Pursuant to Article 121(1) and (3) of the 1982 United Nations Convention on the Law of the Sea," March 23, 2016, at www .assidmer.net/doc/SCSTF-Amicus-Curiae-Brief-final.pdf (accessed December 2, 2018).
[139] *Id.*, paras. 25–28.
[140] *Id.*, paras. 23–24.
[141] *Id.*, para 29.
[142] *Id.*, para 30.
[143] *Id.*, paras. 33–34.
[144] *Id.*, paras. 35–39.
[145] SCS Merit Award, para. 615.

Tribunal concluded that the Spratly features, including Taiping Island, "are not capable of sustaining an economic life of their own within the meaning of Article 121(3)."[146] Clearly, this is a result of the Tribunal's narrow and restrictive interpretation of the concepts of "human habitation" and "economic life of their own," as well as a logic error in the Tribunal's relevant legal reasoning that curiously confused a feature's "capacity to support" human habitation and whether it has actually "supported" human habitation.[147]

12.8 Implications for China's Evolving Approach to International Dispute Settlement

Views are divided as to the role of international law in highly political situations like the South China Sea disputes. Some commentators treat these disputes as purely geopolitical matters which should be left to power politics or, at least, diplomatic means,[148] while others believe international adjudication is appropriate in a politically sensitive case like this one.[149] The Asian background of this case has added complication to the disputes. As Simon Chesterman has observed, "Asian states are the least likely of any regional grouping to be party to most international obligations."[150]

Kristen Boon offered three conditions for "successful arbitration on highly political issues such as cultural issues and boundary disputes":[151]

(i)   Consent of the parties
(ii) The ability of the politicians to sell the process of arbitration to their people
(iii) The arbitral tribunal's ability to tactically manage consent.[152]

---

[146] SCS Merit Award, para. 625.
[147] SCS Merit Award, paras. 618–22.
[148] See generally, R. D. Kaplan, *Asia's Cauldron: The South China Sea and the End of a Stable Pacific* (Random House, 2014).
[149] K. E. Boon, "International Arbitration in Highly Political Situations: The South China Sea Dispute and International Law," 13 *Washington University Global Studies Law Review* (2014), at 487–92.
[150] S Chesterman, "Asia's Ambivalence About International Law and Institutions: Past, Present, and Futures" (2017) 27:4 *European Journal of International Law*, at 945.
[151] Boon, *supra* note 149, at 490.
[152] *Id.*

In essence, the parties have to agree to participate in the arbitration, the politicians need to support the arbitration, and arbitrators need to manage the consent of the parties.[153] Seen within this framework, the *South China Sea Arbitration* is hardly a successful arbitration. However, one has to take note of the positive and practical contributions of the case not only to international rule of law but also to peaceful settlement of disputes in the region. First, the arbitration successfully brought the disputes to the international realm. The international attention drawn by this case to the South China Sea disputes and the "mood of legalization of the dispute settlement" created by the case have put pressure on the parties concerned, especially China, to emphasize the importance of using international law to resolve the disputes. Secondly, the jurisdiction and merit awards have strongly clarified and defined the legal claims of the parties, and have compelled some parties, especially China, to issue more statements to clarify its own claims and position on the disputes. In addition, despite the Chinese government's seemingly strong condemnation of the SCS awards, arguably the awards might have helped unlock the diplomatic impasse between China and the Philippines. After the final award was issued, Philippines's newly elected President Rodrigo Duterte visited China in October 2017. Since then, the relationship between the two countries has significantly improved. Possibly, China's legal defeat in the arbitration has made it understand that it should show good will, reasonableness, and a cooperative stance in its dealings with smaller neighbors, at least from the perspective of maximizing China's national interest in international relations and geopolitics.

One must, however, be cautious in treating the SCS arbitration as a landmark case with superb judgments that may set precedents for future disputes. For sure, to the extent that the awards have defined the claims and clarified certain legal issues, they will shed light on maritime dispute settlement in the future. But it is also important to recognize the weaknesses in both the jurisdiction and merit awards. Two such weaknesses are notable, as previously analyzed. One regards the sovereignty nature of the disputes. That is, the Tribunal took on highly political, sovereignty-related issues without gaining the consent of the parties. The other weakness concerns the Tribunal's narrow and restrictive interpretation of Article 121(3) of UNCLOS.

What is the impact of the case on China's attitude to international law and international dispute settlement? Frankly, it has caused mixed

---

[153] *Id.*, at 490–91.

feelings in China. On the one hand, the legal defeat and the responses from many members of the international community that urged China to comply with the awards have certainly made both the Chinese public and government to begin to appreciate the significance of international law. Although a senior Chinese official described the final award as "nothing but a piece of useless paper,"[154] China's behavior since the arbitration demonstrates that it has taken the awards to heart, otherwise it would not have mounted a sustained and somewhat hysteric legal, political, and diplomatic campaign to discredit the Tribunal and its findings.[155]

Naturally, the awards have also helped fan nationalism in China, strengthening the belief in realism and power politics in international relations. From the very beginning, the SCS arbitration has been depicted in China as a US-led conspiracy to contain China. It is not difficult for conspiracy theories like this to find an audience in China, as the public there has a very strong victim mentality with respect to China's relations with the international community, especially the western world. This victim mentality has led to distrust in international law, as international law was believed to be used by western powers to invade China, extract economic concessions from it, and occupy Chinese territories before the PRC was established. Against this background, to the extent that the Tribunal flatly declared the nine-dash line (and hence China's historic rights) invalid and ruled that Taiping Island is no more than a rock, the "counterproductive effect of the award is to stir up Chinese nationalism while undermining moderate voices represented by professional diplomats," as observed by Zhang Feng.[156]

In the end, the *South China Sea Arbitration* may have given China two takeaways: the appreciation of the importance of using international law, and the understanding that foreign countries – led by the United

---

[154] See B. Dai, "Speech by Dai Bingguo at China-US Dialogue on South China Sea between Chinese and US Think Tanks", May 5, 2016, Washington DC, at www.fmprc.gov.cn /nanhai/eng/wjbxw_1/t1377747.htm (accessed December 2, 2018). See also S. N. Goh, "South China Sea Dispute: New Testing Ground for Asia's Regional Order," *Straits Times*, July 10, 2016, at www.straitstimes.com (accessed December 2, 2018).

[155] See, for example, Xinhua News Agency, *Nanhai Zhudao Shi Zhongguo De* [*South China Sea Islands Belong to China*] (Beijing: Renmin Press) (a collection of reports and commentaries written by the reporters of the Xinhua News Agency, China's state-owned news agency, to criticize and condemn the Tribunal, arbitrators, and awards of the *South China Sea Arbitration*).

[156] F. Zhang, "South China Sea Arbitration Award: Breathtaking (But Counterproductive)," *National Interest*, July 16, 2016, at https://nationalinterest.org/blog/the-buzz/south-china-sea-arbitration-award-breathtaking-17004 (accessed December 2, 2018).

States – are again using international law as a disguise to violate China's sovereignty. A combination of these two factors will strengthen the prevailing attitude of treating international law as a tool to protect China's national interest rather than a serious belief in international rule of law. As noted by Simon Chesterman, China's "embrace of international law arguably continues to be instrumentalist with regard to both domestic and international policy objectives."[157] The *South China Sea Arbitration* can hardly change this attitude but may still be a step forward, at least in the sense that it has pushed China to realize that it has to take international law more seriously.

---

[157] Chesterman, *supra* note 150, at 952.

INDEX

For EU product safety concerns, contact us at Calle de José Abascal, 56–1°,
28003 Madrid, Spain or eugpsr@cambridge.org.

www.ingramcontent.com/pod-product-compliance
Ingram Content Group UK Ltd.
Pitfield, Milton Keynes, MK11 3LW, UK
UKHW020401140625
459647UK00020B/2587